WAR
HORSE

American War Horses, *Chuck DeHaan, oil on canvas, 2002.*

WAR HORSE

MOUNTING THE CAVALRY
WITH AMERICA'S FINEST HORSES

PHIL LIVINGSTON & ED ROBERTS

BRIGHT SKY PRESS

Albany, Texas

bright sky press

Albany, Texas

10   9   8   7   6   5   4   3   2   1

Library of Congress Cataloging-in-Publication

Livingston, Phil
    War horse : mounting the cavalry with America's finest horses / Phil Livingston & Ed Roberts.
      p. cm.
    Includes bibliographical references and index.
    ISBN 1-931721-21-1 (alk. paper)
    1. United States. Army—Remount service—History. 2. War horses—United
  States—History. I. Roberts, Ed (Edward R.), 1934- II. Title.

UC603 .L578 2003
357'.2'0973—dc21

                                2002042670

Front Cover Painting *American War Horses,* Chuck DeHaan, oil on canvas, 2002. Created for the cover of *War Horse* by Chuck DeHaan, Graford, Texas. The painting features a century of American cavalrymen and their mounts from the Civil War, with a sword-wielding Confederate in gray (1861–1865), a blue-clad trooper carrying a guidon in the Indian Wars (1865–1890), to the sergeant of 1940 armed with a Colt 45 automatic—all charging together.

Back cover photographs by Scott Trees and courtesy *The Western Horseman.*

Book and cover design by Isabel Lasater Hernandez

Printed in China through Asia Pacific Offset

CONTENTS

Lieutenant S. C. Robertson, Chief of the Crow Scouts, *1890. Watercolor and graphite on paper. 1961.274. Frederic S. Remington, Amon Carter Museum, Fort Worth, Texas*

☊
WHY THIS BOOK
WAS WRITTEN

This book had its beginnings just before World War II exploded the world into the machine age. Two small boys, one in Oklahoma and the other in California, stood at the roadside and watched cavalry regiments pass by on maneuvers. The locales and times differed but the result was the same. Neither was ever able to forget the long lines of horses, the dusty uniforms, the clink of equipment or the fluttering guidons. Perhaps they realized that they were seeing the end of an era.

Like countless other individuals before them, both boys were infected with the "horse bug." Over the years they were to buy, sell, train and just go look at, innumerable horses. Throughout their careers, the dim memories of the cavalry mounts seen so long ago remained, unconsciously giving them a standard of comparison.

As with most horsemen, they were constantly searching for a better mount, one that could do the job under saddle more efficiently, stay sound in spite of hard use and have sufficient speed when needed. This search led first to a study of practical conformation. That was followed by the understanding that certain bloodlines seemed to produce that conformation. The athletic ability and mental outlook that made a horse a top performer was also related to breeding. Frequently, the pedigree of a desirable individual traced back to one of the U.S. Remount stallions that had stood at stud in America during the 1920s, 1930s and 1940s. That raised the questions of, "What was the Remount?" and, "How did such numbers of those good horses come into being?"

With those questions in mind, the by-then grown boys began piecing the Remount story together. Old magazine articles, dust-covered files and the information stored in the minds of the few remaining individuals who had experienced the end of the Cavalry and the Remount Program all contributed their facts. Little by little, the story began to come together and speculation became knowledge. A study of Quarter Horse,

Palomino, Appaloosa and Paint pedigrees revealed that many of those good animals had one or more Remount forbearers. All of this information confirmed the fact that the Remount Program *had* been the basis for western horse breeding during the years between the two World Wars. It had given ranchers an economic reason to raise better horses. Too many fine animals traced back to Remount stallions for there to be any doubt.

By the time these two boys met, some forty years after they had seen those columns of cavalry, each felt that a book about the Army Remount Service, and its contributions to American horse breeding, was long overdue. What started as a casual conversation about a common interest blossomed. Serious talks, shared files, brittle magazines pulled from storage boxes and hours spent pouring over old pedigrees to trace a particular horse back to a certain Remount stallion began to lead to a single goal. There were trips to pick the memories of former Remount cowboys or cavalrymen, to dig through seldom opened file cabinets or stand on the site of a deactivated Remount depot. As word of their project filtered out to the horse world, stories, articles, family records and old photographs began to pour in from men and women who remembered the program and the horses. Those individuals recognized the contributions that the Remount Program had made to the development of the present horse pool and were eager to help tell the story.

From the two boys who once stood at the roadside watching the cavalry march by, goes a "Thanks" to the men who conceived and put into operation the Army Horse Breeding Program. Those far-seeing individuals built better than they knew. While their goal was to develop a pool of military-acceptable cavalry and field artillery horses, as well as pack and draft mules, they laid the foundation for the American riding horse of today and of the future as nothing else could have. Through their efforts, and through those of the men who rode and cared for the animals, horsemanship in America was kept alive in a world that had turned its back on the animal that had helped to build modern civilization.

From Fort Worth, Texas—once the site of one
of the largest horse and mule markets in the world

Phil Livingston   *Ed Roberts*

Cavalry in an Arizona Sand-Storm, *1889. Oil on canvas. 1961.244.*
Frederic S. Remington, Amon Carter Museum, Fort Worth, Texas

A Cavalryman's Breakfast on the Plains, *circa 1892. Oil on canvas. 1961.227.*
Frederic S. Remington, Amon Carter Museum, Fort Worth, Texas

PREFACE

Americans as a people do not immerse themselves in history. This is good in many ways, as such a people does not wallow in the past. Furthermore, we are a relatively new people and as such, prefer to think of today and an even better future than our past. In doing so we lose out on a great deal of fascinating information which could help un understand ourselves better.

We have fought a great many wars, while remaining anti-militaristic. We study and read about those wars because looking at our conflicts helps us to see ourselves. This granted, we are fond of technology, look to it to make our lives better and are justly proud of the role it has played when we did have to fight. Sometimes though we lose sight of historical truths which do not fall into the category of the technical, but remain in the field of flesh and blood.

This has happened with the history of Americans and their military horses. We are fascinated with the technical so we carefully study the improvements in internal combustion engines, armor plate, the chemical secrets of explosives, the penetrating power of our projectiles and uncountable details of our machinery which we fight, making it bigger and faster and safer and more destructive.

For upwards of a hundred years, there was another product improvement struggle going on, because just not so long ago, we didn't have so many machines and they wouldn't carry a soldier all the places he had to go. A number of very determined and dedicated men applied themselves to what became a national effort to improve the cavalry (and the draft) horse. These were not machines for which a new alloy could be mixed in a steel foundry, or could be altered to take any kind of motor-fuel, but living beings, living partners in warfare. Great minds in Washington and elsewhere knew of the battlefield losses in previous wars, knew there would be greater losses in tomorrow's wars, and in a constant struggle that lasted a hundred years, succeeded: they were able to improve the breed and prepare the United States soldier to have a greater number of larger stronger, more resilient and tougher animals than any country had ever had before. In doing this they also improved the characteristics of the other horses in America, and their mark is seen on almost every category of horse in use in the United States today. The features so determinedly sought by the military horsemen turn out to be those which are desirable in THE HORSE overall. There is hardly a GREAT horse of any category that, in his bloodline, does not boast of a sire or several sires, placed in action by the US Army, as it prepared America for another great military struggle.

The story of this long effort, stubbornly continued over a century by dedicated men often against certain pressures from Washington (horsemen have and still do, undergo a certain level of jealousy from non-riders) and in the face of danger to their careers, is the story that Phil Livingston and Ed Roberts tell. Livingston, cowboy, writer, historian, son of a cavalryman, and Roberts, Executive Secretary of the American Paint Horse Association for 26 years, cattleman and historian, have done so. Both are horsemen in every way that we know how to interpret the word and take a deep interest in improving the capabilities of the animal. Casual samplers, this is not for you. This book has it all: the men, the sires, the century-long effort, the determination, the statistics; all the features that make up a true and original piece of scholarship are here. Through the lists of locations, purchases, bloodlines, the administrative struggles, the strong leadership bucking Depression funk, and the strong and deep scholarship, the reader gets a whiff of dust and the stables, hears those hooves pounding battlefield and terrain, sees the bright sabers sparkle and then dim before blued gun-barrels, and is moved anew at the long partnership of soldier and horse.

Americans do not know enough about their history. We need this book.

Raymond G. Smith,
Ph.D. The Catholic University of America;
Adjunct Professor of History and instructor in U.S. and
Western Civilization at several Washington, D.C.-area
colleges; retired US Army, Vietnam veteran;
and published articles on US and medieval history.

Photograph by Scott Trees

YL Ebony Bey, a registered Arabian descended from *Witez II, is used as a ranch stallion by the YL Ranch, John and Sharon Matthews, Albany, Texas. Through this stallion, and others like him, the legacy of the Remount Service continues into the 21st century.

Photograph courtesy U.S. Army

Sergeant Herman Keauth, retired trooper, holds Chief, the last Cavalry horse on active service, at the Cavalry Memorial dedication, Fort Riley, Kansas, 1959.

Ω
CHAPTER 1

REMOUNTS—AND THE REASONS
FOR THE U.S. REMOUNT SERVICE

*"The big horse market was the army. You could get $200 for a gelding
while a cow and calf only sold for $40–$50. One day I sold 185 horses to the
Army Remount Service."*

Hank Wiescamp

Webster's Dictionary defines "Remount" as "a fresh horse to take the place
of one lost or disabled." The definition was the basis of the Remount
Service and U.S. Army's Horse Breeding Program. In the process of
developing a solid Remount program, one that kept the soldiers mounted on the best
possible horseflesh, the army also made a positive contribution to the light horses in
America. That contribution has lasted for more than a century.

The U.S. Remount Service was activated in 1908, when horses and mules were
primary means of military transportation. The original purpose was to purchase suitable
animals for the troops. This was not always possible and a breeding program was
developed utilizing civilian breeders and government-owned stallions. While many
thousands of horses and mules were utilized during World War I (1914–1918), mechanization made an appearance on the battlefield and indicated the future. As trucks and
tanks became more effective, along with heavier cannons, reassignment of the uses of
cavalry were made. Scouting and harassment became the primary functions, rather than
all-out attack to support infantry. During the 1920s and 1930s, mechanization of the
army was on the rise and the cavalry began to decline in importance, gradually
eliminating the need for a pool of horseflesh. In spite of this, the Remount Service
intensified efforts to produce an effective military animal, utilizing civilian horsemen as

breeders. The program succeeded remarkably well even though the need was gradually disappearing. In the process, the Remount Program laid a foundation for quality in America's light horses as nothing else could have.

Today's American horsemen owe a major debt to the far-thinking individuals who conceived the U.S. Remount Service and convinced the Congress to fund the

Photograph courtesy of The Western Horseman

United States 6th Cavalry on the march across the plains of Mexico during the Punitive Expedition in 1916, one of the most grueling cavalry trials in American history. Additional horses on lead reins are included in the column.

program. The purpose was to develop a pool of military-acceptable horses and mules that could be purchased from civilian breeders in time of need. While the original goal was horses for military use, the efforts of these men influenced the American light horse industry far beyond what they envisioned. Many of today's Quarter Horses, Palominos, Appaloosas, Paints and racehorses trace back to one or more Remount stallions that stood throughout America during the 1920s, 1930s and 1940s. The majority of

these stallions were Thoroughbreds, but Arabians, Morgans, Standardbreds and American Saddlebreds added their genes to the pool. The result was a "usin'-kind"

Photograph by Hellbusch

Plaudit, AQHA 1,657, registered both as a Quarter Horses and as a Palomino, this son of the Remount stallion King Plaudit (TB) was out of Colorado Queen by Old Nick. He sired numerous Quarter Horse and Palomino foals during his 28 years at stud. Left to right: Joan Harms, Mr. Leon Harms, Mrs. Leon Harms.

of horse, that is, an animal functionally conformed to perform satisfactorily under saddle, well-balanced, well-sprung ribs and deep heart girth to provide plenty of lung capacity, a set of withers to hold the saddle in place, legs of sufficient bone to stay sound and a foot large enough to provide a solid foundation. The animal should also be reasonably athletic, have a gentle disposition and a willing mind. Geldings, the product of Remount stallions crossed on the mixed-breed mares owned by farmers and ranchers, were not only purchased by the army but

also improved ranch remudas, played polo, served as hunters and jumpers and became police mounts far from their native ranges. They were a cash crop for the people who raised them. The daughters of Remount stallions were used under saddle, sold or turned back into the broodmare bands to add their contributions to future generations of horses.

An example of the influence that a single Remount stallion could have is King Plaudit, (TB), a son of the 1898 Kentucky Derby Winner, Plaudit. While the bay stallion stood in Colorado during the late 1920s and 1930s, he sired numerous ranch geldings, broodmares and at least one outstanding stallion. The latter was Plaudit, American Quarter Horse Association (AQHA) No. 1,657, named after his grandsire. Foaled in 1930, on the Meeker, Colorado, ranch of Tom Mills, and well before the formation of either the American Quarter Horse Association or the Palomino Horse Breeders Association (PHBA), the prepotent Palomino stallion produced numerous offspring. In twenty-eight crops, Plaudit sired 187 AQHA-registered offspring as well as a number recorded in the PHBA. Among the better-known individuals by him were: Question

Photograph courtesy U.S. Army

Remount stallion King Plaudit (TB) was sired by Plaudit (TB), winner of the 1898 Kentucky Derby, out of Wild Thistle (TB). King Plaudit sired numerous outstanding horses during his career, including Plaudit, AQHA No. 1,657, named for his grandsire.

Mark; Miss Helen (dam of Gold Mount, who sired Maddon's Bright Eyes, and Skipper's Lad, sire of Skipa Star); Scooter W.; Mexicala Rose; Santa Maria; Del Monte; Cimarron; Smokey Moore; Hal Plaudit and Golden Plaudit. Through the generations, the blood of King Plaudit (TB) has influenced countless breeding programs and continued the U.S. Remount Service's contribution to America's horses.

Many large cattle ranchers took advantage of the army's breeding program to raise better saddle horses. Not only did they have more effective horses but they improved employee relations. They had learned that having a good string of saddle horses was an added inducement towards keeping top cowboys on the payroll. A number of those ranches expanded their breeding programs beyond what was necessary to raise their own remounts. The managers discovered that there was always a market for good saddle horses, including the army.

In recalling his reasons for entering the horse business back in the early 1930s, premier Quarter Horse Breeder Hank Wiescamp of Alamosa, Colorado, remembered, "The big horse market at the time was the army. You could get $200 for a gelding. A cow and a calf sold for $40–$50 and a new car for $1,000 so you could purchase a new car for five geldings. One day alone, I sold 185 horses to the Army Remount Service."[1]

Photograph by Skeet Richardson

Jesse James, AQHA No. 2,257, the 1951 National Cutting Horse Association Reserve World Champion Cutting Horse and a popular sire. Jesse James was sired by Red and out of Reno May, a daughter of the Remount Stallion Reno Bay (TB). He is shown here after winning the Open Cutting contest at the 1950 Southwestern Exposition and Fat Stock Show in Fort Worth, Texas, with Snooks Burton in the saddle.

Photograph by Howdyshell

Music Mount, AQHA No. 5,229, son of Gold Mount by Brush Mount by Chimney Sweep (TB), and out of Panzy by Madder Music (TB), was a triple dose of Remount breeding. Music Mount was a popular sire of Halter and Performance Quarter Horses in the Northwest.

Because of the size of the registry, the largest impact of Remount stallions has been upon the American Quarter Horse. The first Secretary of the Association, Robert M. Denhardt, wrote in his book, *Foundation Sires of the American Quarter Horse*, of the development of the registry, the tracing of authentic Quarter Horse bloodlines and the impact of Remount sires, "We assumed that most outside blood would be Thoroughbred from Remount horses such as Uncle Jimmie Gray or from ranch stallions of undetermined breeding."[2]

Descendants of Remount stallions that are well-known in Quarter Horse pedigrees include: Miss Bank by Captains Courageous (TB); Jesse James, out of Reno May by Reno Bay (TB); Sugar Bars, out of Frontera Sugar by Rey by Captains Courageous (TB); Oklahoma Star by Dennis Reed (TB); Bear Hug by Norfleet by *Brettenholm (TB); Skipper W. by Nick Shoemaker, who was out of Skipalong Weiscamp by Lani Chief (TB); Joe Reed II, out of Nellene by Fleeting Time (TB); Bart B.S. out of a daughter of Doc Horn (TB); Lightning Bar, out of Della P. by Doc Horn (TB); Music Mount, who traced back to Chimney Sweep (TB), King Plaudit (TB) and Madder Music (TB); Rebel Cause, a grandson of Miss Bank by Captains Courageous (TB); Buddy Nile by Fleeting Time (TB); Plaudit by King Plaudit (TB); Maddon's Bright Eyes, a great-granddaughter of Chimney Sweep (TB) on the top side of her pedigree and out of Plaudette by Plaudit by King Plaudit (TB); Marion's Girl, out of Joan Scarbauer by Tallwood (TB); Croton Oil, out of Randle's Lady by Doc Horn (TB); Quick M Silver, by Brush Mount by Chimney Sweep (TB) and out of Blue Bonnet Moore who traced back to King Plaudit (TB); Ed Echols, out of Dorothy E. by Flying Squirrel (TB); Hollywood Jac 86, out of Miss Hollywood who was, in turn, out of Miss Buggins 86 by Buggins (TB); Decketta, winner of the 1964 All American Futurity Race, who was out of Lady Thomas Wilson who was out of Bonny by Cattail (TB); Mr. Gun Smoke, a descendant of both Chimney Sweep (TB) and Dennis Reed (TB); and Blondy's Dude who traced back to King Plaudit (TB). An example of how intense the Remount influence could be is the 1979 AQHA World Show Super Horse Diamond Sparkle who is 5 X 5 X 7 X 6 line-bred to Plaudit who was sired by King Plaudit (TB).

Photograph by Larry Kenny

Skeeter, World Champion Cutting Horse, 1950 and 1951, shown winning the "Cow Palace Cutting" event. Receiving the saddle and award is owner/rider Phil Williams, Tokio, Texas, and Cow Palace representative, Porter Sesnon. Skeeter was foaled in 1939, sired by the Remount stallion, Sidecar (TB), out of Skeeterette by Fightin' Joe (TB), another Remount stallion.

Alamo, Lone Star and Major Speck, early-day South Texas sprinters, were sons of the prepotent Uncle Jimmie Gray (TB).[3]

Some of the Appaloosas tracing back to Remount stallions are: Joker B., out of Blue Vitriol by Brown Dick by Derring Doe (TB) and out of Leopard who was a granddaughter of Primero (TB); Bright Eyes Brother, a great-grandson of Chimney Sweep (TB); Mansfield Comanche, a descendant of Dr. Howard (TB); the foundation sire Hands Up by Vinita London (TB) and Bobbie N., the dam of National Champion Broodmare Bobbette N., a great-granddaughter of Zev (TB), winner of the 1924 Kentucky Derby.[4]

Included on the list of Remount-influenced American Paint Horses are: Yellow Mount, tracing back to Chimney Sweep (TB) and Skip Hi out of Sky Hi by Advantage (TB).[5]

Palominos carrying Remount breeding, such as Question Mark, Cimarron, Plaudette, Monte Carlo and Phillips 66, are all by Plaudit by King Plaudit (TB). Gold Mount was by Brush Mount by Chimney Sweep (TB).[6] Booger Bear, by Black Bear (TB) by Runtlar and out of a Berry Ketchum Quarter mare was another great one. In addition to being a ranch and top rodeo mount, he was a show winner and prolific sire. One of the best-known Palominos was Trigger Jr., who carried Roy Rogers across the television and movie screens in numerous Saturday episodes during the 1950s. He was a grandson of Sir Barton (TB), the first Triple Crown Winner and later a Remount sire.[7]

There were countless other individuals by Remount stallions and out of unregistered mares that distinguished themselves under saddle. Among them were: Dutch, a top Pacific Coast Stock Horse of the 1940s, and Dick, another California campaigner of the late 1940s and early 1950s.[8] Red Bird and Bonny Lass, top calf roping mounts of the 1950s at the professional level were both sired by King Raffles (TB).[9] Skeeter, National Cutting Horse Association (NCHA) World Champion Cutting Horse of 1950–51, was also Remount-bred, being sired by Sidecar (TB) and out of Skeeterette by Fighting Joe (TB).[10] There is no doubt that, without the infusion of fine blood that the army's quest for cavalry mounts made available to the private breeder, America's saddle horses would not have obtained the quality that they did and have maintained until today.

Photograph by DeVere, courtesy Dan Taylor

Dan Taylor of Doole, Texas, competes on Red Bird, in the 1950 San Angelo Rodeo. Red Bird was by King Raffles (TB), a Remount stallion handled by Tommy Cochran of Belton, Texas. Taylor purchased Red Bird from Doc Spence, Gatesville, Texas.

Dan Taylor of Doole, Texas, a professional calf roper during the 1950s, remembered the aforementioned Red Bird who carried him to many rodeo winnings: "Red Bird stood 14 hands, 3 inches and weighed 1,150 pounds. He had legs like oil well casing pipe, wore a cut-off No. 2 shoe and had withers that would really hold a saddle. I hauled him all over the country, used him hard and he never took a lame step."[11]

Developing a dependable source of remounts has plagued man ever since he began to ride horseback thousands of years ago. As a hunter and warrior, he was only as good as the horse under him. That meant that he must be riding one with strength, stamina and the conformation to stay sound in spite of hard use. Without such a mount, the rider would soon be afoot. There also had to be a constant supply of similar animals to replace those ridden down, crippled or killed. Rather than depending upon horses captured from the wild herds, man began to raise his own. He learned that breeding the best to the best produced a superior mount. The need for more effective horses also gave rise to improved training techniques and the development of stronger, more comfortable riding equipment. A supply of horses was always critical for any army. Some of the first written communications between military men that have been discovered document the remount problem.[12]

For more than 4,000 years armies have utilized the horse in war. The Assyrians consolidated their world with the use of both cavalry and chariot horses. Alexander the

Great surged out of his native Macedonia to conquer the nations as far East as India and Persia while barbarian cavalry overran Rome and destroyed that civilization. The effective use of horses, and pack mules, marked the successful campaigns of the great generals throughout history.

It is generally accepted that horsemanship and horse husbandry began on the Gobi Desert in what is now Mongolia. The nomadic horsemen of the steppe left no records to prove or disprove the theory but all evidence points in that direction. With the horse domesticated, these peoples quickly evolved into herdsmen rather than hunters and occasional farmers. They moved constantly, following the grass that fed their immense herds of cattle, sheep and horses. The scattered tribes became formidable warriors, protecting and increasing their pastures. The speed and mobility that the horse gave them conquered neighboring tribes and extended the Mongol kingdom. Banded together under the leadership of Genghis Khan, the Mongols were a fierce fighting force that subdued China, India and even spread as far into Europe as Hungary and Poland. In addition to his string of remounts, each warrior owned several mares nursing foals. Each morning and evening the mares were milked, providing rations for their owner. To these nomads (Mongolians, Samaritans, proto-Turks and Chinese), the horse became a way of life and a cult object since they not only lived on the animals but by them as well. The very possession of the animal dictated their lifestyle and allowed them to maintain and expand their vast domains of grass.[13]

Pen and Ink drawing by Phil Livingston

The Mongol raiders who swooped down on China from the Gobi Desert were terrible adversaries. Riding 'high on their horses,' and with short stirrups, the Mongols were able to effectively use a sword, lance or double-arc bow.

The nomadic Chinese tribes below the Gobi Desert gradually settled down and became farmers and merchants rather than herdsmen. They built up a sophisticated civilization based upon both agriculture and the trade headquartered in their walled cities. To defend that civilization, the rulers of the city states maintained large armies. Those armies were primarily infantry with a few mounted messengers and outriders. The speed of an attack, or a change in tactics, was limited to how fast a man was able to walk. Against the galloping rush of the Mongols, the army was limited in effectiveness and unable to respond to a flanking movement from the enemy. To counter this lack of mobility, the Chinese military leaders developed one of the most devastating tools of war that the world had seen up until that time—the chariot. That vehicle was a lighter, more

maneuverable, horse-powered adaptation of the ox-drawn cart that farmers used. The chariot provided speedy transportation of one or more archers, plus the driver, across the battlefield for mobile firepower. A massed chariot assault upon foot troops provided the shock effect necessary to kill, maim and scatter them. The Chinese frequently painted and sculpted reproductions of their ultimate weapon. Ceramic statuettes of chariots, dating from 3500 B.C. have been found, along with the symbols of deified horses, of the Fu-Hsi Dynasty. The

Pen and Ink drawing by Phil Livingston

The Chinese utilized the chariot as an effective tool of war. Not only was there the 'shock effect' of a vehicle pulled behind two running horses but an archer also supplied mobile fire power.

remains of two-wheeled chariots complete with shafts for harnessing a pair of horses to it have been exhumed not far from the present North China city of Bejing.[14] Huge armies of earthenware soldiers and cavalry mounts of the Xia Dynasty were recently excavated at Mount Li, in the Hui region of Ningxia.

The chariot, in various forms, was of major military importance to the Samaritans, Hittites, Mitannia, Assyrians, Egyptians, Chinese, Persians and Romans who utilized it to conquer much of their known world. It contributed strongly to the successes of the many wars that these peoples carried on during their periods of greatness. Mobility, firepower, shock and speed, all of prime importance in battles against infantry, were provided by a chariot charge. There was no actual cavalry at the time, only messengers and mounted patrols with light swords and spears and utilized as auxiliary corps for surprise attacks.

The true cavalry was to sweep down from the Gobi Desert as the Mongols attempted to conquer China. For centuries the battle raged, the attackers sometimes overrunning a Chinese province, ruling for a time and extracting tribute before withdrawing or being driven out. During the Twelfth Century B.C., Genghis Khan and his armies did overrun all of China and governed for several hundred years. This period was known as the Mongol Dynasty.

While the Mongols were formidable warriors and spread their empire across Asia, warfare was still "each man for himself." Attacks were not an organized grouping of mounted elements designed for maximum shock but rather a charge en masse. The wild riders from the North used bows and arrows, lances and short swords as they spurred their horses over the enemy infantry. This type of attack by mounted units forced the Chinese to abandon the chariots, each supported by a squad or more of slow infantry, and change to a tactic that could effectively counter the more mobile Mongols. The Chinese Emperor Wuling, about 300 B.C., substituted armored riders armed with javelins, a sword and the double-arc bow for chariots and the venerable infantry, meeting the enemy on its own terms. This gave the Chinese the ability to attack, or counter-attack, with the same speed as the Mongols. The real creator of heavy cavalry was Emperor Wu-ti (141–87 B.C.). He replaced the bow with the two-edged sword and the javelin and the long lance in addition to protecting his soldiers with heavier armor. He also adopted the saddle and the stirrup from his "raised-on-a-horse" enemies.[15] This provided his cavalrymen with security and support when mounted, putting them on a more equal basis with the Mongols.[16]

Pen and Ink drawing by Phil Livingston

Alexander the Great of Macedonia conquered much of his known world, expanding his empire as far as India. The effective use of cavalry was one of the primary reasons for his success.

Cavalry tactics began to include the devastating charge by massed riders armed with long spears rather than a disorganized attack by a group of individuals. The shock of a heavy cavalry attack upon a body of infantry was usually enough to destroy and disperse them while opposing light cavalry was scattered. This tactic brought about the disciplined and ordered unity of the battlefield, rather than a haphazard, each-man-for himself-clash of armies. The use of heavy cavalry also led to the additional effectiveness of the army, the breeding of horses capable of carrying the weight of a rider with added equipment and solid but flexible armor. To make this new type of warfare effective and lasting, a steady supply of remounts had to be maintained. That required the development of planned breeding and training establishments.[17]

Recorded history has many accounts of battles that were won, or lost, because of the availability of cavalry, chariots or a supply of remounts. Alexander the Great of Macedonia, Greece, Rome, the Gauls, Etruscans, various Germanic tribes and the

Britons all successfully utilized the horse in battle. The concept of speed and the disruption of enemy supply lines (light cavalry) and the shock of a frontal attack (heavy cavalry and/or chariots) to support the massed infantry were often the deciding factors. In order to utilize these elements, the army must have a steady stream of remounts.

Successful use of chariots required flat, dry plains where the vehicles could maneuver at top speed. This is why they were so effective in China, the Middle East and North Africa. The forested hills and wet weather of what was to become Germany and France made them impractical in Europe. During the Middle Ages, heavy cavalry was utilized to support infantry. These units could maneuver around the enemy as well as provide the shock effect of a frontal attack. Since only the wealthy could afford horses and the necessary support for them, the feeling arose that "the man on horseback" was of prime importance and more important than one who walked. This led to the concept of individual combat among principal warriors, the code of chivalry and the knight in armor. What had begun as an expedient of war became a social form of life with status for the knights and rules of conduct for all levels of civilization.

A war horse of the medieval period was required to carry nearly 900 pounds—knight, armor, saddle, equine armor and trappings and weapons—and was necessarily large, sixteen hands or more and weighing 1,400-plus pounds. Size, not speed, was the criteria since the charge between two knights was seldom more than a lumbering trot. The "shock effect" of a well-aimed knight's lance, backed by all that weight, was the reason that the opponent was unhorsed. The added size and weight was also one of the major effects that heavy cavalry had in a charge on massed infantry. Breeding of such horses was of prime importance. Much attention was paid to feeding, training and shoeing of the war horse. In addition to these war mounts, there were other types of horses bred during that time for agriculture, packing, general riding and hunting.[18]

Pen and Ink drawing by Phil Livingston
During the Crusades of the 12th Century, European knights, loaded down with steel armor and mounted on large, slow horses, were out-maneuvered by the Moors. The warriors from the desert were riding quick, agile horses, used short stirrups and were able to effectively handle their weapons.

In 710 A.D the Moslems-Moors from North Africa invaded Spain. The following year, to solidify their initial conquest, a powerful army of more than 7,000 Moorish troops crossed the Strait of Gibraltar. These troops were soon followed by 5,000 additional cavalry. The first battle that the Moors fought against the Spanish armies was at Guadeleta. It lasted for three days and culminated in victory for the invaders. According to Dhobi, the Moorish historian, the defeat of the Spanish army was due to their inadequate cavalry. The Europeans were too few, too slow and too cumbersome.[19]

This was not the only time that the heavy cavalry of Europe had lost to the maneuverability of Asian horsemen. The Christian Crusaders, in their vain attempts to recover the Holy Land from Moslem control during the Twelfth and Thirteenth Centuries, had faced the same problem with the same results.

At the time of the Moorish invasion, the European knights rode with very long stirrups, almost as if they were riding bareback, *a la brida*. Their mounts were the "Great Horse" of Europe and were neither fast nor agile. The saddle was set behind the horse's withers and both mount and rider were covered with heavy metal armor that limited mobility and speed. The Moors placed the saddle well forward on the horse's withers and rode with their knees bent, which allowed them more flexibility, *a la jineta*. The rider could stand in the stirrups

Pen and Ink drawing by Phil Livingston
The Spanish exploration of America was the story of horsemen and their mounts. Cortez, DeSoto, Coronado, Ornate, DeAnza and other Spanish captains took as many horses with them on their expeditions as possible.

and maneuver his upper body to swing a sword or handle a bow as well as duck the slash of an opposing warrior's weapon. The style of riding has survived until the present and few horsemen ride with stirrups so long that they cannot stand in the saddle. The horses were smaller, lighter and much faster (primarily of Arabian, Persian and Barb breeding) and were more maneuverable than those of the Spanish knights.[20]

Spain remained under Moorish influence until the early Fifteenth Century when the armies of King Ferdinand V and Queen Isabella pushed the invaders back across the Mediterranean Sea. During the nearly 700 years the Arabs were in Spain, the Spanish adopted many of their ways. The most notable contributions were in the area of horse breeding and horsemanship. The cross between the European Great Horse and the light, quick imports from Africa produced a superior war and utility horse. By 1500, the Spanish Horse was renowned all over Europe as the finest mount available. In those years, Spain became a nation of horsemen and the word for gentleman, *caballero*, meant horseman.[21]

The discovery of the Americas by Columbus in 1492 sparked an age of Spanish exploration. In spite of the difficulty of sea transportation, the war horse was in the forefront of the expanding Spanish world. Cortez began his conquest of Mexico in 1519 with just sixteen war horses he had transshipped from Cuba. He readily admitted later that without the horses, conquering the Aztec Indians with his small force would have been impossible. As the Spanish spread north into what has become Mexico and the United States, and south to Argentina, there was a steady need for military remounts. In Cuba, and later Mexico, horse breeding rapidly became one of the premier industries, along with raising cattle, sheep and hogs. The military expeditions that explored the unknown Americas required horses and each commander took as many remounts with him as possible. One example was the Marqués de San Miguel de Aguayo's expedition in 1719, to reconquer Texas, called Nuevas Filipinas at the time. He left the state of Coahuila, Mexico, with 500 men and 6,600 horses.[22] The Spanish were well aware of how important horses were to their success and tried to keep them from falling into Indian hands. That was a vain effort. By the middle 1700s, the horse had spread through the Indian tribes of Mexico, in both North and South America, and was running wild in huge herds on the open plains.[23]

Pen and Ink drawing by Phil Livingston

This Trooper of the U.S. Army 2nd Cavalry, in 1840, was assigned to Texas, to contain raiding Indians. The 2nd Cavalry, formed from an earlier unit of Dragoons (mounted infantry), was one of the first American cavalry troops.

It was on the plains of North America that the horse became the central figure in the Indian lifestyle. By 1800 the majority of the tribes owned herds of horses and had developed a culture that mirrored that of the earlier tribes on the Gobi Desert. The primary difference was that the American Indians never became herdsmen. They simply followed the huge herds of bison and remained hunters. Horses gave the Indians greater mobility and speed, which enabled them to enlarge their hunting domains. Horses also became a symbol of wealth, with the individual who owned large numbers of the animals having more status within the tribe than one who did not. Horses were traded for every item of commerce and even used as the medium of exchange when a wife was purchased—the more horses that were traded for her, the more she was valued.

War took on a new dimension with the horse since a war party could range further afield. Horse stealing was also a major part of a brave's life and the thrill of taking a horse, or horses, tied to an enemy's lodge at night meant more than herding a band away from camp.

In 1803 President Thomas Jefferson's Louisiana Purchase gave the United States title to over 800,000 square miles of territory between the Mississippi River and the Rocky Mountains. Formerly claimed by France, the area was largely unexplored by white men. To provide knowledge of the new purchase, President Jefferson sent Lewis and Clark on a two-year exploring expedition. While most of the trip was made on foot or by keel boats pulled up the Mississippi River by the explorers, horses acquired from the Indian tribes of the Rocky Mountains were used to some extent.[24]

There is little mention of military horsemanship during the American Revolution of 1776 or the War of 1812.[25] The first was fought primarily by American frontiersmen on foot who utilized guerrilla tactics against the ordered infantry of England. The few horses used were for scouting, to carry messages or to haul supplies. There was no organized cavalry. In fact, General George Washington was known to have opposed cavalry tactics and depended upon his infantry to fight in the wooded hills of the Eastern seaboard.[26] In 1792 Congress authorized the formation of a single company of dragoons, mounted infantry, a second in 1796 and a full regiment in 1798. The function of these dragoons was primarily to protect the settlers against the Indians. The second war against the British in 1812 was fought on the seas, with scattered infantry and artillery engagements on land such as the Battle of New Orleans. The dragoons played a very limited part in this conflict. Perhaps the fact that the British had no cavalry on American soil during the two-and-one-half-year war removed the need for mounted troops in the eyes of the American commanders. At the end of the war, with the nation crying for economy, Congress cut the mounted arm to a single regiment of eight troops, and in 1816, abolished it completely.[27]

It wasn't until 1832, that the fledgling United States Government again recognized the importance of mounted soldiers. A battalion, six companies, of mounted rangers were organized. The men furnished their own horses, clothing, equipment and arms. The rapid mobility provided by such troops was the only way in which the immense new lands that the nation had acquired could be controlled. The following year, Congress disbanded the mounted rangers and grudgingly allotted funds to create, equip and mount a regiment of dragoons. The primary purpose of the dragoons was to confront the mounted Indian tribes on the Western Plains.[28] Correspondence among army officers of the dragoons recounts the age-old, constantly reoccurring problem of obtaining suitable remounts in any quantity.

By 1810 the Americans had crossed the Mississippi River and were on the Great Plains. Trade with the Spanish settlement of Santa Fe, as well as with the trappers in the Rocky

Mountains for furs, was the first commercial use of the area. Trade goods were transported by pack horse or lumbering wagons pulled by either mules or oxen. To cope with the Plains Indians, Congress authorized the establishment of several frontier forts manned by infantry. Supporting the infantry were three mounted regiments of dragoons, scattered from Texas to Oregon. Realizing that the army at its then-existing strength could not effectively cope with the "Indian

Photograph courtesy Calvin Allen
Cavalry officer and troopers of the 1870s or 1880s.

problem," Congress authorized two new bodies of mounted troops. The two regiments were designated the First and Second Regiments of Cavalry. The latter was assigned to the Department of Texas.[29] The Second Cavalry's mission was to protect and support the settlers against both Indians and Mexican bandits. This organization adopted the successful techniques used by the earlier-formed Texas Rangers. The superior firepower of both the revolving pistol and repeating rifle, as well as the speed of movement, were major tools in their campaigns. Many of the officers who served with the Second Cavalry went on to distinguished service in the Civil War, on both sides, and never forgot the fighting lessons learned on the Texas plains.

The Civil War, 1861–1865, was a series of bloody battles that were frequently punctuated by cavalry raids or attacks on supply lines. The Union Army had 370-some Volunteer Cavalry Regiments in the field during the war, only six Regular Regiments, while the Confederacy utilized 137 Volunteer Cavalry Regiments.[30] Over 650,000 horses were used by both armies. The majority of the animals were killed or wounded in action or died from exhaustion, lack of feed, exposure to the elements or overwork. At the peak of the war, the Union Army was replacing more than 500 a horses week. In the first eight months of 1864 the Army of the Potomac used up 40,000 horses—an average of two remounts for each man.[31] During the last stages of the conflict, almost anything with four legs was considered suitable for a cavalry mount or to pull either a cannon or supply wagon. A soldier was only as good as his horse, unless he was an infantryman, and then he was dependent upon horse power for his supplies.

Following the Civil War and the opening of the Indian Campaigns in the West, military leaders immediately began calling for remounts. However, civilian breeders did not have the quality nor the quantity of horseflesh available. The war had reduced breeding stock to a very low level and it took time to rebuild. Most soldiers in the Department of the West rode horses purchased locally rather than imports from the states. There were simply not enough of the latter to mount the entire cavalry.

Most of the western Indian tribes developed large herds of horses and were able to change mounts regularly. This, combined with an intimate knowledge of the terrain, gave them the mobility to attack or retreat at will and always be mounted on a fresh horse. The army, limited to one mount per man and operating in unfamiliar country, could not successfully compete and spent much of the time in futile pursuit. Only by surprise attacks on Indian camps, the capture or elimination of the horse herds and the destruction of the food supply—the buffalo—did the U.S. Army finally win. An example of eliminating the Indians remounts was demonstrated on the Texas plains by Colonel Randal MacKenzie in 1874. He surprised the Comanches and a number of Kiowas in their winter camp at the Palo Duro Canyon. After attacking and scattering the Indians, he destroyed over 1,000 head of captured horses. He could not afford to have the Comanches steal them back and continue to make war. MacKenzie's methods were brutal, but effective. Putting the Comanches afoot helped to bring about a close to the Comanche Wars on the South Plains when Chief Quanah Parker surrendered in June of 1875.[32]

Photograph by Mathew Brady
A Union officer sits his mount during the Civil War. This is a serviceable military mount, regardless of the period in which he was used.

Horse power for the quartermaster and field artillery of an army, in the form of both draft and pack animals, plus cavalry mounts have often been the deciding factor in the success of a military campaign. During his Russian expedition of 1812, Napoleon crossed the Niemen River with 187,121 horses, 60,000 of which were cavalry. Between the Niemen and Vilna rivers, 10,000 died because of bad roads and lack of food. Another 92,000 succumbed before the first snowfall, primarily from starvation. Six months later, Napoleon's cavalry retreated back across the Niemen with only 1,600 horses. Another example was the Crimean War of 1855. The British and French lost many horses from starvation. Within only a few months, the British cavalry and artillery horses were reduced from 5,048 to 2,258.[33]

Photograph courtesy The Western Horseman
These pre-World War I, U.S. Army supply wagons with a 6-mule hitch, as well as pack trains, transported goods and supplies in the field.

The South African Boer War between the Dutch Settlers—Boers—and the British (1899–1902) utilized over 500,000 horses. Some 150,000 did not survive, either from overuse, poor care or death from disease resulting from a bite by the tsetse fly. Many of the animals were purchased in the United States for the British army by William Anson.[34] Eventually over 100,000 horses and 85,000 mules were acquired and shipped to South Africa. Those volume sales brought about a financial windfall to Western horse breeders. The large-scale purchases of animals did emphasize, however, that while America had thousands of horses, only a small percentage were of truly military quality. John Molesworth of Clarendon, Texas, and a horse buyer for William Anson, observed, "Horses were divided into two classes, A and B. The former were paid for at the rate of $110 per head and the latter up to $95 per head, although many were purchased for as low as $30 per head."[35]

The U.S. Congress declared war on Spain on April 1, 1898. That meant that once again American men, horses and mules would be called into action. At that time, the army, which had been primarily on garrison duty, had only 2,221 mules. Twenty-one were pack stock, the balance were draft animals. Supply officer Colonel C. P. Mullen estimated that for the Cuban campaign 5,000 wagons with 23,500 mules to pull them plus 100 pack trains would be needed.[36]

Photograph courtesy U.S. Army
U.S. Cavalry horses were kept in narrow stalls aboard ship during the voyage to Cuba, during the Spanish-American War, 1898. Slats helped horses keep their footing when feeding from the deck.

Lt. Tom Cruse was immediately sent to St. Louis, Missouri to purchase 1,780 pack mules. His purchases finally totaled 16,681 horses and 20,182 mules. Eventually, 16,483 horses and 19,550 mules were issued for military use during the Spanish-American War.[37]

The American army landed at Daiquiri, Cuba, [...] .orced the ships to stand out from land. The only way to unload the animals was to push them overboard and hope that they swam to shore. Some became confused, swam out to sea and drowned. U.S. forces remained in Cuba until 1902. Animal transportation of supplies, both by wagon and pack train, was used the entire time.[38]

During the late spring and summer of 1898 the United States put down the Philippine Insurrection. At that time, 2,000 regular troops, 1,300 volunteers and 300 pack mules were sent to the Philippine Islands. From August 1898 through November 1900, the United States government was to send 6,275 horses and 3,259 mules to the Philippine Islands for military use. The islands became a territory of the United States and were continually garrisoned by American troops until 1947 when the Philippines became an independent nation. In the nearly half-century of involvement, thousands of cavalry and draft horses, along with pack and draft mules, were shipped there from the port of San Francisco.[39]

Photograph courtesy U.S. Army

L Troop 6th Cavalry U.S. Army patrols near the Great Wall of China, not far from the Ming Tombs, during the Boxer Rebellion, 1921. U.S. soldiers were sent to China to guard American citizens and diplomatic legations.

In the summer of 1900, pack and wagon mules accompanied the Ninth Infantry Regiment to China from Luzon, the Philippines. The purpose was to help put down the Boxer Rebellion against all foreigners in China. The Sixth Cavalry was also committed to the expedition, receiving mounts from the United States just in time to embark aboard ship for Tientsin. The American troops, and mules, made an excellent showing.[40]

World War I, 1914–1918, was the last world conflict in which cavalry horses played a major role. It was, however, to be another thirty years before the bugles sounded the final Taps for the mounted service. American-bred animals were used on both sides in the war. By 1910, buyers from European nations were crisscrossing the United States, purchasing military mounts, draft animals and mules. The large horse markets at Fort Worth, Texas; Kansas City, Kansas; St. Louis, Missouri; Denver, Colorado; Miles City, Montana; Ft. Smith, Arkansas; and Sacramento, California, all moved thousands of horses to military buyers. During the period from November 1, 1914, to July 29, 1915, foreign governments purchased an estimated 200,000 horses in the U.S.[41] In anticipation of the coming war, the American army entered the picture in 1914, ultimately acquiring over 500,000 horses for service during 1914–1918. Of that half-million-plus horses, some 68,000 were killed in France alone.[42] At an average price of $150 per head, military purchases pumped some $82.5 million into America's agricultural economy in just four years.

Mules for military use were also an important market. Great Britain was a major buyer, relying upon the services of Guyton and Harrington, Lathrop, Missouri, to supply them. During the Boer War, the firm supplied the British Army with 55,061 mules. For World War I use, Guyton and Harrington exported 180,000 of the long-eared soldiers.[43]

The U.S. Army also got into the market after America entered the war in the spring of 1917. At that time, the army possessed 27,624 draft and pack mules. By September, 35,068 trained animals were awaiting shipment to France.[44] At the conclusion of the war, the American army sold 121,465 horses and 56,207 mules in Europe. Thousands more were sold in the United States during the first six months following the war, with another 50,000 disposed of before the end of May 1919.[45] During World War I, the German military forces used more than 14 million horses. The British lost some 256,000 animals during their battles in Europe.[46]

Before America entered the war in Europe, the U.S. Cavalry was engaged along the border and in Mexico. On March 9, 1916, the Mexican revolutionary General Pancho

Villa crossed the International Border at Columbus, New Mexico, and attacked the town. Units from the Seventh and Tenth U.S. Cavalry, under the command of Brigadier General John J. "Black Jack" Pershing, immediately moved into Mexico and pushed the opposing forces back from the border. This was called the Punitive Expedition, one of the most grueling tests of mounted forces that has ever been

Photograph courtesy U.S. Army
U.S. Cavalry is on the march near Marfa, Texas, during the undertaken by American forces. On the
Punitive Expedition to Mexico, 1916.

second day of the campaign, the American cavalry units traveled sixty-eight miles in thirteen hours through desert and mountain terrain. During the ten months that the Punitive Expedition was in Mexico, the troops were in constant movement and tested their mounts to the limit.[47]

Following the Villa incident, American cavalry was assigned along the Mexican border in Texas, New Mexico and Arizona. These troops patrolled against Mexican bandits, smugglers or illegal immigrants. During and immediately after World War I there were numerous raids on isolated American ranches. Units of the Fifth, Seventh, Eighth and Tenth Cavalry all served on the border with distinction until the middle 1930s when their duties were taken over by the Texas Rangers and the U.S. Customs and Immigration River Guards. Troops were stationed at Marfa, Ruidoso and Fort Bliss (El Paso) Texas and at Fort Huachuca, Arizona.[48] The rugged country along the Rio Grande River made it impossible for any type of military unit other than cavalry to operate effectively.

While the coming military mechanization was easy to recognize following the "War to End All Wars," the army continued to include horsepower in future plans. Cavalry, pack artillery, field artillery and pack trains, were all utilized. Horses and mules could go almost anywhere that a man could walk, carry a heavier load, and move faster.

Photograph courtesy Phil Livingston

Russian troops use horse-drawn wagons to bring artillery quickly to the front lines while fighting against Germany in 1942.

Trucks, automobiles, tanks and mechanized artillery were limited in numbers, there was a shortage of fuel and lubricating oils as well as dependable, trained personnel, and they could only operate on graded roads. Horses definitely had their place as far as the military was concerned. In fact, planners for the coming World War II envisioned a need for 200,000 horses and mules.

The interest in horse power was not confined to just the American army. Cavalry was employed as a major element during the Spanish Civil War by Generalissimo Franco during the 1930s. In spite of outside aid, principally mechanized, he increased his horse cavalry from five to sixty squadrons.[49] The Japanese utilized both cavalry and horse-drawn field artillery during their Chinese campaigns in the late 1930s. They also planned for an increased military horse breeding program in China with a projected 7,500 stallions in service by 1945.[50] During the same period the German army had more than 791,000 horses, both riding and draft types, in military reserve. More than 200,000 horses were used during the Polish campaign alone.[51] To meet these military demands, the Germans maintained extensive breeding operations that produced some of the finest cavalry mounts that the world had ever seen. During World War II, 1939–1945, the German military machine used 2.75 million horses.[52] The heralded German "Blitzkrieg" attack with tanks across Poland and Franch was supported by horse-drawn wagons.

The Russian forces were also dependent upon horseflesh, deploying a total of 3.5 million animals during World War II. During the Battle of Stalingrad more than 52,000 head were lost.[53] The Russian cavalry played a decisive role in the defense of both

Moscow and Stalingrad, striking swift, devastating blows, then quickly withdrawing and melting into the countryside.[54]

The final mounted charge in American military history was made in January of 1942. A cavalry platoon of Philippine Scouts attached to the U.S. Army attacked, and routed, Japanese forces in the Philippine Islands.[56] The American motion picture industry even got into the act with the low-budget film, *Texas to Bataan*. This forgotten "oater" (a slang term for a cheap Western in the 1930s and 1940s) recounted the adventures of a trio of Texas cowboys taking a boat load of army horses to the Philippine Islands.[57] By the time that the film was issued, the Philippines had fallen to the Japanese.

Photograph courtesy The Western Horseman
The cavalry camp and picket lines, Fort Davis, Texas, 1916, as the U.S. Army guards the border against Mexican bandits.

Following U.S. involvement in World War II on December 7, 1941, the U.S. Coast Guard drew horses from the Remount Service for beach patrol to guard against hostile landings from submarines. A mounted sentry could cover more ground than one on foot, with the added advantage of speed. Other military units used horses in the same, effective manner, guarding bases and prisoner of war camps. This was the primary American military use of horses during the war.[59]

Several hundred horses were procured in Australia and issued to the rapidly formed American Division to defend the Island of New Caledonia. There was no combat there and the horses were eventually shipped to Burma. After service there, the animals were marched over the Burma Road into China for issue to the Nationalist Chinese Army.[60]

American mules were, however, shipped to India where they were utilized by American, British, Nationalist Chinese and native forces as pack animals against the Japanese. Pack mules from America, as well as locally obtained animals, were used by troops fighting in the Italian mountains. For the first time in American military history, more mules than horses were in use since cavalry units were fought as mechanized infantry.

American soldiers utilized locally purchased mules in Tunisia during 1942–43 and throughout the later mountain battles in Sicily and Italy. Those mules packed supplies in and casualties out where terrain made motor vehicles useless.[61] At Algiers, North Africa, a small detachment of mules and wagons leased from the French Foreign Legion transshipped supplies from one airplane to another during 1943 and 1944. That kept the materiel pipeline open for the European front in spite of limited vehicle availability.[62] During 1943 and 1944, 7,800 American mules were shipped to India for duty as pack animals in the China-Burma-India theater of operations. In December of 1944 and February, 1945, some 2,500 of those animals were flown in C-47 air transports over the Himalaya Mountains to Kunming, China. The balance made the trip over the Burma Road on foot.[63] These incidences from World War II are discussed in detail in Chapter 6, The War Years: 1941–1945.

A few of the mules given to the Chinese saw later service during the Korean War of 1950–51. Several were captured from Red Chinese by U.S. troops and pressed into service carrying supplies, ammunition and water. They were identified by the Preston Brands on their necks.[64] One mule was branded 08K0. He was captured from the Red Chinese by members of the First Cavalry Division in 1951. According to American military records, he had been foaled in the United States, purchased by the army and trained at Fort Robinson, Nebraska, in 1945. He was transported to India where he served with American troops in the China-Burma-India theater of operations. Following the Japanese surrender in 1945, 08K0 was taken to China and turned over to the Nationalist Chinese Army. After the Communist government took over China in the late 1940s, he was claimed by the Red Army. Brand Number 08K0 went to Korea with Communist troops where he was eventually recaptured and used by the First Cavalry.[65] See also Chapter 8, p. 225, for more discussion of 08K0.

A number of high-ranking American officers who fought in World War II had strong feelings that both cavalry and pack mules had a place in the various theaters of operation. Included were General Dwight D. Eisenhower, who said, "Horse cavalry units could have been effectively utilized in Tunisia if they had been available." General O. N. Bradley said, "In contemplated operations in mountainous terrain, plans should include facilities for supply by pack train." General George S. Patton said,

> It is the considered opinion, not only of myself but of many other general officers who took their origin from the infantry and artillery, that had we possessed an American cavalry division with pack artillery in Tunisia and in Sicily, not a German would have escaped. Horse cavalry possesses an additional gear ratio which permits it to attain sufficient speed through mountainous country to get behind and hold the enemy until the more powerful infantry and tanks can come up and destroy him.[66]

As effective as both cavalry and pack trains had proven to be, they were not utilized as extensively as they could have been. Regardless of the support from prominent general officers, the horse and mule units were disbanded and soldiers transferred to other outfits. By 1944, the cavalry of the United States Army had been dehorsed and was being fought as mechanized infantry. The effectiveness of cavalry was not, however, completely forgotten by military planners. As late as 1944, the War Department was discussing using horse cavalry in the final stages against Japan. In preparation of that, nearly 800 pack mules had been shipped to Hawaii for the proposed campaign on the China coast. A successful conclusion to this planned offensive would then lead to the attack on Japan. The use of the atomic bomb settled that question. The mules were eventually shipped to China as part of the agricultural United Nations Relief and Recovery Administration (UNRRA) program.[67]

Photograph courtesy U.S. Army
U.S. Army pack mules in the Philippine Islands during the 1930s travel in a loose string behind a bell mare and attended by mule-riding soldiers.

While horses and mules were no longer utilized in global conflicts, they did have a place in regional wars fought in mountainous and primitive areas. In 1949, the U.S. Government supplied Greek forces with over 10,000 American mules for use against Communists.[68] During 1951–54, the U.S. Army purchased and shipped more than 12,000 American horses and mules as part of a Turkish military assistance program.[69]

Horses also played an important part in Afghanistan's battle against Russian occupation in the 1980s. The Afghanistan forces effectively countered Russian helicopters by packing supplies into the rugged mountains with horses as well as riding the animals.[70] Doctor Fazlullah, Chief Commander of the Mujahideen in the Lowgar Province of Afghanistan, observed, "Without the horse, we could not defeat the Russian force. The horse is vital to us. He carries whatever we need from Pakistan to conduct our war."[71]

By the middle of the Twentieth Century, a military tradition tracing back some 4,000 years had finally "cased the colors" and ridden off into the sunset. The mounted cavalry, the pack artillery, the long strings of pack mules and the lumbering supply wagons, as well as the need for remounts, had been phased out of modern warfare. The concept of mobility, of speed and shock in the attack was, however, not obsolete. The cavalryman mounted on his horse was replaced first by the tank, used so successfully during World War II by German Field Marshal Erwin Rommel in North Africa and by the American General George S. Patton Jr., both in North Africa and in France. The next remount was the helicopter that came into military service during the Korean Conflict of 1950 and then during the 1960s in Vietnam. The latter combined both the supply function of the pack mule with the speed and mobility of a cavalry attack. The military insignia that indicates the branch of service for the men who utilize the flying "remounts" still features the crossed sabers of the cavalry.

The sheer volume of military horses and mules utilized by America for over a century and a half is impressive. Little attention has been paid to the economic impact that the cavalry and related branches of the service, along with the supply units needed, have had on the country. Saddle, pack and draft animals were always a viable commodity, especially during times of war. Breeders, dealers, suppliers of fodder, tack and other equipment all benefitted from the dollars spent to keep the military mounted and equipped. America also exported large numbers of horses and mules to foreign armies. Mention has already been made of William Anson purchasing more that 85,000 mules and 100,000-plus horses for the British Army during the Boer War of 1899–1902. The years prior to World War I also found foreign buyers traveling across the nation to purchase cavalry remounts and draft mules. The American army also bought more than 500,000 head. This was all an economic blessing to the ranchers who raised large numbers of good horses, not just for military consumption but for the civilian market as well. A horse that was an effective "usin' horse" on a ranch, hunter, polo mount, pleasure horse or was suitable between the shafts of a doctor's buggy also made a superior cavalry mount. There was a steady market for those ranch-raised geldings.

Mules were always in strong demand, furnishing the power for farming, pulling heavy wagons on city streets, lumbering or working underground in the mines. At the military level, those big-eared soldiers pulled wagons, packed supplies and even carried soldiers from time to time.

Early newspapers made much of the warrior/war horse association and kept the public aware of equine stars and their famous riders. At various times in America's history, the names of the following horses were almost as well known as those of their riders:

> Baldy, ridden by Union General George Meade during the Civil War
> Black Tom, ridden by Colonel Charles May during the Mexican War
> Blueskin, ridden by General George Washington during the Revolutionary War
> Cincinnati, ridden by General Ulysses S. Grant during the Civil War
> Comanche, ridden by Captain Miles Keogh to the Battle of the Little Big
>   Horn. Comanche was the only survivor of the U.S. Army military force.

Jeff and Kidron, ridden by General John J. "Black Jack" Pershing in Europe
during World War I

King Philip, ridden by General Nathan B. Forrest during the Civil War

Little Sorrel, ridden by General Stonewall Jackson during the Civil War

Old Whitey, ridden by General Zachary Taylor during the Mexican War

Rienzi, ridden by General Philip Sheridan during the Civil War

Traveller, ridden by General Robert E. Lee during the Civil War

Vic, ridden by General George A. Custer to the Battle of the Little Big Horn.
It was later reported that Vic had been seen ridden by an Indian brave.[72]

The mounted cavalry, the rattling cannons and caissons, the pack mules and pack artillery, as well as the long wagon trains, are all gone except in a few memories, the pages of books or the movie screen. The military accomplishments of the men who rode and used those animals have not been forgotten, however. The horse provided a military concept that revolutionized battle-speed, mobility, shock in an attack—and was often the pivotal point in a combat. But, to be continually effective, this type of warfare required a steady stream of remounts to replace those lost. For countless centuries, military men addressed the problem, and, in many cases, developed a superior horse in the process.

While the American army did not confront the remount problem, other than purchasing what was available from civilian breeders, until early in the Twentieth Century when the demise of the cavalry was already approaching, American breeders rapidly developed a type of horse that was both militarily and commercially acceptable. The decisions made in the breeding pens more than a century ago are still influencing the horses of today. The blood of many outstanding Remount stallions flows in the veins of numerous modern ranch, rodeo, show, cutting, polo, racing and pleasure mounts in America.

Chapter 1: Sources and Notes

1. H. J. "Hank" Wiescamp, interview by Ed Roberts, Alamosa, Colorado, June 28, 1993.
2. Robert M. Denhardt, *Foundation Sires of the American Quarter Horse* (Norman: University of Oklahoma Press, 1976), 11.
3. See *American Quarter Horse Association Stud Books*, Amarillo, Texas. See also Robert M. Denhardt, *Foundation Sires of the American Quarter Horse* (Norman: University of Oklahoma Press, 1976).
4. See Appaloosa Horse Club Stud Books, Moscow, Idaho. Also, Frank Holmes, "Bobbie N. F-2675," *Appaloosa Journal* (May 1993): 3.
5. See American Paint Horse Association Stud Books, Fort Worth, Texas.
6. See Palomino Horse Association Stud Books, Tulsa, Oklahoma. See also Dr. H. Arthur Zappe, "A Palomino of Note-Plaudit," *Western Horseman* (January–February 1948): 8-9.
7. Naomi K. Chesky, "In Search of a Palomino," *The Fence Post* (January 3, 1994): 4.
8. Jo-Ann Rosser Barnett, *Cow Horse Hall of Fame* (The Working Cow Horse Breeders of Yuba-Sutter Counties, Inc., 1979), 87–111.
9. Willard H. Porter, *13 Flat* (Cranbury, New Jersey: A. S. Barnes and Company, 1967), 67, 148. Also from the authors' personal knowledge of how horses were bred.
10. Larry Thornton, "Sonny Dee Bar," *Southern Horseman* (July 1993): 38. It was also well-known among cutters/horsemen that Skeeter was Remount top and bottom.
11. Dan Doole Taylor, interview with Phil Livingston, August 14, 1993.
12. Luigi Gianoli, *Horses and Horsemanship Through the Ages* (New York: Crown Publishers, 1967), 13.
13. Ibid., 10–12.
14. Ibid., 11–12.
15. The "raised-on-a-horse" Mongols rode horseback from the time they were very small children. Other than eating—which they sometimes did in the saddle—and sleeping, their livelihood (herding flocks, traveling, fighting) and recreation (racing, hunting, contests) was all performed from the back of a horse.
16. Gianoli, *Horses and Horsemanship*, 17–18.
17. Ibid.
18. Ibid., 76–95.
19. Robert M. Denhardt, *The Horse of the Americas* (Norman: University of Oklahoma Press, 1947), 15.
20. Ibid., 18.
21. Ibid., 20.
22. Paul I. Wellman, *Glory, God and Gold* (New York: Doubleday and Company, 1954), 165.
23. Denhardt, Horse of the Americas, 33–90.
24. Meriwether Lewis and William Clark, *The Journals of Lewis and Clark* (New York: Signet Books, The New American Library, Inc., 1964), 234, 239, 303–06, 309.
25. Randy Steffen, *United States Military Saddles* (Norman: University of Oklahoma Press), vi.
26. Glen Vernaum, *Man on Horseback* (Lincoln: University of Nebraska Press, 1972), 266–67.
27. Steffen, *United States Military Saddles*, 14–15.
28. Ibid.
29. Ibid.
30. Monique and Hans Dossenback, *The Noble Horse* (New York: Crown Publishers, 1987), 167. Also, Thomas R. Bueckner, Curator, Fort Robinson Museum, Fort Robinson, Nebraska, personal letter to Ed Roberts, November 25, 1996.
31. Major General William Harding Carter, U.S.A., "The Story of the Horse," *The National Geographic Magazine* (November 1923): 553.
32. Benjamin Capps, *The Indians* (New York: Time-Life Books, 1973), 194.
33. Carter, "The Story of the Horse," 553.
34. William Anson was an English lord who came to Texas at the turn of the century and established a ranch near San Angelo, Texas. He developed a large business selling polo horses on America's eastern coast. In 1899 he purchased a son of the original Rondo and began breeding Quarter Horses. Among stallions that he owned or bred were: Harmon Baker by Peter McCue, Concho Colonel, Brown Jug, Ballymooney and Sam Jones. He was a student of bloodlines and was the first person to write about the Quarter Horse as a separate breed.
35. Dr. John Ashton, "Billy Anson and the Quarter Horse," *The Cattleman* (September 1946): 33. Also, Dossenback, *The Noble Horse*, 170.
36. Emmett M. Essin, *Shavetails & Bell Sharps* (Lincoln: University of Nebraska Press, 1997), 124–128.
37. Ibid.
38. Ibid.
39. Ibid, 132–34.
40. Phil Livingston grew up in the "Old Army" as the son of Colonel C. E. Livingston and thus knew of much of this information.
41. J'Nell L. Pate, *Livestock Legacy: The Fort Worth Stockyards, 1887–1987* (College Station: Texas A & M Press, 1988), 99.
42. Dossenback, *The Noble Horse*, 99.
43. Essin, *Shavetails & Bell Sharps*, 147.
44. Ibid., 150.

45. Ibid., 156.

46. Dossenback, *The Noble Horse*, 170.

47. Ibid., 171.

48. United States Cavalry; Patton Museum Society Publication No. 2; Patton Museum of Cavalry and Armor, Fort Knox, Kentucky.

49. Lt. Col. Edwin N. Hardy, "The Remount Service and the Army Breeding Plan," *The Quartermaster Review* (March–April 1940): 7.

50. Colonel Thomas J. Johnson, "The Army Horse, Model 1940," *The Blood-Horse* (August 10, 1940): 15.

51. Ibid.

52. Dossenback, *The Noble Horse*, 171.

53. Ibid.

54. M. E. Ensminger, *Horses and Horsemanship* (Danville, Illinois: The Interstate Printers and Publishers, 1963), 11.

55. Edwin Price Ramsey and Stephen J. Rivel, *The Secret War of Ed Ramsey* (Pleasantville, New York: Reader's Digest, March 1992), 127.

56. *Movies by Mail Catalog* (Silver City, New Mexico), 55.

57. Anna M. Waller, *Horses and Mules and National Defense* (U.S. Army Office of the Quartermaster General, SVIII-3-009, 1958), 19.

58. General Wayne O. Kester, "Horses and Mules Also Fought," *Horse Illustrated* (October 1991): 8.

59. Ibid., 8–9. Also, Ray H. Erhardt, "The Remount Service of the Office of the Quartermaster General, U.S. Army 1908–1954," unpublished manuscript, 1990.

60. Colonel C. E. Livingston, interview with Phil Livingston, June 1990.

61. Erhardt, "The Remount Service of the Office of the Quartermaster General, U.S. Army 1908–1954," 4. Also, Dr. Lee T. Railsbeck, Manhatten, Kansas, personal interview April 1991.

62. Emmett M. Essin, "Army Mules in World War II—the Last Hurrah?" *The Brayer* (undated copy): 110.

63. Waller, *Horses and Mules and National Defense*, 31.

64. Ibid., 22.

65. Ibid., 24.

66. Ibid., 39.

67. Ibid.

68. Hunter Ryan, "Afghan War Horses," *The Western Horseman* (January 1988): 35.

69. Ibid., 34

70. Waller, *Horses and Mules and National Defense*, 75.

* An asterisk in front of a horse's name means it was imported.

The Floating Picket Line

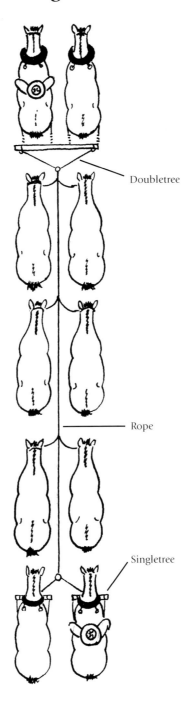

Doubletree

Rope

Singletree

Courtesy of the Quartermaster Corps Horse Guide

The floating picket line permits the exercising of 30 to 50 horses with a minimum of personnel. Both lead horses and rear horses are harnessed, and a rider is mounted every fifth pair of horses.

Photograph courtesy U.S. Army
Soldiers and their mounts stand at attention in front of one of the barns at Fort Reno, Oklahoma, after World War I.

CHAPTER 2

THE HISTORY AND PURPOSE
OF THE U.S. REMOUNT SERVICE

*"From my personal observation, after twenty-eight years in the army, it
is my opinion that the quality and stamina of horses have been tremendously
improved in America."*

Colonel C. E. Wilkerson
Army Remount Purchasing Officer

Born of necessity, the United States Army Quartermaster Corps Remount
Service, and the resulting horse breeding program, was one of the most
successful military procurement programs developed. It solved, at little cost
to the government, a major supply problem which had plagued armies ever since man
first began to wage war on horseback. That problem was maintaining a sufficient
number of horses and mules with which to operate. Unfortunately, during the nearly
forty years that the program was in operation, the need for the end product was
eliminated. The gasoline-powered combustion engine and the resulting mechanization
of the military made horses obsolete on the battlefield. The problems of supply in
rugged country where vehicles could not operate during World War II kept pack mules
a viable, but limited, tool in some areas.

The U.S. Remount Service helped private breeders develop a pool of military-
acceptable mounts that could be drawn upon in time of need. The program also
upgraded American horseflesh and provided ranchers with a commercially acceptable
animal which was suitable for ranch, police and sporting use such as polo, hunting, the

showring, rodeo and pleasure riding. Those breeders had a product to sell, even when America's economy was at a low ebb.

Activated in 1908 as a branch of the Quartermaster Corps, the U.S. Remount Service purchased, processed, trained and issued horses and mules to the cavalry, infantry, pack and field artillery and the transportation corps. It also supplied horses and mules to the National Guard and colleges (Texas A & M, Virginia Military Institute, New Mexico Military Institute, The Citadel, Culver Military Institute and a few others) with a Reserve Officers Training Corps. That was an enlargement of the Quartermaster Corps assigned mission, as it had been from 1775, of meeting all of the materiel needs of the American soldier.[1]

Originally, horses and mules were not included in Quartermaster Corps supply lists. Animals were acquired through requisition upon the respective branch of service (cavalry, infantry, pack and field artillery, or transportation). Actual purchase was made by politically appointed purchasing boards. The necessary fiscal appropriation was made directly to the respective board by the army. The personnel serving on those boards were not always knowledgeable about horseflesh nor, frequently, did they have the interests and the needs of the military first. Money was a factor between civilian horse contractors, purchasing boards and the military. The margin of profit to the contractor versus the quality of the animals was often a point of contention. There were no specified prices or clear-cut requirements as to the types of animals supplied to meet a certain requisition. Consequently, many of the horses and mules delivered were of questionable quality. This was the practice from 1832, when the first battalion of mounted dragoons was organized, until the middle of the Civil War.[2]

Photograph courtesy The Western Horseman
This troop horse is shown fully outfitted for use in the field, circa 1916. This animal shows the improved conformation over the majority of western horses of the period.

When the Civil War erupted, Union Army military animal purchases were divided into two areas. The Quartermaster General's office procured draft horses and mules while the Cavalry Bureau purchased cavalry mounts. Both branches utilized the contractor system. Many difficulties were encountered in purchasing and the care of military animals. There was a lack of knowledge of the use and maintenance of animals by the troops, and it was reflected in the loss of horses due to malnutrition, disease, neglect or overuse. The situation became so bad that special inspectors were appointed and given wide latitude to correct problems. Orders were even issued authorizing transfer of cavalry officers, and whole cavalry commands, to the infantry if the men were found neglecting their animals.[3]

On July 28, 1863, the Union Army set up the Cavalry Bureau within the Office of the Quartermaster General. By then, Union forces were requiring up to 500 remounts per week. Under the existing direct requisition/purchase/delivery system, fighting units were receiving many animals which were not satisfactory. The Cavalry Bureau was to solve the problem. The Cavalry Bureau was staffed predominately by cavalry and field artillery officers (who knew the requirements for a military horse or mule) and took over the duties of the civilian purchasing boards. The bureau inspected, selected, purchased and processed animals before issuing them to the troops.

Photograph by Mathew Brady

General U.S. Grant used these favorite mounts during the Civil War, 1861–1865, Cincinatti, (left) and Little Jeff Davis (right).

As the war progressed, Union receiving stations for the purchased horses and mules were located at: Giesboro, South Carolina; The District of Columbia; Nashville, Tennessee; Greenville, Louisiana; Harrisburg, Pennsylvania; and St. Louis, Missouri.

Those stations were staffed by military horsemen, responsible only to the Cavalry Bureau. They selected the animals, purchased and delivered them to the proper receiving station. The receiving station processed and issued the horses to requisitioning units. This procedure insured the suitability of the animals for active service. The quality of military horses and mules improved, until the end of the war in 1865 when the Cavalry Bureau was closed for reasons of economy.[4]

In 1865, the direct requisition/purchase/delivery system was reinstated, with the expected poor results. Not only were there no official standards for military horseflesh, but there were no stocks of acceptable animals to choose from. During four years of war a large percentage of the better horses had been used up. Civilian breeders had not had time to rebuild their inventories. The limited supply of quality horses coupled with a strong civilian market that was willing to pay more than the army could offer frequently left soldiers riding less than satisfactory mounts. Many of the remounts raised and purchased east of the Mississippi were not equal to the rugged campaigning during the Indian campaigns in the West. Those horses had neither the sturdy conformation nor the endurance that strenuous use on the plains demanded. Officers rode private mounts, frequently of Thoroughbred breeding, but issue animals were seldom of the same quality. Numerous enlisted cavalrymen from the close of the Civil War until the 1890s rode native horses purchased from local dealers. Some of those mounts were adequate, able to carry the weight of a trooper, weapons, tack, extra ammunition, spare horseshoes, blanket roll, picket line and rations that could total up to 250 pounds. So loaded, a horse was expected to march thirty miles per day, often on sparse food and water. In the event of a forced march, the distance could stretch to sixty miles. It was no wonder that many animals broke down.[5]

The concept of a military Remount Depot program was first proposed in the Quartermaster General's annual report for the 1868 fiscal year. It suggested that horses bred in the states required a year's acclimation in the west. A stock farm should be established and a year's supply of horses kept there. The Quartermaster General recommended that it would be to the advantage of the service if such a stock farm be established in Texas and another on the western plains since the Indian campaigns were in progress at the time. He suggested that all mares in service be collected at those two points and money appropriated for the purchase of a few good stallions. In a short period, the farms would supply remounts at less than the market price, of better quality and animals acclimated to the district in which they would serve. There is no record that these recommendations were even considered.[6]

Photograph courtesy U.S. Army
Union soldiers practice firing over their prone mounts during the Civil War, 1861–1865.

In 1884, a recommendation was made in the Quartermaster General's Annual Report for the establishment of a Remount Depot at Levenworth, Kansas. The depot would be under the supervision of the Quartermaster General and would supply the entire service with riding, pack and draft animals. The officer in charge of the depot would have the authority to purchase animals as needed. The normal depot functions of training, shoeing and conditioning would be carried out. This would provide a pool of suitable horses to be issued as needed. No record is available if the depot was ever established.[7]

Prior to 1900, few civilian breeders west of the Mississippi River produced quality horses in volume. Ranchers of the period raised lots of horses but the majority were marginal. Individuals who raised quality animals had little problem in disposing of their product on civilian markets at premium prices. Such operations imported top stallions and bred up their saddle stock. The cross of Thoroughbred, Saddlebred and Morgan stallions on native mares resulted in an animal with the size, functional conformation, bone and stamina to perform satisfactorily.

The major market was geldings. Thousands of them were raised, trained and shipped to eastern markets. In addition to the military, western-bred horses played polo, galloped on fox hunts, were pleasure mounts and carried police officers in major cities. They also pulled buggies for deliverymen and doctors. Fillies produced by ranch breeding programs could also be sold as saddle animals or utilized as broodmares. In the southern states mule production was a big business. Many draft or medium-weight mares not only worked in harness but were bred to high-class jacks and raised an annual mule foal as well.

One ranch which raised and marketed large numbers of both horses and mules was the well-known King Ranch of South Texas. The operation was renowned for the quality of its remudas, and for shipping hundreds of saddle geldings and mares, as well as mules, to eastern markets. Captain Richard King stated, "Horses made a success of this ranch."[8]

Pen and Ink drawing by Phil Livingston
A U.S. Army Cavalry trooper, circa 1876, is mounted and outfitted for service in the field.

Operations such as the King Ranch were relatively few in number. Most ranchers produced horses in a haphazard manner or purchased saddle stock. Western America had thousands of horses but only a small percentage could really be called first class. Military buyers took the best of what was available, within their limited price structure.[9]

The American saddle horse industry received an economic boost during the South African Boer War of 1899–1902, when the British government commissioned William "Billy" Anson to purchase horses and mules for military use. Because the tsetse fly was prevalent on the South African veldt, equine mortality was extremely high. Large numbers of horses had to be replaced. As part of his buying program, Anson established depots throughout Texas where the animals his agents purchased could be processed and shipped for use by the British Army.[10]

By the beginning of the twentieth century, American military planners were aware of the limited availability of quality horseflesh. British army purchases had depleted the stock of acceptable animals. Breeders of large numbers of horses were not upgrading their stock rapidly enough to meet the army's, and civilian, needs. Army leaders knew that a pool of serviceable horses and mules must be produced and available for future use. The conflict developing in Europe—World War I, 1914–1918—would require large numbers of military horses. The Chief of Cavalry also believed that a standard for military animals must be drawn up. America had a large horse population, but the majority were lacking the qualities for military use.[11]

A writer in a military publication of the time emphasized the fact:

> There are thousands of scrub horses, from 14-2 to 16 hands and weighing from 750 to 1,250 pounds, now being raised in the United States. They are of poor type and are undesirable in conformation, disposition and endurance. It is true that they are being used to some extent, because of a dearth of good horses, but no one likes them or wants them. These scrubs bring no price commercially, nor are they suitable for the army, and it costs as much to raise them as it does a good horse.[12]

Writing in the September–October 1930 *Quartermaster Review*, Lt. Colonel Charles L. Scott remembered:

> To appreciate what the Remount Service has done for the cavalry by its recent work requires us to go back a number of years. With this object in mind, I now recall the inefficient system of purchasing in vogue when I joined the cavalry twenty-five years ago (1905). Under that system our horses were generally bought by a regimental or post board from the lowest bidder. The board usually consisted of officers who happened to be available without regard to their ability as horsemen. The successful bidder had just one object in mind and that was to show and sell the very cheapest horse that the board would accept.
>
> I can also vividly recall the short necked, beefy withered, straight pasterned, poor moving horses obtained under this incompetent system. I can visualize the protest that would go up today if the cavalry were to receive them as remounts.[13]

In his 1907 Report for the Fiscal Year, the Quartermaster General, Major General James B. Aleshire, made extensive recommendations to the United States Congress. He pointed out that the acquisition of suitable horses and mules was severely limited under the current civilian production and military purchasing programs. General Aleshire strongly recommended that the responsibility for the entire army be delegated to the Quartermaster Corps, rather than leaving it to the individual branches of the service. He stated in part:

> It is believed that the results contemplated in providing for open market purchases at posts can best be obtained and the greatest advantages secured to both horse raisers and the army by the establishment of a Remount Service, to be a separate division of The Quartermaster General's Office, designated Remount Division, specially selected by the Secretary of War, on the recommendation of The Quartermaster General of the Army, who would supervise all purchases of animals.
>
> There should be a main office (headquarters) located in The Quartermaster General's Office, and three or more remount depots, to be properly organized, located and equipped, and the same number of remount districts; all to be under supervision and control of the officer in charge of the remount division and subject to his inspection. To each of the three remount depots would be assigned a remount district, and each depot and its tributary districts would be in charge of the Quartermaster Department, preferably detailed from the cavalry or field artillery and especially adapted for this duty. Each depot would be provided such employees and equipment as needed to perform its functions.
>
> Under the supervision of the officer in charge of the remount division, the officer in charge of each remount depot would have control of all matters pertaining to the management thereof, and be accountable and responsible for all animals, supplies, property, and funds necessary to the successful operation of the depot.
>
> He would personally superintend the care and handling of the horses under his charge and see to it that the horses were well-fed and cared for, gently and kindly handled at all times, and properly exercised and broken. When directed by proper authority, he would purchase young horses to conform to specifications, within the district assigned to his remount depot, to which they would be shipped.
>
> He would be required to acquaint himself with, and keep a record of, the number and class of horses, how bred (if possible), by whom owned, where located, and generally complete data of the horse and mule

production of his district, and be prepared to direct a purchasing officer, or go himself, to the place most suitable for the establishment of sub-depots in case of an emergency, and where the best horses could be found.[14]

Congress concurred with Major General Aleshire's recommendation. In 1908, the United States Remount Service was activated. The service was within the Office of the Quartermaster General, under the Transportation branch, and was charged with providing horses and mules for the entire army.[15]

The creation of the U.S. Remount Service was the first step in attempting to solve the army's remount problem. Horse and mule specifications, purchase, conditioning and issue were put under one government bureau. It eliminated the civilian contractor who was more concerned with profit than what a trooper would ride. The Remount Service was staffed by career military men who were aware of the duties that a horse or mule must fulfill and the types of animals necessary to perform them. The goal was to provide the army with a mount which would give long, efficient service.[16]

Prior to the establishment of the Remount program various writers expressed their views on the subject. The Chief of the U.S. Bureau of Animal Industry was favorably quoted in an article published in a 1912 edition of *The Spur*:

> Two arguments have been advanced against this plan [proposed Army Horse Breeding Program] ... the first that it is unnecessary because horses of the desired type are plentiful, the second that by adding the amount suggested for the breeding plan appropriation [$250,000 the first year and $100,000 in succeeding years] to the amount now appropriated to the purchase of horses for the army, and thus adding $50 to $100 to the average price paid for horses, the necessary number could easily be obtained. The writer believes that the figures for the relative numbers of pure-bred draft stallions in various states effectively answers the first argument. It must be pointed out that there are now probably enough horses annually available for the requirements of the present peace footing of the army. The country should, in wisdom, however, provide for a reasonably sufficient supply in case of war, and it should take steps to check the unquestionable decrease in the breeding of light horses. Cavalry is of the utmost importance in warfare, and we must sooner or later encourage the breeding of horses for the mounted service of the United States Army or dismount the cavalry. The second argument voices a popular appeal which carries considerable

weight, but it is very doubtful whether it would in any measure bring about the desired result. Let it be repeated that the army is now paying good prices to farmers for the horses it buys. Officers claim that they are paying somewhat more than farmers have usually received for such horses. One hundred and fifty dollars for an unbroken three-year-old colt, or $125 for a two year old are not starvation prices as farmer's colts run. The purchasing officers are buying in the face of the competition of other buyers. For the government to add gratuitously $50 to $100 to the price now paid would be reckless and wasteful extravagance. This argument has been advanced by persons who do not seem to realize the difference between the direct system of buying young horses for the remount stations and the old system of buying by contract mature horses for direct issue to the troops. The former eliminates the middleman's profit and gives the farmer a fair price; the latter gave the farmer a price which was far below what a good mature horse was worth, and the whole system worked against getting good horses. If the contract system were only considered, adding $50 to $100 to a minimum price might have some effect, but the contractor would probably be the principal gainer. The price paid by the army for horses is now governed by supply and demand, just as that of any other commodity. Again, if a given sum were added to the average purchase price and the country plunged into war, where large numbers of horses were needed, $50 to $100, nor twice these amounts, would not supply the demand unless horses of draft breeding were taken. Witness the New York Police Department, with a contract price of $372.50 per head, scouring the country for seventy-five saddle horses per year of certain definite specifications.[17]

The writer continued:

One of the most discouraging features of the halfbred industry in the blue grass section of Virginia in the past has been the fact that only one in six colts foaled has size and class enough to bring good money [referring to the 16-hand specifications for a hunter-jumper prospect] and the farmer has been at a loss as to what to do with the smaller and less favored colt. As the army desires a troop horse ranging from 15-1 to 15-3 hands, a market has now been found for the smaller horse and many farmers are not only willing but anxious to raise them for sale to the government as unbroken three year olds for $150. They feel there is more money in this than fattening steers for the market. It should be remembered that heretofore breeders have paid a stud fee ranging from $10 up. The government, under its proposed breeding scheme, intends to give the service to the farmer and offers to take the colt off his hands for a fair profit, the price to be fixed by states and regulated by the market. During the last season, but two government stallions were present in Virginia. They arrived during the season and one of them, Octagon, almost immediately came down with a bad case of distemper and was of little use. No moneys were available for a systematic canvass of the country in furtherance of the breeding scheme and for the registration of mares, the writer was the only person present to approve and register mares for service. As much other work had to be done, but little time was available for this. As a result, many mares that would have been bred to these stallions were sent to others. In spite of all these drawbacks, fifty-two mares were registered and the large majority bred.[18]

One of the first moves the Remount Service made was to develop acceptable horse and mule standards. Until then, there had been no clear-cut criteria for military animals. These standards included riding and caisson horses (medium-weight, active animals to pull a two-wheeled ammunition wagon with a cannon as a trailer) that the army termed artillery rider and draft animals, as well as saddle, pack and draft mules.

Photograph courtesy The Western Horseman
U.S. Cavalry is shown on patrol, circa 1916. Note the uniformity of the mounts and the equipment they must carry.

Cavalry mounts were to be a functional, well-balanced horse that stood 15–15.2 hands and weighed between 1,000 and 1,200 pounds. The animal had to have a deep heart girth to provide plenty of lung capacity and well-defined withers to keep the saddle in place. Legs had to have sufficient bone to stand up under long hours of marching, sloping pasterns to provide an easy ride and round, hard feet. A short-coupled horse was preferred as it carried weight better than a longer-bodied one. Naturally, no major conformational defects or potential unsoundness were allowed. The highest type of military horse was the same animal that was in civilian demand as a hunter or jumper, polo pony, police or pleasure mount. When the

Remount Service was activated, horses of that type were selling for $150 per head and up, and the army was willing to pay it. That was when private soldiers were being paid less than twenty dollars per month. The fact that the government would pay considerably more for a prospective cavalry mount than a soldier received each month was indicative of the importance placed on good horseflesh.[19]

Photograph courtesy The Western Horseman

A U.S. Army officer is mounted and ready for garrison duty immediately after World War I. The privately owned officers' chargers were normally several grades above the average troop horse and were also used for recreation such as jumping, hunting and polo.

Geldings, and that is all that the army would purchase for troop service, were to be bay, brown, black, chestnut or sorrel, with a minimum of white markings. Only a few outstanding gray horses were accepted. Duns, palominos, roans or varicolored animals were not even considered. Solid-colored horses were not only easier to find but presented a more uniform appearance when massed in troops than did lighter or varicolored animals. They were also harder for an enemy to see at a distance or against vegetation. The reason for geldings was simple. In a large group, geldings got along better with each other than a mixed saddle string—geldings *and* mares—would. A single mare could keep an entire troop of geldings continually upset and fighting over her. Stallions were not used because of the behavior problems.

Geldings had to be three years of age or older, meet the conformation, soundness and color criteria, well-broken and ready to use. The bulk of purchases were designated as troop horses and assigned to the various units within different branches of the service. School horses were older, four years or older, more settled and went to service schools, the National Guard units and colleges that had Reserve Officer Training Corp programs.

The majority of officers purchased their own mounts, either on the outside or from the army within the levies of remounts delivered to a post. Officers' chargers were predominately Thoroughbred or Thoroughbred-cross animals and were of higher caliber than troop horses. Officers of all field branches rode horseback and rivalry for a top officer's charger was high. Following World War I, after the Remount Breeding Program had become established, a number of these officers chargers were mares bred on one of the three Branch Remount Depots. Many officer's chargers did double duty, performing their military duties and serving as jumpers or polo mounts during off hours. Officers and their mounts competed at various levels, both within the army and against civilian riders. A few exceptional horses went on to the Olympic Games in Jumping, Dressage and the Three-Day Event. Until after World II, equestrian teams from competing nations were almost always military personnel riding military horses.[20] One such horse was Remount-bred, Jenny Camp, ridden by Captain Thompson with success in the Three-day Event during the 1936 Olympics at Berlin, Germany. Jenny Camp was eventually retired as a brood mare at Front Royal, Virginia, and was finally buried in the horse cemetery. Other Olympic qualifiers were Don, ridden by Major W. B. Bradford and Dakota ridden by Captain C. W. Raguse.[21]

Artillery riders were 15 to 16 hands and weighed from 1,200 to 1,300 pounds. These horses could be used both under saddle and as light draft animals pulling caissons. A four-up caisson team always had a rider on each of the near-side horses. These horses were large, but very active, and would be considered a heavy hunter type in the civilian world.[22] Naturally, the military criteria for sex, conformation, soundness and color was maintained. Most artillery teams were composed of matching colors.

Draft horses were the medium-sized "chunks" that were popular with farmers. The heavy draft breeds Shire, Percheron and Belgian were too large and not active enough for the purpose but half-bred crosses were effective utility horses. Many draft animals

Photograph courtesy The Western Horseman
A pack string is loaded and ready to move out. Cargo was roped to the Phillips Pack Saddle by experienced packers. U.S. Army 5th Cavalry maneuvers in the Big Bend of Texas, 1915.

were mares which, when crossed with high-quality, light stallions, produced a very serviceable saddle horse that could double as an artillery rider.[23]

Mules were also purchased in large quantities. These were classified as: pack mules (some were utilized as riding animals by soldiers handling pack strings); artillery mules (which required a larger animal to pack a small cannon) and draft mules to pull wagons. Pack and artillery pack mules fell under the civilian classification of Cotton Mules, approximately 14-2 to 15 hands and 1,000 plus pounds. Draft mules were in the general farm mule category (15-2 to 16 hands and 1,100 to 1,250 pounds). Like civilian buyers, the army was interested in the choice and good grades in each classification. No animals with major blemishes, unsoundness or off-colors were accepted.[24]

The Remount Service made no effort to influence civilian mule breeding practices or quality. There was such a commercial demand for good mules that a sufficient quantity of the required grades was available for military buyers. In farming regions of America, large numbers of work mares not only pulled plows and wagons but were annually bred to produce a mule foal.[25]

Prior to World War I, the army had no official involvement in the actual production of horses and mules. Military representatives purchased what was available and came the closest to meeting their requirements within their price range.

In order to effectively handle the purchasing of military animals, the Remount Service set up seven purchasing boards in key horse-population areas across the country. Each office was staffed by a team of horse-knowledgeable army officers, including a

Photograph courtesy The Western Horseman
Wagon Master, supply wagons and outriders pass in review. Mule-drawn wagons were utilized by the U.S. Army through the end of World War I when trucks took over the duty.

military veterinarian, and a small cadre of enlisted men. A buying team—two officers and the veterinarian—periodically visited farmers and ranchers within a purchasing area who might have prospective horses to sell. They also arranged for showings in central locations where owners could display their horses and worked with dealers at the various horse and mule markets. These purchasing boards were located at: Boise, Idaho; Colorado Springs, Colorado; Front Royal, Virginia; Lexington, Kentucky; Sacramento, California; San Angelo, Texas; and Sheridan, Wyoming.

The primary problem facing the purchasing boards was finding the raw material which would meet the army's standards within the price limits. The comment was made that "America had thousands of horses and mules but only a small percentage were of military quality."[26] This lack of quality was further emphasized by a comment from Colonel Fred L. Hamilton, who was to become Chief of the Remount Service following World War II. He wrote, "The year 1920 found me a young cavalry officer, a student at the cavalry school at Fort Riley, Kansas. One look at the saddle string and my unpopular comment was, 'Small wonder that Sitting Bull caught Custer.'"

Colonel Hamilton continued:

> In mid-winter our hopes went up. Remounts were due in, and we reasoned
> that they had to be better than the horses we had. It was false optimism,

for actually they were worse. Three carloads from Fort Keogh, Montana, and half the ranchmen in the state must have unloaded. Smooth-mouthed spooks that had never felt a strap and had seldom seen a man, old stags and feather-legged ponies, they were all there; the kind that once roamed our ranges in the thousands. [27]

Later, as a buyer for the young U.S. Remount Service, Colonel Hamilton was faced with attempting to fill his orders as well as improve the quality of military horses. It was a difficult task. The inferior grade of horses in general use by the army during the 1920s was not the fault of anyone in the army supply services. Better horses did not exist in the United States in numbers. Hamilton looked at too many supposed prospects to have any illusions on that idea. "The horses I found at most locations were usually the kind that looked 'right good' to Joe but 'in town' weren't worth their hides. I bought many of them with zeal for the future of the horse business," he wrote.[28]

Developing a pool of saddle and light draft horses which would be available in time of military need was the major problem facing the fledgling U.S. Remount Service. The army couldn't buy horses that didn't exist. Beginning in 1904, a number of tentative research projects were quietly instigated by the U.S. Government, hoping they might have a favorable bearing on the problem.[29] (See Chapter 3, page 67, for more detail.)

The activities of foreign buyers from 1914 until 1917 and America's entrance into World War I in 1917 convinced military planners of the need to improve America's horse breeding programs. In order to have a well-mounted and effective army, there had to be a way to counter the remount shortage. The only solution seemed to be for the army to raise its own horses, or help civilian breeders do the job for them. A form of the latter plan was in operation from 1908 and during the World War I years. The program was revised and expanded in 1920 and stayed in operation until the Remount Service was disbanded in 1948.

Concurrent with the development of a pool of military-acceptable horses was the need to develop a civilian market for animals not needed by the army. Breeders had to be able to sell the excess horses to army needs, at a good price, or it would not be economically viable to raise them. This meant that the half-bred horse (half Thoroughbred, half grade), as a utility and sporting mount had to be strongly promoted. Civilian horsemen had to be sold on the idea of good horseflesh rather than just riding what was available. The U.S. Remount Service was successful in doing this. Colonel Fred L. Hamilton wrote:

Our own primary interest was the creation of a reserve of military-type horses, a reserve that then seemed highly essential. But we knew that the army buying in peacetime would not support an industry adequate to possible wartime needs. A market had to be created and encouraged, and of necessity, it had to be, largely, a luxury market.[30]

The second step in improving the army's horses was the development and maintenance of permanent Remount depots to process incoming equine recruits. At these locations, horses and mules could be evaluated, conditioned, trained and issued to the units. In time of war, the Remount Service was also responsible for setting up temporary depots, both in America and abroad, to process and issue military animals to the fighting troops. The permanent depots were: Fort Reno, Oklahoma, 1908, servicing the military units operating in the Central and Southwestern states; Fort Keogh, Montana, 1908, servicing the Northwestern, Mountain and Northern Central districts; Front Royal, Virginia, 1911, a reception and issue center for military units East of the Mississippi River.

In 1916, because of impending trouble with Mexico, Fort Sam Houston at San Antonio, Texas, and Fort Bliss at El Paso, Texas, were designated temporary Remount Depots to supply the troops operating along the Mexican Border. They were closed in 1918, following World War I. In 1919, Fort Robinson, Nebraska was opened to service the Northwest and Mountain districts. It gradually took over the functions of Fort Keogh, which was eventually closed.[31]

Photograph courtesy The Western Horseman
The bugler of Troop D 6th Cavalry practices commands and signals prior to World War I. All commands were communicated by bugle and troop horses soon learned to respond. The mount is typical of many military horses of the time before the Remount Breeding Program began to show results. Note the US branded on the left shoulder.

The Branch Remount Depots functioned under Quartermaster Corps control on a trial-and-error basis. There were no regulations to govern duties of personnel, no tables of organization or tables of allowance prescribed for equipment or supplies. Military personnel were assigned to the depots with little regard for previous horse experience. Veterinarian and farrier services were often obtained through the old military tradition of contract civilian personnel. Various procedures of operation were worked out by individuals actually doing the jobs and the standards by which remount horses and mules were purchased were those of depot personnel. It was a haphazard system, but it worked.[32]

The Remount Depots were originally developed as a processing center for horses and mules purchased for later use. The concept of the army breeding its own remounts was not officially considered. Some members of Congress must have, however, realized that a breeding program would be considered at a later date.

An interesting sentence was included in the Annual Appropriation Act in 1909, 1910 and 1911 under the heading of: "Horse, Cavalry, Artillery and Engineers." The sentence, which covered the amount of money to be appropriated for equine purchases, also included, "Provided, that no part of this appropriation shall be used for breeding purposes." The sentence had not appeared before nor did it appear in the wording of the Appropriation Act after 1911. It was almost as if Congress was looking ahead and attempting to keep the army out of the horse breeding business by holding the purse strings tight.[33]

By the time the United States entered World War I in 1917, the Remount Program of purchasing-processing-issue was well organized and functioning smoothly. As soon as war was declared, the Remount Service was rapidly enlarged to accommodate thousands of horses and mules utilized at home and abroad. However, it was not a major user of people. The total personnel involved in the Remount Service by the close of the war totaled 948 officers, 30,661 enlisted men and 789 civilians. There were seventy-two different Remount Depots operating with a total capacity of 292,700 animals. During the war years 1914–1918, some 571,000 horses and mules passed through the Remount Service.[34]

Although the American army had the facilities, the personnel and the procedures to purchase, process and issue large numbers of horses and mules through the Remount Service, the necessary quantity of military-acceptable animals was not readily available. Breeders of the type of animals preferred by the military had not built up their inventories from the inroads made by the British army for use in the Boer War. Foreign buyers were also competing for military animals. As early as 1910, buyers representing European nations were active in the United States, purchasing remounts for the coming World War I. Germany, Austria, France and England were all well aware that the numbers of horses produced by their government programs were not sufficient.

The buying activity intensified after war was declared. An example of this during the brief period from November 14, 1914, until July 29, 1915, was at the Fort Worth, Texas, Horse and Mule Market. Representatives of European armies spent more than five million dollars for prospective remounts at this single location. This was a conservative figure based on an average price of $150 per head. By June of 1915, foreign governments had purchased over 200,000 horses and mules in the United States.[35] This represented an estimated $30,000,000 in sales.

Mrs. Nita McCain, former owner of *The North Fort Worth News*, wrote:

> The war created more activity in the stockyards, especially horse and mule sales as foreign governments engaged in the Great War purchased cavalry animals. Thriving mule sales soon attracted attention. From her window, one of the reporters of *The North Fort Worth News*, whose offices stood just west of the coliseum on Exchange Avenue, could often count among those buying mules as many as fifteen different uniforms from as many nations.[36]

Volume buying by foreign armies substantially reduced the number of military-acceptable horses and mules available when the American army entered the market in 1914. Ultimately, the U.S. forces purchased well over 500,000 horses.[37] A large number of these animals were not totally acceptable but were the best of what was available.

After the close of World War I, the supply of military-quality horses was worse than before. Purchases, both American and foreign, had greatly reduced the prospective remount pool. Army buyers scoured the country, with poor results. In 1920, Colonel E. J. Purfield was assigned the duty of purchasing cavalry horses in the Northwest. He wrote:

> When we opened one of the first Remount Purchasing Headquarters at Boise, Idaho, in 1920, we had orders to buy 2,000 regular army cavalry horses and 2,000 National Guard cavalry horses. Our territory comprised the states of Washington, Oregon, Idaho, Montana and Wyoming, all far above average horse country. In our efforts to fill our first purchasing order, we traveled continuously for three months, inspecting in all, 927 horses. Of these, only 141 passed our inspection and were accepted for purchase. As a general rule, the horses inspected were selected from many times that number by qualified civilian horsemen who, in turn, congregated them at shipping points for our inspection.

Colonel Purfield continued:

> We were not looking for a super horse, just a decent looking riding horse 15 to 16 hands in height and weighing 1,000 to 1,200 pounds. We needed a horse which might be expected to give a man a comfortable ride and last

through one day's march. We were so glad to see a good type of riding horse, regardless of how little work he had under saddle, that we purchased some which later proved to be outlaws. Some four-to-eight-year-old horses shown to us had been ridden only once or twice.[38]

Two decades later in 1941, Colonel Edwin Hardy, Chief of the Remount Division, was charged with purchasing some 27,000 horses for the military buildup prior to World War II. In just a few months, army buyers acquired 20,000 animals suitable for army service. This put the purchasing teams so far ahead of the facilities available to receive and process the animals that they stopped buying. The remainder of the order was to be filled when the army's need was more immediate.

Colonel Hardy was pleased that such a pool of good horses were available. He noted that approximately seventy-two percent of the animals purchased had Remount-owned sires or grandsires. Obviously, the Army Horse Breeding Program had paid dividends.[39] Colonel C. E. Wilkerson, former Remount officer, said, "From my personal observation, from twenty-eight years in the army, it is my opinion that the quality and stamina of horses has been improved tremendously in America."[40]

The Army Horse Breeding Program was officially started in 1913 when well-bred stallions owned by both the army and the Department of Agriculture were made available to privately owned mares. Originally, the stallions were maintained at the Branch Remount Depots, primarily Front Royal, Virginia, and the mares transported to them. Following World War I the program was revised for wider representation across the country and the stallions were assigned to civilian agents, under the supervision of the Branch Remount Depots. Government-owned stallions stood to the general public at the agents' farms or ranches in almost every state. The revised program was in force from 1920 until 1948.

The half-bred geldings—by registered Thoroughbred, Saddlebred, Morgan or Arabian stallions and out of ranch-bred mares—were purchased as prospective cavalry or field artillery animals. Each horse had to meet military specifications and be within the specified price limits. No guarantee was made to buy geldings sired by Remount stallions, but they frequently met all requirements. The Remount-sired colts and fillies not purchased by the army remained the property of the breeder and were disposed of as he saw fit. This nation-wide effort rapidly developed a supply of suitable horses for the military to draw upon. Since these were high-class animals, there was a strong civilian market and it was economically viable for breeders to produce a top horse. At the peak of the Remount program in 1940, there were more than 700 government-owned stallions standing at civilian farms and ranches across the country. Many of today's horses trace their ancestry to one or more Remount stallions.[41]

Remount stallions were obtained by either donation from patriotic civilian breeders or by outright purchase. Frequently, the price that the army paid for an outstanding stallion was far below his actual market value. The owner wished to see the horse add to the national defense/horse breeding effort. Numerous public spirited individuals donated more than one stallion to the program. The most generous was Colonel E. R. Bradley who contributed more than thirty stallions from his well-known Idle Hour Stud Farm over a twenty-year period.[42]

Branch Remount Depots were responsible for the placement of stallions with civilian agents. Annual visits by the army officer in charge of the branch depot to each agent kept the Remount aware of the horse's condition and the type of foals that he was siring. Individual horses were rotated from agent to agent, from community to community and frequently from region to region in an effort to prevent over-saturation of specific blood. Stallions were issued to an agent in the spring, received back to the branch depot at the end of the breeding season, conditioned and then reissued to a different agent the following spring.[43] Some stallions might spend two or three years with a specific agent but eventually were transferred.

Maintenance of the stallions was at the Branch Remount Depots when they were not in the hands of civilian agents. Basic conditioning, training, test breeding and other activities were all carried on at the depots. Remount Service officers carried on regular communications with agents recommending the use of the stallions under saddle as to feeding, breeding techniques and training of the resulting foals to increase their worth. In many cases, these efforts resulted in improved equine management practices, such as regular worming, proper hoof maintenance and health programs. At the depots, research into equine diseases, artificial insemination of broodmares, lip tattooing rather than hot iron branding for identification, improved feeding and training techniques were all under way. Many of those practices worked their way into the civilian world and some are still in use.

The success of the U.S Remount Service and the Army Horse Breeding Program was highly appreciated by both military and civilian horsemen. It functioned well for peacetime procurement and produced the necessary, but unused animals, for World War II. Overflow production went into the civilian world and improved America's saddle horses as nothing else could have. The Quartermaster General of the Army appropriately referred to the Remount Service as "A Public Trust," a feeling that was echoed by the prominent civilian breeders who served, at the request of the U.S. Secretary of War, on the Remount Board.[44]

August Belmont, one of America's leading Thoroughbred breeders, expressed his views at a 1920 meeting of the Remount Board:

> This breeding plan is a splendid idea. It is practical and workable. The only doubts that arise in my mind are: will the Remount Service, in its constantly shifting personnel, be able to follow a uniform policy and be sufficiently patient and consistent to handle such a highly technical and difficult work as horse breeding? Will the War Department, subject as it is to constant legislation and changes of policy, maintain its interest in this work or will it build this valuable work up, then lose interest and tear it down? If this breeding is started correctly, and then destroyed from any cause, it will be a calamity for the breeder and the horse industry of our nation.[45]

Mr. Belmont accurately foresaw the future.

The United States Remount Service Horse Breeding Program succeeded remarkably well, and, in doing so, left America with a legacy of good horses. The top stallions utilized in the program have influenced American horseflesh for many generations. While the restrictions of the breeding program were not as stringent as those in Europe—Germany, Austria, Poland and France—Remount personnel developed specifications for a serviceable horse. Without the benefit of the Army Horse Breeding Program, there is no way to contemplate what type of horses America would have today.

Chapter 2: Sources and Notes

1. Ray K. Erhardt, "The Remount Service of the Office of the Quartermaster General, United States Army, 1908–1954: A Narrative Review," 1990, unpublished paper, 1.
2. Ibid., 2.
3. Major A. A. Cederwald, "The Remount Service Past and Present," *The Quartermaster Review* (November–December 1928): 28.
4. Erhardt, "Remount Service of Office of Quartermaster General," 2. Also, Colonel William H. Carter, *Horses, Saddles and Bridles* (Baltimore: Lord Baltimore Press, 1902), 96–97.
5. Ibid.
6. Cederwald, "The Remount Service Past and Present," 26.
7. Ibid.
8. Tom Lea, *The King Ranch*, Volume II (Boston: Little, Brown and Company, 1957), 655.
9. Albert D. Manchester, "Decendants of the Remount," *The Western Horseman* (October 1986): 60.
10. Dr. John Ashton, "Billy Anson and the Quarter Horse," *The Cattleman* (September 1946): 36.
11. Major General James B. Aleshire, Quartermaster General, United States Army, report to Congress, 1912, unnumbered copy.
12. Copy of Army Report, no date, unnumbered.
13. Lt. Colonel Charles L. Scott, "The Remount Service, What it Has Done for the Cavalry, the Riding Horse Industry and the Farmer," *The Quartermaster Review* (September–October 1930): 11.
14. Cederwald, "The Remount Service Past and Present," 26–27.
15. "Organization of Remount Service," September 1921, mimeographed copy, unnumbered.
16. Anna Waller, "Horses and Mules and National Defense" (U.S. Army, Office of the Quartermaster General, XVIII-3-009, 1958), 5.
17. Captain C. H. Conrad Jr., "The Army Remount Problem," *The Spur* (1912): 29.
18. Ibid.
19. Waller, *Horses and Mules and National Defense*, 3–9.
20. Michael Condes, "When the USET Was Military," *The Cavalry Journal* (June 1, 1992): 2.
21. Lieutenant R. W. Curtis, "Olympic Equestrians," *The Remount* (October 1936): 2.
22. Remount Technical Manual No. TM10-395, 1941.
23. Ibid.
24. J. O. Williams, "Mule Production," Farmer's Bulletin No. 1341, U.S. Department of Agriculture (July 1948): 19–20.
25. Ibid., 7-9.
26. Erhardt, "The Remount Service of the Office of the Quartermaster General," 1.
27. Colonel Fred L. Hamilton, "The Remount Story," *The Western Horseman* (December, 1950): 8.
28. Ibid., 9.
29. Erhardt, "The Remount Service of the Office of the Quartermaster General," 2.
30. Hamilton, "The Remount Story," 9.
31. Erhardt, "The Remount Service of the Office of the Quartermaster General," 2.
32. Ibid., 2–3.
33. "Organization of Remount Service," September 1921, mimeographed copy, unnumbered.
34. Hope Ryden, *America's Last Wild Horses* (New York: E. P. Dutton & Co., 1970), 200–201.
35. J'Nell L. Pate, *Livestock Legacy: The Fort Worth Stockyards* (College Station: Texas A & M Press, 1990), 99.
36. Ibid.
37. Monique and Hans Dossenback, *The Noble Horse* (New York: Crown Publishers, 1983), 170.
38. Colonel E. J. Purfield, "Thirty Years of Remount Service," *The Western Horseman* (August 1949): 9.
39. *The Blood-Horse* (February 1941): 372.
40. Bill Gray, "War Takes Horses," *The Cattleman* (September 1943): 72.
41. Miller J. Stewart, "The Government's Gift to the Private Horse Breeder," *Horseman* (March 1972): 74.
42. *The Blood-Horse*, various issues list the gifts, including: (August 29, 1931): 256; (October 3, 1931): 395; (October 31, 1931): 512; (May 7, 1932): 676; (June 25, 1932): 870; (November 14, 1936): 532; (November 1, 1941): 587; (June 13, 1942): 842; (November 14, 1942): 613; (December 12, 1942): 749.
43. *Technical Manual: Remount No. TM 10-395* (War Department, December 18, 1941): 4–5.
44. Scott, "The Remount Service, What it Has Done for the Cavalry, the Riding Horse Industry and the Farmer," 16.
45. Ibid.

Photograph courtesy U.S. Army

At the gallop, a cavalry platoon moves up to the action along the Texas-Mexican border during the 1920s.

CHAPTER 3

THE ARMY ENTERS
THE BREEDING BUSINESS

"For several years it has been difficult for the United States Army to maintain an adequate supply of suitable horses and, if the efficiency of the cavalry is to be maintained, it will be necessary for the government to develop a systematic plan to encourage the breeding of horses suitable for the army."

U.S. Secretary of Agriculture
April 13, 1911

Well before the United States Army entered World War I on May 6, 1917, military personnel were aware that horses suitable for cavalry and artillery purposes were none too plentiful. Proposals to remedy the situation were made as early as 1868 but no progress had been made. It wasn't until 1904 that steps were taken to develop a pool of cavalry horses that could be purchased when needed. Quality animals were available but the numbers were not substantial enough to meet the needs of the army. That situation was gradually improving although the demands of World War I would deplete the supply. Draft horses could be obtained in sufficient numbers since there was a commercial use for them and breeders were meeting that need. Pack and draft mules were also in good supply for the same reasons. Military planners felt that it would take strong government intervention to up-grade the quality of saddle horses as well as develop a sufficient quantity to draw on in time of need. The majority of individuals raising large numbers of horses were using mediocre stallions on common mares and letting "nature take its course." In addition to the lack of good stallions available, there was the time-lapse involved in horse production. It took four to five years from the time that a mare was bred before a usable gelding was ready for issue. Another problem was the fact that from each foal crop approximately 50% were fillies, and the army did not purchase saddle mares for troop use.

The first breeding program sponsored by federal agencies began in 1904. The United States Bureau of Animal Industry, in cooperation with the Colorado Agricultural Experiment Station, attempted to develop a strain of utility horses. The Standardbred was the primary breed chosen, along with infusions of American Saddlebred and Morgan to supply stamina, serviceable saddle horse conformation and traveling ability that the two latter breeds possessed. These stallions were bred to native mares. In July of 1919, the project was moved to Buffalo, Wyoming, to continue in cooperation with the state of Wyoming. While the combination of bloodlines produced a horse suitable for civilian use, the effort did not result in a desirable cavalry mount.[1]

The Bureau of Animal Industry began to breed purebred Morgan horses in 1906. This work was conducted at the government farm near Middlebury, Vermont. The output was limited, but it was a step towards the production of better horses and supervised breeding practices. The horses foaled there provided a purebred Morgan base for other breeding programs. The farm, and the Morgan horses on it, were originally a gift from Colonel James Battell to the United States Government.[2]

In 1914 the Bureau of Animal Industry assisted the Bureau of the Interior with a horse breeding project on the Cheyenne River Indian Reservation in South Dakota. Two Saddlebred, two Standardbred and eight Percheron stallions were purchased and put into service on native mares. The project was the result of efforts by Major Francis Wolcott, who proposed the project as early as 1904. He felt that the program would be of two-fold benefit—providing the Cheyenne Indians with a product which they could sell and the U.S. Army with acceptable horses.[3] The project was well received but the resulting horses were often not of the quality required for cavalry mounts.

The Jockey Club of New York began to contribute to saddle horse quality of New York in May of 1906, when it created the Breeding Bureau. The plan of the Breeding Bureau was to place Thoroughbred stallions in every county of New York state. This program was for the benefit of the citizens of New York. Stallions were selected with great care as to size, soundness, age, disposition and general suitability to mate with the mares in the localities where they were placed. This was done with the knowledge that an infusion of Thoroughbred blood would greatly improve the general character of saddle horses.[4] These Thoroughbred stallions were provided at no cost to individuals who stood them. Concerned owners, the majority active in Thoroughbred breeding and racing, donated stallions to the program. All promotion was by the Breeding Bureau of the Jockey Club of New York. The keeper of each stallion received all service fees (ten dollars per mare) with his expense that of maintaining the stallion and breeding mares. The program was primarily confined to the Genesee Valley of New York. The Genesee Valley Breeder's Association was formed by participating horsemen, accurate records maintained and a *Half-bred Stud Book* developed and approved by the Jockey Club. This *Stud Book* was first published in 1918. By 1919 a total of 7,769 mares had been bred to Thoroughbred stallions supplied by the Breeding Bureau.[5]

These watering cavalry mounts at Fort Reno, Oklahoma, circa 1930, exhibit uniformity of conformation as a result of the Remount Breeding Program.

The efforts of the Breeding Bureau were closely watched by the military as a possible solution to the remount problem. None of the previously mentioned programs had proven successful and the influx of Thoroughbred blood was considered a step in the right direction. Even with the interest in New York, the output of the right type of horses was minimal. Quality in the necessary numbers was not available on a national level.

Early in 1910, the concept of a governmental breeding program for military remounts was presented to the Quartermaster General and the Bureau of Animal Industry. The concept had been quietly practiced and evaluated for several years, with the approval of the Secretary of War and the Department of Agriculture, through the various breeding plans already mentioned. The idea was simple and basic: breed a stallion of superior genes and conformation to a mare with excellent bloodlines and build. The combination should produce a functional horse.[6] The concept was approved by the necessary government agencies and steps put into practice to develop the program—but where was the seedstock to come from?

By March 1910, the War Department was requesting the cooperation of the Secretary of Agriculture in developing the plan to enable the army to obtain suitable riding horses. The request resulted in each department appointing a representative to help outline such a plan. The move was set forth in the Department of Agriculture, Bureau of Animal Industry Circular No. 178, dated April 19, 1911. In the circular, the U.S. Secretary of Agriculture noted that for several years it had been difficult for the United States Army to maintain an adequate supply of suitable horses, and if the efficiency of the cavalry was to be maintained, it would be necessary for the government to develop a systematic plan to encourage the breeding of horses suitable for the army.[7]

The concept met with Congressional approval. On April 23, 1912, Senator Carroll S. Page of Vermont submitted a horse breeding amendment to the Agriculture Appropriation bill in the Senate. The bill passed through both Houses of Congress and was signed into law by William H. Taft, President of the United States. The army's horse breeding project was official.[8] Representatives of both the Bureau of Animal Industry and the army were assigned to oversee the project. The Department of Agriculture was represented by Mr. George Rommel, Chief of the Animal Husbandry Division of the Bureau of Animal Industry. The War Department selected Captain Casper H. Conrad Jr., Third Cavalry, detailed to the Quartermaster Department in connection with the purchase of remounts. The plan for breeding remount horses was prepared by Mr. Rommel with assistance from Captain Conrad and other army officers stationed in Washington, D.C.

The committee's recommendations were:

The country should be divided into four or more breeding districts and stallions assigned as required.

The mare should not be bred to a government stallion until she has been approved as being of the type suitable to produce military remounts. Common conformational unsoundness, the tendency to which may be transmitted from one generation to another, should disqualify the mare. Even more important would be the necessity to refuse a mare on account of manifest faults of conformation, action or quality.

The terms of service would be free. The owner of the mare would enter into a contract to give the War Department an option on the resulting foal the year that it was three years old (estimating a horse to be one year old on the 1st of January after it is foaled). The price would be fixed before the mare was bred. This was if a horse colt was produced and it was a prospective cavalry mount. A provision was included in the contract that the mare must remain the owner's property until the foal was weaned and that in case the foal was sold before the War Department had exercised its option, a service fee of twenty-five dollars would be paid by the breeder of the foal to the War Department. Provisions were made, however, to cover such emergencies as the death of the owner, etc.

The price contracted to be paid for remounts was to be fixed annually in each state by a Board of Arbitration before the breeding season opened. For example, in January or February 1912, the board would meet in each state in which breeding was carried out and agree upon the price to be paid for remounts bred in that state for that year. This procedure would be followed annually.

The Breeding Board would be administered by the Bureau of Animal Industry of the Department of Agriculture, through the Chief of the Animal Husbandry Division. The division would direct the work under the supervision of the Chief of the Bureau, and keep the breeding records and reports on the development of the foals. No later than January 1 of each year, the division would furnish a report to the War Department on the actual number of three-year-old geldings in each breeding district that were available for purchase, as well as the probable number of those that would make satisfactory mounts. A competent animal husbandryman would be employed, with headquarters in Washington, D.C., as well as a traveling inspector of breeding stallions, to keep the department in close touch with the work. Regular reports would be submitted from breeding districts and evaluated.[9]

Immediately upon activation of the plan, a campaign was instigated to accumulate stallions with the quality and siring ability to produce acceptable military saddle horses. A Congressional appropriation for the 1913 fiscal year of $50,000 was assigned to the Department of Agriculture for the purchase of such stallions. Requests were also made to leading civilian breeders by ranking military personnel and political figures for donations of suitable stallions. Thirty-three stallions were purchased by the USDA during the 1913 fiscal year. These stallions were of Thoroughbred, Morgan, Saddlebred and Standardbred breeding. Five Morgan stallions were donated by the U.S. Morgan Farm, Middlebury, Vermont. An additional six stallions, all Thoroughbreds, were donated by two leading civilian horsemen.[10]

Five of the stallions were donated by August Belmont: *Henry of Navarre, Octagon, Belfry II, Dandy Rock and Foot Print. Johnson Camden donated Boola Boola. In 1894 *Henry of Navarre outran the mighty Domino and Clifford in a match race at Morris Park. Both *Henry of Navarre and Octagon died at Front Royal and were buried in the horse graveyard. A tombstone has been erected over each grave.[11]

Photograph courtesy Phil Livingston
Henry of Navarre (TB) was one of the first six stallions donated to the U.S. Army Remount Service in 1912 by Mr. August Belmont.
Henry of Navarre stood at Front Royal, Virginia, the rest of his life and is buried there in the animal cemetery.

The Government Breeding Program began with forty-four stallions, all of high quality and capable of siring an acceptable cavalry mount. Since the Remount Service Headquarters was located in Washington, D.C., the original stallions stood on America's east coast. The Bureau of Animal Industry divided the breeding operation into three districts: 1) Vermont and New Hampshire, 2) Virginia and West Virginia, and

3) Kentucky and Tennessee. In the first district, all stallions were Morgans. In the second district, the stallions were Saddlebred, Thoroughbred and Standardbred. In the third district, the stallions were Standardbreds and Saddlebreds. This move reflected the prevailing breed interest in each district.[12]

All government-owned stallions were stabled at the specified depot or breeding headquarters for the entire year. Mares were delivered to the location where the stallions were standing. They were maintained at government expense during breeding, prenatal care and the birth of the foals. Mares and their foals were then returned to the owners. Foals remained the property of the mare owner. As three year olds, the trained geldings could be sold to the government at the agreed-upon price or, if not purchased by the army, be disposed of on the civilian market. Fillies could be sold at any age.

Photograph courtesy Phil Livingston
Cruzard (TB), foaled 1923, sired by Crudados, out of Famosa, is shown here while standing at the J.M. Wyman Ranch, Meeker, Colorado.

The breeding program was enthusiastically greeted by horsemen. Some 1,500 mares were presented at various breeding stations during the 1912 breeding season. The following year, 1913, a total of 606 foals were produced. This low number demonstrated flaws in the program. All the mares nominated the previous year had been accepted and bred. However, many of them had not been returned to the stallion to be checked safe in foal and had not conceived. After a close inspection, a large majority of them were found to be unsuitable for breeding to the purebred stallions in the army stable.

The ideal cavalry mount was to stand 15-2 to 16-2 hands, weigh 1,100 to 1,300 pounds, be of serviceable conformation with sufficient bone and be a dark, solid color. A percentage of the mares of that first breeding season were not able to produce a foal which would fulfill those requirements after reaching maturity. In addition, stabling the stallions and broodmares for a year was expensive—in feed, facilities and the necessary manpower for their care.[13]

In his report to Congress for the 1913 fiscal year the Quartermaster General, United States Army, stated:

The interest shown in the proposed scheme of the Agricultural Department to furnish improved stud service under an agreement of sale to the government had been very marked. The scheme had been tentatively put into effect in the vicinity of Front Royal, VA, using the stallions recently presented to the government, and a sufficient number of suitable mares present and bred under the agreement.[14]

The first appropriation of $50,000 to carry out the breeding plan was made by Congress to the Department of Agriculture for the 1913 fiscal year. The following appropriations were made in the succeeding years:

Fiscal Year	Appropriation
1913	$50,000
1914	$50,000
1915	$30,000
1916	$25,000
1917	$25,000
1918	$22,940
1919	$36,940
1920	$36,940[15]

The results of the breeding program, as well as the response from horsemen owning mares in the Northeastern portion of the United States where the government-owned stallions were standing, was acceptable. During the seven years from the inception of the program in 1913 until the program was revised in 1920, the statistics were:

Year	No. of Mares Bred	No. of Foals Obtained	Breeding Percentage
1913	1,572	606	38.5%
1914	2,014	918	45.6%
1915	2,158	948	43.9%
1916	2,019	930	46.0%
1917	1,694	728	42.9%
1918	1,129	475	42.0%
1919	692	–	–
1920	600	205	34.1%[16]

In 1917, under the Remount Program, the army purchased 180 three-year-old colts which had been foaled in 1914. Of foals born in 1915, the army purchased 131 colts in 1918. During August and September of 1919, 931 three-year-old colts were inspected by the army, of which seventy-two were accepted and purchased. In June of 1920, 234 three-year-old colts were inspected and ninety-two purchased for military service.[17]

While the number of acceptable cavalry-type horses obtained under this program was not large, considering the total volume of mares bred and the amount of effort and money expended, the results were encouraging. The major problem was the quality of mares brought to the stallions. "Like Begets Like" and a large percentage of the broodmares were not of the quality to produce cavalry-acceptable horses. The low foaling percentages of the mares further reduced the number of acceptable animals produced. Another contributing factor was that of each foal crop, approximately fifty percent were fillies. Still, the military was satisfied that the Remount program was headed in the right direction.

Reporting to Congress in 1915 the Quartermaster General commented:

> The system of breeding horses for the military service, conducted by the Bureau of Animal Industry, Department of Agriculture, will, if its development is continued and extended along the present lines, form the basis for the Remount system and will result in a great improvement in the quality of horses supplied. Reports indicate that there has been a steady improvement in the type, breeding and appearance of young horses purchased by the War Department as the result of the Remount Service.[18]

The following year, in 1916, the Report contained the statement:

> The quality of horses purchased during the past fiscal year showed a marked improvement over those bought previously, due in part to the stallions provided by the Department of Agriculture and the better knowledge that farmers and breeders have of the type of horses desired as a result of coming in contact with the Remount officers who can advise them as to the type of animals required by the army. However, the breeding of suitable horses for military purposes could be greatly improved and their number increased if the appropriations were increased as to enable the Department of Agriculture to purchase additional stallions and extend the present plan of breeding.[19]

Then, as now, requests were constantly made to Congress for increased funding of government programs.

The 1917 Congressional Report on the status of the Remount Program contained the following comments regarding the type of stallions to be used:

> The majority of the Thoroughbred stallions now standing at Remount Depots are horses that have been presented by patriotic individuals with the idea in view of improving the breeding of the army horses. They have not, however, been selected as "individuals" from a standpoint of conformation to serve this purpose. They are in this respect rather lacking in bone and substance and are not the type of horses which are apt to reproduce the type of animal desired. These horses either had an enviable racing career or have been thought valuable on account of their bloodlines. What is needed is the "individual," even though not so fashionably bred.[20]

This meant that many of the stallions did not have the serviceable conformation and heavy bone required to stay sound under prolonged use. A cavalry mount had to be an example of "Form Follows Function" and the only way to obtain that type of horse was to breed a stallion of the necessary conformation to a mare of the same type.

The most fragile portion of a horse are the front legs, and unless there is sufficient bone—large, flat, dense—the animal is prone to suffer injury or unsoundness and become unserviceable. Many purebred Thoroughbred and Saddlebred horses are deficient in having that type of bone and will not stand up under the weight of a saddle, rider and the required equipment during day-after-day service. That meant that light-boned stallions should be bred to heavy-boned mares, preferably of ½ or ¼ draft blood to produce the type of conformation desired.

The Quartermaster General continued in his 1917 report:

> It should be made possible to purchase from racing establishments or breeders, stallions of desirable conformation and type, which have not developed sufficient speed to give them any value as race horses, but would be valuable to the government as sires, and they could be acquired at a very reasonable figure. Attention should be paid to the family of the "individual" under consideration and it should be ascertained if his forbearers have been "horses of substance."
>
> These stallions should be owned by the government and stationed at

Remount Depots where proper supervision of the mares presented by the farmers would be exerted. This is a weak point of the present system, that entirely undesirable mares receive service from these Thoroughbred stallions with the result of a very inferior product.[21]

The Quartermaster General made it very plain in his 1917 Congressional Report that the army was not interested in continuing the purchase of animals that were not of functional conformation. The goal of the program was to produce a usable product rather than just increase the nation's horse population.[22]

Photograph courtesy The Western Horseman

Tim McGee (TB), foaled in 1915, sired by McGee, out of Cheek, is shown at Front Royal Virginia Remount Depot.

In spite of the favorable comments made by the Quartermaster General regarding the success of the program, neither the army nor the civilian breeders were completely happy with the guaranteed price for a three-year-old gelding. The army was feeding the stallions and the mares, but based upon the 1917, 1918, 1919 and 1920 records, only a very small percentage of the colts produced were purchased by the military. The army wanted a larger return on the investment in the form of more acceptable animals. Breeders felt that more animals should be purchased and that the military should not be skimming the cream from each colt crop. Those animals which the army did buy were of sufficient quality to command premium prices on the civilian market.

In 1920, the buying program was revamped. A total of 310 agreements to purchase three-year-old colts sired by government stallions were canceled. All existing contracts scheduled to expire in 1923 would be honored, but no new ones would be written. In the future, preference would be given to colts sired by Department of Agriculture and Remount stallions but there would be no guarantee to buy. Under the new purchase program, Remount Service officers would visit collecting centers so that area breeders would have the opportunity to sell their horses directly to the army. That way, they could receive the full price at little expense of showing their horses.[23]

The Quartermaster General also felt that the draft mares already on the various depots should be bred. Many of them were of excellent type and when crossed with

Thoroughbred-type stallions, should produce a horse suitable for military use. The mares could function in harness for most of the year and raise a colt at the same time.

The Quartermaster General wrote on April 27, 1918:

> During the past few months, it has developed that a considerable number of these mares, now at the various Auxiliary Remount Depots, are in foal. When it was found practical, a number of them were shipped to Fort Reno and Front Royal. Special arrangements have been made to take care of the others by leasing land in the vicinity of the different depots.

He continued:

> As there are a large number of these mares at the various Remount Depots, only the very best and the most suitable will be selected for this purpose. The expense of this undertaking will be practically nothing, as the mares are now owned by the government and must be maintained in any event. In fact, it will cost less to keep them during the year at one of the permanent Remount Depots than it will to maintain them elsewhere during the eight months until the foals are old enough to wean.
>
> It is recommended that authority be granted the Acting Quartermaster General to:
>
> a) Send selected mares from the Auxiliary Remount Depots to Fort Reno, Oklahoma, Fort Keogh, Montana, and Front Royal, Virginia, for the purpose of breeding cavalry horses.
>
> b) To take up the question of obtaining suitable stallions from interested and patriotic owners who have expressed their interest in the undertaking and to accept in the name of the government any animals which may be offered at a nominal cost of one dollar each and to transport them to permanent Remount Depots.
>
> Authority is also requested to purchase as many stallions as may be required, not to exceed twenty, at a cost not to exceed one thousand dollars each.
>
> It is believed that this plan will not interfere with the interests of the farmer and breeders, as it only proposed to breed the cavalry type of horse. There is no difficulty experienced by our purchasing officers in obtaining the required number of light and heavy draft horses.[24]

The Secretary of War approved the above recommendations on May 18, 1918, with the provision that "only those Remount Depots should be used for this purpose where the animals can be maintained in proper conditions on pasture in the open for most of the year."[25]

The first official horse breeding actually done by the army was in 1918 under the above authority. Up until then, the program had been under the control of the Bureau of Animal Industry, Department of Agriculture. Thirty-nine Thoroughbred stallions were secured, four by purchase and the balance by gift. Approximately 1,500 army mares were shipped to the permanent Remount Depots at Front Royal, Virginia, Fort Reno, Oklahoma, and Fort Keogh, Montana. The program was not put into operation until too late in the breeding season to show any marked result in 1919.[26]

Painting courtesy of the Jockey Club, Lexington, Kentucky
Sir Barton (TB), first winner of the Triple Crown of Thoroughbred racing, was donated to the U.S. Army Remount Service and used as a stallion for many years, ending his days near Douglas, Wyoming.

In 1919 the program was reevaluated. After examination of the 1,500 mares selected in 1918, it was determined that a large majority of them were unsuitable for crossing with light stallions. It was also decided that the maintenance was too expensive for the government to continue. The undesirable mares were reissued to the services or sold. In 1919 the 600 remaining mares were bred. There were 205 foals born in 1920 with forty-four lost to contagious abortion which became prevalent on all three depots. The 205 foals obtained were from selected mares and by excellent sires. They gave great promise of developing into exceedingly high class horses of the type which could not have been obtained at the contract price paid by the army.[27] While the quality of the foals was extremely high, there must have been some concern regarding the low conception and foaling rates. Slightly more than one-third of the mares bred produced a foal, and the odds were strong that fifty percent of them were fillies. That meant that management, breeding and health practices had to be improved if a larger percentage of the mares were to raise a usable foal.

The breeding program authorized by the Secretary of War started May 15, 1918, and was a war measure as World War I was in progress. It was necessary to obtain Congressional permission if military horse breeding was to continue. As soon as peace was declared in 1918, military horsemen began lobbying for the program to stay in operation.[28]

The U.S. Remount Service also attempted to take advantage of the herds of wild and semi-wild horses that roamed the rangelands of Montana, Wyoming, Colorado, Utah and Nevada. These animals were considered a pool of horseflesh to draw upon if needed. During the World War I years, Remount stallions were systematically planted in wild herds to up-grade the resulting foal crops. These stallions, primarily of Thoroughbred breeding, crossed on wild mares and produced a larger, tougher horse that would be suitable for military use. Shortly after the war ended in 1918, the plan was abandoned. Few of the resulting foals were ever utilized by the military. They did improve local ranch remudas whenever they could be captured and broken to saddle.[29]

Military horsemen were not the only individuals concerned about the quality of America's saddle horses. A number of civilian breeders recognized that steps had to be taken to upgrade the nation's light horses or there would be few satisfactory animals available in the future. Pioneer Quarter Horse breeder Coke Blake, Pryor, Oklahoma, was one of those individuals aware of the problem and donated one or more outstanding stallions. Writing to Colonel Armstrong of the U.S. Army shortly after the end of World War I, Blake stated:

> More than 20 years ago I foresaw the evil which is upon us today, and being desirous of being subservient to my fellow man and to perpetuate in the archives of time a name that would live long years after I had passed to the Great Beyond, and believing that beauty, power, speed and intelligence all go hand in hand, I took offspring from four families of Quarter Horses, namely Cold Deck, Bertrand, White Lightning and Brimmer, the result of which I call the Blake Horse. They have proven superior to all horses with which they have come in contact in agricultural pursuits as saddle horses, roping or quarter racing. I will donate one of these horses to the government to be tested in the "Endurance Race" and for breeding. Should you grant this request which I so greatly desire, the horse is at your command.[30]

The army granted Blake's request and the breeder donated Tramp, a son of the great Tubal Cain. The stallion was used at the Fort Reno, Oklahoma Remount Depot for a number of years.[31]

Another stallion that made his contributions to Western horseflesh was Sir Barton (TB), winner of the 1919 Kentucky Derby, the Preakness and the Belmont, making him the first Triple Crown Winner. The son of Star Shoot-Lady Sterling was donated to the

U.S. Remount Service in 1932. When Sir Barton first arrived at Fort Robinson he was used as a teasing stallion. This was not because of his breeding, conformation or race record but his size. At the time the policy laid down by the Chief of Remount in Washington, D.C., was to use only as depot stallions individuals standing 16 hands or better. That was in hopes of producing some good Olympic jumping prospects at the depots. That policy was later abandoned and Sir Barton went on to a long career at stud.[32] He died on the ranch of Remount agent Doctor Hylton of Esterbrook, Wyoming, in 1937, at the age of twenty-one. A stone monument was placed over his grave. Eventually the monument was moved to the Wyoming State Fairgrounds at Douglas. The horse's bones were later moved to Washington Park in Douglas and a statue, along with a plaque, placed over them.[33]

In 1919, with World War I over, Congress tightened the purse strings on defense expenditures and considered canceling the Army Horse Breeding Program. By then, military leaders had become convinced that the program was necessary to develop a pool of suitable animals. That was in the face of developing mechanization of the military. Those individuals mounted an all-out campaign to see that the horse breeding program was continued. Their aim was to develop a program as effective as those of Germany and France prior to World War I. Ranking officers marshalled the support of Congressional members, as well as politically influential civilian horsemen. They managed to not only have the program reinstated but expanded to encompass the private breeding sector. That was done by placing well-bred, government-owned stallions in the hands of private breeders across the country. Their efforts saw the U.S. Army Horse Breeding Program reactivated in 1920 with an increased budget of $150,000, the continuance of the Branch Remount Depots and the assignment of experienced personnel to administer them.[34]

During the twenty-plus years that the U.S. Army Horse Breeding Program was in existence the quality of American horseflesh improved dramatically. By the time the program had been in existence for a decade in 1930, western breeders who utilized Remount stallions had taken over the production of polo, hunting and pleasure riding horses as well as up-graded their own saddle mounts.

Livestock publications and local newspapers all carried articles on Remount stallions, breeders or activities. The editors knew the economic contribution that the horse business made to their communities and to the livestock industry in general. The *Denver Daily Record Stockman* commented under the headline "Polo Breeds Come West" that "Western Ranches are Taking the Lead in Polo Pony Production Away from East— Cow Men are Appreciating Quality Range Horses. The East is giving 'way to the ranches and the farms of the West in the breeding of Polo Ponies, according to Major Henry

Leonard of Colorado Springs, writing in *The Sportsman*." The article ended with "Ranchmen in the western states are producing a goodly number of really high class ponies combining quality with substance."[35] The publication also wrote that "Pillory and Howee Doing Part to Supply Great West's Ranches With High Quality Horse Flesh." Both Pillory and Howee were Thoroughbred Remount Service stallions standing near Julesburg, Colorado.[36]

Other Remount stallions that the *Denver Daily Record Stockman* mentioned editorially during the 1930s included Golden Fagot (TB), Delaware (TB) and Silver Star (Saddlebred)[37], Bluecoat (TB).[38] Area businesses and publications were well aware of the impact that good horses had upon the economy and did all that they could to promote local interest.

The Remount Program succeeded so well that good usin' geldings, the result of Remount stallions being crossed on local mares and the kind that the army would buy, were available in volume. One horseman who grew up during the 1920s and 1930s, A. J. "Jack" Campbell of Douglas, Wyoming, served in the Remount Service at Fort Robinson, Nebraska, during World War II, bought and sold thousands of horses during his career as an auctioneer and later became a leading Quarter Horse and Paint breeder. He commented:

KING PLAUDIT

One of the leaders in America among the Thorobred Stallions of the U. S. A. Remount Association is a dweller in the beautiful and productive WHITE RIVER VALLEY. He typifies the spirit of the Meeker country and its advanced breeding in horses, cattle and sheep. We are backing the White River Valley and its productions.

□□□

FIRST STATE BANK *of* MEEKER

A Bank Owned and Controlled by Local Capital By Men Who Have Made Success A Habit

J. N. NEAL, President
JOHN R. CLARK, Vice President
A. E. FORDHAM, Cashier

Photograph courtesy The Record-Stockman

Many western towns were well-aware of the economic impact that sales from good horses generated for the community. This newspaper advertisement placed by the First State Bank of Meeker, Colorado, pays tribute to the U.S. Army Remount stallion King Plaudit (TB).

> We always figured that we'd have those good, functional geldings around forever … you know the athletic kind that stood 15–15-2 hands high, weighed 1,100 pounds plus, cinched big and had withers that stood up about 4 inches to hold the saddle in place. Those horses had a lot of bone as well as feet and legs that would last forever.[39]

He was wrong. After the closing of the Remount Service, the majority of horses bred by civilian horsemen lost the size, bone, functional conformation and usability that the Remount-bred horses had.

While the Army Horse Breeding Program was reactivated and functioned effectively for the next quarter of a century, it was not without spasmodic opposition. Various enemies of horse racing and betting, the continued use of horses as a military tool in the face of increasing mechanization, opponents of government intervention into private enterprise and advocates for the need of federal economy through the elimination of one facet of the military all attacked the program at one time or another. Each time, America's horse publications and friends of the Remount rallied to the cause with political pressure on elected officials who held the purse strings. It was not until 1948 that the Remount Program was finally eliminated and the horses dispersed upon the civilian market.

One of the first skirmishes was documented in *The Blood-Horse* about an Associated Press article disproving the charges of the anti-racing fanatics that, "Thoroughbred horses were merely gambling tools and that they were useless for other purposes." This was an attempt to close the race tracks and suppress betting. The Associated Press article supported the claims made by *The Blood-Horse* that, without betting there would be no racing; without racing there would be no breeding on a scale sufficient to furnish the nation with Thoroughbred sires from which to breed remounts for the cavalry, an highly important and altogether necessary arm of the United States Army.[40]

By the following year, *The Blood-Horse* was pointing out in an editorial, "There are figures in Congress who would, for no good reason at all, further decrease or eliminate [the Remount Budget] entirely."[41]

In January of 1931 the publication called attention to the fact that a sub-committee on appropriations in the House of Representatives had recommended a reduction to $120,000 of the appropriation for horse breeding for the fiscal year beginning July 1, 1931. This was a reduction of $30,000 from the previous allotment of $150,000 and was considered a serious blow to the entire light horse industry. The editor of *The Blood-Horse* advocated that all horsemen contact their Senators and Representatives immediately, urging that the appropriation be restored to the necessary $150,000.[42]

Evidently, enough pressure was put on the politicians to stop the action. The budget was left at $150,000 for 1932. That was sufficient to maintain some 700 Remount Stallions and leave an excess for replacement purchases.[43]

Two years later in February 1933, Congress was in the news again when the Committee on Appropriations of the House of Representatives failed to include anything in the 1933 Armed Forces Appropriation for the army to purchase remounts. Supporters of the cavalry promptly called the oversight to the attention of their Congressmen and Senators. When the bill did come up for a vote in the House on June 21, the $82,500 carried in the 1932 bill for horse and mule purchases was reduced to $50,000.

That was a reduction of $32,500 but still left money to buy needed remounts. Leading the fight for the restoration of the original amount was Representative Virgil Chapman with support from Representative Vinson, both of Kentucky. They had the backing of Representatives from Virginia, Maryland and a number of the Western states, as well as such prominent generals as Pershing, Summerall, Harboard, DeWitt and others.[44]

The leader of the opposition was Representative Ross Collins of Mississippi. In spite of his efforts, the breeding appropriation of $50,000 was unchanged.[45] *The Blood-Horse* kept suggesting that horsemen continue their write-in campaign to elected officials regarding the importance of the Remount Program.

Photograph courtesy King Ranch Museum

Lovely Manners (TB), foaled 1924, by Sweep, out of *Lady Sournoise, was used as a stud by the King Ranch, Kingsville, Texas, during the 1930s.

On September l, 1934, there was a brief flurry about the proposed closing, for economy's sake, of the Lexington Kentucky Breeding and Purchasing Office, as well as the stables. A week later, an announcement appeared in *The Blood-Horse* that the office, perhaps the most influential in the United States since the majority of stallions were purchased through it, would remain open.[46]

Another area of argument, within the military, was fought between those who advocated discarding the cavalry in favor of the new armor branch which utilized tanks and the necessary support vehicles. They felt that the day of the horse in war was over. Army Chief of Staff, General Douglas MacArthur, was one of those who looked upon armor as the cavalry of the future. As Chief of Staff from 1930 to 1935, he was faced with the development of a new and potentially effective weapon within the restraints of a limited budget-developing mechanization in the form of armor, transportation and the new air force. Realizing that tanks were the cavalry of the future, General MacArthur ordered the destruction of excess cavalry mounts. One of the units ordered to destroy a portion of their horses was the Fourth Cavalry stationed at Fort Hauchuca, Arizona. Detailed to drive a herd of horses out onto the desert where they would be destroyed, four old cavalry sergeants and a lieutenant rebelled. They felt it was an inhumane move. The men not only deserted from the service but drove the animals north, heading for Canada. Those five men and the horses were able to make the trek, eluding pursuing military units and crossing the border into Canada to safety. The story was later recounted in the 1995 made-for-television movie *In Pursuit of Honor*, written by Dennis Lynn Clark who heard the story from two of the individuals participating in the incident.[47]

Photograph courtesy Phil Livingston

This broodmare band and foals are typical of mares crossed with U.S. Army Remount stallions to produce mares for farm and ranch use, and geldings for sale to the U.S. Army, providing financial income for the breeder.

The cavalry adapted to the changing times in the 1930s by using large livestock trailers called "portees." These could carry eight horses at a time, along with their riders and equipment. Cavalry officers felt that the horse could be transported by trailer as long as roads were available, then unloaded and ridden in the rougher terrain. That would give speed of movement, mobility in areas where vehicles could not operate and the scouting abilities that cavalry could provide.

The cavalry mounted a public relations campaign pointing out the effectiveness of animal use in the military. The horse and mule inventories of the major foreign armies, their use and America's relatively poor capabilities to counter them were all questioned. In a speech before the Horse and Mule Association of America on December 3, 1941, Major General John K. Herr, Chief of Cavalry, U.S. Army, discussed the advantages of mounted forces in the field, compared American units against the German, Japanese and Russian armies and listed the number of animals utilized by each nation.

Nation	Cavalry	Draft & Pack	Total
Russia	200,000	800,000	1,000,000
Japan	50,000	325,000	375,000
Germany	50,000	910,000	960,000
America*	25,000	12,000	50,000 [48]

*In Remount Depots and for Administrative use—13,000

Major General Herr pointed out that the German army utilized mounted reconnaissance groups attached to marching infantry divisions as well as a scouting platoon of thirty horsemen attached to each marching infantry regiment. America had neither and he was strong in his feelings that the United States Army was handicapped by the lack of reconnaissance ability.[49] This thinking was later substantiated by the comments of American generals during World War II such as Bradley, Patton, Truscott and Eisenhower. All were faced with fighting battles in mountainous terrain without cavalry or pack support.[50]

While World War II was to prove the effectiveness of machines in warfare, there were numerous instances where cavalry, pack animals and mule-powered wagons could have been, or were, an effective fighting tool for American forces. Although the army was gradually "dehorsed" during the late 1930s, it was not until December 7, 1941, and the resulting Declaration of War, that the final answer was written for the mounted branch and the supporting Remount Service.

In spite of dissension within the military, of attack from both civilian and political enemies, the Remount Service achieved its assigned mission. During the 1920s and 1930s, a steady improvement of America's horseflesh came about, providing the army with more effective remounts and giving breeders something to sell. It was during those two decades that the U.S. Remount Service made a positive contribution to the United States.

Chapter 3: Sources and Notes

1. Mimeographed copy of U.S. Army Report, no date, unnumbered, in possession of author.
2. *The Morgan Horse* (August 1993): 66.
3. U.S. Army document on the History and Function of the U.S. Remount Service, 1921, mimeographed copy in possession of the author.
4. Ibid.
5. *Half-Bred Stud Book*, Volume I (Avon, New York: Genesee Valley Breeders Association, 1925), 1.
6. U.S. Army report, 1921.
7. Ibid.
8. Ibid.
9. Ibid.
10. Ibid.
11. Ibid.
12. Ibid.
13. Quartermaster General, Technical Manual No. 10-395, Section 1, "Remount" (War Department, December 18, 1941): 36. Also, Miller J. Stewart, "The Government's Gift to the Private Horse Breeder," *The Horseman* (March 1972), 73.
14. U.S. Army report, no date.
15. Ibid.
16. Ibid.
17. Ibid.
18. Ibid.
19. Ibid.
20. Ibid.
21. Ibid.
22. Ibid.
23. Ibid.
24. Ibid.
25. ibid.
26. Ibid.
27. Ibid.
28. Ibid.
29. Hope Ryden, *America's Last Wild Horses* (New York: E.P. Dutton & Co., 1970), 200.
30. Freeman Blake Toga, "The Blake Horse" *The Quarter Horse Journal* (March 1984): unnumbered copy.
31. Ibid.
32. "Sir Barton," *The Blood-Horse* (April 20, 1991): 2074.
33. Naomi E. Chesky, "He'll always be the first," *The Douglas Budget Record* (September 15, 1993): unnumbered copy.
34. Major A. A. Cedarwald, "The Remount Service Past and Present," *The Quartermaster Review* (November–December 1928): 29.
35. *The Denver Daily Record Stockman*, Stock Show Edition (1930): 76.
36. *The Denver Daily Record Stockman*, 1930 Stock Show Edition (1938): 99.
37. Ibid., 76.
38. *The Denver Daily Record Stockman*, Stock Show Edition (1930): 152.
39. A. J. "Jack" Campbell, Douglas, Wyoming, interview with Phil Livingston, July 1993.
40. *The Blood-Horse* (June 29, 1929): 21.
41. *The Blood-Horse* (September 27, 1930): 1123.
42. *The Blood-Horse* (January 17, 1931).
43. *The Blood-Horse* (January 28, 1933): 116.
44. *The Blood-Horse* (February 4, 1933): 139; (March 18, 1933): 146; (February 18, 1933): 223; (July 22, 1933).
45. Ibid.
46. *The Blood-Horse* (September 1, 1934): 223; (September 8, 1934): 247.
47. Dennis Lynn Clark, *In Pursuit of Honor*, HBO made-for-television movie, 1995. The military files on the incident are still closed. The script was written in the 1960s, originally for John Wayne, but the author could not get the financing for the project. An article in the *Los Angeles Times* gave the story. Clark was a boy living on a Montana ranch during World War II when he heard the story from two of the five men involved, who had stolen the herd of Second Cavalry horses and driven them to Canada and safety while eluding a strong military pursuit. Two of them later sneaked back into the States and were working for his father on the ranch. They were both still listed as deserters from the army. Clark wrote the story after they were both dead. Livingston asked his father if, during his cavalry service as an officer in the 1930s, he had heard about the incident. Livingston writes that although his father was ninety-four at the time, confined to a wheel chair and almost blind, he drew himself up to attention and in his steely command voice stated, "We were ordered not to talk about it!"

48. Major General John K. Herr, "Why Should the United States Lag Behind Other Great Powers in the Military Use of Animals?" Speech to the Horse and Mule Association of America, Inc. December 3, 1941. Printed in Booklet No. 265 (Chicago: Horse and Mule Association of America, Inc., 1941), 2.
49. Ibid., 2–3.
50. Anna Waller, "Horses and Mules and National Defense" (Department of the Army, Office of the Quartermaster General, No. XVIII-3-0009, 1958), 22–23.

Photograph courtesy The Western Horseman

U.S. Army 6th Cavalry prepares for a long and treacherous march in the Big Bend region of Texas. Supplying such large numbers of horses needed for the cavalry and artillery was the mission of the U.S. Remount Service.

Photograph courtesy U.S. Army

U.S. Army 2nd Cavalry troopers swim their horses across the Smokey Hill River during maneuvers in 1941. The ability of cavalry to overcome natural obstacles that would stop, or slow down, vehicles made horses an effective fighting and scouting force.

Ω

CHAPTER 4

THE PROGRAM COMES OF AGE:
1920–1940

"I would like to say a word of appreciation for the good work of the Remount Association, cooperating with the Remount Department. It is impossible to over-estimate how much this move is affecting the intelligent breeding of riding horses. The liberal and sane methods employed, up-to-date and reasonable, will have a wonderful influence on the American riding horse of the future. Speaking for myself, I can only say that through this means I now have the use of a stallion to continue my breeding operations—a horse which I could not have found myself, though I have been searching and inquiring for some time for such an animal. This is only one of the many instances, and its effect has been not only to supply many needed stallions, to put life into an industry which was nearly defunct."

William Anson

Cristoval, Texas

Pioneer Quarter Horse Breeder[1]

The original Army Horse Breeding Program was designed to bring the mares to the stallions. Those stallions were stabled and maintained by the U.S. Government on the Branch Remount Depots. The first breeding headquarters were at Front Royal, Virginia, since the original stallions were obtained on the East Coast. Stallions were also located in New England and the mid-South on sub-depots. Not only were the stallions stabled there but the government maintained the mares during the year that it took to produce a foal. Under the revised program of 1920, the stallions were dispersed to civilian agents from the Remount Depots in Virginia, Oklahoma, Montana and Nebraska. That move made high quality stallions available throughout the nation. At the time that the Horse Breeding Program was continued by Congress after World War I, the Remount Service owned sixty high-quality stallions and the Bureau of Animal Industry twenty-seven. Additional purchases of suitable stallions were made as well as donations solicited from civilian horsemen. A number of the latter responded by presenting the Remount Service with exceptionally well-bred individuals.

After 1920, U.S. Remount Service stallions were divided between Front Royal, Virginia; Fort Reno, Oklahoma; Fort Keogh, Montana; and Fort Robinson, Nebraska (activated as a Remount Depot in 1919). The officer in charge of each depot assigned stallions to civilian agents within his district. Each agent accepted the loan of a stallion, agreed to house and maintain the animal, and breed him to his own, and other people's mares for a minimum stud fee of ten dollars per mare. The accumulated breeding fees were the agent's payment for standing the stallion. The Remount Service did reserve the right to inspect the presented mares as to their suitability for breeding and meeting the army's standards. That proviso met little opposition among the nation's horsemen since they felt that animals produced through the Remount Program would result in a more saleable foal. The Army Horse Breeding Program made available at the regional level much finer stallions than the normal individual would have access to and at a cost which all could afford.

Under the written contract between the Remount Service and each civilian agent, the stallion was boarded out, relieving the government of the expense of stabling, feeding and handling the animal as well as the mares brought to him. Each stallion was the responsibility of the agent. The only reservation the army placed upon the agent was the opportunity to purchase the three-year-old geldings sired by the Remount stallion, at the prevailing military price, providing the owner wished to sell. The fillies were the mare owner's property from the time of birth.[2]

The Army Horse Breeding Program was considered a success by both military and civilian horsemen. The quality of mounts which became available to the army by the late 1920s was exceptional. Detailed records maintained by the Remount Service made possible well-researched breeding programs. The high-quality fillies produced by Remount stallions and good dams resulted in excellent broodmare bands for civilian breeders at all levels.[3]

The result of this government backed breeding program was a functional, solidly conformed utility horse that stood 14-2 to 15-2 hands and weighed between 1,000 and 1,200 pounds. These saddle horses cinched big to provide lots of breathing room, had well-defined withers and excellent feet and legs. Field artillery riders met the same criteria but stood 15-2 to 16 hands and weighed from 1,250 to 1,600 pounds.[4]

According to Lt. Colonel Thomas J. Johnson, Chief of Remount in 1935, the Remount Program produced "horses made to order." The resulting half-breds had the size, bone and endurance of a functional saddle horse to meet military and sporting requirements. These horses were produced by breeding top-quality stallions to mares of similar type. Good horses were an example of "blood will tell" and he cited the pedigrees and conformation of numerous Remount stallions and their offspring to prove his point.[5]

By the end of the 1920s, the criteria for a cavalry mount was so well known that the average horseman could look at an animal and accurately judge if the army buyers would pass it. Remount-quality horses looked enough alike to have been almost a separate breed.[6]

Officers purchased their horses privately, frequently from a levy on a Remount depot. They normally rode a mount that was a grade above the troop horses issued to the enlisted men. The designation "officer's charger" denoted a

Photograph courtesy Ms. Bette Thurston Mecham
This Remount stallion, Nebo (TB) by Goodley, stood at the farm of Remount Agent Burt Thurston, Morgan, Utah, during the 1930s. Burt Thurston is mounted.

superior individual that could be of Olympic caliber. A number of the officers' mounts were very high quality mares, often the result of a Remount stallion being crossed on a daughter of another Remount stallion.[7] A large percentage of these horses were superbly trained since it was a point of pride to the majority of officers to be well mounted. The horses were not only used for military functions but served as recreational mounts as well. Pole and barrel racing, jumping, flat racing and polo were all part of the troop and post horse activity. The shows were scheduled on a regular basis. Both officers and enlisted men competed and the rivalry between companies and troops was high.

The June 1920 Congressional Breeding Appropriation of $36,940 did not become available until July 1, 1920. That was too late to finance the breeding of many mares for early foals in 1921. In spite of the delay, the combined efforts of the Remount Service and the Bureau of Animal Industry resulted in breeding 1,250 mares that belonged to both civilians and the Remount Service. Upon completion of the 1920 breeding season, the Bureau of Animal Industry transferred ownership of all government stallions standing in Vermont, New Hampshire, Virginia, West Virginia, Kentucky and Tennessee to the U.S. Remount Service. That transfer included: six Thoroughbreds, five Morgans, six Saddlebreds and six Standardbreds. The stallions were later distributed to civilian agents through the Branch Remount Depots.[8] The transfer of stallions removed the Bureau of Animal Industry from the horse breeding program and left it a strictly army effort.

An asset to the Army Horse Breeding Program was the service of Mr. C. A. Bell, an animal husbandry expert. He transferred to the U.S. Remount Service from the Bureau of Animal Industry, Department of Agriculture, on October 16, 1920. In that capacity, he developed and put into use many of the breeding procedures that made the program a success. Mr. Bell was well-qualified to work in the production of military mounts as he had served as a Captain of the Remount Service during World War I.[9]

As soon as the 1920 breeding season was completed, the Remount Service began to prepare for 1921. The plan, developed by Major Charles L. Scott, went into force and operated smoothly with little change for the next twenty years. Major Scott had been in charge of the Army Horse Breeding plans since 1919. The carefully thought-out program operated as follows:

A. When not being utilized for breeding purposes by civilian agents, the stallions were kept at the various Branch Remount Depots of: Front Royal, Virginia, Fort Keogh, Montana, Fort Robinson, Nebraska, and Fort Reno, Oklahoma. These stallions were assigned to a Remount District by Chief of the Remount Service upon the request of the officer in charge of the district. From there the horses were distributed to civilian agents throughout each breeding and purchasing district by the officer in charge. The agents stood the stallions to their own and other horsemen's mares. Each agent signed a contract with the U.S. Remount Service, making him responsible for the animal's upkeep and well-being during the period that he kept him. The agent also maintained records on the number of mares bred and the resulting foals. The placement of these stallions was the responsibility of the officer in charge of each breeding and procurement district. He had to know the horsemen in his district who would take a strong interest in breeding the stallion to quality mares. The stud fee was paid to the agent by the mare owner as the agent's compensation for handling the stallion. Agents worked closely with the officer in charge of breeding in their district. When possible, the agent accompanied the officer in charge and the military veterinarian on annual inspections of mares bred to and foals sired by the Remount Service stallion in his care.

B. The stallions sent out to the breeding centers each year were those which had already proven suitable at stud. Stallions about which there was some doubt as to fertility or siring ability were test-bred to Remount Service mares before being issued. The resulting foals were evaluated the following year. The officer in charge of breeding in each district recommended which stallions were to be retained at the Remount Depot for local use.

All stallions assigned to breeding centers were carefully inspected by the officer in charge of the district and the military veterinarian before being issued. At that time, the two officers determined the maximum number of mares each stallion should serve. This recommendation was passed onto the civilian agent who would stand the stallion.

C. Stud fees were charged on all stallions and the fee was the same as that normally charged for civilian stallions in an area. Those fees were set by the officer in charge of breeding in each district and collected by his local agents (individuals who were standing the stallion).

D. The officer in charge of breeding, accompanied by the military veterinarian and the local agent, was authorized to approve the mares to be bred to Remount Service stallions. The mares were to be of good disposition, physically sound with no hereditary conformational defects and be of such type and conformation that assured satisfactory results. No unsuitable mares were to be bred to Remount Service stallions. After a mare had passed inspection, the owner was given a certificate of suitability by the officer in charge of breeding in each zone (Remount Service Form No. 9). A careful description of the mare was made on Remount Service Form No. 11 and kept on file at the area Remount Purchasing and Breeding Headquarters. The certificate could be revoked at any time by the officer in charge if the mare developed a disease or defect that made her unsuitable for breeding to Remount Service stallions.

Photograph courtesy Ms. Bette Thurston Mecham

Goodley (TB), 1933, by *Waygood and out of Chesney Lass, is shown with Remount Agent Burt Thurston, Morgan, Utah, at halter.

E. The offspring of privately owned mares were the property of the owner of the mare and could be disposed of in any manner and at any time that the owner saw fit. In order, however, to encourage horse breeding and to establish a market within each breeding area, the Remount purchasing officers would inspect and purchase such offspring of Remount Service stallions in each area as was needed, provided that the animals conformed to army specifications.

F. Before the beginning of the breeding season, the officer in charge of breeding, the military veterinarian and agent would inspect the stabling facilities for each stallion in his care. Clean, well-ventilated stalls, along with an exercise corral were required.

G. After all the arrangements had been made, the stallion assigned to the breeding center was turned over to the agent upon his signature of a receipt. The agent in charge of the stallion was responsible for the care and actual breeding of the animal to approved mares. These stallions were normally shipped by train with the agent taking delivery of the horse at the railhead nearest his farm or ranch. By the middle 1930s, stock trailers which could be pulled behind small trucks were in use. Stallions were often transported by trailer to the individual agent if he was located near a Branch Remount Depot.

Photograph courtesy Gordon Moore

A pure-bred Arabian Remount stallion at Fort Robinson, Nebraska during the early 1940s was one of a number of Arabian stallions in the program, many donated by leading breeders from around the United States.

The agent in charge of each stallion received careful instruction in the use of all equipment utilized in breeding. After the stallion arrived at the location where he would stand, the agent made all the arrangements to bring the mares in for breeding. This was in accordance with the instructions from the officer in charge of breeding in the zone where the stallion stood.

In some cases, the stallions were sent out on the road to serve a number of mares. This was in the charge of the agent. He visited the various mare owners and made arrangements in advance. He, or one of his employees, transported the stallion to the different farms and ranches where approved mares would be waiting. Every effort was made to serve the total number of mares approved for the individual stallion. Whenever a mare was bred, a certificate of service (R.S. Form No. 9) was issued to the owner. Second and third services, if necessary, were noted on the same form. No payment was required for second and third services.

At the beginning of each breeding season, sufficient stallions were sent to the various breeding centers to service the available, approved mares in the area.

H. Many work animals at the various depots were superior mares. At the beginning of the program, no mares were kept for breeding purposes alone. Those light draft mares were bred to produce a foal annually as well as work in harness. Several of the stallions selected by the officer in charge of breeding in each zone were retained at each permanent Remount Depot for use on these mares. One of the principal objects of breeding these government mares, other than the production of potential military horses, was that the suitability of a stallion could be evaluated (by either natural cover or artificial impregnation). Testing of the stallions before issuing them to civilian agents, eliminated many potential problems. If conditions warranted it and suitable mares were available, enough stallions to breed all mares within a radius of twenty-five miles would be assigned to each Branch Remount Depot. The stallions would be managed from the depot by the office in charge of breeding in that zone, utilizing depot personnel.

I. The record of a foal, while still a suckling, was kept on the mare record. Once the foal was weaned, another record (R.S. Form No. 10) was filled out. The officer in charge of each zone was required to maintain close contact with the owners of the foals and mares, keeping his records up-to-date to determine the suitability of a stallion or mare for breeding purposes. After the foal was weaned and recorded as an individual, it was inspected annually until it reached four years, unless sold by the owner, to determine progress and development. This detailed record keeping documented the productivity of both sire and dam. It did much to give the Army Horse Breeding Program credibility. It is from these records that the pedigrees of many modern horses are traced back to various Remount stallions.

J. The officer in charge of a zone, accompanied by the military veterinarian and the respective local agent when practical, inspected all foals born in his zone at least once a year. The military veterinarian was able to inspect the foals at any time that he deemed it necessary. At each inspection, advice was offered by the inspecting officers to the agent as to the care, trimming of feet, correction of defects in the legs or any other matters affecting the well-being of both the mare and the foal.

These inspections were well-coordinated and all persons supervising the breeding programs became familiar with the conditions in their zone. Agents learned procedures and practices that the military desired as well as the type of animal required for purchase. The inspectors had ample opportunity to assess the work and the capabilities of each agent. This knowledge was utilized when passing on him for the stewardship of future Remount Service stallions.[10]

Even with regular inspections and instruction to the agents on the care of Remount Service stallions, some animals did die or had to be destroyed. Statistics maintained by the office of the quartermaster general showed that very few stallions died of old age. The majority of those lost were destroyed because of poor care or injuries resulting from carelessness by handlers.[11]

As with any other government operation, reports in triplicate were mandatory. These ranged from monthly to quarterly to annual to special, all of which had to be filed to keep the program supervisors in Washington, D.C., aware of the situation in each area.

When the 1921 breeding season began on April 20, the Remount Service owned 160 stallions. One hundred thirty-four were Thoroughbred. The remainder were Arabian, Saddlebred, Morgan and Standardbred. Eighty-five of the Thoroughbreds had been donated by civilian racing organizations such as the Kentucky Racing Commission, the Maryland Jockey Club, the New York Jockey Club, the Kentucky Breeders Association and the Jockey Club. Seventy-five of the stallions had been purchased on the open market, often at prices far below their actual value.[12]

Included in this first group of stallions were such top individuals as Gordon Russell (TB), donated by the Kentucky Racing Commission who would distinguish himself as one of the greatest Remount sires[13]; King Plaudit (TB), by the Kentucky Derby winner Plaudit, whose blood was to become the basis for the famous Shoemaker and Wiescamp Quarter Horses two generations later[14]; Man of Honor (TB), sired by Dearing Doe and out of a Peter McCue daughter[15]; Uncle Jimmie Grey (TB), by Bonnie Joe, who sired speed across the Southwest in the 1920s and 1930s and the sons of Star Shoot (TB): Brookland, Defense and Rifle Shooter.[16] Many of these Thoroughbred stallions were themselves sons of such outstanding individuals as Sweep, Ogden, Rock Sand, Fair Play and Ben Brush.[17] While the majority of the stallions were Thoroughbred, Saddlebred sires such as Bourbon King and Rex Peavine were represented along with Morgans sired by Headlight Morgan and Scotland as well as Arabians by Jahil, Nimar and Abu Keyd.[18]

A number of public-spirited horsemen such as August Belmont, Pierre Lorillard Jr. and Colonel E. R. Bradley donated many stallions to the Remount Program. Bradley's contribution of more than thirty Thoroughbred stallions, included: Behave Yourself, Bet Mosie, Buckeye Poet (the first Remount stallion stood by Hank Wiescamp of Alamosa, Colorado) and the well-known Black Toney.[19]

Other American horsemen who gave stallions to the Remount Service were: Harry Warner, head of Warner Brothers Motion Picture Studios, along with C. S. "Seabiscuit" Howard and his son Lin.[20] Colonel F. W. Koester, officer in charge of the Western Remount division, said,

> Several very prominent American breeders, purely because of their selfish
> interest in, and respect for, the Remount Program, made a habit of giving
> me first crack at horses—excellent, sound individuals—that they found
> wanting in their racing stable but which had all the physical qualities we

needed for Remount breeding…. I was authorized to pay as much as $1000 for these stud prospects, which was a fraction of what they would have brought in the sales ring. Among the fine future Remount sires obtained in this manner: the Man O' War horses, Warrior Son and H.M. War, Final Appeal, Toney Boots, Flechazo and Nuisance.[21]

At the beginning of the Remount program in 1913, the value of the donated stallions was conservatively listed at $300,000. The average price paid for the individual horses purchased was $860, but that did not reflect the true value of each animal. Some had been practically given to the Remount with the understanding that the U.S. Government pay only the amount due for their upkeep. Others were secured at races written especially for stallions suitable for Remount service. The purses offered at those races were often as high as $1,500, with the provision that the winning horse was sold to the government for $750. The total value of the stallions owned by the Remount in 1921 was estimated at $440,000, a more than twenty-five percent increase in both numbers and value.[22] Those stallions were first distributed to the Branch Remount Depots and then to the breeding

Photograph courtesy U.S. Army

A Remount stallion is exhibited during a Fort Reno Field Day. This animal typifies the quality of the Remount stallions as up-graded saddle horses in the areas where they stood.

centers which were managed by civilian agents. It would be several years before the results would be seen and evaluated, but the potential for improved military and civilian saddle horses was great.

The majority of civilian agents were enthusiastic about the quality of the stallions provided to them. A number of them took the time to write the officers in charge of purchasing and breeding in their zone, passing on their opinions of the stallions. On March 1, 1921, Goslet Gallatin of Sheridan, Wyoming, wrote to Major W. H. Neil of Boise, Idaho, "I am more than delighted with Meator. He is a beauty and I expect to get fine colts from him." On March 30, 1921, Roy M. Pittman of Ashland, Montana wrote to Major Neil, "I have not seen the stallion Roly that Luther Dunning received but have heard several men say that he was the finest horse they ever saw. I am very glad he got this horse and hope it will not be long until the breeding appropriation is raised. We certainly do need to raise better horses."[23]

Luther Dunning's N Open A Ranch near Ashland, Montana, was a source of top saddle horses, polo ponies, hunter-jumpers and Army Remounts for over thirty years. In addition to Roly, Dunning used the Remount stallions Saratoga, Secret Greetings and Do or Die. While Dunning was not well known to most horsemen, his horses were and shipments went from Montana to Chicago, Illinois, Louisville, Kentucky, and to polo trainers on the East Coast. The American team polo pony Sailor was a Dunning-bred mount.[24]

On March 30, 1921, Colonel C. E. Hawkins of Kansas city, Missouri, received the following letter from J. W. Neuhes of Medora, North Dakota, "I received the stallion Son of the Wind in good condition and am very well pleased. He sure is a dandy and I don't see but what we should get a good many mares of good type to breed to him. Everyone who has seen him says he is a dandy." On April 6, 1921, Colonel Hawkins received the following letter from Philip J. Sale of Genry, Missouri, "Everyone is perfectly crazy about the horse Rococo and I could breed 100 good decent mares easily. I could use another horse, Colonel Hawkins, if it could be arranged. He is in splendid condition and I am glad to be of service to you."[25]

Photograph courtesy Gordon Moore

This typical two-year-old filly was a product of Remount breeding, at Fort Robinson, Nebraska, during the closing years of the Remount Program. Mares of this type were invaluable in the development of superior ranch remudas as well as producing foals which were later registered in the AQHA, the Appaloosa and Palomino associations.

While representatives of the majority of the popular light horse breeds were utilized in the Remount Service stud, the Thoroughbred was selected as the foundation stock to improve the quality of military horses in the United States. Time and test had proven that the breed had the disposition, intelligence, endurance, conformation and adaptability to do the job. It was also pointed out that the Thoroughbred horse came in all sizes and shapes, varying from a thick, compact type (Ariel) to a taller, slimmer and more leggy individual (Phar Lap). The military was primarily interested in those individuals of the first type, well-balanced with considerable substance and standing between 15 to 15-2 hands.[26]

While the Thoroughbred was the favored breed, the U.S. Remount Service did utilize other stallions. Those included were: Cleveland Bay, Arabian and Arabian-kind (developed in Europe), Morgan, Morabs (a blending of Morgan and Arabian), Lippizaners, Anglo Arabs (Thoroughbred and Arabian) and a few American Saddlebreds. Standardbreds were not used because the trot or pace were the primary gaits. The Remount's criteria was, "Any *good* horse is a *good* horse!" Military buyers were interested in a functional mount rather than the breeding of the individual.[27]

Colonel Grove Cullum of the U.S. Remount Service, wrote:

> From this varied background, mingling together in the hardy environment of the range country, was drawn the bands of native Western brood mares which the Remount Service at the beginning of its efforts found for its Thoroughbred sires. From the beginning of these efforts Remount officers discovered that while many ranchmen were looking for better stallions they did not know quite what they needed. To cite an instance, when I was first placed in charge of the Southern Remount Zone, a great majority of the applicants for Government sires expressed a preference for Morgans, Arabs, Quarter Horses, Hambletonians, etc. But, by the time that I left there, four years later, by actual count ninety-eight percent of the applications were for registered Thoroughbreds.[28]

Colonel Fred L. Hamilton, Chief of the U.S. Remount Service at the end of World War II, added his comments:

> In the late twenties and early thirties, the stampede for Thoroughbred blood was on. Texas was the first to go overboard, and at one time we had nearly 150 Thoroughbred stallions in that state alone. Everyone suddenly waked up to the fact that a Thoroughbred sire, almost any Thoroughbred with four legs, was better than the monstrosities that they had been using. Where at one time it had been difficult to find agents for government stallions, suddenly the applicants exceeded the supply. Putting the horses out was easy. Thereafter, getting them away from a community meant war, or at least a barrage of brickbats from the community's senators and congressmen.[29]

Civilian agents who stood Remount stallions received regular information from the army on the care, feeding and breeding of the horse. Suggestions as to the type of mares that should be bred to a specific stallion came from the officer in charge of the Purchasing and Breeding Zone and the military veterinarian during their regular visits. That information was reinforced by printed matter that was either mailed to the agent or left during visits from the officer in charge. There was also frequent correspondence between the military and the agent, reflecting the high degree of confidence that was placed in those men.[30]

Publications, such as *The Blood-Horse*, editorialized on the purchase of stallions by the Remount Service and listed the Branch Remount Depot where the horse would be assigned. When a civilian agent sold a stallion to the Remount Service, that fact was also reported, as well as his tenure as an agent. An example of such a sale was the Army's purchase of a son of Star Set (TB) for $4,000 from R. S. Waring of San Angelo, Texas.[31]

The area Purchasing and Breeding Office worked through agents when searching for potential army horses and mules. The agents, because of their local knowledge, either recommended various ranches where acceptable animals might be found or helped set up a showing where individuals could bring their horses for the military inspectors/purchasers to see. Frequently, this was at the ranch of an agent. In some cases, agents purchased animals that they felt were acceptable and then resold them to the army at a profit.[32]

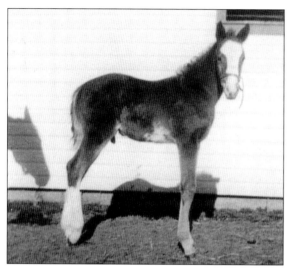

Photograph courtesy Gordon Moore
This Thoroughbred colt was bred under the Remount Program at Fort Robinson, Nebraska, during the early 1940s.

Agents were notified of such events as shows, endurance rides, polo matches or other activities where Remount-type horses could be exhibited. The purpose of these events was to demonstrate the superior qualities of the horses, making them more attractive to the general public as a sporting and utility mount. Even during the early years of the program, the Remount Service was looking ahead to the day when more acceptable horses would be produced than could be consumed by the army except in time of war. There had to be a civilian market for the animals in order to give the agents a reason to breed them.[33]

Principals of Breeding which were insisted on at all Breeding Centers:

1. Not necessarily more horses but better ones.
2. Careful selection of mares as to type, soundness and disposition. Violent crosses, such as on coarse draft mares, are not permitted.
3. Elimination of mares that prove poor mothers, or that produce weedy colts, providing the results from mating with other mares shows that the stallion is not at fault.
4. Good care and feeding of both mares and colts.
5. Proper handling, gentling and breaking of colts from birth to maturity.[34]

Agents were required to fill out the certificate of service for each mare bred, to submit a monthly report of the number of mares bred to the stallion that they were standing as well as various annual reports. Those were all forwarded to the officer in charge within the district. In turn, he sent reports from his zone to the Remount Service offices, Office of the Quartermaster General, U.S. Army, Washington, D.C. As was/is normal with any project connected with the U.S. Government, the paperwork piled up.[35]

For several years after the formation of the Remount Program, agents were allowed to pasture-breed the stallions. Many good sires did not last long under the rugged range conditions found in the western states. They became crippled, fell off of cliffs, were bitten by rattlesnakes, were injured fighting with wild stallions or died of exposure. By 1925, agents were required to keep Remount stallions in suitable quarters. This move increased the life and the effectiveness of the stallions.[36]

Hand breeding was practiced as it not only protected the stallions from the stress of pasture life and injuries but gave a higher conception rate. At the time that each stallion was issued the agent received a special breeding halter, a set of breeding hobbles to be used on the mare and instructions on how to use the equipment.[37]

In 1918 Mrs. Francis Wadsworth founded the *Half-bred Stud Book*. This organization was an outgrowth of the Genesee Valley Breeders Association, headquartered at Avon, New York. It was sanctioned by the New York Jockey Club and was open to horses sired by Thoroughbred stallions or out of Thoroughbred mares. The purpose was to maintain a record of the bloodlines and give recognition to the various individuals who bred and used the Half-bred animals. Horses with Half-bred registration papers were extensively used in jumping, hunting, polo and other sporting activities as they had been found to carry the desirable performance characteristics necessary for those equine sports. The formation of the *Stud Book* was the beginning of Half-bred registrations in America, although Thoroughbred cross had been widely used for many years. The fact that an animal was registered carried an economic benefit as well. A premium was paid for individuals of known parentage that carried the genetic combination for functional conformation, athletic ability and the mental capabilities to perform well under saddle. A number of Half-bred stallions and mares were used in the development of Appaloosa, Paint, Palomino and Quarter Horse breeding programs. The *Half-Bred Stud Book* registry and records were taken over by the American Remount Association in 1934.[38]

Agents standing Remount stallions were encouraged to join the American Remount Association, founded in November of 1918, by General C. L Scott.[39] With a charter membership of eighty-eight and headquartered in Washington, D.C., it was dedicated to enhancing the public awareness to the suitability of Remount-bred horses for sporting use as well as enlarging the economic benefits for the people who bred them. The membership was originally limited to army officers but was soon opened to anyone who was interested in the improvement of light horses through the use of well-bred stallions. The group not only included civilian Remount agents but individuals prominent in Thoroughbred racing. Horsemen such as: A. B. Hancock, Pierre Lorillard Jr., General H. C. Whitehead, Samuel Riddle, Colonel E. R. Bradley, August Belmont, Mr. and Mrs. Payne Whitney, F. Ambrose Clark and Harry S. Hart were all enthusiastic members. By the middle 1930s, the organization had grown to approximately 4,000 members, both in the United States and abroad.[40]

The interest in America's military horseflesh was characterized by the gentlemen who served as officers of the American Remount Association. They were all men of national stature and means, with a deep devotion to fine horses. President was Pierre Lorillard Jr., of Tuxedo Park, New York; 1st Vice President was Carleton F. Burke, of Los Angeles, California; 2nd Vice President was Arthur B. Hancock, of Paris, Kentucky; 3rd Vice President was F. Ambrose Clark, of Cooperstown, New York; Chairman, Executive Committee was Henry Leonard, of Washington, D.C.; Secretary-Treasurer was A. A. Cederwald, of Washington, D.C.; Assistant Secretary was M. E. Brown, of Washington, D.C.[41]

A bi-monthly publication, *The Horse,* was printed and distributed by the American Remount Association. It called attention to where the various Remount stallions were standing, their breeding, the performance of their foals at shows, on the polo field, jumping, hunting, endurance riding or at military exercises, and subjects of general interest to all horsemen. Selected books of interest to horsemen were also offered for sale.

Of major interest to both the army and supporters of the Remount Association was convincing Western stockmen that half-bred Thoroughbreds made good stock horses. Numerous articles in the various horse publications were devoted to that effort. Respected ranchers were interviewed and written about with special attention paid to their reasons for riding Remount-bred horses.

John Hopkins, of Glenwood Springs, who ranched in western Colorado was quoted:

> This talk about the Thoroughbred not being fitted for cow work is pure bunk. He's not only fitted for it—he is, in my opinion, the only horse that is. He has everything that a cowman needs—plenty of bottom, plenty of intelligence, plenty of speed and plenty of weight-carrying ability.
>
> At the ranch we want all the Thoroughbred blood we can get into our cow horses. Most of ours are three-quarterbred at least, a few seven-eighths.

We've ridden these hot bloods for years, and I doubt if we could have got the job done without them.[42]

The activities of the Remount Association were important enough to horsemen to be documented in other publications. Information appeared in: *The Blood-Horse, The Morgan, The Thoroughbred Record, The Cavalry Journal, Breeder's Gazette, The Show Horse Chronicle, Town and Country, The Rider and Driver* and *The Daily Racing Form* as well as various local newspapers across the nation.

Light horses for riding purposes or active, medium-sized "chunks" to pull caissons were the only type of horse that the Remount service was attempting to influence. Animals of this type all benefitted from the infusion of improved blood. There were sufficient quality draft horses produced by civilian breeders to supply the military when necessary.

Mules were also needed by the military but the strong commercial demand for the animals maintained a ready commissary for the army. Many daughters of Remount stallions were crossed with high-class jacks to produce the lighter commercial classifications of mules and upgraded the quality of those animals. While mules had played an important part in American military history, it was not until World War II that the demand for the animals became greater than that for horses.[43]

By the end of the 1921 breeding season, the basic Army Remount Horse Breeding Plan was in place and would remain "as is" until the program was transferred to the U.S. Department of Agriculture in April, 1948.

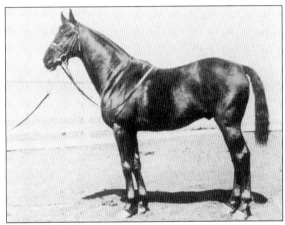

Photograph courtesy The Western Horseman

Kind Sir (TB), one of the early Remount stallions, is shown at the Front Royal Remount Depot, Front Royal, Virginia.

From the original 160 stallions distributed in 1921, the number expanded to well over 700 in 1941. By 1929, the army was purchasing approximately 100 stallions a year as replacements or to enlarge the program.[44]

Concurrently with increased interest in army horse breeding was declining military use of the animal. Mechanization had begun to invade the battlefield. World War I had proven that tanks could provide the shock and mobility of cavalry, with increased fire power. A convoy of trucks could carry far more supplies faster than either wagon or pack train, provided that the terrain was flat or that the vehicles didn't bog down in mud. Motorcycles had also begun to take over some of the scouting duties of horsemen. The young air force demonstrated a new dimension in reconnaissance, traditionally a cavalry function. The men who guided the Remount Service were well aware of those technological advances, but felt that the horse arm was still an effective military tool. To counter the cries that horses took too long to get to a point, the cavalry was beginning to use trucks (portees) to transport units rapidly to the furthest unloading point, from where the unit would function in the traditional cavalry manner.

By the late 1920s the emphasis of the breeding program had shifted from a cavalry mount to a superior Half-bred horse for general public use. The criteria of the animal was the same, only the civilian use broadened. A horse which would meet military requirements was also a prospect as a hunter, jumper, endurance or pleasure mount and stock horse. The horse-owning public, primarily recreational riders, had to be convinced that "blood would tell" to create a market for the half-bred animals. That was the only way in which a pool of military-acceptable horses would be available to meet the increased demand of war. While tanks and trucks were a rapidly expanding part of the army, the time-honored use of cavalry and pack strings was still a part of long-range planning. By the 1930s, professional soldiers were already looking ahead to the next global conflict and considering how it would be fought.

Summary of Breeding Results from 1921 Through 1927

Year	No. of Stallions in Service	No. of Mares Bred	No. of Foals Secured
1921	159	4,100	2,460
1922	219	6,800	4,080
1923	236	7,500	4,500
1924	277	8,700	5,220
1925	308	9,900	5,940
1926	382	11,800	9,260
1927	452	14,000	9,800
Total	2,033	62,800	40,260
Yearly Average	290	8,971	5,751

During the 1928 breeding season, 540 stallions were at stud in forty states, Hawaii, Puerto Rico, and the Canal Zone. It was estimated that they would be bred to approximately 20,000 mares. The resulting 1929 foal crop would be at least 14,000 head.[45]

By 1930, stallions owned by the U.S. Remount Service were siring over 12,000 foals annually with an estimated value of $2,000,000. Of those foals, 10,000 would be utilized by civilian horsemen in various areas. The civilian market was estimated to need approximately 30,000 replacement horses each year.[46] Military consumption remained at 2,500–3,000 annually in peacetime, with the percentage of those sired by Remount stallions steadily increasing. By 1932, a study released by the American Remount Association noted that over forty percent of the horses in military use were sired by Remount Service stallions.[47]

Between 1921 and 1948 leading ranchers and horse breeders in America took advantage of the Remount program. The economic benefits were too strong for a successful ranching operation not to participate. Some individuals stood a Remount stallion to their own and to public mares. Others, large cattle operations that used many horses in their activities, maintained a Remount stallion on their own mares to sire ranch mounts. The excess geldings were sold to the army, other ranchers and dealers. Included in the long list were: Texas-Burnett Estate, Guthrie; King Ranch, Kingsville; Spur Ranch, Guthrie; JA Ranch, Clarendon; SMS Ranch, Seymour; William M. "Port" Daggett, Pecos; Pitchfork Land and Cattle Co., Guthrie; L. J. "Buster" Burns, Yoakum; Bryan Hunt, Sonora; E. S. P. Brainard, Canadian; Pfefferling Brothers, San Antonio; New Mexico: CS Ranch, Cimarron; Tesquite Ranch, Tesquite; Bell Ranch, Bell; Colorado: H. J. "Hank" Wiescamp, Alamosa; Marshall Peavy, West Plains; Coke T. Roberds, Hayden; Nebraska: Hans Fogh, Strool; Pine Ridge Indian Agency, Pine Ridge; George McGinley, Keystone; Montana: Luther Dunning, Ashland; Wyoming: Ed McCarty, Chugwater; Kansas: E. C. Roberts, Strong City; Hawaii: Parker Ranch, Honolulu.[48]

Hank Wiescamp, Alamosa, Colorado, summed up the advantages of raising and selling horses and mules to the army in his answer to the question, "Was the basic gelding market to the army at that time a major reason why you were in the horse business?" Wiescamp responded,

> Oh yes, that was my big market then. You could get $200 apiece for a gelding and that was a pretty good price. You could buy a cow and calf for $40 and a new car for $1,000. That meant that you could get a new car for the price of five geldings. One day alone, I sold 187 geldings to the Remount.
>
> Horses were selling to the army anywhere from $160 up to $200 while the mules were pretty well set at $200 per head. That was during the 1930s and early 1940s.[49]

The Colorado horseman continued that he had sold 110 pack mules to the army on one day. He had raised a few and bought the rest to put together railroad carloads for the military buyers before and during World War II.[50]

The CS Cattle Company (Cimarron Ranch), Cimarron, New Mexico, utilized Remount stallions extensively in their breeding program from the time that the service was begun until it was phased out in 1948. Included in the stallion battery were such individuals as: Forever Young (TB) by Peter Pan, Donnay (TB) by Dannacena, Half Pint (TB) by Spanish Prince, Energy (TB) by Colonel Vennie, Buckeye Poet (TB) by Black Toney, Besom (TB) by Golden Broom and Chimney Sweep (TB) by Whisk Broom II. Those stallions, crossed on the CS band of select mares, produced an outstanding group of horses that were popular polo, ranch, rodeo and pleasure mounts as well as hunters and race horses up to one-half mile.[51]

Photograph courtesy U.S. Army

Chimney Sweep (TB), a brown stallion sired by Whisk Broom II and out of Polly Flinders, stood as a Remount stallion at the CS Cattle Company in Cimarron, New Mexico. His blood ran in the veins of such Quarter Horses as Music Mount, Maddon's Bright Eyes, Quick M Silver and Mr. Gun Smoke, as well as American Paint Horse stallion Yellow Mount and the Palomino Gold Mount.

Beginning in 1934 the CS Ranch held an annual Polo Pony Show. The show included a class for polo pony prospects under five years of age; polo ponies over five years and carrying a rider up to 160 pounds and another for a rider up to 200 pounds. There was also a 300-yard race for polo ponies, a stake race, a jumping class for hunters, a remount class, a cowpony class and breeding classes for mares with foal, yearlings, two year olds and stallions. A polo tournament was also held with teams from the CS Ranch, the YO, Texline, Colorado Springs, the Philmont Ranch and Las Vegas competing over the four days. There was also an exhibition of work horses plus a rodeo and a full slate of races up to three-eights mile. Exhibitors and spectators came from all over New Mexico, Colorado and states surrounding to look at the good horses, enjoy the festivities and visit fellow horsemen.[52]

Another well-known ranching operation that utilized Remount stallions and then bred their daughters to out-cross stallions was the Burnett Estate of Texas. Daughters of both Buggins (TB) and King O'Neil II (TB) were bred to Joe Hancock and other Quarter Horse stallions to produce a strain of outstanding military, ranch and rodeo horses.[53] Colonel Joseph H. Dornblaser VC, officer in charge of Southwestern Remount Area, commented, "I once saw a whole polo team mounted on ponies sired by King O'Neill II and all looking alike as peas in a pod."[54]

The Pitchfork Ranch, a neighbor of the Burnett operation, utilized Joe Bailey's King P-7260 as a herd sire for many years. The good gray stallion, a son of Gonzales Joe Bailey P-4, was out of Miss Tommy 58, a granddaughter of King O'Neil II (TB). The Pitchfork also used Southern Gent (TB), purchased in 1947 at the Remount Dispersal Sale at Fort Robinson, Nebraska. Southern Gent (TB) was by Open Door (TB) and out of Virginia Lassy by the Remount Stallion Chilhowee (TB), second placer at the 1924 Kentucky Derby. After the loss of Southern Gent, the Pitchfork purchased his half-brother, Gay Gent (TB), by Red Bug (TB) and out of Virginia Lassy.[55]

D. Burns, manager of the Pitchfork, claimed that good ranch horses paid dividends in more ways than one. They rendered a service that helped to operate the ranch, they provided a product to sell and they attracted, and kept, good cowboys.[56]

Agents worked closely with the military in the production of good horses. They realized that the Army Horse Breeding Program was not only an opportunity to utilize some of the finest blood in the nation in their own herds but gave them a product to sell. To keep their programs fresh and to prevent in-breeding, most of the agents changed stallions on a regular basis. Colonel Joseph H. Dornblaser VC, said, "Some of our agents have had as many as seven or eight stallions over a period of twenty-five years."[57]

All of the listed operations utilized Remount stallions to improve the quality of their horseflesh and give them a product to turn into cash—something that was not always easy to find in the years between World War I and II. Many of those progressive horsemen went on to become important breeders in the various equine breed association which began to spring up in the late 1930s and 1940s. A large number

Photograph courtesy Nebraska Historical Society

This gelding, typical of the quality purchased by the army for service as a troop horse, was evidently a new recruit since he did not have either a US brand on the left shoulder or a Preston ID brand on his neck.

of the mares which they utilized in their breeding programs, and registered the offspring as Quarter Horse, Palomino or Appaloosa, were daughters of Remount stallions.

Some of the horsemen who stood Remount Service stallions included: Rex Ellsworth, Safford, Arizona (later became a Thoroughbred breeder, owning Swaps, winner of the 1955 Kentucky Derby); H. K. Linger, Hooper, Colorado, Executive Secretary of the American Quarter Horse Association, 1957–1968; the Jack Ranch at Cholame, California; Big Timber, Montana rancher, author and later Trustee of the

Cowboy Hall of Fame, "Spike" Van Cleve; B. C. "Cap" Mossman, Roswell, New Mexico, early-day lawman and later manager of the famous Hashknife Ranch in Arizona; The Philmont Ranch, Cimarron, New Mexico, owned by the Phillips family of Oklahoma and owner of the famous Plaudit; Joe F. Crow, Bartlesville, Oklahoma rancher, Quarter Horse breeder and well-known single steer roper; Hans Fogh, Strool, South Dakota, long-time Quarter Horse breeder during the 1940s, 1950s and 1960s.

In Texas there was the Scharbauer Cattle Company at Midland, where the well-known cutting mare, Marion's Girl, was bred. Owner Clarence Scharbauer would later serve as President of the American Quarter Horse Association as well as be associated with Alysheba, winner of the 1987 Kentucky Derby; Robert J. Kleberg of the famed King Ranch; Beeville rancher "Rocky" Reagan; Quarter Horse breeder Foy Procter of Midland; J. F. Hutchins, manager of the Shanghai Pierce Estate at Pierce, one of the founders of the American Quarter Horse Association and President in 1942–43; the Matador Land and Cattle Company at Channing and G. R. "Rollie" White of Brady.

In a number of cases Remount Stallion stud fees and the sale of their colts to both the army and civilian horsemen helped keep a family afloat during the depression years of the 1930s. There was a limited market for cattle but good horses did sell. Dr. Bill Jackson, of Stephenville, Texas, former president, American Paint Horse Association, remarked,

> My father, Robert Jackson, and his brother, Willie, stood Remount stallions in Stevens County, Texas, during the depression years. The stud fees, plus the sale of Remount-bred polo horses that they shipped back East, fed the family for several years. There were lots of half-bred horses in our country (Central Texas) at the time, sired by Remount stallions and out of native mares and they were good mounts.[58]

Remount stallions also stood at universities, agricultural colleges and U.S. Government agencies as well at the Branch Remount Depots. Government stallions were in use at those institutions from the early years of the project until it was liquidated in 1948. Included in the stud battery were: Madder Music (TB) New Mexico Military Institute, Roswell, New Mexico, 1928; Rogon Jr. (TB) Oklahoma A & M College, Stillwater, Oklahoma, 1928; Star Hampton (TB) Colorado Agricultural College, Fort Collins, Colorado, 1931–1934; Oley (TB), Parmelee (TB), Portsul (TB) and Winning His Way (TB) Blackfoot Indian Agency, Browning Montana, 1931; Southern Cross (TB) U.S. Department of Agriculture, Fort Keogh, Montana, 1931; Reno Commander (TB) Oklahoma A & M College, Stillwater, Oklahoma, 1931–1934; Brilliant Jester (TB) Pierre

Polo Club, Pierre, South Dakota, 1931; Rosin (Morgan) U.S. Department of Agriculture, Missoula, Montana, 1934; Don Diego (TB) Utah State College, Logan, Utah, 1934; Rock Heather (TB) College of Agriculture, Cedar City, Utah, 1934; Lawrence M (TB) University of California, Davis, California, 1948; Defense Act (TB) Colorado State Reformatory, Buena Vista, Colorado, 1948; Farana (Arabian) University of Idaho, Moscow, Idaho, 1948; Eagle Pass (TB) University of Illinois, Urbana, Illinois, 1948; Dashalong (TB) U.S. Range Experiment Station, Miles City, Montana, 1948; Varro (TB) Flathead Indian Agency, Dixon, Montana, 1948; Advantage (TB) New Mexico Military Institute, Roswell, New Mexico, 1948; Swanton (Morgan) Pine Ridge Indian Agency, Pine Ridge, South Dakota, 1948; Ormesby (TB) Parker Ranch, Territory of Hawaii, 1948; Reno Umaydit (TB) Texas A & M College, College Station, Texas, 1948; Homme Rouge (TB) Utah State Agricultural College, Logan, Utah, 1948; Sahara Wynn (TB) Military Attaché of Venezuela, Washington, D.C., 1948; Muallim (TB) Washington State College, Pullman, Washington, 1948.[59]

 Most stallions were utilized by a number of agents in different locals during their years of service. The Remount policy was to move a stallion when his daughters became old enough to breed. In this way, a stallion could have seven or eight homes during his active years and influence horses in several locations.

The career of one stallion, and the contributions that he made during his long tenure in the Remount Service, could be considered typical. Plodder—Thoroughbred, Br. with "small star," 1916. Borgia out of LaCalma by Tiger. 15-l hands, 1,075 pounds, Brand IS66, purchased from C. T. Boots, Milpitas, California on September 11, 1921 by Remount Service Lt. Colonel A. N. McClure.[60]

Plodder was assigned to Agent W. A. Guymon, Huntington, Utah, and delivered on December 1, 1921. That was the first season that Remount Service stallions were in Utah and he was one of six assigned for the 1922 season. In addition to Plodder, the stallions were: Marse Henry, assigned March 1921; Albert H., assigned April 1921; White Shield, assigned April 1921; Trophy, assigned October 1921; Lieut. Hixon, assigned December 1921.[61]

Shortly after the stallion went to Mr. Guymon, the agent wrote,

> The government stallion you shipped me sometime ago arrived in good condition; but, as you said, he was playful and very nervous when I first took him off the car. Now he has gotten used to his new home, he has quieted down as much as could be expected for a horse of his kind. The boys and I are quite satisfied with him and feel that we will be well paid for the effort we made in getting him here.[62]

Plodder remained at the Guymon's until November of 1922, when, after the death of W. A. Guymon, he was assigned to S. L. Aiken. He stayed there until the end of 1929. When agent Aiken received Plodder, he wrote the following in a letter to the Remount Headquarters, "Don't hunt for anything better. We have adopted him as one of the family. He seems to be almost human. The more we have to do with him, the better we like him." Aiken later wrote, "We are highly pleased and think more of him all the time. We would not trade him for Man O' War."[63]

In 1930, Plodder went to Idaho Falls, Idaho, to Leo Fifield, where he remained for a year. Then, he moved to Blackfoot, Idaho, with Everett C. Colburn (the rodeo stock contractor active during the 1930s, 1940s and 1950s) for another two years. Gilbert Hunt, American Falls, Idaho, used Plodder four years from November 1932 to December 1936. His next move was to Rollin Showell at Stone, Idaho, who kept him until November 1938. Next, G. T Rasband of Heber City, Utah used the stallion until the fall of 1940 when he was returned to headquarters for a rest and "overhauling." According to Captain George R. Henderson, who knew the horse well and watched his long career at stud,

> Plodder is very near the ideal stallion for the Remount Service. His colts were all good. He was a wonderful producer of high-class riding horses. He sired no really poor ones that I've ever known. Good size, plain, quiet, willing and useful animals were the kind that Plodder got. Very few of his get were ever rejected by buyers. Other stallions might outshow him, but few could outbreed him.[64]

During his nineteen-year career in the stud, Plodder was bred to a total of 597 mares, sired 307 foals (1940 and 1941 seasons not reported) with a fifty-four percent ratio.[65]

There were 183 stallions, including Plodder, utilized in the program when it was reorganized in 1921. Many of them stayed in service for a long period of time and influenced the quality of horses in the areas where they stood. Several of these individuals were:

King Plaudit—Br. stallion, 16 hands, 1,100 lbs. Foaled 1916, by Plaudit out of Wild Thistle by Knight of the Thistle. Purchased in 1921, by Major C. L. Scott and assigned to C. C. Stillman of New York, New York. For the breeding season of 1922, King Plaudit was shipped to Ralph Brooks, Denver, Colorado. In 1923, the stallion passed to Sam Himes, Rifle, Colorado. In 1924, King Plaudit was transferred to Arthur Wilber of Meeker, Colorado. He stayed there until 1934, siring an average of 50 foals per year.[66]

Marse Mouse—Ch. stallion, 15 hands, 3 inches; 1,150 lbs. Foaled 1915, by Marse

Abe out of Miss White Mouse by Bright Phoebus. Purchased March 30, 1921, by Col. A. N. McClure. He spent his entire Remount service career in California with the agents George Millerick, Shellville; Chas. S. Howard (eventually owner of the great Seabiscuit (TB) and Fair Truckle (TB) who was outrun by Barbra B. at Hollywood Park in 1942), Ridgewood; O. S. Pitts, Bishop; E. A. McKee, Three Rivers, and Harry Balfe, Clovis. During eleven years in the stud, Marse Mouse sired an average of twenty-five foals per year.[67]

Runflor—Ch. stallion, 15 hands, 3 inches; 1,100 lbs. Foaled 1918, by Runnymeded out of Han Florry by Handsome. Purchased in 1921 and placed with W. J. Moore, San Saba, Texas, through 1924, he sired a reported sixty-five foals. In 1925, twenty-nine foals were reported and in 1927, forty-seven were reported. After the 1927 breeding season Runflor was transferred to W. L. Fisher of Marfa, Texas, where he stayed until February 1931. He was returned to Fort Reno for conditioning and then placed with Paul E. Anderson of Anadarko, Oklahoma. He was considered one of the finest breeding horses in the Southwest and his foals proved suitable for almost anything.[68]

Sands of Time—Ch. stallion, 16 hands, 1,100 lbs. Foaled 1916, by Beach Sand out of Alma K. by Conrand. Acquired in 1921, and sent to Front Royal for test breeding where he sired two foals. Placed with Fred L. Albin, Kiowa, Colorado, from 1922 through 1926, where he averaged thirty-five foals per year. Transferred to Lawrence Phipps, Jr., Denver, Colorado, for the 1927 season. Sands of Time was placed with R. W. Johnson, Parker, Colorado, in 1928, and was still there in 1934. He sired a number of outstanding polo ponies in the Denver-Colorado Springs vicinity.[69]

Irish Dancer—Ch. stallion, 15 hands, 3½ inches; 1,100 lbs. Foaled 1917, by Colt out of Ballet Girl by St. Leonards. Purchased in 1921 and sent to Front Royal to be test bred. Assigned to Mrs. Hazel O'Reilly, Horse Creek, Wyoming, 1922 until 1931. Transferred to Earl Vanderbuilt of Cheyenne, Wyoming. He averaged twenty-five foals a year and was considered one of the most successful sires in the Northwest.[70]

Delaware—Bay stallion; 16 hands, 1,100 lbs. Foaled in 1916, by Ormondale out of Livonia by Star Shoot. Donated to the Remount in 1921, by A. C. Schwartz and sent to C. C. Stillman, Cornwall, New York. In 1922, Delaware was assigned to C. D. Cary, Cheyenne, Wyoming, where he was still standing in 1934. He averaged eighteen foals per year.[71]

Out the Way—Br. stallion; 16 hands, 1 inch; 1,200 lbs. Foaled 1915, by Peter Pan out of Sweep Away by Wild Mint. Purchased June 30, 1921, through the elimination races on the Kentucky tracks. Originally assigned to Fred H. McElhone, Upperville, Virginia, from 1922 through 1927, where he sired 176 foals. He was transferred to F. W. Sharp, The Plains, Virginia, in 1928, and the following year to David Sharp, Berwyn, Pennsylvania. Out the Way sired many steeplechashers and hunters in the Virginia hunt country.[72]

Gordon Russell—Bay stallion; 16 hands; 1,100 lbs. Foaled 1910, by Marchmont 2nd out of Tokalon by Tammany. Donated to the Remount Service on October 27, 1920, by the Kentucky Racing Association. From 1921 until 1923, he was left in Kentucky. During 1924 and 1925, he stood at Front Royal, Virginia. He was in the hands of B. G. Ray, Happy Creek, Virginia, from 1926 through 1928, where he produced approximately 100 foals. In 1928 and 1929, he was in New York. Gordon Russell was sent to Fort Robinson in 1930, and utilized for Depot breeding. Among the many outstanding horses he sired were the Olympic winners Jennie Camp and her full brother, Don R. Gordon Russell, has been considered one of the greatest sires the Remount Service ever had.[73]

Marse Henry—Br. stallion, 16 hands, 1 inch; 1,200 lbs. Foaled 1913, by Ben Brush out of Nun's Cloth by Melton. Donated to the Remount Service in 1920 by the Breeding Bureau of the Jockey Club, New York. He stood the 1921 to 1924 seasons with George Henderson, Joseph, Utah. Late in 1924, he was transferred to C. W. Bailey, Escalante, Utah, where he remained until 1927, when he was returned to Mr. Henderson. He then transferred to S. L. Aiken, Castle Dale, Utah, where he died in 1932.[74]

Uncle Jimmie Gray—Blk. stallion, 15 hands, 1 inch; 1,050 lbs. Foaled 1909, by Bonnie Joe out of Mary Hill by Bowling Green. (A half-sister, Useeit, was the dam of Kentucky Derby Winner Black Gold.) Purchased by the Remount Service in 1921, after successfully racing until he was twelve (138 starts with forty-two wins, twenty-six places and showing twenty-four times). Uncle Jimmie Gray was assigned to Ed Pfefferling of Pfefferling Brothers Horse and Mule Barn, San Antonio, Texas. He remained there for the rest of his life, dying at twenty-nine. He was a prolific sire of speed from almost any kind of mare and was listed as the Leading Maternal Grandsire of Register of Merit Quarter Running Horses in 1947. His blood lived on through: Tommy Gray, sire of Chain Lay; Major Speck, sire of Lane's Flicka, Gallant Maid and Major D; and Golden Girl, dam of Flicka—all speedy Quarter racers in the 1930s and early 1940s.[75]

A number of Arabian breeders were also strong supporters of the Army Breeding Program. They felt that, even though the army was concentrating upon Thoroughbred stallions, there was a place for the Arabian. In 1941 the Directors of the Arabian Horse Club of America each donated one or more horses to the U.S. Remount Service. Those were horses of unquestioned quality, the type that generally was not for sale. Those horses were maintained at Fort Robinson for several years, and gave the Northwest Breeding District a shot of some of the finest Arabian blood in the world. In 1944, after Kellogg's Arabian Horse Farm in Pomona, California, was given to the army as a Remount Depot, the entire group, which had increased to twenty-four, was shipped there. The original horses were:

Horse	Donor
Zewa No. 1681	Henry B. Babson
Babolna No. 1498 and 1941 foal	J. M. Dickinson
Night No. 578	Albert W. Harris
Horma No. 636	Albert W. Harris
Kehefe No. 768	Albert W. Harris
Katar No. 724	Albert W. Harris
Surana No. 1356	W.K. Kellogg
Rifnetta No. 1660	W.K. Kellogg
Sonata No. 1661	W.K. Kellogg
Mirzaia No. 1010	Roger A. Selby
Ragia No. 1375	L.W. Van Fleet[76]

There is no doubt that those stallions, and others like them, helped to upgrade the quality of American horseflesh where they stood at stud. Horsemen took advantage of both the fact that the quality stallions were available and the low ten dollar stud fee.

In 1931, *The Blood-Horse* magazine listed the Remount stallions standing in America. Of the 596 Government-owned stallions, Texas had the most with 134, followed by Montana with forty-four, Oklahoma with forty-two, Wyoming with thirty-eight. Other states had fewer stallions. Included on the list were such well-known individuals as: King Plaudit, Danger Rock, Doc Horn, War Plume, Gordon Russell, Uncle Jimmie Grey, Beau Geste and Lion d'Or.[77] Other publications which editorialized on the Remount Service and Remount-bred horses were: *Horse and Horseman, The Thoroughbred Record, The Morgan Horse, Town and Country, The Rider and Driver, The Thoroughbred Journal* and *American Horsebreeder*.

While the Remount Program was certainly a success in the quality of horses produced and the development of remounts for the army to draw upon, some members of government were in favor of closing the service down. The cost to the tax payers was the usual reason given, but advocates of an all-mechanized Army, the anti-racing establishment and breeders in favor of the elimination of competition to privately-owned stallions all spoke out against continuation of the Remount. In spite of this, supporters always marshalled enough backing to keep it functioning, even during the dreary 1930s.

In December of 1931, writing in *The Blood-Horse*, Pierre Lorillard Jr., President of the American Remount Association, announced that membership support was vital to insure that Congress would appropriate sufficient funds to continue the Horse Breeding Program. America's economy was in trouble and the Remount Program was one of the first government programs to be looked on as unnecessary. He wrote: "The irreducible minimum is $120,000 for the next fiscal year, which is a reduction of $12,500 from the amount available for the current year. With exercise of rigid economy … [that amount] will permit the maintenance of 700 stallions, but would allow no expansion beyond that number." Lorillard continued with the facts that the Remount Service had begun operation in 1921 with 159 stallion in seven states. Eleven years later there were 693 stallions standing in forty states. Since the beginning, the Remount Program had bred a total of 126,900 mares with a production of 85,000 foals (7,739 annually). The aggregate expenditure for the maintenance and operation of the stallions during the eleven years of the Breeding Plan's existence was $1,576,997. However, stud fees to the amount of $227,710 offset the cost, bringing the total down to $1,349,287 for an average annual expenditure of $122,662 and the average yearly cost of maintaining a stallion, including the original purchase price, cost of transportation and maintenance to $272.25. His final salvo was,

> The total value of donations of stallions and other breeding animals by members of this Association and other public-spirited citizens—men and women—is conservatively estimated at $350,000. Additional sums have been received from the same source for the donation of prizes at horse shows and fairs to encourage the breeding, so that the government has already been the beneficiary of the generosity of the friends of the breeding plan by nearly $400,000.[78]

By 1937, the results of the Army Horse Breeding Program were very conclusive.

Remount Area	Mares Bred in 1936	Foals Foals of 1937	% of Foals	Mares Bred in 1937	Mares Stallions at Stud	Mares per Stallion
Eastern Area	775	497	64.1	923	44	21.0
East Central	832	369	44.4	783	43	18.2
North Central	2,216	1,174	53.0	2,021	92	22.0
South Central	4,667	3,116	66.8	4,665	171	27.3
South Western	1,904	1,102	57.9	1,723	81	21.3
North Western	3,702	2,328	62.9	3,358	130	25.8
Western Area	2,450	1,540	62.9	2,422	93	26.0
Front Royal	89	48	53.9	113	6	18.8

Fort Reno	61	48	78.7	77	4	19.2
Fort Robinson	65	49	75.4	69	5	13.8
Total	16,761	10,271	61.3	16,154	669	24.1

Breed of Stallion

Thoroughbred	15,996	9,820	61.4	15,433	630	24.5
Arabian	365	227	62.2	330	19	17.4
Morgan	309	172	55.7	269	16	16.8
Saddlebred	86	49	57.0	92	3	30.6
East Prussian	5	3	60.0	26	1	26.0
Total	16,761	10,271	61.3	16,154	669	24.1[79]

Tabulation Showing Results Obtained From Remount Breeding Plan

Since Inception in 1921 through 1937

Year	Approp.	Expended	No. Studs Used	Mares per Stud	Total Mares Bred	Total Foals Secured	Value of Foals[a]
1921	$250,000	$176,271	159	26	4,100	2,460	$369,000
1922	150,000	132,728	219	31	6,800	4,080	612,000
1923	150,000	106,347	236	32	7,500	4,500	675,000
1924	150,000	140,245	277	31	8,700	5,220	783,000
1925	150,000	145,348	308	32	9,900	5,940	891,000
1926	150,000	149,385	382	31	11,800	7,080	1,062,000
1927	150,000	149,546	454	28	12,800	7,680	1,154,000
1928	150,000	148,414	527	28	14,800	8,880	1,332,000
1929	150,000	149,407	544	27	14,800	8,880	1,332,000
1930	150,000	149,636	576	28	16,100	9,660	1,449,000
1931	132,500	129,670	630	26	16,500	9,900	1,485,000
1932	132,500	132,378	638	26	16,600	9,960	1,494,000
1933	119,795	115,105	678	27	18,300	10,300	1,647,000
1934	116,577	46,646	691	25	17,100	10,260	1,539,000
1935	71,215	70,420	685	24	16,600	9,960	1,494,000
1936	72,155	72,114	658	25	16,500	9,900	1,485,000
1937	72,155	71,682	650	27	17,500	10,500	1,575,000
Total	$2,316,897	$2,085,342	8,312	472	226,400	135,840	$20,376,000
Ave:	136,288	122,667	489	27	13,318	7,991	1,198,700[80]

[a] Valued at $150 head average

Jumping ahead to 1939, Remount Service stallions, (both at depots with agents) produced 10,193 foals from 16,492 mares bred in 1938 for a 61.8% ratio. Of this total, 15,709 mares were bred to Thoroughbred stallions and 9,782 (62.3%) produced foals the following year. The average number of mares per Thoroughbred stallion was 26.2. Other stallions used were Arabian, Morgan, Saddlebred and East Prussian.[81] As might be expected however, promoters of other breeds criticized the Army for its choice of the Thoroughbred-type horse.

The above information showed that the Army Horse Breeding Program was considered a success by the nation's horsemen. The number of foals produced annually was growing as more and more breeders took their good mares to Remount stallions. It also showed that, overall, the Thoroughbred was considered the most desirable cross to produce a horse for both civilian and military saddle use.

In spite of limited appropriations from Congress, the U.S. Remount Service produced viable results. Following the original appropriation of $250,000 in 1921, the Government reduced the figure to $150,000 for 1922. That appropriation remained the same until 1931 when it was cut to $132,500. In 1933, the budget was again reduced to $119,795, the following year to $116,577 and, in 1935 to $71,215. In 1936 the appropriation was raised slightly to $72,155 and then repeated in 1937.

Not one time did the Remount Service spend the entire annual appropriation. For example, in 1921 only $176,271 of the $250,000 appropriated was spent; in 1931 $129,670 of the total of $132,500 and in 1934 the Service stayed at $46,646 of the total allocation of $116,577 while in 1937 it spent $71,682 of the total of $72,156. While staying under budget, the Remount Service continued to increase the number of stallions available. Beginning in 1931, there were well over 600 stallions standing and it reached 691 in 1934, when they served 17,100 mares that foaled 10,260 colts and fillies, worth an estimated $1,539,000, the following year.[82]

Much credit for the success of the Army Horse Breeding Program must go to the American Remount Association and the civilian donors of the top stallions. Even with this assistance, it is hard to see how the Service stayed within its budgets since the money allocated had to cover the cost of stallions and their maintenance and transportation, the wages of civilian employees, the operational expenses of Remount Depots and the purchases and maintenance of the broodmare bands kept at the depots. It was one of the few cases of a government program working successfully within the financial limits imposed upon it.

Chapter 4: Sources and Notes

1. William Anson, "Quarter-of-a-Mile Running Horses," in *The Quarter Horse*, ed Bob Denhardt (Fort Worth: The American Quarter Horse Association, 1941), 123.
2. Ray K. Erhardt, "The Remount Service of the Office of the Quartermaster General, United States Army 1908–1954," unpublished paper, 1990, 3.
3. Lt. Colonel Thomas J. Johnson, Chief of Remount, "Horses Made to Order, The Job of the Remount Service," *The Quartermaster Review* (September–October 1935): 8–9.
4. Ibid., 9.
5. Lt. Colonel Thomas J. Johnson, Chief of Remount, "Blood Will Tell," *The Quartermaster Review* (March–April 1936): 18–20.
6. Albert D. Manchester, "Decendants of the Remount," *The Western Horseman* (October 1986): 60–61.
7. Fort Reno Diary 7/1/39–11/29/41, mimeographed daily report composed by the Officer of the Day.
7. U.S. Army document on the History and Function of the Remount Service, 1921, mimeographed copy in possession of the author.
8. "Breeding in 1920," U.S. Army document, mimeographed, unnumbered pages.
9. Ibid.
10. Ibid.
11. Quartermaster General, Technical Manual No. 10-395, Section 1, "Remount" (December 18, 1941), 5.
12. U.S. Army document, 1921.
13. "Gordon Russell," *The Horse* (September–October 1937): 10.
14. Pat Close, "The Man Behind the Wiescamp Horses," *The Western Horseman* (March 1979): 23.
15. Bob Denhardt, *The Quarter Horse* (Fort Worth: The American Quarter Horse Association, 1941), 72.
16. Robert Moorman Denhardt, *Quarter Horse: A Story of Two Centuries* (Norman: University of Oklahoma Press, 1967), 79, 88.
17. Lt. Colonel S. C. Reynolds, "The Survival of the Fittest," The Horse (March–April 1934): 11.
18. Ibid.
19. Colonel E. J. Purfield, "Thirty Years of the Remount Service," *The Western Horseman* (August 1948): 8–9, 50.
20. Colonel F. W. Koester, "A Historical Perspective on the U.S. Army Remount Service," unpublished manuscript, Fort Robinson Museum, Crawford, Nebraska, 13.
21. Ibid, 13–14.
22. U.S. Army document, 1921.
23. Ibid.
24. Professor W. Howard Forsyth, "The NA Thoroughbred Horse Ranch," *The Remount* (September–October 1929): 20–21.
25. U.S. Army document, 1921
26. Colonel Joseph H. Dornblaser, "Remount Breeding in the Southwest," *The Cattleman* (September 1946): 161.
27. Koester, "Historical Perspective on U.S. Army Remount Service," 14.
28. Colonel Grove Cullum, "Importance of Racing and the Remount," in *The Quarter Horse*, ed Bob Denhardt (Fort Worth: The American Quarter Horse Association, 1941): 129.
29. Colonel Fred L. Hamilton, "The Remount Story," *The Western Horseman* (December 1950): 9–10.
30. Major A. A. Cederwald, Secretary of the American Remount Association, Personal letter to Frank D. Reed, Forder, Colorado, advising him that he had been elected to membership in the American Remount Association, July 1922. Mr. Reed stood several Remount stallions during the 1920s and 1930s. Copy in author files.
31. *The Blood-Horse* (June 8, 1929): 17.
32. H. J. "Hank" Wiescamp, Alamosa, Colorado, interview with Ed Roberts, June 1993.
33. *The Blood-Horse*, reporting that the Remount Service had purchased a 3-year-old stallion from Hans Fogh, South Dakota (December 9, 1944): 865.
34. "An Outline of the Army Plan for the Encouragement of Breeding Light Horses," American Remount Association, 1923, four-page folder, 3.
35. U.S. Army document, 1921.
36. Purfield, "Thirty Years of the Remount Service," 51.
37. Quartermaster General, "Operation of the Remount Breeding Service," Technical Manual TM 10-390 (February 28, 1941): 20.
38. Phil Ray, "The Remount Registry," *The Western Horseman* (October 1964): 65.
39. Phil Ray, "The Remount Association and the Half-bred Studbook," *The Chronicle of the Horse* (March 20, 1964): 63.
40. *The Blood-Horse* (July 6, 1929): 21.
41. Koester, "Historical Perspective on U.S. Army Remount Service," 11.
42. Charles B. Roth, "The Thoroughbred a Cow Horse?" *The Horse* (February 1936): 15.
43. U.S. Army document, 1921.
44. Erhardt, "Remount Service of the Office of the Quartermaster General, United States Army 1908–1954," 3.
45. Tom Buecker, "The Dismounting of the Fourth Cavalry at Fort Robinson, 1942," *Nebraskan*, 1989, 12.
46. "Distribution of Remount Stallions by States for the 1928 Breeding Season," (Washington, D.C., American Remount

Association, 1928), loose-leaf mimeographed copy, 9.

46. *The Blood-Horse* (November 15, 1930): 1349.

47. *The Blood-Horse* (January 2, 1932): 22.

48. Compiled by Ed Roberts from various Remount Stallion listings.

49. Wiescamp interview, June 1993.

50. Ibid.

51. Les Davis, CS Ranch Remount Stallion pedigrees and letter to Ed Roberts, December 17, 1992.

52. Brownlow Wilson, "Cimarron Horse Activities," *The Horse* (May–June 1935): 24–25.

53. Colonel H. Dornblaser, "Remount Breeding in the Southwest," *The Cattleman* (September 1946): 162.

54. Ibid., 161–62.

55. Frank Reeves, "Cow Horses: How an Up-to-Date Ranch Has Developed a Remuda of Top Cow Horses and How They Are Used in Modern Ranching," *The Cattleman* (September 1955): 64–65.

56. Ibid., 36.

57. Dornblaser, "Remount Breeding," 161.

58. Dr. Bill Jackson, Stephenville, interview with Phil Livingston, August 25, 1996.

59. Compiled by Ed Roberts from various Remount Stallion listings.

60. Captain George R. Henderson, "Plodder," *The Horse* (September 10, 1941): 13.

61. Ibid.

62. Ibid., 13–14.

63. ibid., 14.

64. Ibid.

65. Ibid., 15.

66. Reynolds, "The Survival of the Fittest," 7.

67. Ibid., 7–8.

68. Ibid., 8.

69. Ibid., 9.

70. Ibid.

71. Ibid., 9–10.

72. Ibid., 10.

73. Ibid., 10–11.

74. Ibid., 11.

75. Ralph Dye, "Uncle Jimmie Gray Made His Mark," *Lone Star Horse Report* (April, 1994): 11, 19.

76. Gladys Brown Edwards, The Arabian War Horse to Show Horse (Denver, Colorado: Arabian Horse Trust, 1980), 113.

77. *The Blood-Horse* (July 28, 1931): unnumbered copy.

78. *The Blood-Horse* (December 12, 1931): 713.

79. *The Horse* (September–October, 1937): 16.

80. Ibid., 5.

81. *The Blood-Horse* (April 27, 1940): 656.

82. David Remley, "More Speed and More Bottom: Breeding Improved Western Horses in the Late 19th and early 20th Centuries" unpublished manuscript, 1994, 19.

Organizational Structure of the Remount Service
1921 (Peacetime)

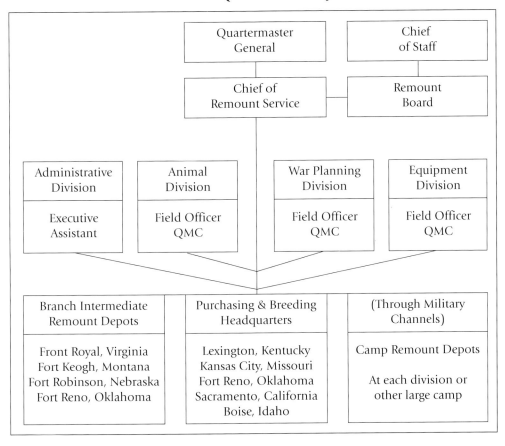

Photograph courtesy Jack Campbell

Horse barns and corrals are filled during the 1945 sales at Fort Robinson, Nebraska. "There were twice as many pens on the other side of the long barn. The horses were driven through a long cement chute and out onto a broad floor in the large saddling room to be sold," remembers Jack Campbell.

Ω

U.S. REMOUNT SERVICE ORGANIZATION AND PROCEDURES

"As long as a horse passed the conformation inspection, the test for wind and could be ridden past the inspecting officers, the Army wasn't too particular about how hard he bucked."

Lanham Riley
Remount Cowboy, 1942

While the Army Horse Breeding Plan was ultimately to reshape the quality of light horses in America, it was only a part of the Remount Service. As a section of the Quartermaster Corps, U.S. Army, the Remount Section was primarily charged with the purchase, processing and distribution of saddle, pack and draft animals for the entire army. The development of a pool of animals that could be purchased in time of need was a secondary responsibility of the section.

The Remount Service bought horses and mules only upon the directive from the War Department to fill the requirements of the various units. It was not the mission of the Remount to decide how many animals were required but to procure them as directed. Should the War Department call upon the Remount to obtain a large number of horses, the mission would be accomplished only because of the success of the Army Horse Breeding Program by civilian breeders.[1]

Remount buyers visited ranches and breeding farms, attended auctions, worked with large dealers and arranged for showings where individuals with one or more potential military horses could bring them for inspection and possible purchase. The dates of these showings were advertised in area newspapers or on local radio stations to notify horsemen. The use of a stallion agent's facilities for a showing was strongly recommended since the event helped to solidify his position among area horsemen.[2]

A showing could be animals on a single ranch if the offerings were large enough. Lanham Riley, Aledo, Texas, horseman, later a rodeo roper, performance horse trainer and show judge, remembered Remount buyers visiting the 6666 Ranch, Guthrie, Texas, early in 1942. They inspected a corral of geldings being offered as possible army horses. The 6666 used two Remount stallions, King O'Neill II (TB) and Buggins (TB), during the 1930s, and raised more ranch horses than they needed. The army was an outlet for surplus animals.[3]

More frequently, a showing was at a central point where a large number of horses could be displayed. Sometimes these showings would have several hundred horses collected for inspection and possible purchase. Regardless of the number inspected, each horse received a fair look and only those that met the military criteria were purchased. Each transaction was for the individual horse, rather than for a group. Consideration was given only to the animal's suitability.[4]

It was the army's policy to purchase animals first from breeders. This allowed the breeder to obtain a higher price (within the army limits) and encouraged him to produce better animals. Dealers had to deliver animals of equal quality, and at the same price, as bona fide breeders.[5]

Purchases were made for the Regular Army, the National Guard and the Reserve Officer's Training Corps at various colleges. For the last two categories, horses five years old and older were preferred and had to be gentle. No more than ten percent of the riding horses acquired for the Regular Army could be well grown out three year olds of exceptional suitability. Those were purchased between July 1 and December 31 to allow as much growth as possible. No three-year-old draft horses or mules were to be purchased since military buyers felt that they were too young to stand up under training.[6]

Other army "do's and don'ts" included suggesting that breeders keep their best fillies for broodmares rather than selling them. Up to fifteen percent of the total riding horse purchase could be saddle mares. Those had to be top individuals. Mares of that type became officers' chargers since geldings were used as troop horses. Only outstanding gray horses were considered and had to be either a school or Olympic prospect. Roans, Paints, Duns and horses with excessive white stockings or faces were not considered.[7]

Purchased animals were paint-branded with identification numbers and shipped to the nearest Remount Depot. There, the level of training assessed, they were conditioned and eventually issued to the requisitioning units. Since shipment was by rail, every effort was made to purchase military animals in carload lots.[8] Horses and mules assigned to a unit were sometimes returned to a depot for evaluation, rest and then reissue. All of this activity meant that a knowledgeable crew of horsemen was assigned to each depot and continually worked with animals in various stages of training and condition.

As with every army function, each step was carefully planned and detailed in a training manual. Specifications, purchasing, care and conditioning, selection of issue animals, breeding, training and transport were all covered in such manuals. Purchasing, conditioning, training, issuing and retraining were under control of the Chief of Remount Services. He reported to the Quartermaster General of the Army in Washington, D.C. The Quartermaster General was advised by the Remount Board, a twenty-five-man group composed of army officers representing different combat branches and service corps, plus twelve prominent civilian horsemen who had the interests of military horseflesh at heart.[9]

Under the Chief of Remount Services were regional purchasing and breeding headquarters. Each office was staffed with a Purchasing Board consisting of three qualified officers (two detailed to the Quartermaster Corps but normally cavalry or field artillery), and one veterinary corps officer. Several enlisted men and civilian employees to care for the animals were assigned to each board. There were five centrally located Purchasing and Breeding Headquarters. When extensive purchasing was in progress, additional purchasing boards were set up in areas which would require heavy attention from the buyers.

The United States was divided into seven Breeding and Purchasing Districts. Buying and stallion issue offices were located in major equine population areas. The seven Branch Remount Depots received, conditioned and issued horses and mules for the army and issued, received and maintained stallions for civilian agents.

These Regional Purchasing and Breeding Headquarters were located at:

Kansas City, Missouri—Territory assigned: North Dakota, South Dakota, Minnesota, Wisconsin, Nebraska, Iowa, Illinois, Indiana, Michigan, Colorado, Kansas and Mississippi.

Lexington, Kentucky—Territory assigned: Maine, New Hampshire, Vermont, Massachusetts, Connecticut, Rhode Island, New York, New Jersey, Pennsylvania, Delaware, Maryland, Ohio, West Virginia, Virginia, Kentucky, Tennessee, North Carolina, South Carolina, Alabama, Georgia and Florida. (The officer in charge of this board played an important role in shaping the Remount Program Breeding Plan since he made the majority of stallion purchases.)

Fort Reno, Oklahoma—Territory assigned: New Mexico, Oklahoma, Arkansas, Texas, Louisiana and Mississippi.

Boise, Idaho—Territory assigned: Washington, Oregon, Idaho, Montana and Wyoming. Sacramento, California—Territory assigned: California, Utah, Nevada and Arizona.[10]

In 1941, the United States was divided into seven Remount Areas. The purchasing board was also located at the headquarters for each area. The Remount Areas were:

Eastern-Connecticut, Delaware, Maine, Maryland, Massachusetts, New Hampshire, New Jersey, New York, Pennsylvania, Rhode Island, Vermont, Virginia and the Island of Puerto Rico. Headquarters: Front Royal, Virginia.

East Central-Alabama, Florida, Georgia, Illinois, Indiana, Kentucky, Louisiana, Michigan, Mississippi, North Carolina, Ohio, South Carolina, Tennessee, West Virginia and Wisconsin. Headquarters: Lexington, Kentucky.

North Central-Arkansas, Iowa, Kansas, Minnesota, Missouri, Nebraska, North Dakota and South Dakota. Headquarters: Kansas City, Missouri.

South Central-Oklahoma and Texas. Headquarters: San Angelo, Texas.

Northwestern-Idaho, Montana, Utah and Wyoming. Headquarters: Salt Lake City, Utah.

Southwestern-Arizona, Colorado and New Mexico. Headquarters: Colorado Springs, Colorado.

Western-California, Nevada, Oregon, Washington and Hawaii. Headquarters: San Mateo, California.[11]

The officer in charge of each regional headquarters arranged for purchasing boards to inspect and purchase horses and mules. He was responsible for all breeding activities. In the latter capacity, he visited civilian agents, assigned stallions, inspected facilities, mares and foals and worked with local horsemen to promote Remount stallions and their offspring. As the representative of the Army Horse Breeding Program, he contacted and cooperated with county agents, agricultural and livestock societies, educational institutions and maintained personal contact with horsemen in his region.[12] He also kept himself informed of quality civilian stallions in his area and, if possible, acquired them for the Remount.

Branch Intermediate Remount Depots were set up to process new animals so that when they were issued each one was in fit condition and sufficiently trained for immediate use. All preliminary health procedures, shoeing, branding, record keeping and training were carried out at the depot level. The animals were issued as requisitioned to the various army units, National Guard and colleges with military training programs. Government stallions were maintained at the Branch Remount Depots between breeding seasons, issued and then reclaimed from agents. Some test breeding was done, using new stallions on government-owned mares to prove their fertility. At first these were draft mares but the depots rapidly developed broodmare bands sired by Remount stallions or donated individuals that were exceedingly well-bred. The resulting foals were trained by depot personnel and geldings issued to one of the services. Remount-bred fillies were either trained under saddle, put into the breeding program or sold.[13] This activity resulted in a great deal of animal movement at each depot. Railroad carloads of horses and mules arrived, or were shipped out, on a weekly basis and thousands of animals moved through each depot during a year.

Permanent Remount Depots were normally staffed with four commissioned officers and eighty-nine enlisted men. Additional enlisted personnel or employed civilians were utilized when needed. The personnel list was based upon 500 animals on hand and 500 acres under cultivation. Additional personnel were added as the number of animals confined and acres composing the depot increased. Because of the amount of acreage involved, Remount Depots were located away from large cities and on a major railroad line. Each depot was a self-contained world with sufficient housing, schooling, medical and entertainment facilities for the personnel.[14]

Photograph courtesy U.S. Army

The original veterinary hospital, Fort Reno, Oklahoma, was built in 1915.

Each military post had a Remount Depot to service units stationed there. The size of the operation depended upon the branch of service (infantry, cavalry, field or pack artillery), the number of personnel and the duties of the post.

In addition to the peace-time Remount Service personnel, an augmented list for wartime was prepared. This included: Port Remount Officers; Transport Remount Officers; Headquarters Office, Communication Zone Office; Chief Remount Officer, Advance Section; Headquarters of a Group of Remount Depots; Remount Officers with Troops; Remount Squadrons; Camp Remount Depots of 4,800 and 7,200 capacity; Debarkation Remount Depots of 2,400 and 3,200 capacity; Field Remount Depots of 400, 1,200, 2,400 and 3,200 capacity.[15]

The primary function of permanent Remount Depots was:

a. To receive, condition, train (to a limited degree), and issue horses and mules as required by the army.

b. To condition and test-breed Remount stallions for use in the Army Horse Breeding Program.

c. To conduct training as required for all personnel, commissioned and enlisted, in Remount duties.

The secondary function was to conduct a limited amount of breeding as a means,

a. To instruct Remount personnel to enable them to properly supervise breeding activities at the various Remount areas.

b. To produce superior horses for special purposes for the army.

c. To produce suitable Remount stallions for use in the Army Horse Breeding Plan.

d. To provide replacements for depot brood mare bands.[16]

The Permanent Remount Depots were:

1. Fort Reno, Oklahoma

The first of the permanent Remount Depots was located seven miles west of El Reno, Oklahoma. Set apart from public domain by an Act of Congress, May 1906, the 8,406 rolling acres was turned over to the U.S. Army Quartermaster Corps. The facility had a maximum capacity of 15,000 horses and mules, in addition to all of the necessary service buildings, corrals and shipping pens. The depot was on a major railroad line and was located to supply the West, East and Gulf Coast ports as well as interior military installations.[17]

Photograph courtesy U.S. Army

This aerial view of main headquarters of Fort Reno Remount Depot, El Reno, Oklahoma, includes the administrative buildings, military quarters, barns, feeding pens, veterinary hospital and other facilities. Fort Reno was founded in 1908.

The stated mission of the Fort Reno Remount Depot was: To receive, process and issue horses and mules for military service. To receive, condition and issue stallions used in connection with the Army Horse Breeding Program. To train personnel in animal administration and animal management with additional instruction in horse shoeing and saddlery repair. The facility also trained Remount troops in horsemanship and horse handling, and, when requested, trained officers and enlisted men in animal packing.[18]

Fort Reno was established in 1874 for the purpose of keeping peace among the Indians in Oklahoma Territory and to protect the citizens in adjoining territories. The reservation was originally included in the limits of the Cheyenne and Arapaho Reservations by an Executive Order dated October 19, 1869. The first garrison included Troop E, Sixth Cavalry and four companies of the Fifth Infantry.[19]

The Cheyenne and Arapaho Indian Agencies were located on the north bank of the river, about a mile and a half from the post. From the time of its establishment, Fort Reno was an important base for the troops in the various Indian campaigns throughout the Southwest. It was also used as a detention point for captured and surrendered

Indians for many years. A number of the northern Indians were sent to Fort Reno in 1877, from both Fort Robinson and Fort Keogh when the Sioux surrendered.[20]

In 1908, fencing of the depot was begun and was completed by 1910. This fencing was horseproof, of post and heavy board or post and woven wire. Farming began in 1908 and was extended until more than 1,800 acres were under cultivation.[21]

The main buildings were red brick, in the traditional military design, and located around a huge parade ground. Outside barns, hay sheds and other buildings were brick or board construction. The depot was a self-contained unit. Some contract civilian workers lived on the depot while others commuted from nearby El Reno.[22]

In 1948 the Army Horse Breeding Program was transferred to the U.S. Department of Agriculture and phased out. The Department of Agriculture utilized the facilities as a beef cattle research station. A foreign aid program was in effect at the time to purchase, process and ship 1,000 pack mules to Greece. Fort Reno was used as a distribution point. The program was later enlarged and by the time that the last Remount personnel left Fort Reno in December of 1949, approximately 10,000 mules had been sent abroad.[23]

A similar program was inaugurated in 1951 and the animal processing facilities were loaned to the Department of the Army by the Department of Agriculture. By May of 1954, approximately 12,000 horses and mules were purchased, processed and shipped to Turkey. This was the last military use of the property.[24]

2. Front Royal, Virginia

Activated on August 30, 1911, Front Royal was located three miles southwest of Front Royal, Virginia, in the Shenandoah Valley. The property was originally composed of forty-two different farms. The acreage was acquired solely for the purpose of developing a permanent Remount Depot. Buildings and utilities were laid out to effectively handle large numbers of horses and mules. When the installation was activated, it contained 5,062 acres. Acreage was removed from the depot in 1939 and added to the Shenandoah National Park. In July 1945, the name was changed to the Aleshire Quartermaster Depot in honor of Major General James B. Aleshire, Quartermaster General, U.S. Army, from 1907 until 1916, and instrumental in bringing the Army Remount Program into existence.[25]

The depot was created to receive, process and issue horses and mules for the military service and to receive, condition and issue stallions used in the Army Horse Breeding Program. It was also designed to train personnel in animal administration and animal management as well as instruct personnel in horse shoeing and saddlery repair.[26]

Since Front Royal was located near the Lexington Kentucky Purchasing Office, the majority of the Thoroughbred stallions purchased passed through the facility. A large number of stallion runs were located adjacent to the main compound in addition to the barn reserved for the animals being used on mares from the depot breeding herd. This provided the army with a convenient location to condition the stallions before issuing them to either Fort Reno or Fort Robinson where they would be assigned to civilian agents.[27]

Situated on the side of a hill, the major complex was tightly integrated. A showplace, located just eighty miles from Washington, D.C., the brick buildings had red

Photograph by Ed Roberts
This red brick horse barn is still in use at Fort Robinson, Nebraska.

tile roofs. The stallion barn featured 20 foot x 20 foot box stalls, with tongue and groove wooden lining. Perimeter fencing was cement posts (cast on the depot) with four 2 inch x 10 inch oak planks. Outside barns had supporting hay sheds. Each paddock or pasture had round cement water troughs with spring water piped from a central source. All pastures were connected by a series of wide lanes that led to the working corrals and barns. Horses arriving by rail were unloaded at Front Royal and then driven some eight miles over the mountains to the receiving corrals. Maxie Cameron, who grew up at Front Royal, remembered standing on a high hill, next to the animal cemetery, and looking out across the valley towards the lane funneling into the working corrals. Sometimes a herd of several hundred animals would come galloping off the mountain behind the outriders. The trip was reversed when a shipment was to be made and the animals were trailed to the rail-loading facilities at Front Royal.[28]

An animal graveyard situated near the old race track contains headstones commemorating the Remount Service stallions Henry of Navarre (TB) and Chilhowee (TB), favored officers chargers, and Olympic mounts such as Jenny Camp.[29]

Following the closing of the Remount Service the depot was transferred to the U.S. Department of Agriculture for a beef cattle research center. In 1975 the property became the National Zoo's Conservation and Research Center for the preservation of endangered species of wildlife.[30]

3. Fort Keogh, Montana

Opened in 1876, the fort was named for Captain Miles Keogh, commander of Company I, 7th Cavalry, who was killed in June of that year during the Battle of the Little Big Horn. The military reservation encompassed 100 square miles. In 1879 the

War Department released approximately ten square miles for the establishment of the town of Miles City, Montana. In 1912 the fort was designated a Remount Depot. During World War I (1914–1917) more horses and mules were processed there than at any other depot. At the end of the war, Fort Keogh was abandoned by the military. The Remount Services handled by Fort Keogh were taken over by the recently activated Fort Robinson, Nebraska, in 1919.[31]

In April of 1924, Congress passed an Act which designated 56,300 acres of the Fort Keogh Reservation as the U.S. Range Livestock Experiment Station. This was for the experimental raising of livestock and the growing of forage crops for livestock use.[32]

On July 20, 1925, the second government Morgan Horse Breeding Program was established on the U.S. Range Livestock Experiment Station. Unlike the first U.S. Morgan Horse Farm at Middlebury, Vermont, which was created to breed cavalry and civilian sporting animals, this endeavor produced working stock horses. Between 1925 and 1939, approximately four percent of all Morgan Horses registered in the United States were bred on this ranch.[33]

4. Fort Robinson Quartermaster Depot, Nebraska

Established at the recommendation of General Phil Sheridan to General Ulysses S. Grant, then President of the United States, on March 8, 1874, Camp Robinson was located on the White River in northwestern Nebraska. It was named in honor of First Lieutenant Levi H. Robinson, who had been killed by the Sioux Indians. The military post was not on Indian lands but was just below the limits of the Red Cloud Sioux Indian Reservation. The reservation was set apart from public lands by the Treaty of 1869 and located south of the Black Hills in South Dakota. Camp Robinson was continually garrisoned until 1910 when the Tenth Cavalry stationed there was transferred to the Mexican border during the Poncho Villa campaign. It was then abandoned.[34]

Photograph by Ed Roberts

The Handling Barn at Fort Robinson, Nebraska, where horses and mules entered through the door on the right side and went through a long series of cement and pipe chutes to be hot iron branded, wormed, tested for Dorine and sprayed with medications to prevent mange and other diseases. At that time, permanent identification cards were completed and filed. The animals were then turned into large feeding pens for a period of conditioning.

The Remount Depot was established November 22, 1919, three miles from Crawford, Nebraska. The 23,040 acres were set aside from public domain to take advantage of the strong native pasture in the region. Large numbers of horses and mules had accumulated at division Remount Depots

Military buyers knew exactly what type of animals they would purchase, could rapidly evaluate conformation and potential unsoundnesses and were quick to make up their minds. An animal either met the requirements or it didn't and no time was wasted in making the decision. Sometimes they walked down the line of horses and pointed out the individuals that they wanted to take a closer look at. Other times they would tie a paper tag to the halter, indicating what the price would be if the horse was purchased. If the owner was willing to accept that price, the inspection continued.[43]

Aaron Dudley, Chino, California, remembered watching Colonel Koester purchase horses at the Los Angeles Horse and Mule Auction prior to World War II:

> The Colonel was all spit and polish, striding up and down a line of horses and ignoring the dust on his shiny cavalry boots. He carried a riding crop in one hand which he used to point out the animals that interested him. An aid followed closely with a clip board to mark down the horses purchased. He bought fast and shrugged off the complaining owners of rejected horses.[44]

Other buyers had their own methods of inspecting horses. Chuck DeHaan of Graford, Texas, remembered a conversation with one of those individuals long after the Remount Service had been phased out. The buyer had developed a trick to help him move through a large number of horses in a hurry:

> Mac Quen told me that the army was always in a hurry, so he didn't have much time to spend on any one horse. He'd have the sellers line their horses up. On ranches that he dealt with on a regular basis, he'd have the agent build a long rail, about hock-high so he wouldn't get kicked, for the horses to be backed up to. He'd walk down the line and raise each horse's tail up over his back. If the tail was limp, Mac would pass the animal out. A horse that clamped his tail down was marked for a closer inspection. He told me that a limp-tailed horse just didn't have the "try" to make a good army horse. He figured that he passed out some nice ones but he just didn't have the time to check one too closely. He also didn't care for a horse with limp, floppy ears. In his opinion, they weren't alert or have the desire to perform under saddle.[45]

A visual inspection was the first step, with the officers waving out animals that did not meet the basic criteria. This included horses that were too small, too large, too young or old (the army normally only purchased geldings four to eight years of age for cavalry or artillery troop horses), were not sound or were blemished.[46]

The second step was a check on the way of going. Inspectors stood some hundred feet apart. The horse was led, at a walk, towards one officer who looked to see if it traveled straight in front. His partner stood behind and watched from the rear. When the horse reached the first officer, it was turned and trotted back to the second. Horses that winged out, toed in or had some other traveling defect were culled. If the horse passed the second test, he was saddled and galloped past the officers to check his breathing under speed. This was not only to determine if the horse was windbroken but to be sure that it could be saddled and ridden. Depending upon how badly the army needed remounts, horses sometimes

Photograph courtesy U.S. Army

U.S. Army mules, freshly shod and with manes and tails trimmed, await shipment from Hawaii to China following World War II.

didn't have to be too well broken to pass inspection. In fact, some of them bucked past the inspecting officers. Stable sergeants and Remount cowboys all had stories of outlaw horses that turned up at the depots.[47]

Mules were not ridden but had to pass a conformation check, travel well and be gentle to handle on the ground. Draft mules were occasionally shown in harness but it was not mandatory. When possible, mules were purchased in volume lots through the large, central livestock markets such as the Fort Worth Horse and Mule Auction in Fort Worth, Texas; Kansas City, Kansas; St. Louis, Missouri; and Ft. Smith, Arkansas. The basic military price was adhered to and the animals purchased in volume had to conform to all military requirements. If, upon closer inspection, some individuals did not meet those specifications, they were resold through the same auction.[48]

Horses and mules that passed inspection were approved for purchase at the declared price. This was originally $150 per head for saddle horses but was later increased to $165. During World War I, when suitable animals were in short supply, the price went as high as $175 each. During the 1930s and during the short buying activity prior to World War II, prices rose to $200 per head. Payment was either by military voucher, which was redeemable at any bank, or the seller filled out a military form. This was sent in by the purchasing board to the regional office for processing and payment.[49]

Upon purchase, the animals were turned over to the army representatives who arranged rail transportation to the nearest Branch Remount Depot. Before shipment, the new animals were number-branded with either white paint or silver nitrate. This was to provide identification of where it was purchased, age and description, and matched the temporary number on the identification card that accompanied each animal. The temporary brand did not exceed three eight-inch high digits plus the buyer's brand letter and was placed on the left side of the back.[50]

The majority of stallions acquired by the U.S. Remount Service were purchased, although many were donated to the Remount by public-spirited horsemen. A number of the stallions were acquired at a figure less than their actual value since the owners wished to see them make a contribution to the Remount program. In some areas, special races were written for prospective Remount stallions, with the winner being purchased by the army for a minimum amount. Since the majority of the Remount stallions were Thoroughbred, and the Thoroughbred industry was centered in Kentucky, the Lexington Purchasing and Breeding Headquarters was of prime importance. The officer heading this headquarters was responsible for the acquisition of a large number of stallions each year and had to be a top horseman. His decisions would affect the success of the horse breeding program. After the Army Horse Breeding Program had been in operation for some years, military stallion buyers sometimes had the opportunity to purchase one or more sons of a Remount stallion, sometimes from a civilian agent.[51]

Photograph courtesy Gordon Moore

An officer holds one of the Remount stallions at Fort Robinson, during World War II. Officers quarters are in the background.

All stallions, either purchased or donated, received the same thorough inspection as troop animals. If the stallion was to be donated, the offer was forwarded to the Quartermaster General. The inspecting officer included his recommendations as to the animal's suitability. Stallions could not be accepted for donation unless they met the same requirements of stallions to be purchased except as to age.[52] D. Todd Gresham observed that, "Whether purchased or received as a gift, each stallion was processed before issue to make sure that he was in good physical condition, potent and possessed good breeding manners and discipline. The physical examination included a blood test for dourine and contagious and infectious abortion."[53]

The purchase or donation of stallions was frequently reported in one or more of the various horse publications. In the case of Thoroughbred stallions, *The Blood-Horse* magazine often published a short article listing the previous owner of the animal and which Remount Depot it was being assigned to. Often a synopsis of the stallion's racing record was included.[54]

Photograph courtesy U.S. Army

A "typy" Remount-bred mare at Fort Robinson Remount Depot exhibits the qualities which ensured the Army of good saddle horses.

The majority of broodmares on permanent Remount Depots were daughters of army-owned stallions. Some were, however, donated. These mares were subject to the same close inspection of both stallions and issue horses. In addition, they would not be accepted unless they were considered to be better in type and conformation than the average of the existing broodmare bands or have an outstanding performance record. Donors also had to agree at the time of issue to destruction of the mare when she was no longer considered desirable as a broodmare.[55]

Animals on permanent Remount Depots were classified as follows: a. Issue Animals—this included horses and mules for general issue to the army; b. Issue Stallions—included stallions for general issue to agents; c. Depot Breeding Stock—stallions and mares used for depot breeding; d. Depot-raised Animals—the produce of depot breeding from sucklings to four year olds; e. Animals for Depot Use—horses and mules used for depot operations.[56]

Recruit horses and mules arrived by railroad car from the purchasing point to the designated Branch Remount Depot for processing. Processing consisted of three steps: 1. Receipt 2. Conditioning, training and maintenance 3. Issue

1. Receipt: The animals were immediately quarantined for twenty-one days to reduce the spread of contagious diseases. Animals purchased at approximately the same time were grouped in segregated areas until the end of the quarantine. During this period all animals were dipped for skin diseases, wormed, inoculated against equine encephalomyelitis (sleeping sickness) and malleined (tested for glanders). The temporary paint or silver nitrate brands applied at the time of purchase were replaced with hot iron brands (US on the left shoulder and an individual I.D. Preston Brand on the left neck). Blocks of brand numbers were assigned to Remount areas and Remount Depots by the quartermaster general. Feet were checked, trimmed and balanced, the mane and tail clipped in the military manner and the level of training determined. An

individual permanent record card was filled out for each animal, utilizing the information on the temporary card. This card was an accurate description, age at time of purchase, serial number and point of purchase, and moved with the animal during its entire military career. At the end of the quarantine period, the horses and mules were again dipped and wormed.[57]

2. Conditioning, training and maintenance: Animals were assigned to a pasture where they were fed a carefully balanced ration. In addition to good pasture, high-quality hay and ten to fifteen pounds of grain per animal, in not less than two rations per day, were fed in big troughs and hay racks. The animals were carefully watched to prevent sickness and injury. The purpose was to bring them to a high degree of flesh before starting the training program. Periodically all animals were brought in to the corrals so that manes and fetlocks could be clipped and tails thinned. Brands were clipped for quick identification and the feet trimmed. Following conditioning, the recruits moved to the second phase—training and maintenance. The new soldiers had to be trained and fitted for the particular task to which they would be assigned. This was carefully organized to insure that each animal would be tractable to handle, and gentle to ride or drive by the time of issue. Riding-type horses were ridden and taught the basic commands under saddle. The heavier artillery-type animals were ridden and worked in harness. Draft mules were worked in harness and pack mules were ridden, packed and trained to follow a bell mare. Some horses were kept at headquarters and ridden regularly, either on pasture patrol or in the various military functions that were a part of Depot life.[58]

Photograph courtesy The Western Horseman

A cavalry mount receives new shoes from the company farrier. Horse shoeing/farrier schools were maintained at all three Branch Remount Depots to train military farriers.

3. Issue: (by the order of the Quartermaster General to the depot commander issuing animals to units of the regular army, the National Guard and the Reserve Officers' Training Corps) The selected animals were brought in from pasture approximately two weeks before shipment. During this period, they were given special feeding and grooming, as well as a refresher training course, and inspection for any faults which might disqualify them for the work for which they were selected. Feet were trimmed and balanced, fetlocks clipped and manes and tails pulled and thinned in the military manner. Immediately before shipment, each animal was wormed and given a lime and sulphur dip to prevent ringworm infection.[59]

Since all three of the Branch Remount Depots had continuous horse shoeing schools, there was no problem in finding qualified personnel to care for the horses' feet. Fledgling farriers were able to practice their craft on all types of horses and mules. During the eight-week course they rapidly became adept in handling good and bad actors as well as identifying and solving the numerous foot problems that could develop where large numbers of animals were maintained. Corrective shoeing was minimal since only horses and mules with good feet and legs were purchased. Since every military unit that used horses had a farrier, students were constantly cycling in

Photograph courtesy Gordon Moore

Jumping was a major part of military horse training, shown in progress on the jumping course at Fort Robinson, Nebraska.

and out.[60] Many of these men continued to use their training after military service and became professional farriers, practicing at race tracks, breeding establishments and for the general public.[61]

The Remount Service was originally concerned with purchasing only trained animals for use under saddle or in harness. As noted, a horse had to be galloped past the purchasing team in order to test his wind, check the way of going and judge the level of training. The majority of horses purchased were well-broken and presented no problems. However, a percentage of horses offered for sale were rough string animals from ranch remudas, and while they could be saddled and ridden by a top hand, they were more interested in bucking. Army buyers hated to turn a well-made horse back, especially during war time when cavalry mounts might be in short supply, so some outlaws ended up at the breaking pens with Remount cowboys "settin' the hair" on them. Those that couldn't be reformed were either resold to the public or ended up as rations for army dogs.[62]

Lanham Riley remembered his years as a Remount cowboy in the early 1940s, first at Fort Reno, Oklahoma, and then at Front Royal, Virginia.

> As long as a horse passed the conformation inspection, the test for wind and could be ridden past the inspecting officers, the army wasn't too particular about how hard they bucked. I guess that they figured that us soldier cowboys were tougher than the horses. We straightened a lot of those broncs out and they made pretty good horses.[63]

The training program emphasized basic handling, manners, leads and the development of the four-mile-per-hour walk, a trot and lope. This training also aided in

conditioning the animals for issue. Once the horses were distributed to the requisitioning units, they became accustomed to their place in the troop, bugle calls, gun fire, and had a willingness to negotiate any type of terrain. The ability to jump was important and most cavalry mounts would attempt to clear any obstacle they were aimed at. This talent was demonstrated at the frequent inter-company shows and playdays.

Photograph courtesy A. J. 'Jack' Campbell

A. J. 'Jack' Campbell, home on leave from Fort Robinson during World War II, sits on Reno Mandate, a Remount stallion his father was standing.

While the "handle" of the average cavalry mount was not comparable to that of a good ranch horse, they were extremely responsive. Issue horses were ridden with a mild Pelham-type bit or a ring snaffle so they had to have a good mouth. A sure and reliable mount was more valued than a flash-reined animal.[64]

Because of his extensive horse background, A. J. "Jack" Campbell, Douglas, Wyoming, enlisted in the cavalry at the outbreak of World War II. He was assigned to Fort Robinson, Nebraska, and spent four years training remount horses as well as breaking pack mules. He observed:

> The soldiers who were doing the riding got to try every new horse that came on the Post and it didn't take too long for each of us to have a pretty good saddle string. If we found one that we liked better than what we were riding, we turned the old one out and claimed the new one. We rode pastures on them to check the horses and mules that were being conditioned, snubbed broncs, pulled pack mules around, competed in Post Playdays where we had pole and barrel races, jumped, played polo and all the rest. We even took a relay team to the Cheyenne Frontier Days Rodeo one year and won that. There were some really outstanding saddle geldings that came through Fort Robinson.[65]

The larger horses which were used to pull cannons and caissons (artillery riders) were broken to harness and then driven, as well as ridden. (A caisson and cannon were pulled by a four-up team with a rider on each of the left-hand-near-side-horses and two soldiers on the caisson box). The horses were usually paired up at the depot and then issued that way. In addition to becoming bridlewise and learning to pull as a team, the animals became accustomed to artillery fire. Other horses were trained as pack animals, to carry both the .50 and .30 caliber machine guns, ammunition, rations, water or even a litter for casualties. Training at the Remount Depot was to ready the animals for actual use after they were issued.[66]

Training pack and saddle mules was another facet of the program. The majority of the mules purchased by the army were only halter-broken, and Remount cowboys had their work cut out for them. They had to teach those animals to lead, to follow a bell mare and to stand and accept the pack saddle and load. A white or gray mare was used to lead the pack string since the mules would "mother up" and follow her anywhere.[67]

Several thousand four- to eight-year-old prospective pack mules were purchased

Photograph courtesy U.S. Army

Mules are loaded aboard ship in temporary stalls below deck. These 780 mules are being shipped to China for farm use following World War II by UNRRA.

early in Campbell's enlistment. They stood 14-3 to 15-2 hands high and weighed 1,000 to 1,200 pounds. They were all of stocky build, with short, strong backs and loins, low withers, large barrels and straight, strong legs. He said,

> We had to teach those mules to let us catch them without roping, to let us handle their feet, be groomed and clipped, and then to stand while they were being saddled and packed. We blindfolded and hobbled most of them so that they'd stand. It was a rodeo every day at Fort Robinson. Those mules came from all over the country and most of them didn't take too kindly to military life. We did manage to make good pack animals out of most of them.[68]

Campbell laughed as he remembered the fights that he and other Remount cowboys had with the long-eared soldiers. Convincing some of the mules that it was to their best interest to cooperate was often a time-consuming chore. Jack and his fellow "mule skinners" did their jobs well since American mules performed creditably in Italy, the South Pacific Islands, India, Burma and China during World War II.[69]

The army used mules to pull wagons until the late 1930s and many long-eared recruits were hitched up for the first time at one of the Remount Depots. As long as much of America's farming was powered by mules, especially in the South, there was a plentiful supply for army buyers to choose from.[70]

Another job at the depots was training the foals raised from the Remount mares. Each depot, with approximately forty to sixty head of carefully selected mares and two or three stallions, was actually a Remount Service laboratory. Over the years, numerous first-class horses were bred and trained at the depots and every effort was made to give those foals an early acquaintance of humans and a good set of manners. Halter breaking, leading and foot handling started early, usually when the foal was only a few weeks old, and continued on a daily basis. The result was a well-trained, well-mannered horse that had no fear of man.[71]

Training young horses was a continuous thing. A saddle was introduced their two-year-old year and they were ridden for a short period of time. Regular training was continued as three year olds. Each horse was handled quietly to maintain his confidence in men. By the time each gelding turned four, and was issued, he was a well-trained saddle horse. Many of them became officer's chargers, and in addition to their military duties, were used as jumpers and polo mounts.

While equine veterinary medicine had been of prime importance to the nation until after World War I, the practice languished as America moved into the machine age. During the 1920s, cars, trucks and tractors gradually took over transportation and farming. Veterinary schools changed their emphasis to food animals and equine care was eliminated from teaching and research.

Only in the army, and a few Thoroughbred and Standardbred breeding centers, did equine practice continue to thrive. The U.S. Remount Depots (Front Royal, Fort Robinson and Fort Reno) were more than just breeding and processing centers. Research, teaching and demonstration were all practiced and the lessons learned were passed on to the rest of the equine veterinary community. Much of the practical equine veterinary knowledge of today was first observed, learned and documented on the depots by the army.[72]

The Army Veterinary Service was activated in 1916. It was only after thousands of animals had been lost during World War I that it became functional in support of the combat arms. Records show that 234,000 animals were issued to American troops during the four-year conflict in Europe. In less than one year, 42,000 were lost and untold thousands rendered unfit for service due to disease and poor management. The military learned from that experience and applied the lessons to equine management on the Remount Depots and in the field units during the balance of the horses' service in the army.[73]

Faced with the care of large numbers of animals, regular health programs were put into practice. Quarantine of new animals, regular worming, testing and treating animals for glanders, dipping for skin diseases, floating of teeth and careful shoeing at set intervals were normal practices. Depot veterinarians experimented with new medicines and techniques and developed procedures that are still in effect today. Artificial insemination was successfully experimented with on the depots during the 1930s, increasing the number of mares that a single stallion could impregnate each year.[74]

While military horsemen were looking towards the future and what continued experimentation and research could bring, they also utilized the knowledge accumulated by horsemen during the proceeding century. Many of the practical

Photograph courtesy of Phil Livingston

This equestrian operating table in the veterinary hospital at Fort Robinson was typical of the 'state of the art' facilities at each of the Branch Remount Depots.

remedies were still used and the applications of time-tested drugs administered. An army publication of 1926 listed over fifty basic drugs that were available to equine practitioners, many of them effective on a variety of ailments. Heat, cold and moisture were also used since the therapeutic affects were well understood.[75]

The veterinary hospital at Fort Robinson, Nebraska, was state of the art for the time. Included in the facilities was a stall with a cement floor that could be filled with mud to keep the heat down in a horse's feet.[76]

Prior to World War II, a vaccine for eastern and western encephalomyelitis was developed for use on army horses. That proved to be a breakthrough for all future virus vaccine production. The new tetanus toxoid was successfully tried on both US and French army horses and became a regular inoculation. When World War II broke out in 1941, sufficient data had been accumulated to convince the surgeon general that tetanus toxoid could be used to immunize humans as well as horses. It became a part of the group of inoculations that all solders were given. Only three or four cases of tetanus were recorded among US troops during World War II.[77] Annual vaccination for both equine encephalomyelitis and tetanus is now an accepted management practice by horsemen.

In 1946, veterinarians at the Pomona Remount Depot, Pomona, California, demonstrated the effectiveness of lip tattooing as a means of identification instead of hot iron branding. The procedure had been tried on the Arabian horses kept at the depot. Since then, the system has become widely used in the Thoroughbred and Quarter Horse industries.[78]

The same year, at Front Royal, Virginia, veterinarians proved that Periodic Ophthalmia (Moon Blindness) is related to diet. The disease, known to horsemen for some 2,000 years, resulted in temporary and sometimes permanent blindness. Three years of work at the veterinary research laboratory resulted in the finding that forty milligrams of Riboflavin mixed with the feed controlled the disease.[79]

Photograph courtesy The Western Horseman
A bareback, mounted tug-o-war was a lively event in 1916, near Marfa, Texas. Equestrian sports were important to cavalrymen, teaching horsemanship and fostering competiveness among the soldiers.

Mounted sports were always popular with cavalrymen, not only as a welcome relief from the boredom of garrison life but also to show their ability. Horse shows, gymkhanas, polo, steeplechasing and jumping were all popular contests. These sports added to the continual training programs required to produce effective soldiers and mounts. They demonstrated the aspects of mobility, quick action and bravery from both horse and rider that made the cavalry an efficient fighting force.

Photograph courtesy The Western Horseman
A dinner table jump is an unusual challenge at a cavalry exhibition horse show, 1916. A cavalryman would jump anything! It was important for a cavalry mount to be able to jump at unexpected times and under difficult circumstances. In practice, military mounts cleared tables, hay bales, the hoods of cars and more, in addition to standard jumps.

The horse shows, or field days, could range from only four or five classes held during a single afternoon to forty or fifty spread over several days. Civilians from the surrounding areas were invited as spectators. Western America, especially, was still interested in horsemanship and people turned out to evaluate both horses and riders.[80]

Contests varied from gymkhana type classes, such as a Crazy Costume Class, Best Turned Out Trooper and Mount, Rescue Race or Bull Durham Race (contestants had to roll and light a Bull Durham cigarette during the race) to Polo Pony competition and Open Jumping. Pole Bending, in four-horse heats, Quadrille, Sack Races and Mounted Tug-O-Wars between different platoons were also popular. Some of the classes had a distinctly military flavor such as the Pack Mule Race, where a pack mule had to be packed, and then successfully led through an obstacle course that included several jumps. Many of the classes centered around jumping. The jumps, however, were not those found in a normal show ring. Almost anything and everything that a horse might possibly have to jump under battle conditions was used.[81] Tables, chairs, pup tents, stacked bales of hay, rock and wood barriers as well as conventional fences were all set up and cleared by cavalry mounts. Cavalry jumpers even cleared the hood of a car on occasion. Steeplechasing and drag hunting were other sports that utilized the jumping ability and were frequently a part of the sporting scene on a military post. While foxes were scarce in the West, the coyote made a great substitute and was pursued on many Sunday mornings.

Some of the military horse shows of the 1920s, 1930s and early 1940s were huge. One of the largest was at the Cavalry School, Fort Riley, Kansas. The show was created with the establishment of the school in 1919 and was held annually until the cavalry was dismounted during World War II. The show consisted of nineteen different classes and fourteen races.[82]

Photograph courtesy The Western Horseman

Roman riding was an interesting event at a U.S. Army 6th Cavalry military horse show near Marfa, Texas, 1916.

Horses and riders competing in such shows were shipped in from other military bases. Competition between the different units was strong, and in the case of a show like Fort Riley, it was a case of the best meeting the best.[83] Such contests were where members of America's Olympic Equine Teams were often chosen. Until 1950, when the cavalry was no more, America's Olympic riders and their mounts came from the military. Making appearances for the United States at the 1936 Olympics, held at Berlin, Germany, were such performers as Captain Thompson on Jenny Camp (Remount-bred, eventually retired as a broodmare and finally buried in the horse cemetery at Front Royal, Virginia) taking second place in the three-day event; Captain C. W. Ragus on Dakota, earning fifth place in the Prize of Nations event, and Major W. B. Brandfor on Don R.[84]

Many of the horses and riders that competed on the U.S. Olympic Team became famous. The purpose of the event was to foster horsemanship and further the prestige of the nation. Following the bombing of Pearl Harbor, competition was out of the question, but with the training of a future Olympic team in mind, eleven horses schooled in dressage and Olympic events were shipped from Fort Riley to Fort Robinson for the duration. There the level of training was maintained. After the war, the animals became the nucleus for the rejuvenated team.[85]

Following careers in national and international competition those horses and others brought into use after the close of World War II in 1945, were all retired to pasture at Fort Riley, Kansas. Included in this group were such Olympic stars as: Dinger, Gorando, Dakota, Masquerader and Renzo. Other mounts included those later leased to the U.S Olympic Team after the army ceased to compete. Among those retired were: Totilla, Grey Fox, Swizzlestick, Gambler, Reno Rhythm, Rattler and Bill Biddle. Bill Biddle placed fourth in Olympic Dressage in 1948 and eleventh in 1952.[86]

Photograph courtesy The Western Horseman

Polo was a major cavalry recreation, and teams from the different units competed on a regular basis. Polo in the United States had its beginnings with military contests.

Polo was always an important part of army equine gatherings. It was fast, exciting and tested men and horses to the limit. Many officers had begun the sport during their West Point days and continued to play during their off time. Company, troop and regimental teams developed and were matched against other military posts or civilian clubs. The army Chief of Staff was in favor of the sport, commenting before World War I that, "U.S. Cavalry fighters are going to play polo to obtain poise in the saddle."[87] The army influence kept polo alive in America during the dreary 1930s. The military had the necessary horseflesh, and at one time, approximately 1,500 players. Many times, the first introduction to the sport that a group of civilian horsemen had was through a passing army officer who "just happened to have" several mallets and balls in the trunk of his car. According to Colonel Jim Spurrier, one-time president of the U.S. Horse Cavalry Association, "The Army is to Polo what Johnny Appleseed is to the apple."[88]

Dressage was also practiced by military horsemen. For a number of years, selected officers were sent to the French Cavalry School at Saumar for special training, where they were introduced to dressage. Upon their return to America, many of them incorporated some rudimentary three-phase dressage movements into their training programs to "supple a horse." In fact, the training manual at the Fort Riley Cavalry School, "Horsemanship and Horsemastership," outlines the schooling of an officer's mount to the third level of dressage. Since America's Olympic equestrian teams were military riders on military horses, promising animals were marked for special training.

While that facet of horsemanship never gained the wide popularity of jumping or polo, the U.S Army planted the seed for civilian horsemen to nurture.[89]

The army also took advantage of a number of the better trained performers and their riders for publicity purposes. Some of the horses were real characters with personalities all their own and developed a following among spectators. Area newspapers were quick to pick up on the fact that people liked to read about such animals, as well as see them in action, and devoted columns of space to them.

One such character was Whiskey. He was assigned to the Third Infantry at Fort Snelling, Minnesota in 1921 as a raw recruit from Fort Reno, Oklahoma. Whiskey's temper was bad, his conformation poor and he possessed a staggering gait that made him look as if he was drunk. No one knows how he happened to come face-to-face with Lt. William Hazelrigg, but somehow the two "nicked" and Whiskey became Hazelrigg's personal mount. Under the officer's training the former outlaw became one of the best-known equines in the U.S. Army. He was not only a top military mount, an exceptional jumper and a handy polo pony but also a trick horse. After he became well-known, the army was besieged with invitations for him to perform at events from New York to San Francisco. Whiskey would leap through a hoop of fire, jump impossible objects, lay down on command, pick up scattered handkerchiefs, and bow to or kiss any pretty girl that came close to him. The press loved the horse and devoted numerous articles to his exploits. In 1936, Whiskey was retired to pasture at Fort Snelling. The old performer died in 1943 and was buried between Minneapolis' Veterans Hospital and St. Paul's Federal Building. A stone marker at the spot reads:

Whiskey
A great horse
A stout heart
1911–1943"[90]

Chapter 5: Sources and Notes

1. Captain Charlie B. Team, "The Remount and the Present Situation," *The Cattleman* (September 1942): 98.
2. Quartermaster General, Technical Manual No. 10-395, Section 1, "Remount" (December 18, 1941): 14.
3. Lanham Riley, Aledo, Texas, interview with Phil Livingston, April 15, 1993.
4. Technical Manual No. 10-395, 13.
5. Technical Manual No. 10-395, 12.
6. Technical Manual No. 10-395, 13.
7. "Introduction of an Army Horse," *Cavalry Journal* (July–August, 1942): unnumbered copy.
8. Technical Manual No. 10-395, 13.
9. U.S. Army document on the History and Function of the U.S. Remount Service, 1921, mimeographed copy in possession of the author.
10. "The Remount Service and the Army Breeding Plan," *The Quartermaster Review* (March–April, 1940): 11.
11. Technical Manual No. 10-395, 3.
12. Ibid.
13. *Fort Reno Daily Log*, July 1, 1939–November 29, 1941, mimeographed copy of report written by Officer of the Day.
14. U.S. Army document, 1921.
15. Ibid.
16. Technical Manual No. 10-395, 19.
17. Anna Waller, "Horses and Mules and National Defense" (Department of the Army, Office of the Quartermaster General, XVIII-3-009, 1958), 55.
18. Ibid.
19. Ibid.
20. Ibid., 55–56
21. Ibid., 56.
22. Observations gained by visits to Fort Reno, Oklahoma by authors Ed Roberts and Phil Livingston.
23. Waller, "Horses and Mules and National Defense," 39.
24. Ibid.
25. Ibid., 51.
26. Ibid.
27. Maxie Cameron, Farm Operations Foreman, Conservation and Research Center, Front Royal Remount Depot, interview with Phil Livingston during guided tour, April 10, 1996.
28. Ibid.
29. Ibid. Training of dogs for military use during World War II, as well as the personnel to handle them, was another object of the facility.
30. Ibid.
31. Richard Tower, "The US Range Livestock Experiment Station: The Second Government Morgan Horse Farm," *The Morgan Horse* (1990): 115.
32. Ibid.
33. Ibid.
34. Waller, "Horses and Mules and National Defense," 59.
35. Ibid., 65.
36. Thomas R. Buecker, *Fort Robinson, a Self-Guided Tour* (Nebraska State Historical Society), unnumbered pages.
37. Ibid.
38. Ibid.
39. Waller, "Horses and Mules and National Defense," 53.
40. Mary Jane Parkinson, *The Kellogg Arabian Ranch: The First Fifty Years* (The Arabian Horse Association of Southern California, 1975), 266.
41. Ibid., 323.
42. Technical Manual No. 10-395.
43. Lanham Riley, Aledo, Texas, interview. Also, Aaron Dudley, Chino, California, letter to Phil Livingston, June 23, 1994 and A. J. "Jack" Campbell, Douglas, Wyoming, interview with Phil Livingston, July, 1993.
44. Aaron Dudley, letter.
45. Chuck DeHaan Grafford, Texas, interview with Phil Livingston, February 13, 1995.
46. US Army document, 1921.
47. Ibid.
48. M. L. Hames, "U.S. Army Mules," *The Draft Horse Journal* (Summer, 1993): 137.
49. D. Todd Gresham, "Remount," *The Western Horseman* (May–June 1946): 50.
50. Technical Manual No. 10-395, 29–30.
51. Greshman, "Remount," 50.
52. Ibid.
53. Ibid.

54. *The Blood-Horse*, December 9, 1944, reporting that the Remount Service had purchased a three-year-old stallion from Hans Fogh, South Dakota.

55. Technical Manual No. 10-395, 38.

56. Ibid., 25.

57. Ibid., 26–27.

58. Ibid., 27–29.

59. Ibid.

60. Ibid.

61. "Army Training Horse-Shoers," *The Blood-Horse* (April 22, 1944): 621. Also, visit to Fort Robinson by Ed Roberts and Phil Livingston. Recollections of civilian horse shoers working during the 1940s and 1950s who had learned their trade while serving in the army and attending one of the shoeing schools maintained at a Remount Depot, including Main Hanks and Walt Koch, both of Tooele, Utah.

62. Interviews with former Remount Service cowboys: Lanham Riley, Aledo, Texas; George Brown, Stephenville, Texas; John Burris, Stephenville, Texas; A. J. "Jack" Campbell, Douglas, Wyoming; Bob Rothwell, Weatherford, Texas; interview with Colonel C. E. Livingston, U.S. Army, Retired, Tujunga, California.

63. Lanham Riley interview

64. J. F. Carithers, "The Last of the Horse Soldiers" *The Western Horseman* (March 1994): 151.

65. A. J. "Jack" Campbell, interview.

66. Major Henri A. Luebbermann, "The Army Horse," *The Cattleman* (September, 1941): 108.

67. Team, "The Remount and the Present Situation," 98.

68. A. J. "Jack" Campbell, interview.

69. Ibid.

70. Hames, "U.S. Army Mules," 137.

71. Gresham, "Remount," 52.

72. Brigadier General Wayne O. Kester, DVM, "Development of Equine Veterinary Medicine in the United States," *Journal of American Veterinary Medicine* (July 1976): 52.

73. Ibid., 51.

74. Technical Manual No. 10-390, XVIII-3-011, C1, March 1945, unnumbered insert added to manual.

75. Kester, "Development of Equine Veterinary Medicine," 52.

76. Visit by authors Roberts and Livingston visit to Fort Robinson, Nebraska.

77. Kester, "Development of Equine Veterinary Medicine," 52.

78. Col. F. W. Koester, "New Army Method of Branding," *The Blood-Horse* (June 1, 1946): 1261.

79. "Periodic Ophthalmia Control Achieved," *The Blood-Horse* (January 4, 1946): 1314. Also, Brigadier General R. A. Kelser, "This Is Not Speculation," *The Blood-Horse* (March 16, 1946): 685.

80. Robert D. Thompson, "Cavalry Horse Shows," *The Western Horseman* (January 1986): 87.

81. W. F. Smithers, "The United States Cavalry," folder from Fort Knox, Kentucky: Patton Museum of Cavalry and Armor, Fort Knox, Kentucky, 1960, unnumbered.

82. Thompson, "Cavalry Horse Shows," 89.

83. Ibid.

84. Lieutenant R. W. Curtis, "Olympic Equestrians," *The Horse* (October 1936): unnumbered copy.

85. Major C. D. Ramsel, "Last of their Kind," *The Quartermaster Review* (May–June 1954): unnumbered copy.

86. Ibid.

87. "The Big Picture," *Polo Life* (Spring 1990): 25.

88. David W. Hollis, "Polo and the U.S. Army," *Polo Magazine* (undated copy): 34.

89. Peter Lert, "Dressage Yesterday: The Way It Started in America," *Dressage Today Magazine* (undated copy): 120.

90. Aileen Kilgore Henderson, "Stout Heart," *Equus Magazine* (February 1995): 50.

General George S. Patton, Commanding General of the U.S. Third Army, in St. Martin, Austria, rides Lippizaner Favory Africa, the horse Adolf Hitler had chosen personally to present to Emperor Hirohito of Japan.

Ω

THE WAR YEARS: 1941–1945

"It is the considered opinion, not only of myself but of many other General officers who took their origin from the infantry and artillery, that had we possessed an American cavalry division with pack artillery in Tunisia and in Sicily not a German would have escaped. Horse cavalry possesses an additional gear ratio which permits it to attain sufficient speed through mountainous country to get behind and hold the enemy until the more powerful infantry and tanks can come up and destroy him."

General George S. Patton
United States Army, Sicily[1]

While Patton and other American generals wished for the effectiveness of cavalry and pack units, it was not available during the early years of World War II. The decision had been made during the 1930s to phase out the horse arm and replace it with tanks for assault and motorcycles for scouting. Proponents of supply trucks had ignored the necessity of pack mule trains in rough terrain. Marine shipping space was limited and cannons, trucks, tanks and materiel had priority to North Africa and then Europe. There wasn't shipping space to move horses, mules and the necessary fodder across the oceans.[2]

When America declared war on Germany and Japan in December of 1941, cavalry and pack artillery units were promptly "dehorsed." Of the approximately 40,000 horses purchased and prepared for issue prior to World War II, only forty-nine were ever transported overseas, other than those assigned to pack trains.[3] The usefulness of pack mules was also ignored, but such a need developed that they were re-activated. Pack mules were used during the North African campaign but were obtained locally. It wasn't until 1943 that pack mules were shipped from the United States to Italy, the Pacific Islands and the China-Burma-India theater to supplement those obtained in the area.[4] Before World War II ended in 1945, over 12,000 American mules were shipped abroad for military service and more than 30,500 mules were procured and used by U.S. forces. Of those, nearly 8,000 were purchased and shipped from America to India and Burma. An additional 3,500 American mules went to the United Kingdom for use in Europe.

Photograph courtesy U.S. Army

A mule is loaded aboard ship bound for India during World War II. Over 8,000 pack mules were sent to the China-Burma-India theatre of operations between 1943 and 1945.

The balance of mules were obtained in the theaters of operation.

In 1941, the American army owned approximately 50,000 horses and mules. Of these, 25,000 were assigned to cavalry duty, 12,000 for draft and pack use while the other 13,000 were held in inventory at Remount Depots or for administrative use.[5] It was clear that World War II would break out soon and the army was getting ready to fight. Some military planners, proponents of horse power, envisioned a greatly expanded cavalry, pack artillery and pack supply. They estimated that a maximum of 200,000 animals would be needed.[6] During the 1941 fiscal year the Remount Service purchased 22,720 riding horses, 1,333 draft horses and 4,096 pack mules. The 1941 purchase order was for 27,000 horses, but the purchasing teams stopped buying midway through the year to process those already acquired. The receiving depots could accommodate no more. The number was short of the original estimate but far above the purchases of the 1930s when between 1,500 and 2,000 head were purchased annually.[7] The Remount Division inspected approximately 70,515 horses and purchased 23,989, or approximately thirty-four percent. The average cost was $161.68.[8] The fact that there were so many acceptable horses available was due to the army horse breeding program during the previous two decades.

Immediately prior to World War II, issue of animals did not keep pace with purchases. The cavalry took 13,500 of the 22,000 riding horses procured; the field artillery, 1,800, and the rest of the army 250. The field artillery required 600 draft horses and 2,400 pack mules. By the end of the 1941 fiscal year, the Remount Depots still had an inventory of 28,000 horses.[9]

The following fiscal year, the Remount Service estimated that a limited number of riding horses would be required, as well as a small number of mules. Procurement began in September but stopped when the chief of staff announced that units were to be "dehorsed" and the animals returned to the depots. Approximately 2,900 horses were purchased prior to the decree. That was the last large-scale military horse purchase.[10]

With the influx of animals to the depots, training and conditioning duties increased. Personnel had to be hired, or enlisted, to take care of the animals. Many ranch cowboys signed on as contract horse breakers, riding the new horses to assess the level of training and then putting the finishing touches on them. A number of those good hands went on to the rodeo arena or the horse business after the war. Included in that group were: "Kid" Fletcher, George Brown, A. J. "Jack" Campbell, George Richmond, Lanham Riley, John Burris, "Buster" Cole, Glen Nutter, Billy Wyche and the nine-goal polo player, George Garrett.[11]

Lanham Riley remembered how his service with the Remount came about:

> I was working for the 6666 [Burnett Estate at Guthrie, Texas] in 1940 when a group of army horse buyers came by to look at a bunch of geldings. A number of the geldings were by either Buggins (TB) or King O'Neill II (TB), two Remount studs that the ranch used for several years. I rode some of those horses past the inspectors and I guess that they liked what they saw. Well, we were eatin' dinner at the chuck wagon and one of the inspectors came over to talk. He asked how much I was being paid [$35 a month and meals] and then told me that I could make more money riding Remount horses at Fort Reno, Oklahoma. He gave me the telephone number to call for a job.
>
> The next time that the supply truck came out to camp, I hitched a ride back and went to the store at Guthrie to call. The army offered me a job to ride broncs for them at $175 a month and it sounded great. I went back to the wagon, quit, rolled my bed, sacked my saddle and headed for Fort Reno, Oklahoma. I rode horses for the army there for a couple of months. Then, I was asked if I wanted to transfer to Front Royal, Virginia. I'd never seen that country so I went.
>
> I stayed at Front Royal until the middle of 1943 when most of the horses were surplused and sold. I enlisted in the air force, was trained as a airplane mechanic and sent to San Angelo, Texas. That didn't end my riding though. There were lots of weekend ropings and rodeos in that country and I could always get mounted on somebody's calf horse.[12]

The years following World War I had brought a gradual phasing out of the horse in the American army. Tanks, trucks, automobiles, motorcycles, vehicle-drawn artillery and aircraft took over. By the middle of the 1930s, cavalry was no longer considered an effective attack force. The new role of the horse arm was scouting and harassment, with the secondary purpose of attack. This is the same manner in which Confederate General J.E.B. Stuart used cavalry during the Civil War. He worked behind the Union lines, harassing supply trains, attacking columns of infantry and then retreating, as well as disrupting communications.

As already discussed in Chapter 3, page 81, in 1930, General Douglas MacArthur ordered the destruction of excess cavalry mounts as part of the dehorsing of the army.

In 1935, the Fourth Cavalry, headquartered at Fort Meade, South Dakota, was transformed into a "horse-mechanized corps reconnaissance regiment." The Second Squadron was dismounted and equipped with armored scout cars and motorcycles. Their horses were returned to the Remount Depots. The First Squadron remained horse-mounted. Other cavalry units were transformed in the same manner. By 1940, the horse-mechanized cavalry was the norm. During this time the horse portee was introduced. This was a four-and-one-half-ton truck tractor with a semi-trailer. The trailer would carry a squad of eight horses, their riders and equipment.[13] Horses and men could be transported rapidly over improved roads to a designated point, then unloaded to achieve their mission. The combination of mechanized equipment

Photograph courtesy U.S. Army

The cavalry becomes horse/mechanized. Trucks pulling trailers which will accommodate 8 animals, a squad, and equipment, are attached to cavalry units. These "portees" would transport the troops as far as the road conditions would permit. When the stopping point was reached, the horses were unloaded and the troop would begin functioning as a mounted unit. This combination allowed speed which had not been possible without the truck participation. The 6th Cavalry is shown during maneuvers in Louisiana, 1941, proving the effectiveness of this technique.

and traditional cavalry was considered an effective utilization of the old and the new. The portees were speedy transportation as long as improved roads were available. In rough country, the horses had to provide their own.

The horse portees proved their effectiveness during the 1941 fall maneuvers in Louisiana. The First Cavalry Division used them to move mounted troops from point to point as needed. Unloaded at the end of a passable road, the units marched about a 1,000 miles with little rest, forded rivers swollen by rain to establish a bridgehead for the Sixth Armor Corps and crossed foot bridges that trucks and tanks could not negotiate. During the maneuvers the horse cavalry disrupted "enemy" supply lines, performed scouting duties and supported infantry. This maneuver demonstrated the versatility of horse cavalry in mechanized warfare.[14]

This served to no avail. The die was cast and the cavalryman was put behind the wheel of a jeep, scout car, truck or in a tank. For the old timers, this move was not met with enthusiasm, but orders were orders. Some older cavalrymen never really got over the loss of their horses.

Even while the brass in Washington, D.C., were convinced that the horse cavalry had no place in modern war, the Twenty-Sixth Cavalry was showing them to be wrong. The place—the Philippine Islands; the enemy—the Imperial Japanese Army; the time—January 1942. Japan invaded the Philippines immediately following the attack on Pearl Harbor. The Twenty-Sixth covered the withdrawal of General Jonathan M. Wainwright's American forces from the Lingayen Gulf in North Luzon to the Bataan Peninsula before finally surrendering.

Wainwright later wrote:

> Perhaps the undersigned is the last senior commander to employ mounted cavalry in action against an enemy. In my withdrawal from the Lingayen Gulf in North Luzon to the Bataan Peninsula, the Twenty-Sixth Cavalry splendidly covered the withdrawal of my corps of four Philippine army divisions. Without this gallant little band of horsemen, I doubt if I could have successfully made that withdrawal.[15]

During the withdrawal, on January 16, Lieutenant Edwin Ramsey and a platoon of Philippine Scouts, 264th Cavalry Regiment, charged the village of Morong and routed a larger Japanese force. Ramsey's unit attacked with pistols and rifles, killed a number of the Japanese and forced them back across the river. The action helped to open the way for Wainwright's troops to continue their withdrawal. This was the last mounted charge made by any American Cavalry unit.[16]

Even during wartime some amusing things happened. Two large gray pack mules were used during the delaying action fought by the Philippine Scouts as the army fell back to Bataan. Both had been injured by bomb fragments and were sent to the veterinary hospital. Tied in a bamboo thicket, they immediately attracted attention from low flying Japanese Zero fighter planes returning from other targets and were frequently strafed. Naturally, the mules tore down much of the thicket in their attempts to escape incoming fire.

Major Bertz, commanding officer of the veterinary hospital, decided that the animals were too attractive a target and ordered Corporal Otto Whittington to

Photograph courtesy U.S. Army

Rivers, streams, rough or muddy ground, narrow bridges or inclement weather could halt trucks, but did not slow the mounted troops. The 6th Cavalry has crossed a river, which had halted the mechanized advance during 1941 maneuvers.

camouflage them. Camouflage netting for an overhead cover was non-existent, so the resourceful corporal managed to acquire several cases of old-fashioned green Putman cloth dye. A fifty-five gallon oil drum was filled with water, brought to a boil and the dye dumped in and stirred. When the mixture had cooled, it was applied to the mules using burlap sacks as swabs. The dye ran all over the animals, causing light and dark stripes in mottled camouflage patterns.

Major Bertz, surprised at the result, promptly sent word to all the West Point graduates in the area, since the mule is the mascot of West Point, to come see the first, and probably only, green mules in U.S. Army history. The camouflage effort was wasted, however, since the mules, along with the majority of the cavalry horses, were soon slaughtered for food during the last days before the islands fell to the Japanese.[17]

While a few military experts still considered cavalry as an effective scouting and fighting force, the majority did not. Army-wide dismounting of the cavalry began early in 1942. Fighting units were needed overseas as fast as they could be re-equipped and trained. That spring the Fourth Cavalry Regiment, headquartered at Fort Meade, South Dakota, was ordered to Omaha, Nebraska, to participate in the annual Army Day parade. On April 4th, the regiment, consisting of 386 vehicles, 487 horses and 1,250 men, marched into Omaha and camped at the Ak-Sar-Ben Fair Grounds. The next day Colonel Joseph Tully, commanding officer of the Fourth, received orders that the regiment would be dismounted.[18]

Following the parade at Omaha, the regiment marched back to Fort Meade, stopping at Fort Robinson to turn in mounts. After a final review of honor the horses were transferred back to the Remount Service. Their shoes were pulled and the animals released on depot pastures. They were eventually surplused and sold to the public.[19]

Following the dismounting of the Fourth Cavalry, seven federalized National Guard horse-mechanized units and the Sixth Cavalry Regiment were directed to turn in their horses. The historic First Cavalry Regiment was dehorsed during April and May of 1943. Finally, in March of 1944, the Second Cavalry Division and the Fifty-Sixth

Brigade of the Texas National Guard, the last mounted units in the United States Army, received orders to do the same.[20]

The rapid dismounting of the army was reflected in the swelling inventories at the depots. More animals were being returned than assigned. During the 1942 fiscal year only 6,000 animals were issued compared to 15,000 returned. By June 30, 1942, the depots had more than 21,000 horses on hand despite the curtailment in procurement. The following fiscal year, with the dehorsing program nearing completion, approximately 6,900 animals were returned against 5,200 issued. The excess was not greater due to a request from the Coast Guard to issue more than 3,000 head for beach patrol.[21]

During World War II, the purpose of the Remount Service in the United States was liquidation—not procurement. Through the fiscal years 1941 through 1945, approximately 33,000 horses were returned to the depots. In comparison, less than 31,000 were issued, exclusive of the 3,900 loaned to the Coast Guard. The majority of the animals issued during the earlier years of the war were eventually returned to inventory. Between July 1943 and December 1945, more than 28,000 horses were turned over to disposal agencies for sale to the civilian market. A few of these animals were used under saddle at the depots.[22]

While there were no shipments of military horses abroad during World War II (other than the few attached to pack mule units), a use at home was found for the equine soldiers. Within twenty-four hours after the attack, Colonel F. W. Koester, commanding officer of the Western Remount Area, met with representatives of the Eleventh, Twelfth and Thirteenth Naval Districts on the Pacific Coast to make a detailed survey of coastal security. The purpose was to determine which areas were suitable for patrolling on foot, with sentry dogs, or by men on horseback.[23] The threat of enemy submarines landing agents on America's coastline was very real. The Army, Navy, Coast Guard and the Federal Bureau

Pen and Ink drawing by Phil Livingston
Immediately following the declaration of war in 1941, the U.S. Coast Guard activated a mounted beach patrol to protect the nation against enemy infiltration from the sea. Over 3,000 horses were issued to the Coast Guard from the cavalry. Beach riders carried portable radios and were able to cover a much larger area than a man on foot.

of Investigation combined forces to develop and maintain a mounted beach patrol. Some 3,900 horses were issued from the Remount Depots to mount radio-equipped Coast Guardsmen patrolling the 3,700-plus miles of the East and West Coasts. Mounted guards had a higher and wider field of vision as well as ability to cover twice the ground that a man on foot could during the same time period. Horses could overtake fleeing suspects and easily carry the thirty-five-pound radios in addition to a rider. Horses would negotiate terrain that motorized vehicles could not, and were quieter giving the patrolmen the element of surprise. The duties of a beach rider were to detect and observe enemy vessels operating in coastal waters, report enemy landings and prevent communication from the shore to the enemy at sea.

Photograph courtesy A.J. "Jack" Campbell

Even though the cavalry was "dehorsed" early in World War II, there were thousands of horses on the Remount Depots. These horses at Fort Robinson, Nebraska, are being sorted for shipment to the Coast Guard or Military Police at shipping installations, prisoner-of-war camps and military bases.

Cavalrymen trained the sailors-turned-horsemen how to ride, military veterinarians cared for the horses' health and Fort Reno Remount personnel trained Coast Guardsmen as farriers and saddlers. For three years the sailors rode the beaches. The mounted unit was disbanded in 1944 and the horses sold.[24]

Saddle horses were issued to army guards at prisoner-of-war camps. Shipment of horses continued throughout World War II to such POW camps as Concordia, Kansas; Clarinda, Iowa; Atlanta, Nebraska; Bracewell, Colorado; and Douglas, Wyoming. Many of the Italian or German prisoners were assigned to farming operations, and mounted guards could keep a better watch as well as being more mobile. Horseback patrols were also utilized at military bases, war plants and shipping ports. The Twelfth Naval District, San Francisco, California; the Thirteenth Naval District, Seattle, Washington; Camp Carson, Colorado; Camp Roberts, California; and Aberdeen, Washington, all used the mobility, speed of movement and economy of horses as part of the guard force. Some military bases, as well as hospitals, maintained riding horses as recreation for off-duty personnel.[25]

While the horse was no longer considered a viable military tool by many ranking officers in Washington, D.C., the mule was. African battle experiences during the winter of 1942–43 created the sudden revival of interest in the long-eared soldiers. Animal transport units could supply ammunition, food and water, and, to a lesser degree, move equipment to troops that could not be reached by motor vehicles. Frontline commanders in Tunisia, Africa, were crying for pack mules. When they were available, locally obtained pack animals were used by American troops fighting in mountainous areas.[26] Colonel C. E. Livingston (Ret.), veteran of the North African campaign, observed, "The mules packed supplies up to the front lines and the dead and wounded back down to where the jeeps could carry them to the field hospitals. We couldn't have fought in those mountains without them."[27]

In the 1941 fiscal year, the number of horses purchased for military use outnumbered those of mules by more than 5:1. By 1943, only four horses were purchased and none thereafter. The same year, 10,200 mules were procured. During the last two years of the war, more than 14,000 were purchased.

Fiscal Year	Horse Purchased in United States	Mules Purchased in United States
1941	23,409	4,279
1942	2,859	1,699
1943	4	10,217
1944	0	5,129
1945	0	9,199
Total	26,409	30,523 [28]

As shown in the chart above, the use of horses by the army was rapidly being phased out. Emphasis had shifted to pack mules. The training and processing of the animals was of prime importance at Fort Reno, Oklahoma, and Fort Robinson, Nebraska.

Gordon Moore was stationed at the Nebraska facility during 1942–45 and assigned to the stallion barn. While he didn't directly handle pack mules, he had ample opportunity to watch their antics.

> The C and I gang [soldiers assigned to the Conditioning and Issue Barn] would ride those mules past our stables on the road to the Wood Reserve where they really put the miles on them. Before they managed to get to our stable, about half of the mules would run away, going through the officer's yards and flower gardens. I don't think that went over too good.[29]

Eventually most of the mules settled down and performed well as either saddle or pack animals. They were purchased in the United States, predominantly in the southern states, and trained at either Fort Robinson, Nebraska, or Fort Reno, Oklahoma. The animals were shipped by boat from New York City, New Orleans, the Port of Los Angeles or San Francisco, depending upon the destination—Europe, India or the Pacific Islands. Before World War II ended, fourteen ships were to transport over 8,000 mules more than 300,000 miles. Only two of those ships were sunk by enemy submarines.[30]

Stalls were constructed in the ships' cargo holds for the animals and they were confined there for the entire trip. Often the floors had wood cleats to allow more secure footing as the ship rolled in the waves. During loading, the mules were individually led up a loading ramp and stalled by a handler. Feed and water were provided by soldiers assigned to care for the animals.

Photograph courtesy A.J. "Jack" Campbell

Pack mules were trained at Fort Robinson, Nebraska. Over 17,000 "long-eared soldiers" were trained and issued for service in Italy, France, the Pacific Islands, India, Burma and China.

An incident at Fort Reno in 1943 demonstrated that even though they were in uniform, the bronc busters handling the horses and mules were still "cowboy." An English general arrived to select 3,000 pack mules to ship to British forces in Burma and Italy. After he had made his choices, he was asked if there was anything else that he wanted to see. The general replied that he'd never seen a real bucking bronc ride and was there anyone capable of performing such a feat. The volunteer was "Kid" Fletcher (a rodeo cowboy, World Champion Bull Rider in 1938 and later an inductee to the Cowboy Hall of Fame in Oklahoma City). Fletcher swung up on the black outlaw, spurred it all over the lot, then turned loose, flipped over the horse's head and landed on his heels in front of the British officer. The general's comment was, "Good show, good show!"[31]

Photograph courtesy Gordon Moore

Many of the mules sent to Fort Robinson, Nebraska, for pack and saddle training were not saddle broken. Sergeant Glenn Nutter, one of the "cowboys-in-khaki," shows his abilities aboard a "bronc" mule.

The first pack mules used by American forces were in the Atlas Mountains. While much of North Africa was flat, open plains with few hills or streams—ideal for the tank warfare of the German's East Afrika Corps under General Erwin Rommel—the Atlas Mountains were not. They formed an inverted "V" running southward from Tunis, had few roads and were cut by rivers and streams. When the Germans were pushed back into them, the battle became one of infantry fighting on hilltops. Mechanized supply units were almost helpless.

Major General Clarence R. Huebner, commander of the First Infantry Division, solved the supply problem with pack mules. His request to the Tunisian command was phrased as follows: "To enable the 81 mm mortar and its ammunition to follow the infantry into rough country, mules, equipped with … pack saddles must be available."[32]

The need for animals and personnel trained to handle them had not been anticipated by American military planners and there were no inventories of animals available. Two hundred eighteen mules and twenty-eight horses were rented from the local Arabs at one dollar per day and ninety-five donkeys purchased at $295 to $385 each. Pack saddles were begged, borrowed and probably "scrounged" by American soldiers. The British army furnished a limited supply of forage as reciprocal aid.[33]

Rather than use the traditional pack trains where the loose animals followed a bell mare, each mule was led by a soldier who cared for the animal as well as serving as packer. This practice was followed throughout World War II. Supplied by pack mules, the First Infantry Division success-fully pushed the German forces out of the mountains and defeated them in 1943.

American Generals Dwight Eisenhower and George Patton were vocal in their wish for both cavalry and pack artillery in Tunisia. The Atlas Mountains were an ideal place to use the mobility that the units could have provided and would have ended the African campaign much sooner with fewer American lives lost.[34]

Photograph courtesy U.S. Army

A U.S. Army "pack string" moves supplies in Italy during World War II. Instead of a string of loose, packed mules following a bell mare as had been traditional in the past, each animal had an individual handler who packed, led and cared for the mule.

While information on pack animals in the Atlas Mountains is vague, there is no mystery about the use of mules and wagons in Oran, Algeria, by the American Air Transport Command. The air field at Maison Blanche was selected to serve as the transshipping point from America to Italy, France, England and the Middle East. C-47 transport planes flew from the U.S. to Brazil and then made the long hop across the Atlantic Ocean to North Africa. As the officer in charge of moving supplies, Captain C. E. Livingston was faced with both vehicle breakdowns and bad weather. Trucks were few and replacement parts almost nonexistent. Heavy rains the winter of 1943 turned the dusty fields into quagmires. Planes could land on the metal mats laid down by the engineers, but the trucks bogged down and American soldiers had no

A French Foreign Legion wagon and 3-mule team is used to transport supplies from American C-47 cargo planes in Algiers, North Africa in 1943. The teamsters and loaders were Italian prisoners-of-war, under U.S. Army supervision.

way of effectively moving the cargos. Livingston solved the problem as an old cavalryman would. He leased wagons (called camions) and three-mule teams from the French Foreign Legion at twenty dollars per day per unit. A Moroccan stable sergeant, placed on detached duty by the French, supervised the care of the mules. Italian prisoners of war from a nearby camp were commandeered as drivers and loaders under guarding American soldiers. The "Light Brigade," as laughing soldiers titled the unit, showed the mechanized

American army that mules still had a place until the spring of 1944.[35]

American and British armies invaded Sicily in July 1943. The mountainous island had few roads. Allied forces were without horse cavalry and pack artillery with which they could have encircled the Germans and fired artillery from higher positions. The Germans, with years of combat experience in rough terrain, had found that it took 4,000 animals to effectively supply an infantry division. They not only had the mules but used them. German troops fought a delaying action until they could withdraw across the narrow channel and escape to Italy.[36]

American Seventh Army troops fought far above the jeep line, making supply a major problem. One unit, using the lessons learned in North Africa, organized a pack outfit with 168 mules and donkeys. Mule trains were used more extensively in Sicily than they had been used in Tunisia by the II Corps. Some animals came from Bizerte, others were "liberated" along the line of advance or were rented from civilians. Rented horses and mules went for fifty lire per day with a specified amount paid if the animal was lost or killed. The average rate was $150 per mule, $120 per horse and $40 per donkey. The majority of General Patton's 4,000 animal pack string had been captured in combat and carried the brand of the Italian army. More than a third of the animals were lost or killed by enemy action and numerous others crippled or disabled.[37]

The campaign was finally concluded on August 17, 1943. American Generals George S. Patton and Lucian K. Truscott, both thoroughly trained in horse cavalry and pack animal tactics, complained bitterly that with horse cavalry the escape route could have been cut off and the German troops captured. The escaped Germans were to later fight fiercely on the Italian mainland. Lieutenant General Truscott observed:

> I am firmly convinced that if one squadron of horse cavalry and one pack troop of 200 mules had been available to me at San Stefano on August 1, they would have enabled me to cut off and capture the entire German force opposing me along the north coast road and would have permitted my entry into Messina at least 48 hours earlier.[38]

General Truscott was determined to have horse cavalry for scouting and pack animals to carry supplies and light artillery before committing his troops to the Italian campaign. He organized both cavalry and a supply pack train, the Third Provisional Cavalry Reconnaissance Troop. To staff these units he asked for volunteers. From three Infantry regiments plus Artillery, Engineer, Signal and Medical units came four times as many men as were needed. The majority of horses were captured Italian army mounts, although some were purchased from private individuals. The mules were those captured from the German army in Sicily.[39]

The Fifth Army's mounted troops loaded aboard ship for Italy in September 1943. In the hold of one Landing Ship Transport (LST) were 355 head of animals. The unit reached the Salerno beachhead the next afternoon, and by midnight was unloaded. A shuttle of eighty 6 x 6 two-and-one-half-ton trucks (known as a "deuce 'n a half") transported the men, animals and equipment inland. Pack artillery went into action the next day at dawn. The following day mounted reconnaissance platoons rode out. Cavalry scouted, harassed enemy units and guarded captured troops. The performance of those soldiers and their animals against the Italians was outstanding, in the long traditions of the cavalry and the pack artillery.[40]

Photograph courtesy U.S. Army

A U.S. Army pack mule is loaded with a 30-caliber machine gun by his handler before heading towards the front line. The saddle used is the Phillips Pack Saddle. Notice the bag looped around the mule's neck which carried a gas mask.

Commanding General Mark Clark was quick to see the need for more pack mules. Within a week after arriving in Italy he commented, "I'm impressed with the pack train which the Third Division has. We are going to need more of this type of transportation."[41]

His quartermaster staff searched for 600 local mules. They found 316. The estimated need rapidly rose to 20,000 as American troops moved into the Italian mountains. Twelve hundred mules arrived from Sardinia but they were not enough. Soldiers in the various units scrounged or liberated pack mules wherever they found them. Pack units moved their mules all over Italy in 6 x 6 two-and-one-half-ton trucks. On one occasion, the Tenth Mountain Division commander was worried that the mules might jump over the low side boards. The officer in charge of the Remount Depot answered, "Load the mules up," noting that only one mule had jumped out of a moving truck. "They're just smart enough to stay put." [42]

Photograph courtesy U.S. Army

A U.S. Army pack mule carries a body down the mountain from the front line, Italian front, World War II. The trusty animals "packed-in" supplies, ammunition and water. On the return trip they carried the wounded and dead.

Division commanders were demanding pack mules. The high ground their troops had taken cost many lives and the men still holding that ground either had to be supplied or withdrawn. Jeeps could take supplies only so far. After that, it was pack mules. They carried food, water and ammunition up the mountains to the fighting men and the dead and wounded down. One of the most dramatic and touching stories of the 1943 Italian winter campaign was written by the well-known American correspondent, Ernie Pyle. In a United Press release to American newspapers, he told of a dead American captain being packed down the mountain on a mule. German artillery shells were bursting around the pair as they made their way down the rocky slope with the burden. Pyle recounted the somber reception by the surviving members of the platoon, along with the regard he and the men felt for the packer and his mule. The article was later included in Pyle's book, *GI Joe*. The 1943 Italian campaign has gone down in history as one of the bloodiest, fiercest-fought battles by American troops.

On September 8, 1943, the Italian army surrendered. The fifteen pack mule troops, with 4,000 seasoned mules and their handlers, became available for allied use against the Germans. Those animals, along with the hired local mules and packers, brought the total to approximately twenty troops with 5,400 to 6,000 mules.[43] Before the battle for the Italian mountains was done, the U.S. Quartermaster Remount Service had procured approximately 15,000 pack animals and issued 11,000 of them to the using forces.[44]

American units also captured German and Italian animals and used them without the benefit of official sanction. Mounted couriers were used to deliver messages when radio contact was lost. Riders scouted enemy movements and harassed small units. Surrendered German troops were often marched behind the lines guarded by mounted American soldiers.

Remount Depots in Italy functioned much as they did in the United States. One unit was an example. Under command of infantry officer Donald Willems, the 6742nd QM Remount Depot procured mules, deloused, fed, shod and trained them for issue. The depot secured feed and supplies as well as receiving mules from America once the brass in Washington had finally accepted the need for the four-footed soldiers. One shipment of 2,900 head arrived for the Tenth Mountain Division, and those mules were promptly issued for use.[45]

Below is a statistical breakdown of average daily animal strength, morning report strength of the unit, along with cooperating Italian military and civilian strengths for the period. It showed that animal transportation was a very important part of the Italian campaign for American forces.

Month	Animal Strength	M/R/ Strength	US-ITI	Italian Civilian
October	763	56	191	24
November	933	60	231	42
December	1,494	59	258	51
January	1,605	60	254	52
February 1–15	1,726	57	254	78[46]

Mechanization of the army had reduced the number of experienced packers and most troops had to learn from the bottom up. In Italy, many of the Americans learned from surrendered Italian cavalrymen. In other cases, the men applied the knowledge available in U.S. Army training manuals.

Another factor that helped in effective packing was the improved Phillips Cavalry Pack Saddle and the Phillips Cargo Pack Saddle. They were designed in the late 1920s by Colonel John E. Phillips and could be easily interchanged between horses and mules. They were lighter, distributed weight more evenly and soldiers could be trained more easily to pack them for both guns and cargo.[47]

German forces in Italy surrendered May 4, 1945, bringing to an end the need for mules. As soon as the firing stopped, many of the Italian mules (and some American mules as well), and their handlers, disappeared. Others were given to Italian farmers or were sold to the French. Some mules went to the British on a reverse Lend-Lease. The well-blooded

Thirty-Sixth Infantry Division took 200 mules with them for duty in the French Alps. A part of the 6742nd QM Remount Depot also moved to France and set up accommodations for 600 mules and fifty horses.[48] They served until Germany surrendered on May 7, 1945.

The island of New Caledonia was the supply point for Australia and the Pacific theater of operations. To strengthen security, the Ninety-seventh Field Artillery Battalion was sent there in March of 1942. Funds were made available for purchase of local horses and ponies to serve as pack animals. A Remount Depot was set up

Photograph courtesy A. J. 'Jack' Campbell
Warren Bard ropes a pack mule trainee at Fort Robinson, Nebraska, in 1944. He is using a ¼" nylon glider tow rope, the forerunner of today's nylon lariats. In the background are the guard towers and barracks of the Italian prisoner-of-war camp.

to procure and process them. However, the native animals proved inadequate, lacking the necessary stamina to carry heavy loads. The unit next tried horses from nearby Australia where several hundred were procured, but they were not much better. An order was sent to the states for pack mules.[49]

Three hundred mules were received from Fort Reno, Oklahoma, in August of 1942. Within thirty days the new arrivals were acclimated and trained. In January of 1943, the entire battalion, including the pack mules, was sent to Guadalcanal. That was to become one of the bloodiest battles

of the Pacific War. American forces were fighting in the high, steep foothills and through dense jungle. The pack howitzers the mules carried were desperately needed to counter Japanese artillery. Supplies and ammunition were sent by boat to dumps along the shore, unloaded and then packed in to the men handling the guns. The mules carried supplies for the infantry, relieving soldiers of carrying food, water and ammunition on their backs.[50]

The men who handled the mules developed great respect for the animals. They not only survived the heavy loads, the heat, humidity and the noise of battle well but were quick to detect dangers. Enemy snipers, booby traps and unsafe ground were all detected by the alert animals. Handlers learned early not to drink water that a mule would refuse. One packer remembered: "The water could be clear, but a dead Jap might be lying in it up the mountain. It would be contaminated and not safe to drink. The mules could smell the water and know to leave it alone."[51]

Little historical mention has been made of the use of pack animals during the

Pacific Island campaigns, but without them, it would have been a much longer series of operations with a higher loss of American lives.

Some 8,000 American mules and horses were shipped to India early in 1943. These were to be used by American and British forces to carry supplies in Burma or trans-shipped into China for the Nationalist Army. The sight of the animals to many American troops was a familiar part of the United States that they had left behind.[52]

Colonel L. J. Burns Jr., of Yoakum, Texas, remembered an incident while visiting the unloading point at Karachi, India. A life-long horseman, he had not only been a Remount stallion agent during the 1930s but served as a buyer for the army during the buildup prior to World War II. He recounted, "I was at the unloading dock, looking over the animals, and all of a sudden I spotted a blaze-faced black horse coming down the ramp. I'd purchased him for the army at Belton, Texas, in 1942. It was like seeing an old friend 'way out there in India."[53]

The army established a Remount Depot to handle incoming animals just outside of Calcutta. According to Coy McNabb, a member of the 5332nd Provisional Brigade, nicknamed by the press the "Mars Task Force" which utilized pack howitzer mules in Burma, the depot was huge, covering more than forty acres. "It was like looking at a giant stockyards. Mules from the states—big mules, farm mules, beautiful mules. And, as you drove around and you looked down at those mules from the overhead walkways, it was just like looking at a big stockyard full of cattle and these were all mules—thousands of mules."[54]

Another depot was established at Ramgarh for the 476th Army QM Remount Troop. In 1944 the 475th was split to form the cadre of the 699th Remount, which was moved to Bari Poni, Assam, India. There, the cowboys-turned-soldiers took on the task of breaking the animals to pack and ride. In addition to the 450 mules, the American bronc stompers also had to cope with approximately 400 head of Australian horses. Chuck Booth said, "Breaking them to ride was a lot of fun. They were needed right away, so some of our methods weren't by any means polite and according to Emily Post's book on good manners. We just snubbed them up, saddled them and climbed aboard. I could never figure how these mules could manage to kick a feller in the hip pocket while he was on their backs."[55]

The Remount cowboys even staged a rodeo for the entertainment of American and British troops. Not only soldiers assigned to the depot competed but also as many others as could wrangle a pass and make their way to Bari Poni. The main event was, naturally, wild mule riding with a rope surcingle. The action was wild and both spectators and contestants enjoyed the event.[56]

In February 1942, British General Orde Wingate led a successful harassing mission 200 miles behind the Japanese lines into Burma. His 3,000 men were supported by 1,000 pack mules carrying heavy explosives, weapons, radio equipment and other supplies through the wilderness, mountains, rivers and mud.[57]

Wingate next proposed, and mounted, a similar mission in March 1944, with a new twist. The 77th Brigade (Chindits) consisting of 9,052 troops and 1,360 pack animals would be flown into position behind the Japanese lines using 125 American WACO gliders. The force was to be supplied by air drops. Unfortunately, the landing area was criss-crossed with large logs and a number of the gliders crashed, killing ninety men. No one knows the number of mules injured. One survivor remembered,

> A dozen of us … struggled through the bamboo to reach a crashed glider. We found it on its back, a twisted mass of wreckage. We hacked through the fuselage. A British private climbed out, said the F-word without undue emphasis, and turned to help us. One by one, five other soldiers and an officer followed, each making the same comment. Finally we dragged out two mules. Being devocalized, they could not say anything, but one of them tried to bite me on the arm, and I don't blame him.[58]

The mules that survived were immediately packed and started down the trail with their handlers. In spite of the bad beginning, Wingate's mission was a success, wreaking havoc upon Japanese roads, railroads and ammunition dumps and creating confusion behind the battle lines.[59]

Japanese forces in Burma denied overland access to China via the Burma Road. In order to supply the Nationalist Chinese Army, the supply line had to be opened up. With the approval of American President Franklin D. Roosevelt and British Prime Minister Winston Churchill, Brigadier General Frank Merrill's 5307th Composite Unit (Provisional) undertook the mission of walking some 600 miles through dense jungles, over mountains and across rivers and swamps to capture the airport at Myitkyina, Burma. That would allow a supply road, the Ledo Road, to be constructed linking up with the better-known Burma Road over the Himalayan Mountains and into China. The unit, called "Merrill's Marauders" by the press, left Ledo on February 7, 1944.[60]

The attack force consisted of 2,900 Americans (all volunteers) with 700 pack animals. Unfortunately, only 360 mules were delivered from American Remount Depots. The ship carrying the balance was torpedoed and sunk in the Arabian Sea. The lost mules were substituted with 340 Australian horses. By the time that Myitkyina fell on May 17, only 1,310 men survived and of that number 679 were immediately evacuated because of disease or injury. All the horses, and many of the mules, died during the grueling trek.[61]

Remembering the three-and-one-half month ordeal, the heat, the humidity, the rain, the insects, the jungle rot that affected a man's body and the body-numbing tiredness of fighting through the jungle, Robert Wilson said, "We would have never made it to Myitkyina without the pack mules. The horses died but many of the mules survived. They carried our food, water and ammo through some of the roughest country in the world. The jungle, heat, insects and terrain were terrible."[62]

Photograph courtesy U.S. Army

Australian cavalry horses were used by the U.S. Army 699th Remount Depot, Bari Point, Assam, India. Most of these animals were used by Merrill's Marauders, the 5307th Composite Unit, during the 600-mile trek to capture the Japanese-held airport at Myitkyina, Burma, May 1944.

In 1945, a *Yank* correspondent wrote the following story about a Marauder mule handler and his charge. The animal balked at the bottom of every Burma hill. The handler had to "coax, cajole, cuss and tug" constantly. Finally, at one hill the mule stopped dead and lay down.

"Get up you sonuvabitch," yelled the handler, who had volunteered for the Marauders. "You volunteered for this mission, too."[63]

There was also the story about a Japanese soldier who captured a loose mule and was using the animal as a shield to sneak inside of the American perimeter. "He was doing alright and might have made it if he had not become impatient," remembered one of the Marauders. "Trying to urge his mule to greater speed, he 'poked' it in the rear with his bayonet. Mules don't like that."[64]

Following Merrill's capture of Myitkyina the area surrounding the Ledo and Burma Roads had to be cleared of entrenched Japanese. The purpose was to eliminate opposition and get supplies flowing from India into China as well as reinforcing the few thousand American, British and Chinese forces. The unit assigned the task was the 5332nd Provisional Brigade, the Mars Task Force.[65]

To reinforce the unit, the 124th Cavalry Regiment was transferred from South Texas, dehorsed and sent to India. The 475th Infantry was also assigned, along with a Chinese unit that had American liaison officers. The 612th Field Artillery Battalion (Pack Howitzer) trained at Fort Grueber, Oklahoma, and transferred to India to be attached to the 475th. Also attached were both the Thirty-first and the Thirty-third Quartermaster Pack Troops and half of the Seventh Chinese Animal Transport Co.[66]

After reaching India, the 612th Field Artillery Battalion was attached to the 124th Cavalry, as well as were the 37th, 252nd and 253rd Quartermaster Pack Troop and the second half of the Seventh Chinese Animal Transport Company.[67]

It was a long, grueling campaign by the task force before the Japanese troops were either killed, captured or withdrew. The unit was supplied by air drops but the mules still had to pack everything. Japanese artillery learned to zero in on the area where supply-bearing parachutes landed and the task force was under constant fire. The area was thick jungle, criss-crossed with rivers and streams, hot and humid and with a heavy insect population.

Former Marsman W. B. Woodruff, Jr., of Decatur, Texas, remembered:

> The mules held up wonderfully under the hard use in the jungle and we couldn't have done the job without them. In spite of all the Japanese shelling, our losses were light. The British cut the vocal cords of their mules so they couldn't bray and give away their position to the enemy. We didn't and never had any problems. The mules were too tired. Besides, the chief veterinary officer said that a mule didn't have much fun and we shouldn't destroy what little he does have.[68]

The Mars Task Force cleared the area of Japanese forces and opened the Burma Road for truck transport into China. The mules carrying pack howitzers provided the artillery backup necessary for American troops to get the job done.

It is estimated that 6,000 American mules were shipped to and used in Burma by the Americans, British and American-trained Chinese units. Thousands of Indian mules were used by Indian, British and French troops while the Chinese packed many mules from their country. In addition, native ponies were used by provisional native units on both sides as well as by the Japanese, along with elephants, water buffalo and cattle.[69]

Reports of the campaign, and the memories of the men who fought in it, are full of praise for the pack mules. While the force was supplied by air drop every third day, the supplies and pack howitzers (broken down and carried by six mules) still had to be packed on the backs of the reliable animals. Without animal transportation, the war in Burma could not have been won, even with the tremendous amount of supplies, vehicles, ammunition and personnel which was assigned to it.

By 1944, it was finally understood by the military experts in Washington, D.C., that pack animals were still necessary. It was also evident Japan could not hold out much longer and plans were made for an all-out attack on Japanese units on the Chinese mainland, the final step before the invasion of Japan. Realizing that pack animals would be required, in April the U.S. Army shipped some 800 mules from Fort Robinson, Nebraska, to a Remount Depot on the Hawaiian Islands. There they were readied for use during the Chinese campaign.[70]

In the latter part of 1944, Japanese forces in eastern China began a concentrated drive to the West, threatening both American and Chinese installations in central China. This could nullify the usefulness of several air bases from which the United States Air Force had been operating. Reinforcements to the Chinese troops were required if the Japanese were to be stopped.

Several well trained and equipped Chinese troops were withdrawn from Burma to stem the Japanese advance. Since the Burma Road over the forbidding Himalayan Mountains into China could not be utilized, and marching the units through the jungle was out of the question, the soldiers and their equipment were air lifted hundreds of miles to where they were needed.[71]

The Chinese forces in western and central China relied on pack animals because of the rugged terrain, the scarcity of roads and the lack of motor vehicles and fuel. The need for pack animals was winding down in Burma, there were sufficient numbers, and they could be utilized in China. But, they could not be driven over the Burma Road or through the jungles. The only solution was to fly them into China just as the troops were.[72]

Douglas C-47 transport planes were adapted to carry four to six mules, along with an attendant for each, the man's personal equipment and five days rations for both animals and men. The bucket seats in the aircraft were removed, the floors covered with plywood overlaid by waterproof tarpaulins and a layer of straw. Bamboo poles were rigged for stalls to contain the animals. The mules were also tied to the sides of the plane.[73]

Making the arrangements, adapting the planes and loading the animals was under the supervision of the theater veterinary service, headed by Major Lee T. Railsbeck, DVM. He was supported by twenty-five American veterinary enlisted personnel from several units stationed in Burma, including a number of transplanted cowboys.[74]

The horses and mules, carrying either pack or riding saddles, were loaded on two-and-one-half-ton 6 x 6 cargo trucks by ramp. The trucks were then backed up to the C-47's and the animals led directly aboard and secured. Crews were able to load twenty-five to twenty-eight planes in one-and-a-half-to-two hours. Each aircraft took off immediately after loading for the two-and-a-half-hour flight. In the air the planes sometimes reached altitudes of 20,000 feet to clear mountain peaks.[75]

The first of two series of shipments began in December of 1944, with 1,582 horses and mules flying "The Hump." It required fourteen days to complete. In February 1945, a second series of air shipments was made, carrying 1,100 animals. In all, 2,682 head, requiring more than 600 flights, were transported into China. Only one mule became excited and had to be destroyed. A single plane made an emergency landing when one of the animals broke loose from its stall.[76] Dr. Railsbeck observed, "The animals rode better than expected, were very quiet after being loaded and did not become excited. It just showed you how much sense a mule really had."[77]

Early in 1945 it was evident that Japan could not continue fighting much longer. Japanese forces had been pushed out of Burma and there was little need for the continuing operations of the Mars Task Force. Unneeded soldiers were transferred out of the China-Burma-India (CBI) theater of operations to other areas or sent back to the states. This left the American army with an excess supply of mules.

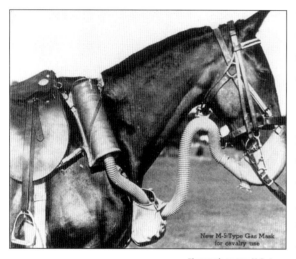

New M-5 Type Gas Mask for cavalry use

Photograph courtesy U.S. Army

A U.S. Army troop horse wears a gas mask. Chemical warfare had invaded the battlefield in World War I, and horses as well as men had to be protected.

The decision was made to give 1,000–2,000 CBI mules in Burma to Chaing Kai-Shek's Nationalist Chinese Army in western China. The dubious assumption was that sufficient feed was available for the large American mules and that Chinese troops had the skills to handle them. The only problem was that the mules had to be moved to China.[78]

In May 1945, Artillery Captain John A. Rand received orders to trek 900 combat-seasoned mules from Myitkyina, Burma, to Kunming, China. That was 750 miles over the Himalayan Mountains. Three sections (300 mules in each one) with a total of 240 men made the journey. To avoid traffic on the Burma Road, a northern route was taken encompassing part of the Old Marco Polo road. This was through heavy jungle overgrowth, over steep, slick trails and in endless cold rains. The trail through the mountains included a long, narrow flight of slippery stone steps worn smooth by centuries of traffic. The slick-shod mules scrambled to maintain their footing on the precarious path. In one section of animals, the dangerous footing over that part of the trail resulted in sixty-six pulled shoes in one day. Farriers traveled with each section, with portable forges and a supply of shoes packed and utilized as needed.[79]

The mules began to tire after a month on the trail, some lagging behind and had to be rounded up at the end of each day. The rate of march was slowed from four to three miles per hour with grazing breaks included. The problem was probably the progression, under stress, of Surra, a vector-borne disease indigenous to areas with heavy mosquito and horsefly populations (equine infectious anemia or "swamp fever") in a few infected mules. After almost three months on the trail, the first section reached Kunming, China, on July 26. The third halted at Tsuyang, 120 miles behind. The second section stopped in between the two groups.[80]

Transfer of the mules to the Chinese was delayed due to heavy floods on the eastern front where the animals were scheduled for use. The overall health of the animals declined and was diagnosed as Surra. After weeks of waiting, and after two Atomic Bombs were dropped on Japan and V-J Day came and went, the decision was made to destroy all of the animals. On August 20, individual mules were led to the edge of a ravine and shot in the head by officers. The carcasses were rolled into the ravine and later covered over with dirt.[81]

The official excuse was "to keep the disease from spreading to the native horses and mules. Those in command feared that any microbe powerful enough to kill big, well-cared-for mules would go through the Chinese stock like wildfire."[82] While the directive was not popular with the soldiers, they followed orders. For years afterward, many of them questioned the reasoning behind the move but were finally reconciled to it. One of the men who had accompanied the mules from Burma, and took part in the disposal, offered another line of reasoning.

He remembered:

> For years I shared a popular belief with others that: 1) the mules were shot because of the expense to our government of shipping them home, and 2) that their handlers and others in charge chose the easy way out. After discussion with a dozen people involved, I now believe what was considered to be in the best interest of the mules dictated the decision.
>
> It is my belief that compassionate veterinarians and affectionate mulemen believed the better fate of their mules was a bullet rather than to face a future of cruelty, overwork, disease and starvation by people, who themselves, were hungry.[83]

Surrender of Japan on September 2, 1945, aboard the U.S.S. *Missouri* brought an end to the war. In December of 1945, the U.S. government agency, Foreign Liquidation Commission, was given full authority to dispose of all horses, mules and equipment at the Remount Depot at Shillong, Assam, India. There were between 2,000 and 3,000 animals at the depot.

The first consignment of horses and mules went to Calcutta and were shipped to Poland, Yugoslavia, Rumania and other European countries. That move was part of America's Lend Lease Agreement to help European nations. The second shipment, mostly mules for farm use, went by ship to China and the Philippines. Approximately 125 horses and seventy-five mules which had contracted Surra were humanely destroyed by American military personnel. Following the disposal and burial of the animals, a farewell rifle volley was fired over the grave by a detail of soldiers as a military tribute of respect.[84]

The 800 pack mules which had been sent to the Hawaiian Islands in 1944, were also declared surplus. Those animals were shipped to China (via the Lend-Lease program) and turned over to the Nationalist Government of Chaing Kai-Shek.[85] A few of those animals later appeared in Korea during the war there. They were used by the Red Chinese, who had acquired them from Nationalist forces following the Communist take-over. Some of them were captured by American units and used as pack stock. (See Chapter 1, page 35 for details of one of the animals.)

In addition to the American mules flown and driven into China for use by the Nationalist Army of Chiang Kai-shek, a military purchasing team was dispatched to Tibet to acquire pack horses. An undisclosed number of native ponies (10–12 hands in height) were acquired by the Sino-American Horse Purchasing Bureau and issued to Chinese troops. For this purpose, a temporary Remount Depot was set up at Ying Kiang Choi, Tibet.[86]

On another front during World War II, the Russian army had not given up horses, even with all the mechanized materiel they were receiving from the United States. At the beginning of the war, the Russian Army had approximately 1,000,000 horses in service, with 200,000 in the cavalry. As previously noted, they were to eventually use 3.5 million animals during the war. Combined with tanks (four to five horsemen per tank), Russian cavalry provided flank protection during attack and were invaluable in an encircling action against infantry. The tanks gave the shock effect and firepower necessary to overrun the enemy while cavalry furnished the speed and mobility to circle and harass the scattering troops. Captain Nicholas Caratneff of the Russian army, said, "Tanks and infantry for a breakthrough. Tanks and cavalry for a breakthrough *and* encirclement." At Stalingrad (now St. Petersburg) a Russian horse cavalry brigade turned the German flanks and rear, creating such disruption that the retreat became a rout. Captain Caratneff proclaimed: "The hammer is our tanks, the sickle our cavalry."[87]

The Russian cavalry played an important part in the defeat of the German army, a highly mechanized and science-minded army that was considered one of the finest in the world. The hit-and-run tactics utilized by the irregular cavalry units provided disruption of German supply and communications. Colonel Fred L. Hamilton, Chief of the Remount, reports,

> I have talked with many regular German officers who served throughout the Russian campaign. All stressed the effectiveness of the Russian Horse Cavalry, both regular and irregular, throughout the campaign. Some were inclined to attribute the failure of the German army supply and the eventual German defeat to the activities of those ever annoying, scrubbily mounted Russian horsed units. The Russian were, I am told, unbelievably adept in hit-and-run tactics, a maneuver so suitable for cavalry in the open warfare that must be fought in wide areas.[88]

To a number of ranking American officers, this type of thinking represented a solid reason why the cavalry should be continued as a part of the American army. Unfortunately, as Colonel Hamilton commented, "In the minds of our leaders, the horse has become classed with the slingslot as an item of military equipment."[89]

Back home, purchasing, training and supplying pack mules to American forces fighting overseas was only a part of the activity on the Remount Depots. Horses and mules cycled in and out from guard duty assignments, training continued and auction sales were conducted to disperse the huge surplus of animals. The latter were important since the horse inventory was still high and military use was limited. While cavalry, pack artillery and pack mule units were utilized abroad, no horses were shipped. The decision to mechanize the military had been made and the horses were to go.

The huge animal populations resulted in overcrowding, especially at Front Royal which was smaller than either Fort Reno or Fort Robinson. Paul Burdett of Missoula, Montana, was an enlisted man at Front Royal and remembered,

> One of the pastures, known as the Intake Pasture, had about 1,000 horses in it. They were horses that had never been issued. During previous years, when massive purchases had overwhelmed the facilities and staff, there had been some horses which could not be gentled and prepared for issue in the requisite time. Those renegades had been sent to Intake and hardly been handled. Some had been there two or three years. Early in 1943 Captain Bill Rand, the Animal Control Officer, decided that the inflow of returning animals had about ended and it was time to do something about those in Intake. He augmented the "Wrangle Gang" with a few extra good

horsemen. For two or three weeks we ran through and rode all those horses. Each pasture had a set of pens and chutes and that made working them a little easier. I know that the Horse Record Cards were marked according to the probable usefulness to the army for each horse. I suspect a lot of the ones from Intake were sent to the canners.[90]

Animals were shipped to the Coast Guard, prisoner-of-war camps and different military posts for guard duty or recreational use, ridden, returned and sold. Depot personnel were kept busy issuing and receiving horses as well as preparing animals for sale. By 1944, approximately 17,000 animals had been disposed of by the Quartermaster Remount Depots through the procurement division of the Treasury Department.[91]

The Monthly Information Letter of Fort Robinson, Nebraska for February 1–February 29, 1944, in Appendix xi, illustrates the activity.

Sales such as the one at Fort Robinson, Nebraska, were undoubtedly also held at Fort Reno, Oklahoma, and at Front Royal, Virginia, during 1944 and early 1945. The army was clearly eliminating surplus animals and preparing to completely do away with horses as a military tool.

In October 1943, the well-known Kellogg's Arabian Horse Farm at Pomona, California, was donated to the U.S. Remount Service by W. K. Kellogg. The outstanding Arabian horses which had been bred there were included in the gift. Located near Los Angeles, the farm was a prime location for staging animals scheduled for shipment to the Pacific Zone of Operations. Purebred Arabian stallions from Kellogg's had previously been donated to the Remount and were standing with civilian agents around the country.[92]

Upon activation, Kellogg's became the headquarters for the Western Remount Area. Colonel F. W. Koester was transferred from San Mateo to continue as officer in charge of the area. In an interview, Colonel Koester commented:

> Our primary work is the production of Arabians and maintaining, rejuvenating and conditioning Remount stallions for placement in the field. When we took over the plant, the first job was "lifting the face of the place" to accomplish our principal task and make way for innovations which are being recognized as a vital service for horsemen of the West.[93]

Included in the renovations which the army promptly made were a new stallion issue barn, a veterinary hospital and research facility, new pastures and pasture renovation, paving of all ranch roads with decomposed granite and a typical stallion barn and corral. The latter, an example for civilian agents, was constructed of eucalyptus logs cut on the ranch.[94]

One of the priority moves was to increase the size of the high-quality broodmare band and acquire replacement stallions. The former was accomplished by keeping depot-raised fillies. Colonel Koester was also enthusiastic about the young stallions being developed on the depot. He felt that they could make a positive contribution to the quality of stock and pleasure horses in the Western Remount Area.[95] The Colonel also purchased Thoroughbred stallions from West Coast breeders when it was advantageous to do so. Often a prominent horseman would donate a stallion to the program.

Following World War II, Kellogg's also served as a receiving and issuing point for the Arabian, Half-Arabian and Lippizaner stallions imported from Germany, Hungary and Poland as "Prizes of War." Lip tattooing as a alternate means of permanent identification was also developed and tested there by army veterinarians.[96]

On August 12, 1944, the five existing Remount purchasing and breeding areas were consolidated into four districts for ease of administration. Mass purchases of horses were no longer being made and mules were primarily being acquired in the South Central Area. That eliminated the need for an additional office. Purchasing offices within each Remount District were eliminated and all breeding and assignment of stallions was handled from the area headquarters.

These Remount Areas were:

Eastern:

Headquarters—Front Royal, Virginia

The area embraced the states of Alabama, Connecticut, Delaware, Florida, Georgia, Illinois, Indiana, Kentucky, Maine, Maryland, Massachusetts, Michigan, Mississippi, New Hampshire, New Jersey, New York, North Carolina, Ohio, Pennsylvania, Rhode Island, South Carolina, Tennessee, Virginia, Vermont, West Virginia and Puerto Rico.

North Central:

Headquarters—Fort Robinson, Nebraska

This area included the states of Iowa, Minnesota, Montana, Nebraska, North Dakota, South Dakota, Wisconsin and Wyoming.

South Central:

Headquarters—Fort Reno, Oklahoma

The states included Arkansas, Colorado, Kansas, Louisiana, Missouri, New Mexico, Oklahoma and Texas.

Western:

Headquarters—Kellogg's, Pomona, California

States administered included Arizona, California, Idaho, Nevada, Oregon, Utah, Washington and the Territory of Hawaii.[97]

Even during the war years, foals bred and raised on the depots were continually trained and ridden by army personnel. Military horsemen were looking ahead to the disposal of the animals and were well aware that only trained horses would have any resale value on the civilian market. At Fort Robinson the two and three year olds were ridden on a regular basis under the supervision of the depot commander. Gordon Moore of Crawford Nebraska, observed:

> Shortly after Front Royal closed down, a few of the enlisted men were sent to Fort Robinson. They were assigned to our stable to ride colts. They were good jumping horse men. Shortly after they arrived, Colonel Carr (Commanding Officer of the depot and a real good horseman), came to our stable and asked that a colt be saddled for him to ride. He gave us a demonstration of how he wanted those colts to be ridden. It was a good demonstration and we all learned something. He also told us that he didn't want anyone jumping the colts. He just wanted good handling and good mannered saddle horses.[98]

The activities of those men resulted in exceedingly high-class, well-trained mounts that would be in demand to civilian horsemen. When those animals appeared on the market they were purchased as pleasure, sporting, ranch and rodeo horses.

While there was a clear-cut message that horses would have no place in the post-war army, the horse breeding program continued to function. Stallions were placed in the hands of agents and research projects were continued and evaluated. The Remount Association and the army maintained a strong position regarding the production of better horses. The association advocated that breeders register their superior foals in either the *Half-bred Stud Book* or one of the purebred stud books if eligible, not only to increase their value but to maintain a record of what good blood produced. These records were invaluable later in determining the breeding behind numerous early-day Quarter Horses, Palominos, Appaloosas and Paint and Pinto horses. Many of the offspring of Remount stallions, especially the Thoroughbreds, made positive contributions to the rapidly growing American Quarter Horse Association as well as the other three associations.

For the produce of a registered Thoroughbred stallion (as the majority of Remount stallions were) and mare, there was the *American Stud Book of the Jockey Club*. Half-Thoroughbreds could be registered in the Half-Thoroughbred section.

Foals by a registered Thoroughbred stallion and a registered Arabian mare could be listed in the Anglo-Arab Section, along with foals by registered Thoroughbred or Arabian stallions and out of a registered Anglo-Arab mare. The same registration was available for colts and fillies by a registered Anglo-Arab stallion out of registered Thoroughbred, Arabian or Anglo-Arab mares.

Foals by a registered Arabian stallion out of mares not registered in the *Arab Stud Book* could be registered in the Half-Arabian section of the *American Arabian Stud Book*.[99]

It was also possible to register a Half-Bred foal, if sired by a registered Thoroughbred or a registered Arabian stallion and out of a mare not registered in either the *American* (Thoroughbred) or the *Arabian Stud Book*. These foals could be registered in the *Half-Bred Stud Book* under the supervision of the American Remount Association. This would provide a permanent record of the breeding of each foal. The American Remount Association even went so far as to advertise in various horse publications.[100]

During the years 1942–1943, 14,240 foals sired by Remount stallions were born on various breeding establishments, ranches and depots. In 1943 a total of 11,066 foals were produced as a result of the army horse breeding program, approximately a twenty percent reduction compared to the previous three years. The downward trend was the result of several factors, including the farm manpower shortage which caused stockmen to breed only their best mares.[101]

The chart below shows the 1944 Breeding year results.

| | Foals | | | Mares Bred | | |
Area	Mares Bred 1943	Foals Reported 1944	% of Foals	Mares Bred Stud	Stallions at Stud	Mares per Stud
Eastern	565	276	48.8	503	28	17.9
Central	883	415	46.9	724	34	21.3
Northwestern	3,013	1,697	56.3	2,721	114	23.9
Southwestern	3,106	1,869	60.2	2,352	102	23.1
West Central	2,845	1,850	65.0	2,278	98	23.2
Western	3,613	2,325	64.4	2,948	128	23.0
Front Royal	84	64	76.2	62	5	12.4
Fort Reno	58	40	68.9	56	4	14.0
Fort Robinson	37	24	64.0	28	2	14.0
Pomona	36	18	50.0	39	2	19.5
Total	14,240	8,578	60.2	11,711	517	22.7

		Foals			*Mares Bred*	
Area	Mares Bred 1943	Foals Reported 1944	% of Foals	Mares Bred Stud	Stallions at Stud	Mares per Stud
Breed						
Thoroughbred	13,503	8,174	60.5	10,808	481	22.5
Arabian	309	175	56.6	591	22	26.9
Anglo-Arab	35	21	60.0	0	0	0
Cleveland Bay	4	1	25.0	5	1	5.0
Morgan	326	171	52.5	273	10	27.3
Saddlebred	63	36	57.1	34	3	11.3
Total	14,240	8,174	60.2	ll,711	517	22.7 [102]

Many of the stallions in Remount service were growing old during the waning days of World War II. With the future of the army horse breeding program in mind, the Remount Division was looking for replacements. Naturally, a high standard of excellence was insisted upon.[103]

In January 1945, *The Blood-Horse* magazine ran an article under the heading of, "The Remount Wants Stallions," noting that Colonel Marion I. Voorhees, officer in charge of the Lexington Kentucky Remount Headquarters, and Colonel William R. Wolfe, veterinarian attached to the Lexington office, would be in New Orleans early in the month looking for stallions. That would be followed by a visit to Miami for several days on the same trip.

The article quoted a letter previously sent by Colonel Voorhees to several race tracks with the following general specifications:

> Price. Up to $2,000. We prefer the best rather than the less suitable at a lesser price.
> Color: Any except grey, or with too much white.
> Height: Above 15.2 to 16 hands in maturity.
> Type: Full-made, deep-bodied, muscular, or relatively short legs, well let down. A great many of the Ariels and *Aethelstan II's are the type most desirable.
> Detail: A racing record is of no importance. Substance, conformation, disposition, way of moving, and hereditary unsoundnesses are very important.[104]

While the foals sired by these stallions would not go to the military, they would become popular with civilian horsemen. The Half-breds were used in the show ring, for hunting and jumping, on polo fields, in rodeo arenas or on ranches for a decade following the close of the Remount program. A number of the Remount stallions were remembered by horsemen for the quality of their offspring in the various fields.

Barbara Mills, of Weatherford, Texas, grew up in Virginia horse country prior to World War II. Not only did she know of the Remount stallions and their popularity with area horsemen but she owned and competed on Golden Victory, a halfbred son of Golden Seal (TB). "I showed him in jumping and equitation classes, rode for pleasure and really enjoyed just plain riding Victory." Mrs. Mills continued, "The Remount stallions were a big influence on Virginia horseflesh at the time. Everyone wanted the halfbreds for pleasure, hunting and jumping or polo mounts since they had the class, the conformation and the athletic ability to do whatever you wanted."[105]

Each depot kept several stallions to be bred to the broodmares maintained there. These could be newly purchased stallions being test bred, or older animals brought in from agents and conditioned before re-issue. Regardless of origin, the stallions were regularly exercised under saddle to keep them in top condition. Gordon Moore of Crawford, Nebraska, remembers,

> For a short time during 1942–43, I exercised the stallions Open Door, Chimney Sweep and Perchance. They were using these stallions on the Thoroughbred mares at the depot. When the stallions at Fort Robinson were sold after the war, Open Door went to the U Cross Ranch at Gordon, Nebraska. I imagine that there are still a number of horses in that country with some of his breeding.[106]

Even with World War II in progress, and in spite of the fact that the army was not purchasing horses, Remount agents continued to stand government stallions and produce good foals. During the 1940s, there were such influential stallions in use as: London Pride by Capt. Cuttle, winner of the English Derby and out of *Flower of Yarrow; Excite; Marca Bala; Over Lord; Biff; Reno Inhale; Virginia Shad and Virginia Valley (both bred at Front Royal, Virginia). Buggins and King O'Neil II, were used on the 6666 and Triangle Ranches at Guthrie, Texas. All these Thoroughbred stallions produced useful sporting, pleasure and stock horses that proved the value of the half-bred animal under saddle. Reno Legend; Reno Norman; Reno Job; Lion D'Or and Olabug were also well-thought of by horsemen as sires of good using mounts.[107] Romolino, by the great Ariel, stood at the King Ranch in South Texas during the war years and sired the speedy Chovasco (Maggie), among others.[108] The Remount Service thought so much of Romolino that they purchased the stallion from the King Ranch. He was resold at a Remount dispersal sale after the war. In Colorado, Hank Wiescamp bred mares (a number of them carrying the blood of King Plaudit) to Galus, Coventry, Captain Alcock, Advantage, Light Carbine and Reighlock before standing Maple Prince at his Alamosa ranch.[109]

Another stallion that influenced Colorado horses was Gudea. A pure Arabian, Gudea (AHC 2004) was foaled at Traveller's Rest, Tennessee. He was sired by the Remount stallion Khyber AHC 1037 and out of Gubba AHC 1326. At that time the Jockey Club was still registering Arabians and part Arabians. Gudea was double registered with the number JC410014. (The Jockey Club closed the stud books to Arabians in 1943.) After his Remount years, Gudea was sold to Tim Miller of De Beque, Colorado, in 1945. He spent the rest of his life on the western slope of the Rocky Mountains, dying in 1964. Interestingly, as the result of being double registered, Gudea sired twenty-six purebred registered Arabians, seventy-five registered Half-Arabians, fifteen registered Quarter Horses and one registered Thoroughbred as well as numerous grade get. His career is a good example of the influence Remount breeding has had upon western horses.[110]

While the army horse breeding program continued to operate in a normal way, all was not well with the Remount Service. Since horses were no longer considered viable for military use, many horsemen questioned the future of the program.

The army made a major effort following World War II to acquire a number of the top European stallions which had been under the control of the Nazi German government. These stallions, if they had been allowed to become a part of the Remount program, would have substantially improved the quality of America's light horses, even in the face of a non-existent military horse market.

That story, along with the closing of the Army Horse Breeding Program, is told in the next chapter.

Chapter 6: Sources and Notes

1. Anna Waller, "Horses and Mules and National Defense" (U.S. Army, Office of the Quartermaster General, XVIII-3-009, 1958), 31.
2. Ibid., 27.
3. Ibid., 19.
4. Mel Bradley, *The Missouri Mule* (Columbia: University of Missouri Press, 1995), 408–10.
5. Waller, "Horses and Mules and National Defense," 16.
6. Major General John K. Herr, "Why Should the United States Lag Behind Other Great Powers in the Military Use of Animals?" Transcript of a speech before the Horse and Mule Association of America, December 3, 1941, 6.
7. Waller, "Horses and Mules and National Defense," 16.
8. "Remount Purchases," *The Blood-Horse* (January 3, 1942): unnumbered copy.
9. Waller, "Horses and Mules and National Defense," 16.
10. Ibid.
11. Lanham Riley, Aledo, Texas, interview with Phil Livingston and Ed Roberts, April, 1993.
12. Ibid.
13. Thomas R. Buecker, "The Dismounting of the Fourth Cavalry at Fort Robinson 1942," *The Rural Electric Nebraskan*, 1989. Also, Crossed Sabers, March 1994, reprint of Buecker article, 12.
14. Herr, "Why Should the United States Lag Behind," 11–12.
15. Bradley, *The Missouri Mule*, 33.
16. Edwin Price Ramsey and Stephen J. Rivel, *The Secret War of Ed Ramsey* (Pleasantville, New York: Reader's Digest, March 1992), 126–27. On January 1, 1996, Lieutenant (now Lieutenant Colonel) Ramsey led another cavalry platoon. He headed the U.S. Cavalry Association's mounted group in the Rose Bowl Parade, Pasadena, California. See also, "Meet Lt. Ramsey—he led last mounted cavalry charge" (Phoenix, Arizona: Council of America's Military Past, 1996): unnumbered copy.
17. Otto Whittington, "Greening of the Mules," *The Brayer* (1995): 19–20.
18. Thomas R. Buecker, "The Dismounting of the Fourth Cavalry at Fort Robinson, 1942" (*The Rural Electric Nebraskan*, 1989): 12–13.
19. The 4th Cavalry was issued M-5 Light Tanks and sent to the Southwest for training. In 1943 the 4th Cavalry went to England and eventually participated in the D-Day Invasion of Europe.
20. Waller, "Horses and Mules and National Defense," 16.
21. Ibid., 19.
22. Ibid. The well-trained horses on the depots did, occasionally, have an unscheduled use for soldiers. Lieutenant Clark Imlay of Grantsville, Utah was sent to Fort Robinson for infantry training. The ranch-raised Imlay saw no sense in walking with all those good horses around. One day his platoon was on a field exercise and the opportunity to play cavalryman arose. He cornered several horses against a fence, picked out one with saddle marks and caught him. Fashioning a hackamore from rope, the enterprising lieutenant rode for the rest of the day. The incident remained one of his most pleasurable World War II memories. Clark Imlay, Grantsville, Utah, tape sent to Phil Livingston, July, 1994.
23. Col. F. W. Koester, "A Historical Perspective of the U.S. Army Remount Service," unpublished manuscript, 1984, 4.
24. Waller, "Horses and Mules and National Defense," 19. See also, Mary Beth Ribeaux, "Sailors on Horseback," *Equus Magazine* (February 1992): 44.
25. Thomas R. Buecker, Curator at the Nebraska State Historical Society Museum, Fort Robinson, Nebraska, letter to Phil Livingston, January 15, 1996.
26. Waller, "Horses and Mules and National Defense," 24.
27. C. E. Livingston, Tujunga, California, conversations with Phil Livingston.
28. Waller, "Horses and Mules and National Defense," 24.
29. Gordon Moore, Crawford, Nebraska, letter to Phil Livingston, October 30, 1996.
30. Bradley, *The Missouri Mule*, 408.
31. Chuck Booth, "Tales of the Remount Cowboys," *Horse and Rider* (March 1984–February 1985): 22–23.
32. Bradley, *The Missouri Mule*, 384.
33. Ibid.
34. Waller, "Horses and Mules and National Defense," 22.
35. Captain C. E. Livingston was the father of author Phillip Livingston, who heard these stories many times from his father.
36. Bradley, *The Missouri Mule*, 384–85. See also, Phil Livingston, "All the Try of an Army Mule," *Western Horseman* (June 1979): 22.
37. Bradley, *The Missouri Mule*, 385.
38. Ibid., 385.
39. Ibid., 385–87.
40. Ibid.
41. Ibid.
42. Ibid.

43. Emmett M. Essin, *Shavetails & Bell Sharps* (Lincoln: University of Nebraska Press), 170.

44. Bradley, *The Missouri Mule,* 408.

45. Ibid., 390.

46. Ibid.

47. Ibid., 388.

48. Ibid., 392.

49. Ibid., 393.

50. Emmitt Essin, "Army Mules in World War II—the Last Hurrah?" *The Brayer* (undated copy): 110.

51. Bradley, The Missouri Mule, 395.

52. Ibid., 408.

53. L. J. Burns, Jr., Yoakum, Texas, conversation with Phil Livingston in 1972.

54. Bradley, *The Missouri Mule,* 409.

55. Booth, "Tales of the Remount Cowboys," 36.

56. Ibid.

57. Bradley, *The Missouri Mule,* 399.

58. Essin, "Army Mules in World War II," 111.

59. Ibid.

60. Bradley, *The Missouri Mule,* 401

61. Ibid.

62. Robert Wilson, Sunland, California, conversation with Phil Livingston during the late 1950s.

63. Essin, "Army Mules in World War II," 111.

64. Ibid.

65. Bradley, *The Missouri Mule,* 401.

66. Ibid.

67. Ibid., 408.

68. W. B. Woodruff, Jr., Decatur, Texas, interview with Phil Livingston, May 14, 1996.

69. Bradley, *The Missouri Mule,* 408.

70. Ibid., 429.

71. Colonel Ralph W. Mohri, V.C., "Flying Animals Over the Burma 'Hump,'" *The Cavalry Journal* (September–October 1945): 43.

72. Ibid.

73. Ibid.

74. Ibid.

75. Ibid., 44.

76. Ibid., 43.

77. Dr. Lee T. Railsbeck, Manhattan, Kansas, interview with the authors, April, 1991.

78. Bradley, *The Missouri Mule,* 428.

79. Ibid., 429–80.

80. Ibid., 430.

81. Ibid., 431.

82. Ibid.

83. Ibid.

84. Ibid.

85. Ibid., 428

86. Essin, "Army Mules in World War II," 112.

87. Bradley, *The Missouri Mule,* 364.

88. Colonel Fred L. Hamilton, "The Remount Story," *The Western Horseman* (January 1951): 44.

89. Ibid.

90. Paul Burdett, Missoula, Montana, letter to Phil Livingston, May 20, 1997.

91. "Arms and the Horse," *The Blood-Horse* (May 27, 1944), 747.

92. Bill Smale, "Western Remount Depot," *Western Livestock Journal* (May 12, 1946), 116.

93. Ibid., 118.

94. Ibid.

95. Mary Jane Parkinson, *The Kellogg Arabian Horse Ranch: The First Fifty Years* (Pomona, California: The Arabian Horse Club of Southern California, 1975), 287.

96. Ibid.

97. Quartermaster Corps Training Manual QMC 22-22: Distribution of Remount Stallions by States—Breeding Season of 1946, Department of the Army, Office of the Quartermaster General. Looseleaf unnumbered copy.

98. Gordon Moore, letter.

99. Quartermaster Corps Manual QMC 22-22.

100. Advertisement, American Remount Association, Western Horseman (September–October 1944): 37

101. "Arms and the Horse," *The Blood-Horse* (May 27, 1944): 747.

102. QMC Manual—QMC 22-2, Distribution of Remount Stallions by States Breeding Season, 1947, unnumbered copy.

103. Ibid.

104. "The Remount Wants Stallions," *The Blood-Horse* (January 6, 1945): 11.

105. Barbara Mills, Weatherford, Texas, interview with Phil Livingston, July 20, 1997.

106. Gordon Moore, letter.

107. Bill Gray, "War Takes Horses," *The Cattleman* (September 1943): 72. Also, Colonel Joseph H. Dornblaser, "Remount Breeding in the Southwest," *The Cattleman* (September 1946): 161.

108. Robert Denhardt, *The King Ranch Quarter Horses* (Norman, Oklahoma: University of Oklahoma Press, 1970), 162, 215, and 219.

109. Frank Holmes, *The Hank Wiescamp Story* (Colorado Springs, Colorado: The Western Horseman, 1996), 32–36.

110. Martha Haven, "Gudea-All-Breed Sire," *The Western Horseman* (October 1965): 74.

Francis the Talking Mule visits with Donald O'Connor in the movie, Francis Goes to West Point.

Ω

CHAPTER 7

TAPS FOR THE REMOUNT
1945–1948

"No American could have taken even a small part in the recent war and then have returned to Washington without being aware of the fact that in the minds of our leaders, the horse has become classed with the slingshot as an item of military equipment. I refuse to believe that some of this thinking stemmed from branch ambition. Whatever its origin, sound or otherwise, I knew of its existence when I returned from the Southwestern Pacific theater to assume my duties as chief of the U.S. Army Remount Service. From all sides came the cry to abolish the army horse and to liquidate the Remount forthwith."

Colonel Fred L. Hamilton
Chief of Remount 1945[1]

The surrender of Germany on May 7, 1945, and of Japan on September 2 of the same year ended hostilities. It also brought problems to the U.S. Remount Service and its supporters. Those problems were:

1) The end of fighting left the American army with large numbers of horses and mules, both in America and abroad.

2) The animals in the U.S. were already being surplused since use of the horse and mule in the post-war army were obsolete.

3) Pack and saddle stock in Europe could be disposed of there since shipping them back to the United States was not economically feasible. Horses and mules captured from German and Italian armies were also to be surplused to civilians in Europe for farming purposes.

4) The outstanding horses at German breeding farms, termed "The Prizes of War," had to be either assimilated into the American Remount Program or dispersed to European breeders.

5) Livestock in Burma and China were to be either given to farmers under the Lend-Lease Program or to allied military forces.

6) The Remount Service was under fire as an unnecessary expense from civilian, political and military enemies. Regardless of the part that horses and mules had played in World War II, many people wanted to abolish the army horse completely and immediately.

7) Even the Army Horse Breeding Program was suddenly viewed as an unnecessary government expense, an intrusion into private enterprise and some individuals felt it should be immediately eliminated.

Colonel Fred L. Hamilton was assigned as Chief of the U.S. Army Remount Service early in 1945, following a long tour of duty in the Southwest Pacific. He was faced with finding solutions to those problems.

Sales of military horses and mules had been in progress ever since 1942, as surplus to military need. Following World War II, disposal of military animals in Europe and Asia was handled through one of the U.S. Government agencies, the Foreign Liquidation Commission. Selling, or giving, those animals to allied governments was aid to the farming problems that the war-torn countries faced. The army inventory in Europe included those obtained from surrendering German and Italian military units. Over 7,000 horses were acquired from the German army. The majority of those animals were dispersed to farmers. A few were utilized by the American military government. The Italian pack mules that had not already "disappeared" were also turned over to farmers.

Photograph courtesy U.S. Army
Pack mules in Hawaii after World War II await shipment to China. These mules were transferred from the U.S. Army to the UNRRA relief program to give Chinese farmers draft animals.

The horses on the Nazi German government breeding farms and Remount Depots were another matter. Technically those animals were "Prizes of War," captured from a hostile enemy government and legally belonged to America under the accepted rules of war. The stallions, mares and young stock in that group represented some of the finest breeding in the world. Horsemen of all nations were clamoring to take possession. Many were the result of the German military horse breeding program which flourished during the two decades between the world wars. A number had been confiscated from German-occupied countries during the war and taken to Germany. Some of the latter could be returned to previous owners, if proper documentation existed. Others would be turned over to allied nations as a nucleus of breeding stock. A few could be shipped to the United States for use in the Army Horse Breeding Program.

Both the Remount Service and the horse breeding program had to be re-evaluated and restructured. If either, or both, were to continue, the programs had to conform to America's immediate political, military, social and economic future. Colonel Fred Hamilton wrote:

> The immediate hue and cry was "expense," always a fine argument. To me the incredibly small cost of the Remount was hardly a vulnerable target from a money angle in the light of what I saw all about me. Furthermore, given a little time for reorientation and reorganization, and with the proper management, the Remount activities could have been made almost self-supporting. However, I know now that certain steps toward that end were viewed with alarm by some horsemen.[2]

When Colonel Hamilton assumed command of the Remount Service in the summer of 1945, certain points predicting the future of the Remount seemed self-evident. After reviewing the situation, Colonel Hamilton concluded:

> 1. In the future the direct, peace-time military supply activities of the Army Remount Service would be almost nil.
> 2. The horse would still play a part in the economic and social life of the nation.
> 3. The military strength of the nation rests largely on the economic and social health of the country.
> 4. The breeding plan, with suitable adjustments, could still make a contribution to that economic health.
> 5. Quite possibly, such indirect contributions to national strength might have no place in the military establishment, and hence governmental light horse activities should be consolidated and streamlined with a view to eventual transfer to a civilian agency.
> 6. Although governmental subsidy for agricultural products was the order of the day, there was little inclination to include the horse among those

products to be subsidized. Hence, the breeding plan, if any, would have to stand on its own feet.

From that line of reasoning, one had to conclude that little of the Remount could be salvaged other than the breeding plan. And, did the horsemen of America want it salvaged and improved?[3]

While horses and mules had performed creditably during World War II, it was very clear that there would be no place for them in the post-war army. Therefore, there would be no need for a supply of remounts. The breeding program, designed to help improve America's civilian horses, was the only thing left which might have value. In 1945, the Remount situation was far from satisfactory. Stallion strength was down from about 700 in 1940 to 450. One third of those horses were seventeen years or older. Colonel Hamilton was convinced that with the projected upswing in horse racing for the peace-time United States, the number of top stallions available to the Remount would be severely limited. Breeders who in the past had donated or sold stallions at a fraction of their worth, would now be keeping the animals. Replacement stallions for the government program would have to be bred by the Remount Service or acquired on the open market at a higher price than before. Breeding stock on the Remount Depots suitable to raise cavalry mounts was not of the caliber to produce stallions that would improve the quality of the general horse population. The outstanding animals captured from the Germans were possibly part of the solution.

Colonel Hamilton was ordered to Germany during the summer of 1945. He was armed with the broad War Department mandate "to select horses from captured army stocks for shipment to the United States."[4]

Former cavalryman and polo player General George S. Patton Jr. was one of the few ranking American officers who understood the usefulness of the horse in military operations, as well as the importance of well-bred animals to the civilian economy. When his Third Army overran Germany, he left detachments of troops behind to guard each captured breeding farm. No sooner had he assumed command of the American Sector following the German surrender than he ordered the 709th Mounted Military Police and the 16th Constably formed. Utilizing captured German cavalry horses, they functioned effectively until 1950.[5] Patton was also the American general most responsible for keeping the captured "Prizes of War" horses in American hands rather than immediately turning them over to the advancing Russians. Under Russian ownership, the animals would have disappeared behind the "Iron Curtain" or have been destroyed.

The story of Nazi Germany's "Super Horses" began well before World War II. The horse, as a cavalry mount or a draft and pack animal, was an important part of the German army. When war in Europe broke out in 1939, over 700,000 horses were in German military use.[6] There was a well-managed breeding program to produce military remounts on Nazi government-operated farms. Even Adolph Hitler was concerned about the quality of German military mounts and stressed the importance of top breeding stock. These horses were of Thoroughbred, Arabian, Anglo-Arab and Lippizaner breeding. The Germans had skimmed the best of the best from government and private breeding farms in Poland, Czechoslovakia, Hungary, Austria and France, as each country was occupied. Controlled horse breeding was carried on by the Germans throughout World War II, records were carefully kept and the identity of the animals well documented. Those horses were captured by, or in several cases turned over to, American forces during the closing days of World War II to prevent them falling into Russian hands. It was reported that the Russians had already shot and eaten some of the German horses by the time Patton's troops reached the various farms. Others were confiscated and shipped to Russian breeding farms or utilized as cavalry mounts.[7] The fact that General George S. Patton Jr. took a personal interest in the future of those horses and gave his official approval for rescue efforts was the major reason for their survival. Many of them were moved by American troops to farms within the American Zone of Germany where they remained under American guard. Gladys Brown Edwards notes, "If General George Patton ... had not been a cavalryman who appreciated good horses, the appeal to save these animals from the on-coming Russian forces might not have been answered."[8]

Photograph courtesy The Western Horseman

This four-year-old grade Thoroughbred at Donnauworth, a Nazi German Army Remount Depot, was just one of a large number of Hungarians, Thoroughbreds, Arabians and grade Arabians the German military had bred, or confiscated from conquered countries during World War II.

When Colonel Hamilton reached Germany the American military government was just coming into being and personnel were vague about the reconstruction problems or had no idea of how to solve them. The fate of captured horses, outstanding though they might be, was of little consequence to most military authorities. Not so to America's recent enemies, Allies or quasi-Allies. Horses were important in Europe and those governments were well aware of the high value of the animals held by American forces.

All those countries were making major efforts to obtain title to them.[9]

By all international rules of land warfare, and interallied agreements, the horses belonged to the United States. They had been captured as property of a hostile government which no longer existed, and, from a legal standpoint, might have all been appropriated by the U.S. Army.[10] That fact was completely ignored by European nations seeking ownership of the animals.

While German cities had suffered heavily from American bombing, much of the countryside was unharmed. German horse breeding establishments showed little war damage since they were located well away from metropolitan areas. The Germans had carried on breeding, racing and registration right up to the surrender, often feeding and caring for the animals better than their people.

Photograph courtesy The Western Horseman
Colonel Fred Hamilton, Chief of U.S. Remount Programs, holds
*Nordlicht (TB), winner of the German Derby. Colonel Hamilton was
in Germany in late 1945 to select horses which would be purchased and
taken to the United States for use by the Remount Service.

There were six major Thoroughbred breeding farms in Germany. Five were located in what became the American Zone; one was in the Russian Zone, and none in the French and British Zones, which might have had a bearing on the protests from these countries against America's acquisition of the horses. Two of the farms were German government-owned while four were private enterprises.[11]

Altefeld, a Nazi government farm some 100 miles northeast of Frankfurt, had been captured by General Patton's Third Army. It was in the charge of the small American detachment Patton had left behind. The ex-German government had assembled the cream of the crop of European Thoroughbreds. These horses had been acquired from a variety of sources and in different ways. Some had been purchased in countries occupied by the Germans and had documentation to prove it. Others had been requisitioned, although the sales could not be classed as voluntary. The animals had been paid for with German marks. A few had been confiscated from the studs of the Aga Khan and Mr. Widener on the basis that these two men were citizens of England and the U.S. Some also came from the French Baron Rothschild's stable. All three nations were enemies of Nazi Germany and property owned by residents was legal contraband.[12]

Colonel Hamilton's decision on the requisitioned and confiscated animals was, "All individual horses at Altefeld, either requisitioned or confiscated and moved into Germany on that basis, were to be returned to their previous owners."[13]

The young stock which had been bred by the Germans, the product of parentage from several sources, were German contraband. The U.S. had the strongest claim since it was the primary power which defeated Germany, but all of the Allied nations, as well as defeated Germany, Hungary, Austria and Czechoslovakia were clamoring for ownership.[14] After returning what animals he could and carefully appraising the remainder, Colonel Hamilton made his choices for America. The selected horses were trucked to the Port of Bremerhaven for shipment to the United States.

Mansback, a Nazi government farm, also under the protection of Patton's soldiers, was the home of excellent purebred Arabians. A number of the older animals had been captured in Poland in 1939. When the Germans withdrew ahead of the advancing Russians, they took the horses with them. Most of those Arabians were moved to Hostau (near the Czechoslovakian border) and taken under the protection of Patton's Third Army at the request of a German army veterinarian who did not want the horses to fall into Russian hands. The animals were soon evacuated to Mansback. That farm was on the border of the Russian sector. Russian soldiers would frequently shoot at American troops working on the farm.[15] It was there that Colonel Hamilton chose several of the Arabians that were to go to the United States. Included were Arabian stallions Lotnik and the well-known *Witez II. The selected animals were transported in box cars, with American soldiers guarding them, to Bremerhaven.[16]

Near Donnauworth, in southern Bavaria, were a group of farms that had long been Nazi Army Remount Depots. There were large numbers of Hungarian horses, Thoroughbreds, grade Thoroughbreds, Arabians and grade Arabians under the protection of General Patton's troops and in the care of Hungarian military personnel. Patton placed Major J. P. Owens, Third Army Remount Officer, in command. Had it not been for Major Owens, most of the horses at Donnauworth would have been sold, taken by the Russians or put to pulling German plows. With few exceptions, those horses had been bred in Hungary and evacuated into Germany ahead of the Russian advance. Whether the Hungarians took the horses to Germany voluntarily, or were coerced, was immaterial. The Germans, Italians and Hungarians were Allies and a common enemy to the United States. The horses at Donnauworth were captured enemy property, and, by the rules of warfare, now belonged to America. Some of these animals were also selected for shipment to the United States.[17]

Isaarland, near Munich, consisted of four or five breeding farms and training establishments that had been the personal interest of the German thug (Hamilton's description) Weber. There were only a few German caretakers with no Americans in authority when Colonel Hamilton visited the area. The colonel was accompanied by a French horseman who was one of the most active members of the French Breeders Syndicate, the governing body of French Thoroughbred breeding and racing. The Frenchman was completely dependent upon the United States Army for transportation, guidance and information. At no other farm visited during the inspection trip did he question the announced identity of any horse until Isaarland was reached. Hundreds of young horses and broodmares were turned out in barren paddocks and starving to death. In that condition, and with no competent German to identify the animals, the Frenchman could not distinguish one from another, although he had trained a number of the older animals.[18]

Photograph courtesy U.S. Army

*The great *Witez II, a Polish-bred Arabian stallion, was a prominent stud in the German Remount breeding program during World War II. *Witez II was brought to the United States, where, after the dissolution of the Remount Program, he became a major influence in Arabian horse breeding.*

Colonel Hamilton arranged for Major Owens, the American officer in charge of Donnauworth, to supervise and staff Isaarland. Only four horses were selected for shipment to America because of doubts of identity. Of the four, one stallion and three mares, the stallion was later assigned to a Remount agent in Texas. Two of the mares, after being carefully tested for disease, were shipped to Fort Reno, Oklahoma, and added to the Half-bred band. The New York Jockey Club was not asked to register any of the four animals. Not so with the French. They promptly claimed most of the animals at Isaarland with no opposition. Those animals were immediately shipped to France.[19]

In addition to the horses at the Nazi government farms, there were many owned by German civilians. A number of those animals were for sale. Because horse feed was almost non-existent and Nazi money had no value, many of those German breeders were willing to sell their animals. The Germans themselves appraised the horses, the prices were paid in Occupation Marks (the only currency legal in Germany at the time) and the sellers received what was frequently a life-saving payment. Approximately a dozen stallions and mares were legally purchased by the United States in this manner. One was *Nordlicht (TB), winner of the German Derby.[20]

One hundred fifty-two top-quality horses were selected from the hundreds available at German depots and breeding farms. They were shipped to America in October of 1945. This group included sixty-five Thoroughbreds, twenty-two pure Arabians, fifteen Anglo Arabians, nine Lippizaners, forty Half-Breds and one Russian stallion. All were appraised and the value entered as a credit to the German government for subsequent interallied reparations settlement.[21] In view of the tremendous, unpayable balance in favor of the United States in this account, the horses cost America nothing.[22] Among this group were the Arabians *Lotnik, Pilot, *Witez II, Tarnik and Wierka.[23] Thoroughbreds included Taj Akbar (bred by the Aga Khan and an exceptional race horse), Taj Shirin, Athanasius and *Nordlicht.[24]

The 152 horses were shipped to America on the Liberty ship *Stephen F. Austin.* Contrary to stories circulated by America's radio and newspapers, the animals did not take preference over American G.I.'s who had served in Europe during the conflict and were eligible to return home. Sixty-five American soldiers, all with high-point service ratings, volunteered to defer earlier return to travel with the horses.[25] At the assembly point of Bremerhaven, each animal was individually crated, lifted aboard ship and then stalled. Some of the Lippizaner mares and young colts were not halter broken, which created numerous problems during loading and on the trip. One Arabian mare foaled while aboard, adding to the inventory. The journey, which was scheduled for ten or twelve days, took a long, stormy twenty-one days to reach Newport News, Virginia. By the time the ship docked, feed was exhausted and drinking water was in short supply.[26] The horses were transferred to the Aleshire Remount Depot, Front Royal, Virginia, and quarantined for ninety days.

On April 7, 1946, a Parade of Horses was held to showcase the animals. Soon afterwards, the Arabians, Half-Arabians, Anglo Arabians and Lippizaners were shipped to Pomona, California.[27] On June 29, 1946, a showing of those animals was held at the Pomona Remount Depot in co-operation with the California Arab Horse Breeders Association. In addition to exhibiting the imported animals, there was a demonstration of lip tattoo branding and an inspection of the depot veterinary facilities.[28] The Thoroughbreds and Half-breds were divided between Fort Robinson and Fort Reno.

While Colonel Hamilton had made his selections from some of the finest horses on the European continent, he had not exhausted the supply. There were still numerous, outstanding animals remaining in Europe. Colonel Hamilton observed, "Many a good one was left in Germany."[29]

Early in 1946 Colonel Hamilton made a second horse-hunting expedition to Europe. Approximately 300 additional Thoroughbreds, Half-Breds and Arabians from Germany, Austria and Italy were acquired. They arrived at Front Royal in September. After quarantine, acclimation and processing, the new arrivals were assigned to either Remount Depots or authorized Remount agents.[30] Included in this group were the stallions *Aventin, by Teddy; Samurai by Orleander (one of the most distinguished

German Thoroughbreds prior to World War II) and a half-dozen mares by Orleander. There were also several Thoroughbreds which French breeders had not claimed because of the impossibility of determining rights of ownership.[31] Colonel Hamilton also brought with him a large quantity of affidavits and other evidences of ownership to prove America's claim to the animals. Colonel Hamilton observed,

> With characteristic German thoroughness, these horses have been bred for temperament, durability and thriftiness for generations. Thoroughbreds and grades alike have been thoroughly tried in many ways, and only those with exceptional records were sent to the government nurseries for breeding. This system of selective breeding is exactly in accordance with the objectives of the American Remount Service. We feel that we can advance our Army Breeding Plan many years through adapting to our own Remount program the experience of the Europeans and the results obtained by them.[32]

No sooner had America indicated interest in the German horses than Russia, and her Allies of Poland, Hungary and Yugoslavia, challenged America's right to any of the animals. The fact that Germany was a defeated nation, which had declared war upon the United States, was of no importance. France was also loudly in the picture, clamoring that many of the horses had been forcibly taken by the Germans and should be immediately returned to France. During the time that Colonel Hamilton was selecting animals for America, foreign nations were lobbying strongly to prevent it and "hollering that they wuz robbed."[33] Colonel Hamilton's actions regarding the individual animals originally from France have already been documented. The problem was the offspring of these horses which had been bred and foaled in Germany. European nations, especially France, wanted all the horses to remain on the Continent. Russia wanted them behind the Iron Curtain.

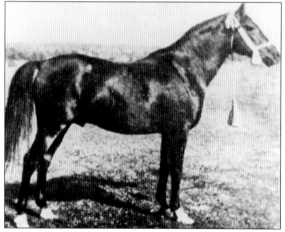

Photograph courtesy The Western Horseman

*Lotnik, a Polish-bred Arabian stallion, was confiscated by the Germans during World War II, and taken to Germany. *Lotnik was one of the stallions which came to the United States as a "Prize of War."*

The French Breeders Syndicate was making numerous claims that ownership and identity of the horses was clouded and that it was not correct to register them under existing circumstances. These questions were not raised about any of horses that were taken to France.

On November 10, 1946, another problem arose. The Jockey Club, which had assisted in the formation of the U.S. Remount Service three decades before, resolved not to recognize or register the horses purchased or requisitioned from German individuals and war authorities by the United States Army.

The Jockey Club said that two factors weighed in the decision which it finally made. They were:

1) The identification of these horses was dependent upon the word of an enemy and the control of certain records of the *German Stud Book* had been taken from those in Germany whom the Jockey Club had dealt with before the war and assumed by the German government, resulting in the necessity for The Jockey Club to refrain from recognizing the *German Stud Book* at all, for the time being.

2) The Jockey Club felt that it would be failing in its primary purpose of protecting the American Thoroughbred horse if it granted registry as requested.[34]

The text of the resolution follows:

> RESOLVED; Because certain German horses have been presented for registration in the *American Stud Book*, the following ruling has been adopted: In view of the following facts, that the German horses presented for registration were requisitioned, or purchased from German individuals and that the knowledge of those requisitioning them or purchasing them as to the identity of the horses is dependent upon the word of an enemy; and other factors which cast a shadow upon the proof of their identity, the stewards of The Jockey Club deem it advisable to decline to register such horses in the *American Stud Book*. And, furthermore, in view of the fact that it is reported that control of certain records of the *German Stud Book* were [sic] taken away from the German authorities which The Jockey Club dealt prior to the war and was taken over by the German Government itself, it is determined that the Jockey Club in behalf of the *American Stud Book* has ceased to recognize the *German Stud Book* for the present, so that no horses imported from Germany with German certificates can be registered in the *Stud Book* here. This applies not only to horses taken by the German army from France during its occupation of France as loot and to their produce, but also to horses of German origin. It does not apply to horses taken from France as loot and have been repatriated into France and of which the

Syndicat des Eleveurs de Chevaux de Sang, which has been formed in France to insure the identity of the repatriated horses, will give their approval to reestablish into the *French Stud Book*. Such horses when recognized by the *French Stud Book* will be eligible to the *American Stud Book*, if satisfactory on other basis.

At some future time, if conditions are then satisfactory to the stewards of The Jockey Club, a study will be made to see whether the situation has reconstituted itself to such an extent that the *German Stud Book* can be again recognized on the lines on which it was recognized before the war.

This action was taken in order to protect the American Thoroughbred horse.[35]

The decision by the Jockey Club could be interpreted as an effort to keep the European Thoroughbred stallions from being in a position to compete with American sires. Regardless of how it was viewed, the move effectively eliminated the German Thoroughbred stallions from contributing to the improvement of America's racing Thoroughbreds.

Was it possible that there was collusion between the leading American and French Thoroughbred breeders? Recognition of the European horses, and their availability at stud through the Remount program, would have an adverse effect on the interest in home-bred stallions. The refusal to accept the European Thoroughbreds was viewed from another aspect by one Virginia hunter-jumper breeder. "Well, it suits me," he said, referring to the German Champion *Nordlicht (TB). "If they can't sell him for two or three hundred thousand, maybe he will stand here and I can breed to him for ten dollars."[36]

Photograph courtesy Gordon Moore

Dix Fois (TB), a broodmare from the band at Fort Robinson, Nebraska, was sold in 1945 at the dissolution of the U.S. Army Remount Program.

Colonel Hamilton responded to the Jockey Club's refusal in a January 7, 1947, letter to *The Blood-Horse.* The magazine printed it in the February 8 issue. He questioned: 1. The Jockey Club's right to depreciate property values with no provision for appeal. 2. Whether the French Breeders Syndicate was the authority more acceptable than the United States Army. 3. Whether the Jockey Club had given a fair hearing to the case. 4. He also suggested a disinterested committee of two to study the case.[37]

Colonel Hamilton pointed out that the U.S. Remount Service had data and evidence that would answer many of the questions raised by the Jockey Club. That evidence was not called for prior to the refusal to register the horses nor did the Jockey Club provide any advice on discrepancies in the registration and export certificates submitted to them. The Remount Service was not consulted at any time, even upon receipt of the "all important" letter from the French Breeders Syndicate in October 1945. That was about the same time that the first shipment of horses arrived in the United States.

Hamilton continued with the statement that the French Syndicate had created the impression that there was a mass of conflicting ownership claims on the horses and that even their identity was clouded. In the former, the Remount Service maintained that the International Claims aspects of the situation were well outside of the providence, real or assumed, of the New York Jockey Club.[38]

The majority of the horses at Isaarland claimed by the French were shipped to France where they were registered in the French Breeders Syndicate studbook and later raced. The young horses foaled in Germany must have been identified on the word of Germans and evidence passed to the French by American Officers. If there were any horses whose identity might possibly be questionable, it was the Isaarland horses.

Colonel Hamilton also raised the questions:

> 1. Was it reasonable for the French Breeders Syndicate, working with information acquired from and through the American army to sit in judgement of the horses selected by the American army?
>
> 2. Were they morally qualified to do so when they registered young horses with poorer credentials than those in America whose credentials they protested?
>
> 3. By what line of reasoning did German Records and the words of Nazis become purified and more acceptable by passing through the hands of the French Breeders Syndicate, an organization with no known official standing?[39]

As previously noted, he suggested that the matter be referred to a disinterested committee of two. The Jockey Club and the Remount Service would each designate a man who was an experienced horseman of national reputation. Neither individual would be in any way associated with either the Jockey Club or the Remount Service and both would be Americans. Those two men would inventory and evaluate the evidence in the hands of the Remount, inspect the horses, and, if need be, travel to Germany to substantiate the facts or bring German horsemen to America.[40]

The Jockey Club ignored the suggestion and did not register any of the German horses at the time, which eliminated the registry of the offspring of those horses and prevented them from racing on American tracks.

On August 11, 1948, in United States court for the southern district of New York, a complaint for mandatory injunction was filed against the Jockey Club by Ford E. Young Jr. Mr. Young was seeking aid from the court in obtaining the registration of two foals, a filly by *Nordlicht-Reno Kit by London Pride, and a colt by *Aventin-Golden Tone by Golden Guinea. Both stallions were brought to the United States from Germany by the U.S. Remount Service and both mares were registered Thoroughbreds.

In his complaint, the plaintiff alleged:

> The refusal of the defendant corporation [The Jockey Club] to register aforementioned stallions, constitutes an abuse of the monopolistic powers possessed by the membership of defendant corporation.... [Unless the colt and filly are registered] the plaintiff will suffer irreparable injury in that the value of said filly and colt unregistered will not be nearly as great as their value would be if registered ... [Unless they are registered, The Jockey Club] ... will be allowed to and by its arbitrary action will restrain trade among the several states that in the forenamed filly and colt will not be eligible to race in competition with other Thoroughbred horses.

Mr. Young also alleged that

> The Remount Service has applied to defendant to register these stallions. Plaintiff believes ... that the Remount Service has established the identity and ownership of these stallions beyond any reasonable doubt and has complied with every reasonable requirement which might be a condition precent to the registering of these stallions.[41]

According to Colonel Hamilton, American registration of the German Thoroughbreds would have been an official endorsement of the quality of the horses in question. Registration, and the successful racing of the offspring of those horses, would have given private breeders a logical reason to take their best mares to Remount stallions. Recognition by the Jockey Club would have been a fine boost to the Remount Service, a boost sorely needed if the program was to continue. To him, the failure to recognize the horses spelt doom for the Remount. [42]

The United States Department of State favored the restitution claims of European nations, both Allied and enemy, over the army's strong objections. Early in 1947, a departmental proclamation was made to return the animals to Europe. This move may have been the result of the army's decision to no longer utilize horse power plus a wish to be divorced from the breeding program, from civilian pressure to eliminate competition to American stallions, from the Jockey Club's refusal to recognize the European Thoroughbreds, or an effort to promote favorable international relations by the State Department with Russia, Austria and Hungary. Plans were quietly formulated to assemble the first shipment of European horses from the various Remount Depots at New Orleans, Louisiana. They would be loaded on a ship (also carrying 500 mules bound for Greece under the Lend-Lease Program) on November 6, 1947. The final destination was Trieste, Italy. There, they would be returned to the appropriate governments of the nations from where they had originated. Since Hungary and Poland were both under Russian domination by then, the horses would be out of sight. Behind the Iron Curtain, there would be no difficulty in solving the ownership problems.[43]

Photograph courtesy Gordon Moore

Open Door (TB), by The Porter and out of Mablonde, was a U.S. Remount Service stallion at Fort Robinson, Nebraska, 1942–1943.

There was no formal announcement made beforehand, the State Department preferring to present the move after the fact. Government officials knew that not all Americans would feel that it was the proper solution, and a public discussion would not be in the best interest of the State Department. There was only light coverage of the decision by the newspapers, and by the time magazines printed the story in depth, the shipment would already be at sea. Even the military was gagged so that there could be no adverse publicity. Officers received a special order not to discuss the matter without prior approval of the army's public relations bureau.[44]

Although few stories had appeared in the papers, or were at least noticed, horsemen began to learn of the proposed move by the State Department. Letters arrived at *The Blood-Horse* and other equine-related publications from California, Texas, Virginia, and elsewhere indicating that the Prizes of War were to be returned to Europe. The majority of those letters were *not* in favor of the decision by the State Department.

On October 10, the story broke nationally in newspapers via a United Press release from Washington, D.C.:

> The State Department announced today that it is ready to make amends for an international "horse trade" that backfired on the War Department.

Soon after V-E Day, the army shipped 254 horses found at various German remount stations to the United States. Poland, Hungary, Yugoslavia and Hungary protested that many of the steeds had been looted by the Nazis.

Following negotiations with the interested governments, the State Department said the first shipment of 120 horses will leave this country for Hungary about November 1. Negotiations are continuing on the Polish and Yugoslav claims.[45]

The State Department, forced into early admission of the move, issued an explanation:

The return of horses to the respective owning countries has the support of both the Departments of the Army and State. This position is based on the determination of the Department of State that the horses in question are not properly considered as captured enemy material, as originally supposed, but rather as property looted from countries while they were under German occupation.[46]

This policy was announced long after it had been put into effect and the order sent out to the Remount Service to return the animals to Europe. National attention was suddenly called to the unannounced restitution of the animals to Hungary by the State Department. Newspapers began to assign reporters to the project and stories appeared all over America. Even Fulton Lewis Jr., one of the best-known radio commentators, indignantly blasted the move on his nightly news program. Horsemen began to contact their Senators and Congressmen about the situation, requesting a delay in the proposed shipment.

The Chairman of the Senate Appropriations Committee, Senator Stiles Bridges of New Hampshire, responded and protested the action to the Secretary of State, George C. Marshall. What was supposed to be a minor problem being swept under the rug was rapidly assuming huge proportions for the U.S. Government.[47]

Reacting to both the media blitz and the barrage of public opinion, Congress went into action and delayed the return of the animals. A Senate sub-committee, with Senator Wayne Morris of Oregon as Chairman, Senator Robertson of Wyoming and Senator Maybank of South Carolina as members, investigated the claims and prepared a voluminous report in favor of the army.[48]

On January 13, 1948, the Armed Services Committee of the Senate unanimously "approved the findings of fact and conclusions of law" on the question of the captured horses' ownership. The United States had legal title to the horses both under the "rules of land warfare and under the peace treaty entered into on September 15, 1947, between Hungary and the Allies."[49]

The proposal of the State Department, set forth in a letter of April 7, 1947, that the horses should be sent back to the Hungarian government, was countered with the statement that it "was contrary to sound public policy as these horses are the best military type in the world" and to return them would constitute sending them for use by the Hungarian Army—which was a satellite of Russia—as very valuable military material."[50]

The Congressional sub-committee's finding also applied to the horses claimed by the Polish and Yugoslav governments as well. Consequently, none of the horses involved in the dispute would be returned to Europe as desired by the American State Department.[51] The group of Senators, led by Wayne Morris and Tom Stewart, insisted that any shipment be held up until they were satisfied that it was a necessary and proper procedure. According to *The Blood-Horse* magazine, "they expressed no disapproval of returning private property to private individuals, but they gagged at the idea of sending it to a Russian satellite where there would be no assurance that it would return to the hands of the previous owners."[52]

The countries which claimed the stock had fallen under Communist domination, and Communist Russia was at war with the United States in everything but a military

Photograph courtesy Bette Thurston Mecham

This fine looking Half-bred gelding was sired by a Remount Service stallion at the Thurston ranch, Morgan, Utah, following the end of World War II.

sense. As a result of the Senate group's strong disapproval, the State and War Departments altered their previous instructions to the U.S. Remount Service. The horses stayed in the United States.

As soon as the Prizes of War stallions were assigned to Remount Agents, a cry went up among some of America's horsemen. They felt that it was unfair competition offering stallions of such quality at the low stud fees of ten dollars. The entire Army Horse Breeding Program was suddenly a menace to the earning capacity of home-grown stallions. To this end, all sorts of stories were circulated to discourage the use of Remount stallions. This civilian approach was eventually to be one of the major reasons why the Army Horse Breeding Program was discontinued in 1948.

On October 21, 1946, during a dispersal of military horses at the Aleshire Remount Depot, Front Royal, Virginia, seven German mares and six two year olds of German and

Hungarian breeding were offered for sale. It was announced to the public that these animals were not acceptable for registration with the New York Jockey Club. The top selling individual, the Hungarian mare Seabreeze (TB), by Coronach-Golden Clear, and in foal to *Nordlicht (TB), was sold for $5,000. The thirteen imported horses' sales

totaled $19,100. One hundred forty-two American Thoroughbred broodmares, yearlings, two and three year olds and riding horses were also auctioned off. The entire sale consisted of 153 surplus army horses bringing $153,500 with a $990 average. Over 2,000 people attended the sale, many of them dealers in hunters and jumpers who were looking for prospects or breeding stock.[53]

The military animals in Burma and China did not present the problems the German Prizes of War did. Since they were pack and saddle stock, they could be disposed of with no thought of shipment back to the United States, as noted in Chapter 6.

Photograph courtesy Dan Taylor
Red Bird, ridden by Dan Taylor, was sired by King Raffles (TB), a Remount Stallion standing at Tommy Cochran's ranch, Belton, Texas. Taylor was a champion roper of Rodeo Cowboy Association during the 1940s and 1950s.

Sales of surplus military horses and mules started in 1943 and continued throughout the war. The dispersal of all military animals, other than a very few, was accelerated after the hostilities ceased. These sales were held at Remount Depots, offering as many animals per session as was practical for the depot staff to fit during a given period of time. Examples were:

Fort Robinson, Nebraska—February 24–25, 1944; 500 mules averaging $132.50; 1,067 horses with an average of $61.11 for riding horses; $52.17 for animals suitable for light farm work. Approximately 200 bidders attended. Ferd Owens of Kansas City, Missouri, was the auctioneer.

Fort Robinson, Nebraska—March 23, 1944; 1,274 horses averaging $41.80. Ferd Owens of Kansas City, Missouri, was the auctioneer.

Fort Robinson, Nebraska—September 3, 1944; 400 horses sold to Eli Lilly Company for the making of serum. Unit price was $57.48 per animal.

Fort Robinson, Nebraska—October 26, 1944; 1,017 horses averaging $34.35; 76 mules averaging $91.80. W.R. Ross, Fort Worth, Texas, was the auctioneer.[54]

Both auction and volume sales to a single company were held at all three of the Remount Depots during the war years. The decision had been made that horses and mules had no place—regardless of the contributions they were making in both Europe and Asia at the time—in the army and surplus inventory had to be disposed of.

As early as 1946 the army made it clear that there was no longer a place for the Remount Service in the military. A message was passed from the army to some key Congressmen. The following was from a message telephoned to Maryland Senator Tydings, as reported to *The Blood-Horse* by H. S. Finney:

> With the reduction in procurement functions, the breeding program can now be divorced from the Remount Service and placed under another department. It is believed that this program could be more appropriately operated under the Department of Agriculture, where such responsibilities are more closely related than to the War Department.[55]

Members of Congress began to look for public reactions and suggestions as to which way to move. *The Blood-Horse,* after communicating with a number of individuals well informed on the subject, suggested that the Remount Service be kept in the army. The reasons were that the Department of Agriculture did not want it, only the army had the qualified personnel, and the Remount program was too precious an asset to be moved to a department where it might possibly become subject to political grab.[56]

The question now was, "What to do with the Remount Service?" Neither the Army nor the Department of Agriculture wanted it, regardless of how important the Army Horse Breeding Program might be. That foretold the future, even while a small, dedicated group of army officers and civilian horsemen were fighting to keep it.

Even with the future of the Remount Service, and the breeding program, under discussion, the daily routine at the depots continued. Horses and mules were trained and conditioned or fitted and sold as surplus. Depot breeding programs continued and stallions were issued, and received back, from agents. Some new stallions were even purchased during this period of uncertainty as to whether the program would continue or not.

The October issue of *The Quarter Horse,* published by the National Quarter Horse Breeders Association, printed the following under the headline: "Sons of Ariel In Remount Group":

> Col. Joseph H. Dornblaser, officer in charge of remount activities at the San Angelo depot … gives us the name and location of the breeding sons of Ariel

available to public use through the remount service.... Romolino has been purchased by the U.S. Remount at the Keeneland Fall Sales held in Lexington, for $3400. He was consigned to the sale by the King Ranch. Romolino is by Ariel out of Flying Dust, by High Cloud, and has already been proven to be a sire of sprinters. Prior to his sale by them, Romolino stood at the King Ranch.... His purchase is in line with the Remount's policy of obtaining good tempered stallions of the short-legged, well-muscled type that not only can produce speed on short tracks, but can also sire stock horses and polo ponies. It is to be recalled that the Remount purchased two yearling colts last spring by Ariel. These colts are being developed at Fort Robinson, Nebraska.... Marcabala is with Martin Stiles of Anson, Texas. After June this stallion will be brought in and re-assigned to another agent or sent to Fort Reno, Oklahoma, as a depot sire. He is by Ariel.[57]

It was evident that the Remount Service was making a strong effort to offer the type of stallions that were in demand by civilian breeders. The rise in popularity of the Quarter Horse was already evident along with the infusion of Thoroughbred sprinting blood necessary to win on the short tracks. Remount personnel were meeting that need as well as continuing the

Photograph courtesy U.S. Army

Yearling Remount-bred stallion is shown at Fort Reno, Oklahoma, during World War II.

established policy of improving the quality of America's light horses.

Following the war, the major activity at the various Remount Depots was accelerating the dispersal of the animals on hand. Saddle, draft and pack animals were fitted—conditioned, feet trimmed, manes and tails trimmed—in groups for scheduled sales. Large lots were sold to the Reconstruction Finance Corporation, Kansas City, Missouri, probably "as is," for resale in other parts of the country. Those volume sales were at a set price per head, rather than offered individually at auction, and helped to rapidly clear out the inventory. For example: Fort Robinson, Nebraska—November, 1946, 400 riding horses and 1,820 mules; December, 1946—1,075 riding horses, 125 draft horses and 1,800 mules; January 1947—300 riding horses and 26 draft horses; February 1947—210 riding horses, 30 draft horses and 625 mules; March 1947—799 mules.[58]

There were also auction sales at the Depots where civilian buyers could purchase individual animals. Many horses undoubtedly went to farms, ranches and pleasure riders but it is well-known that the majority were purchased by traders for resale. One person who bought a number of surplus army horses was A. J. "Jack" Campbell. He observed, "[The auctioneers] ran 'em through pretty rapidly and you had to make up your mind on a horse as fast as you saw it. Of course, I'd served at Fort Robinson during the war and knew many of the horses. I bought several loads at different sales held there."[59]

Photograph courtesy Barbara Tinsley Mills

Barbara Tinsley Mills clears a jump on Golden Victory, by Golden Seal (TB) in 1946. Golden Seal, a Remount stallion, was a popular sire of hunters and jumpers in the Virginia horse country during the late 1930s.

The prices that the government received for the surplus horses and mules were bargains to the buyers. The army had paid approximately $200 per head and maintained the animals for several years. Some of the horses had been utilized for guard duty, beach patrol or recreational riding before being surplused, but there was still a large financial loss on each one.

The sales, both in volume lots and at auction, continued into 1947 until the inventory of saddle and draft horses, as well as pack and draft mules was exhausted. Only the Remount stallions, brood mares and young stock raised on the depots was left. Countless well-trained geldings made their ways to ranches or recreational riders in the rapidly growing pleasure horse industry. The US branded on the left shoulder and a Preston Brand on the neck was a common sight during the late 1940s and through the 1950s. The U.S. Forest Service took a number of the surplus pack mules. The animals packed supplies—material and equipment to make repairs to buildings, bridges, fences and other facilities—to remote forest ranger stations, or were used to support fire fighting teams. The Forest Service utilized the same technique that the cavalry had developed prior to World War II—truck the animals as far as possible, unload and pack in.[60]

A large number of former army mounts were utilized by civilian horsemen in a variety of uses. Some went to the polo field or show ring, others earned their oats on ranches and a few were strictly pleasure animals. In each case, they demonstrated their good breeding and solid training.

One US-branded mount was the bay mare, Reno P245. Foaled at Fort Reno, Oklahoma, in 1942, she received her early training under army horsemen. Reno was purchased by George Cohins, Hinsdale, Illinois, at one of the 1947 dispersal sales. Cohins trained the mare for polo and played her successfully until she was twenty. In 1962, feeling that Reno was getting too old for the sport, Cohins sold her to Mrs. Helen M.L. Hall of Oakbrook, Illinois. Mrs. Hall schooled the mare in equitation and rode for pleasure until her show career began.

Showing under a thirteen-year-old girl during 1962, Reno netted five blue ribbons, one red, one yellow and one fifth place. The following year, 1963, with another thirteen year old in the saddle, Reno collected two red ribbons, three yellows and four whites. In 1964, the sixty-eight-year-old Mrs. Hall took over the show campaign and the pair earned three blue ribbons, one red, three yellows, two whites and one green. During three years of showing the capable mare was unplaced only four times.[61]

Photograph from U.S. Army ID card

Spud, a brown gelding bred by D.L. Smith, Claremore, Oklahoma, was sired by Panic (TB), a Remount stallion, and out of a Quarter-type mare, Bay Bess. He was purchased by the U.S. Army in 1941. Spud was acquired by Mr. Stroming, Patterson, New Jersey, in 1944. Below is Spud's Army ID card.

Spud entered the Army by mistake. Bred by Mr. D.L. Smith of Claremore, Oklahoma, the brown gelding was sired by the Remount stallion Panic (TB) and out of a Quarter-type mare named Bay Bess. The mare died shortly after he was foaled and Mr. Smith raised the colt on a bottle. As a two year old, Spud was broken to saddle and developed into a top cowhorse, being used for contest calf and steer roping. In 1941 when army buyers visited the Smith ranch, Spud passed inspection and was mistakenly sold. Mr. Smith tried to buy the animal back but was unable to.

On March 3, 1944, Spud was purchased at an army dispersal sale by Mr. Stroming, Patterson, New Jersey, for $145. Mr. Stroming received the original Army ID card with the animal listing the original purchase. In response to a letter asking for information on the animal, Smith offered to buy him back. Stroming refused and kept the animal for the rest of his life.[62]

Brand 2627		Class Riding		HORSE (MULE) RECORD CARD					DUPLICATE		
SECTION I						GENERAL DESCRIPTION AND PURCHASE RECORD					
Color	Sex	Height	Weight	Foaled	Breed	Sire	Dam	Purchased at—	By—	Price	Date
Br.	Geld.	lb.1½	1075	1937	Unknown	----------	----------	Claremore, Okla.	CBT JWT	$175	5/25/41
Purchased from—			Shipped to—				Remarks by purchasing officer				
D. L. Smith			Reno QM Depot	(For Cav)							
SECTION II						SERVICE RECORD					
	Issued to—			From—		Date			Remarks		
SECTION III					FINAL DISPOSITION						
Date of death, sale, or destruction			Cause of death				Reason for condemnation or destruction				
			Sold Surplus 3-3-44								
WAR DEPARTMENT—Q. M. C. Form 125 (Old No. 417)—Approved May 25, 1924—Rev July 14, 1926											

Another ex-Army horse was Major, a Roman-nosed bay gelding ridden by one of the authors from 1949 to 1952. A smoothly-made individual, other than his head, Major was used as a ranch and hunting mount in addition to pleasure riding. Well-trained and quick on his feet, the gelding was one of the few that would pack out a deer during a successful hunting season. The best that could be determined of his history was that he was purchased at one of the Fort Robinson dispersal sales following World War II. He made his way to Tooele, Utah, where he was acquired by the Livingston family who used him for several years until they were transferred to another army post.[63]

Munroe Tumlinson, of Cresson, Texas, got his start cowboying on West Texas ranches right after World War II. He remembered riding a number of Remount-bred horses, both colts and older saddle stock, during the late 1940s and early 1950s. Many of them were the results of two

Photograph courtesy U.S. Army

The McClellan saddle and equipment carried by a cavalry mount during the Punitive Expedition of 1916 into Mexico varied little from the Civil War until the mid-1940s when the Cavalry was "dehorsed."

decades of up-breeding by progressive ranchers and really showed the quality that improved blood would bring. He observed, "They were about as good a bunch of horses as a man could want. Big, stout, good legs and feet, and most of them had pretty good minds. They'd be good horses today."[64]

The dispersal of horses left the army with a huge inventory of McClellan saddles, bridles, halters, brushes and other equipment. These items were purchased in lots, at sealed bid, by dealers who in turn sold them to retailers. Through the late 1940s and early 1950s, countless advertisements appeared in horse magazines offering the equipment to the general public. For twenty years after the demise of the horse in the military, army issue bridles were a common sight among pleasure riders. One of the authors remembers seeing a barrel of army pelham bits priced at one dollar each in a store during the late 1940s.[65]

On October 21, 1946, the 142 army Thoroughbreds at the Aleshire Remount Depot were sold at auction. This sale included in-foal mares, barren mares, riding horses, yearlings, two year olds and three year olds. This dispersed all the horses in the breeding program at Aleshire. Stallions were transferred to either Fort Reno or Fort Robinson. Those horses represented a quarter of a century of Remount Service breeding.[66] On November 1, 1948, Aleshire was transferred to the Department of Agriculture for use as a beef cattle research farm.

Depot personnel also trained government-bred foals and young stock still on the depots. The future of the Remount might be in jeopardy, but the education of the colts could not wait. Immediately after birth the foal was rubbed dry with a coarse towel. For the first two or three days it was handled frequently to accustom it to men. When the mare was led to the paddock to graze, a helper walked alongside the foal, restraining it with his arm around the neck. A halter was introduced during the first week and used each time the dam and foal went to the paddock. By the end of two weeks, the pupil was used to being led and would follow a handler away from the mare for short periods of time. Regular brushing and handling of the feet and legs helped the foal became used to those activities. By the end of the first month, a foal had learned to trust men as well as acquiring the basic manners that a well-trained horse should have.[67]

Photograph courtesy Phil Livingston

Gold King, PHA Number 3427, PHBA Number 10,201, NQHBA Number 1,448, owned by Dave Cullison, Claremore, Oklahoma, was a popular sire in the late 1940s and 1950s. He was sired by London Pride (TB), a Remount stallion, and out of a Yellow Jacket Quarter Horse mare.

Two year olds were saddled and then lounged. After they were used to a saddle, they were ridden for a few minutes each day by experienced trainers. All the rider expected was for a colt to carry weight and learn to pay attention to the bridle reins. Training was at a walk or a slow trot and care was taken to not overwork the young animals.

Three year olds were ridden regularly, not only in the training arena but they also "went outside" in the big pastures. Jumping was not permitted as it was felt the activity put too much stress on growing bones.[68]

The monthly activity report from Fort Robinson, Nebraska, listed the training activities. The entire program was geared to instill trust and confidence in each young horse through constant, gentle handling.

1947—January: Twenty-four yearlings are taught to stand tied. Seventeen two year olds lounged and ridden under saddle daily, all for the first time. Nine three year olds lounged and ridden under saddle, three for the first time. Four depot-raised four-year-old stallions ridden daily and given some stock horse training. Fourteen issue stallions ridden and trained daily.

February: Twenty-three yearlings haltered, groomed, feet handled and taught to stand tied. Seventeen two year olds lounged and ridden daily. Nine three year olds lounged and ridden daily. Four depot-raised four-year-old stallions ridden daily and given stock horse training. Fifteen issue stallions ridden and trained daily.

March: Twenty-three yearling haltered, groomed, feet handled and taught to stand tied. Sixteen two year olds ridden daily. Nine three year olds ridden daily. Three depot-raised four-year-old stallions ridden daily and given stock horse training. Eight to fifteen issue stallions ridden and trained daily.

The regular program continued for the balance of 1947.[69]

The issue of stallions to civilian agents continued as it had for the past twenty-five years. The main difference was that there were not as many stallions going out to the public. A combination of the older animals dying off, a lack of suitable replacements and a growing interest in Quarter Horses, Palominos and Appaloosas had lessened the demand for Remount stallions. Animals registered in one of the breed associations were important to the rapidly growing pleasure and show horse world. While the Half-bred get of Remount stallions were outstanding under saddle, they were not eligible for participation in a horse show recognized by one of the breed associations.

On November 1, 1946, the Chief of Remount Colonel Fred L. Hamilton issued the following directive regarding breeding policies at the Depots:

1. In Remount Depot breeding operations hereafter, greater emphasis will be placed upon the production of foals suitable for development as country stallions.

2. In these breeding operations, depot commanders will be guided by the requirements of horsemen within the general geographic areas of individual depots.

3. It will be assumed that a selective breeding plan can and will be pursued for five generations.

4. As a matter of policy, the use of untried, unproven stallions at depots will be avoided.

5. Area stallions held at depots for conditioning, and not assigned as depot stallions, will not cover regularly assigned depot broodmares, except with authority from this office.

6. Selection of fillies for retention as broodmares and of colts for later

assignment as stallions will be based on temperament, durability, frugality, and nobility, and in that order.

7. More time will be devoted to progressively rigorous tests designed to determine the qualities mentioned in number 6, above. At a later date, if feasible, inter-depot tests will be arranged.

8. Depots.

a. **Pomona:** It will be the breeding objective of the Pomona QM Remount Depot to produce registered Arabian stallions for country-wide assignment. Operations will be conducted in accordance with the practices of the best commercial horse breeding and training establishments of all countries. A broodmare band of not to exceed fifty (50) registered Arabian mares will be maintained.

b. **Fort Robinson:** It will be the breeding objective of the Fort Robinson QM Remount Depot to produce registered Thoroughbred stallions for assignment to ranchmen. Young horses will be raised under natural conditions consistent with their gentleness, health and development at maturity. The methods of progressive ranchmen will be approximated, with constant attention to economic and sensible improvement therein. A broodmare band of not more than sixty (60) Thoroughbred mares will be maintained.

c. **Front Royal:** It will be the breeding objective of the Aleshire QM Depot, generally, to produce stallions suitable for assignment in the United States east of the Mississippi River. Operations will be conducted as indicted in 8 a., above. A broodmare band of not to exceed forty (40) Thoroughbred mares will be maintained.

d. **Fort Reno:** It will be the breeding objective of the Fort Reno QM Depot to raise Half-bred stallions suitable for assignment to ranchmen, and in those localities where, due to continuous use of purebred stallions, the horse population has become too refined for utilitarian purposes. Here, additional emphasis will be placed upon frugality and durability at the expense of nobility, and in approximating ranch conditions. In the matings, Thoroughbred stallions and pure Arabians will not be mated with pure Arabian mares and/or Thoroughbred mares. In general, "clean" bred individuals will appear in pedigrees in second or third generations only. Under no circumstances will draft stallions or mares be used in these blending operations. A broodmare band of not to exceed one hundred

(100) Half-bred mares and mares of various light breeds will be maintained. The Commanding Officer at Fort Reno will submit annual breeding lists to this office for approval, lists to be submitted as of 1 January, for the subsequent breeding season.

9. Instructions previously issued by this office that are in conflict with the above are hereby rescinded.[70]

It was obvious that Colonel Hamilton was attempting to place the Remount Breeding Plan in a position to serve the horsemen of America in a more effective manner.

On December 18, Colonel Hamilton authorized that the stud fee on Remount stallions would be raised from ten dollars (as it had been from the time the program was developed in 1921) to twenty dollars per mare for the 1947 season. This move was to offset the civilian agent's rising costs of maintaining the stallion.[71]

Even with the uncertain future of the Remount Service, army veterinarians carried on research programs at the depots. Their findings were to become a major part of America's equine health programs:

Periodic Ophthalmia (Moon Blindness): Army veterinarians at Front Royal (Aleshire), Virginia proved that the disease was related to diet. After three years of testing and experimentation, it was shown that 40 milligrams of Riboflavin mixed with a horse's feed successfully

Photograph courtesy Gordon Moore

Star Mark (TB), a Remount stallion, stands at Fort Robinson, Nebraska, during the 1940s.

controlled the disease.[72] Riboflavin is now mixed with prepared horse feeds to prevent the disease.

Identification: In late 1946, the Remount Service announced that tattooing a serial number on the inside of the upper lip, rather than a hot iron brand on the neck, would be utilized as a means of individual identification on incoming animals. The same combination of letters and numbers in a "Preston Brand" would be used. This process had been tested at the Pomona Remount Depot on several hundred horses.[73] This tattoo would not disfigure the animal as a brand on the neck did.

Both the Jockey Club and the Thoroughbred Racing Protective Bureau were enthusiastic of the "positive identification" by the process. The idea was presented to horsemen at Saratoga Springs, New York, on August 13 with a demonstration by

Colonel F. W. Koester, Chief of the Western Remount Division.[74] Lip Tattooing has been adopted as a means of permanent identification for Thoroughbreds, Racing Quarter Horses, Appaloosas and Paints for many years, another legacy of the Remount Service.

Although normal activities continued, the future of the Remount program was in doubt. Military leaders wanted out of the horse business and were lobbying strongly to transfer the breeding program to the Department of Agriculture. Since horses and mules were not considered necessary for military activities, the army saw no reason why the armed services should be responsible for any type of breeding program for the improvement of civilian horseflesh.

Late in 1946, information leaked out of Washington indicating that the Remount Service, the horses and all facilities would be transferred to the Department of Agriculture early the following year. This proposed move was not without opposition from Secretary of Agriculture, Clinton P. Anderson. He raised the objection that "his department did not have the trained personnel necessary for the administration of the Remount Service, which included the supervision and placing of several hundred stallions plus a considerable breeding program of its own." According to *The Blood-Horse* magazine, the transfer would include the military and civilian personnel on the depots.[80] This would provide experienced staffing for the breeding program until USDA employees could be trained.[75] In other words, it had been officially decided to completely divorce the army from the Horse Breeding Program. Once the transfer was in effect, the Department of Agriculture would have sole responsibility for the future of the program, and the Horse Breeding Program was not wanted by that branch of the government.

While the move to the Department of Agriculture was considered the solution to the Remount Service problem, the actual transfer had not been finalized by the middle of 1947. To keep the Remount from being immediately liquidated because of lack of operating funds, an emergency funding bill was implemented. An appropriation of $350,000 was passed by Congress to maintain the program through the current fiscal year. A bill to effect the transfer of the Remount had passed the House of Representatives on June 16, 1947, without a dissenting vote. In the Senate, a similar bill was snarled by Senator Thomas of Oklahoma. He had plans of his own for the Fort Reno facilities and held up the passage. The bill was eventually passed and made the transfer official.[76]

On April 21, 1948, Congress passed House Bill No. 3428, transferring the Remount Service from the United States Army to the Department of Agriculture. The transfer was to be effective July 1, 1948. The action marked the end of forty years of careful horse breeding by the United States Army. During that nearly half a century, the U.S. Remount Service stallions improved the general saddle stock of America as no civilian program could have.

In order to make the transition a smooth one, House Bill No. 3428 did provide that, "Until June 30, 1949, the Secretary of the Army may detail to the Department of Agriculture such military personnel, including officers in the Veterinary Corps of the Medical Department, as he may determine with the Secretary of Agriculture to be desirable to effectuate the purposes of this Act or to safeguard the interest of the United States."[77]

Photograph courtesy U.S. Army

*Formas, a Half-bred Remount stallion at Front Royal, Virginia, was sired by Lancelot (TB) and out of Formamint.

No record can be found of the Department of Agriculture making any attempt to train personnel for the Remount Program. The only individuals utilized during the short association with the USDA were those assigned by the Department of the Army.

Although governmental approach to the horse program changed, the American Remount Association continued to encourage the breeding of good light horses. That organization had worked closely with the army for more than two decades and was determined to fully cooperate with the Department of Agriculture. The Association felt that their efforts, combined with the army, had resulted in a definite improvement of light horses, along with developing a growing appreciation of the light horse as a utility and pleasure animal. The concept of the horse as a companion to man was also fostered by the Remount Association.[78]

Continuation of the American Remount Association publication, *The Horse*, as well as the operation of the three stud books—*The Half-Bred Stud Book, The Half-Arabian Stud Book* and *The Anglo-Arab Stud Book*—was part of the plan. The value of registration was no longer a question in the minds of horse breeders. In fact, it was becoming a necessity for the showing or sale of a horse.[79] The rapid growth of the American Quarter Horse Association, the Appaloosa Horse Club, the Arabian Horse Club and the Palomino Horse Breeders Association were proof of that. Potential buyers wanted documentation of the breeding behind their horses.

With the transfer of the U.S. Remount Service to the Department of Agriculture, the army ended a 4,000 year military partnership with the horse. The Assyrians conquered their world and were, in turn, succeeded by Alexander the Great. Rome fell because of effective barbarian cavalry. In the twelfth century the Mongol forces of Genghis Khan conquered China. All of those successful military campaigns were waged on horseback.

Frederick the Great won the majority of his decisive battles through the effective use of cavalry. The decline of Napoleon began when his cavalry met superior Russian mounted forces. Decisive victories in World War I hinged on mounted troops. For forty centuries, man had utilized the horse, and to a lesser degree, the mule, to help him as a warrior. Now that partnership was gone.[80]

Only three small units with horses and mules were left in the military service. Two of them were the Thirty-fifth Quartermaster Company (Pack) and Battery A of the Fourth Field Artillery Battalion (Pack), both stationed at Camp Carson, Colorado. The third was the Caisson Detail, headquartered at Fort Myer, Virginia, to be used for military funerals at Arlington National Cemetery. It carried on the tradition that a deceased warrior should go to his grave behind horses.

For nearly half a century the U.S. Remount Service successfully fulfilled its objectives. That was primarily because of the dedication of a small group of army officers and enlisted men. Those men knew that for the military to function properly it must have good horses and mules. They devoted their careers to that purpose, frequently living on sub-standard salaries and in less than comfortable quarters.

Immediately upon assuming responsibility for the Remount Service, the Department of Agriculture changed the name to "The Agricultural Remount Service." It was to be administered by a separate organizational unit within the Agricultural Research Administration headquartered in Washington, D.C. Operations would be carried out at the four field installations previously maintained by the army (Aleshire Remount Depot, Front Royal, Virginia; Fort Reno, Oklahoma; Fort Robinson, Nebraska and Kellogg's at Pomona, California).[81]

The USDA proposed, initially, to follow an operational plan similar to the army. A breeding program would be maintained at each installation to produce stallions of the necessary quality for the production of good light horses. Only when new blood was needed would stallions be purchased. Stallions would be issued to civilian agents for the breeding of utility horses on America's farms and ranches. The stud fee on these stallions would be twenty dollars.[82]

While the proposal from the USDA sounded reassuring, the assumption of new responsibility for the horse breeding program was viewed with apprehension by many horsemen. The Secretary of Agriculture was already on record as saying that his department did not want the program nor did it have the necessary trained personnel. He was much more interested in the production of food animals, grains and farm produce than in the continued improvement of America's horses. A number of government officials agreed with the army that the horse was obsolete, even in the face of a growing interest in pleasure riding in both rural and urban areas, and felt that no government assistance was necessary. The program was also viewed by many government employees and politicians as an unnecessary expense. There was also a segment of civilian breeders who were against any type of government horse program because of the competition factor with privately owned stallions.

Evidently, even while the announcements were being made for the continuance of the Remount Service, plans were being quietly laid for liquidation. In view of the sudden cancellation early in 1949, the decision was not an impulse move. The government did not operate that way. Perhaps, the Secretary of Agriculture decided that without army purchases the horse

Photograph courtesy Bette Thurston Mecham
Sun Fast (TB), a Remount stallion is shown with Agent Burt Thurston, Morgan, Utah. He sired many fine horses in the Inter-Mountain region of the American West.

program was not large enough to warrant the federal support that it had received in the past. He may also have been listening to those who felt that a government horse breeding program and the low stud fees received was unfair competition for private breeders. And, very possibly, he was primarily concerned with cutting the breeding program expenditures from his budget.

Amidst this controversy, the Remount Service continued to function. Stallions were sent out to civilian agents for the 1949 breeding season. Plans were made for matings at the depots and the training programs for young horses continued.[83]

On November 1, 1948, there was an indication of what the future held for the Remount Service. The Aleshire Remount Depot at Front Royal, Virginia, was suddenly closed insofar as horses were concerned. The property was to be converted into a beef cattle research center. It was to be operated in co-operation with the US Department of Agriculture and the Virginia Agricultural Experiment Station.[84]

Then, the plan to eliminate the Remount Breeding Program became public. Early in 1949 all civilian stallion agents received a letter from H. A. Marston, a research coordinator in the Department of Agriculture. He ordered that all government-owned stallions be readied for shipment back to the depots. They were to be assembled at either Fort Robinson or Fort Reno and then sold at public auction. Stallions, mares and young stock at the depots would be included in those sales. Agents were ordered to stand by for shipping instructions. The sales were to be held later in the spring, right in the middle of breeding season. Those dates would negate the agreements with horsemen to breed mares to government-owned stallions.[85]

There was an immediate protest from agents. Angry letters were sent to members of Congress, equine magazines and government officials protesting the move. No public announcement of the decision to quickly liquidate the Remount Service was made but the reason for recalling the stallions was clear. Consolidating the stallions for sale was easily seen as complete liquidation and the immediate elimination of the program. Presumably, the Department of Agriculture wished to postpone public protest as long as possible—preferably until after liquidation. This was the same tactic that the State Department had attempted earlier in the move to return the German, Austrian and Hungarian horses to Europe.

Colonel Thomas J. Johnson (Retired), Executive Secretary of the American Remount Association, immediately arranged a meeting with the Secretary of Agriculture and the Secretary of the Budget to protest the move. He pointed out the following:

> There are 403 Remount stallions scattered across the United States in the hands of agents, plus 51 others at the Remount Depots, for a total 454. At the Depots there were approximately 100 useful broodmares still considered useful for breeding, along with nearly as many of their younger offspring.
>
> Concentration of the stallions in the two depots would be an expensive process in itself, and the sale of such a large number at the same time would certainly make the individual prices very low. It is doubtful whether the amount received would equal the expense of shipment and sale.[86]

During this meeting, Colonel Johnson read almost 200 letters from agents protesting the order to the officials. Only five of those letters expressed any doubt that the Remount Program was still definitely needed by America's horsemen. One agent in New York protested in his letter that the stallion that he was standing was "twenty-one years old, but still useful, and has gained local distinction as a sire of good horses. Shipping him to Fort Reno would simply be an expensive way to destroy him."[87]

Colonel Johnson also stated that if the Government-owned stallions were removed, they would be succeeded by inferior horses, or with none at all. The economic loss would far outweigh the small cost of maintaining the breeding program. During the thirty years of the Remount Service, there had been a tremendous improvement in America's working and pleasure horses. To discontinue the program would sacrifice most of that improvement.

In an effort to salvage the breeding program, Colonel Johnson suggested a plan of action to the Department of Agriculture and the Director of the Budget. In it he made the following points:

1. With a horseless Army, the liquidation of Remount activities, other than the stallion program, was probably a necessary move.

2. The stallion program could be maintained, and at a moderate cost, to continue the contributions to America's light horses. That program should be a function of the Department of Agriculture.

3. The most expensive part of the Remount operation was the maintenance of the depot breeding programs. The estimated cost to produce a suitable Remount stallion at one of the depots was at least $6,000.

4. The necessary replacement stallions (approximately forty per year) could be purchased off of race tracks for half that figure. If the depot breeding program was discontinued, a much smaller staff could handle the operation.

5. The estimated annual cost for continuing the purchase, maintenance, placement, inspection, rotation, etc. of stallions was $220,000.[88]

Both the Secretary of Agriculture and the Director of the Budget turned a deaf ear to Colonel Johnson's arguments. The horses were to be sold as quickly as possible and the facilities utilized for beef cattle research.

Senator Wayne Morris, of Oregon, stepped into the picture again. He had earlier been instrumental in stopping the shipment of the Prizes of War back to Europe. The Senator arranged a meeting on April 5, 1949, which was attended by Secretary of Agriculture Charles F. Brannan, Edward J. Overby of the Department of Agriculture, Chief of Remount Colonel R. E. Ireland and about thirty Congressmen and Senators. He was unable to halt the liquidation of the Remount Service but he did convince the officials to set the date back to October 31, 1949, rather than the end of May. That would give civilian agents the opportunity to complete the breeding season before returning the stallions for sale.[89]

A memorandum from Senator Morris, dated April 13, reported the April 5 conference in *The Blood-Horse:*

We found the Secretary very cooperative in agreeing to modify the Department's plans for liquidating the Remount Service this year. He advised us that he would be willing, subject to the granting of the necessary deficiency funds for administrative purposes, to leave the stallions in the hands of the agents for the breeding season with the understanding that they would be liquidated on or before October 31, 1949.

He agreed further that the agents of stallions should have first opportunity to purchase them upon a basis which would take into account the equities which their custody of the stallions had created in them, save and except in the case of those few stallions of exceptional value. In respect to the latter group of stallions it was generally agreed that the Secretary of Agriculture was right when he pointed out to the group that these few stallions, such as Nordic (*Nordlicht?) for example, should be disposed of by either competitive sealed bid or by open public auction, thus assuring all prospective purchasers in the country an equal opportunity to bid on these famous stallions.

On the other hand it was agreed that many of the stallions in the Remount Service should remain, if possible, in communities where they have been stationed, in many instances for several years, and that the agents who have gone to considerable expense and effort in handling these stallions should have the opportunity to buy in direct negotiations with the government.

It is to be understood that if the stallions are allowed to remain in the hands of the agents for this breeding season with final dispersal of them to occur on or before October 31, 1949, the Department of Agriculture will proceed with the disposal of broodmares and colts up to and including two year olds, by June 30 of this year. Announcement of the exact details of such a liquidation program will be issued by the Department of Agriculture in due course of time.[90]

The announcement was also made that Fort Robinson and Fort Reno would be converted into agricultural experiment stations. Pomona (Kellogg's Arabian Horse Farm) was to be returned to the University of California.[91]

The Department of Agriculture wasted no time in scheduling sales of government-owned horses. It was almost as if the USDA wished to get the project liquidated, allow the resulting clamor from the nation's horsemen to die down, and go on about its business. Agents who wished to purchase the stallion, or stallions, which they were standing could negotiate the sale directly with the Department of Agriculture. This was in keeping with the agreement arranged by Senator Morris.

H. W. Marston, research co-ordinator with the USDA wrote: "If the present custodian is not interested in purchasing the stallion, or if his offer is unreasonable, the stallion will be disposed of either by means of sealed bids in his present location, will be brought in for one of the auction sales, or sold at a public sales yard."[92]

The agent standing the stallion at the time had first opportunity to purchase the animal. It is very probable that a few Remount stallions standing at isolated ranches "died" shortly after the directive to return them to the depots was received. The USDA wanted to dispose of the stallions, but if notified of the animal's death, unless it was one of the few extremely valuable ones, would probably not go to the trouble of checking it out too closely.

Photograph courtesy Western Livestock Journal

Trolley Car (TB), a U.S. Remount Service stallion, stood at the W. B. Morris Ranch, San Lucas, California.

Following the close of breeding season, agents not wishing to purchase stallions would return the animals to the assigned depot at government expense. The first two sales (Fort Reno and Fort Robinson) were held immediately after the close of breeding season. They were to liquidate the animals on the depots and included stallions, broodmares, riding horses and young stock.

On May 25, Fort Reno, Oklahoma, one hundred fifty-four stallions, broodmares, yearlings and two year olds from both Fort Reno and Pomona were offered at auction. The group included: eighty-one Thoroughbreds, twelve unregistered Thoroughbreds (European), twelve Arabians, thirty-six Half-breds and one Lippizaner. Fifty-four horses sold for an average of $850.97 per head. The average price for Thoroughbreds was $775; Arabians $1,467.70 and Half-Breds for $660.41. The animals which did not sell would be included in a later offering.

Among the Arabians offered was *Witez II. He was purchased by E. E. Hurlbutt and Fred Arth of California for $8,100. Hurlbutt later bought Arth's interest in *Witez II. The bay stallion was to establish an Arabian dynasty during his long career at stud.[93]

Romolino (TB), by Ariel, was sold to J. W. R. Myers, Dover, Oklahoma, for $1,675. As noted earlier, Romolino was bred by the King Ranch and stood there during the World War II years. In 1946, the King Ranch sold Romolino to the U.S. Remount Service and continued to stand him until he was called in for resale. Some of the other stallions were sold for as little as $250 per head.[94]

Other Thoroughbreds which sold included Excite, by Stimulus out of Arena by St. James, who went to Watt Hardin for $2,525; Wahrika, who sold to L. W. Knudsen for $2,350; and Bramaxo for whom Frank Brophy paid $2,900. The volume buyer was H. H. Munday, Pawhuska, Oklahoma.[95]

On June 3, Fort Robinson, Nebraska, the offering of 129 Thoroughbreds and Half-Breds included stallions, broodmares, yearlings, two year olds and trained saddle horses took place. One hundred twenty-six horses sold for a total of $91,425, averaging $725 per head.

Stallions ranged in price from the $1,200, paid by M. N. Moran of Buffalo, New York, for the unraced Double Swath; $700 from the Pitchfork Land and Cattle Company, Guthrie, Texas, for Southern Gent; down to the $125 spent by H. M. Wallace, Kennel, South Dakota, for Reno Kaffir.[96]

Gid R. Thompson topped the sale paying $3,500 for Indel and Dick McKay successfully bid $3,400 for Tarry Long. H. H. Munday, Pawhuska, Oklahoma, was the volume purchaser taking ten head.[97]

Other purchasers included: A. W. Howard, Lee Aldwell, L. M. Mertz, J. M. Huffington, Raul Orona, H. W. Davis, Henry Culpepper, C. A. Ditmore, Henry Bossman, Ronnell McDaniel, Pitchfork Land and Cattle Company, Edmond Keys, Col. J. M. Adamson and the Hunt Ranch, all from Texas.[98]

The fall sales, primarily of stallions returned by agents, were all grouped closely together during October. The USDA was evidently in a hurry to close down the project.

On October 18, Front Royal, Virginia, among the stallions offered were Auftakt, Barred Umber, Chattillion, Chilly Beau, *Nordlicht, Preisrichter, Paychic, Rival 2nd, Spanish Ghost and Spanish Jean.[99] Although not registered with the Jockey Club, *Nordlicht brought $20,300 from a syndicate of Virginia breeders.[100] *Nordlicht was later purchased and exported back to Europe by a group of French breeders.

On October 21, Fort Robinson, Nebraska, included among the stallions offered for sale were Crescent Pole, Lutaf (Arabian), Open Door, Prince Brideau, Reefer, St. Mirth, Sax Player, Soldier Blues and Wealthy Saint.[101] Total number of horses and prices paid not available.

On October 25, Pomona, California, the stallions listed in the catalog for sale included Athanasius (TB), Stimjul (TB), Taj Akbar (TB) and the seven Arabians, Bari, Damascus, Halanda, Jedran, Lotnik, Pomona Abd El Kadir and Rabiyas.[102] The total number of horses and the prices paid for them, is not available.

On October 28, Fort Reno, Oklahoma, among the stallions offered were: Basalt, Battlewick, Bergkristall, Buster, Jungheer, Kaiserstuhl, Leibwachter, Marcabala,

Moosehead, Plowshare, Rasakkla (Arabian), Recke, Reno Lee, Tagfalter and Valdina Dandy.[103] Total number of horses and the prices paid is not available.

As Colonel Johnson had predicted, the prices paid for the Remount stallions, mares and young stock was low. There were too many animals offered at each sale, and potential buyers were well aware that the USDA was liquidating the program. Almost any bid was accepted. Only a few outstanding individuals, primarily those Thoroughbreds imported from Europe following World War II, sold for prices equal to what American-bred Thoroughbreds were bringing. A number of the older Thoroughbred stallions were acquired for much less than the stud fee paid to produce them.

In spite of the claims made by the Department of Agriculture about continuing the stallion program, the US Remount Service became history on October 31, 1949. For nearly a half century it had survived economic depression, a declining use of the end product, attack from various segments of the military, government and civilian population and a cost-cutting Congress. During those years the efforts of a dedicated group of men had given the United States Army a cavalry mount second to none in the world. While the Remount was no more, the improvement that it made to America's horses would live on for many years.

Chapter 7: Sources and Notes

1. Colonel Fred L. Hamilton, "The Remount Story," *The Western Horseman* (January 1951): 44–45.
2. Ibid., 45.
3. Ibid., 45–46.
4. Colonel Fred L. Hamilton, "The Remount Story," *The Western Horseman* (February 1951): 12.
5. Information from a visit to the Cavalry Museum, Fort Riley, Kansas, by the authors in 1992.
6. Monique and Hans Dossenback, *The Noble Horse,* Part II (New York: Crown Publishers), 171.
7. Hamilton, "The Remount Story" (February 1951): 13. Also Helen Addison Howard, "Germany's Captured Superhorses," *The Western Horseman* (May 1977): 50–52, 146–151.
8. Gladys Brown Edwards, *The Arabian as a War Horse to Show Horse,* (Denver, Colorado: Arabian Horse Trust, 1980), 112.
9. Ibid. The rescues of these horses from advancing Russian forces, and the efforts made to save them by German horsemen and American soldiers, are told in numerous books and articles. One of the best known incidents is the story of the White Lippizaners of the Spanish Riding School in Vienna, Austria, and the breeding stock at the farm. For the latter, General Patton sent a tank-guarded convoy into Czechoslovakia to move the animals and prevent the Russian army from taking them.
10. Hamilton, "The Remount Story" (February 1951): 12.
11. Ibid., 13.
12. "The Thoroughbreds From Germany," *The Blood-Horse* (November 9, 1946): 1174–1179.
13. Hamilton, "The Remount Story" (February 1951): 13.
14. Ibid., 14.
15. Ibid., 12.
16. Ibid., 13–14.
17. Colonel Fred L. Hamilton: "The Remount Clarifies Its Case For Registry of German Horses," *The Blood-Horse* (February 8, 1947): 398.
19. Ibid., 405.
20. Hamilton, "The Remount Story" (February 1951): 40.
21. "Army Importations," *The Blood-Horse* (November 10, 1945): 973.
22. Hamilton, "The Remount Story" (February 1951): 40.
23. Edwards, *Arabian as a War Horse to Show Horse,* 112.
24. "Army Importations," *The Blood-Horse* (November 10, 1945): 973.
25. Ibid.
26. "The Horses from Germany," *The Blood-Horse* (December 1, 1945): 1198.
27. "Remount Shows Captured Horses," *The Blood-Horse* (April 13, 1946): 918.
28. Mary Jane Parkinson, *The Kellogg Arabian Horse Ranch: The First Fifty Years* (Pomona, California: The Arabian Horse Club of Southern California, 1975), 288.
29. Hamilton, "The Remount Story" (February 1951): 40.
30. "More Horses from Germany," *The Blood-Horse* (July 27, 1946): unnumbered copy.
31. Ibid. Also see, "QMC Shipping 300 Blooded Horses," *The Cattleman* (September 1946): unnumbered copy.
32. Hamilton, "The Remount Story" (February 1951): 13.
33. Ibid., 12.
34. "Recognition Refused German Imports," *The Blood-Horse* (November 9, 1946): 1024.
35. Ibid.
36. Ibid.
37. "The Remount Clarifies Its Case for Registry of German Horses," *The Blood-Horse* (February 8, 1947): unnumbered copy.
38. Ibid.
39. Ibid.
40. Ibid.
41. "The Case for the German Horses," *The Blood-Horse* (September 18, 1948): 689. The authors have been unable to find documentation recording the outcome of this court case.
42. Hamilton, "The Remount Story" (February 1951): 41.
43. "Hungarian Rhapsody, With Russian Influence," *The Blood-Horse* (October 25, 1945): unnumbered copy.
44. Ibid.
45. Ibid.
46. Ibid.
47. Ibid.
48. Helen Addison Howard, "Germany's Captured Superhorses," *The Western Horseman* (May 1977): 148.
49. Ibid.
50. Ibid.
51. Ibid.
52. "Old Story Revived," *The Blood-Horse* (October 8, 1949): 64.

53. "Sale at Front Royal," *The Blood-Horse* (October 26, 1946): 1024.

54. Monthly Information Letter (Form No. 3-SPQOR-4-F) Fort Robinson, Nebraska (1 March 1944; 1 April 1944; 1 October 1944; 1 November 1944).

55. "The Remount and the Army," *The Blood-Horse* (March 30, 1946): 798.

56. Ibid.

57. "Sons of Ariel in Remount Group," *The Quarter Horse* (October 1947): unnumbered copy.

58. Monthly Information Letter (Form No. 3-SPQOR-4-F) Fort Robinson, Nebraska (1 December 1945; 4 January 1946; 1 February 1946; 1 March 1946; 1 April 1946).

59. A. J. "Jack" Campbell, Douglas, Wyoming, interview with Phil Livingston, July 1993.

60. Jane Reed Benson, "Thirty-two Years in the Mule Business" folder of The USDA/Forest Service, 1977.

61. Robert J. Marik, "Reno US P254," *Western Horseman* (September 1969): 38.

62. Letter from D. L. Smith, Claremore, Oklahoma, dated September 20, 1946. Letter and photo courtsey of Stroming family, January 2, 1995, via Jim Crocker, Fort Worth, Texas.

63. Recollections of Phil Livingston.

64. Monroe Tumlinson, Cresson, Texas, conversation with Phil Livingston, September 1996.

65. Recollections by both authors.

66. Sale Catalog; Aleshire Remount Depot, Front Royal, Virginia, October 21, 1946.

67. D. Todd Gresham, "Training Remount Foals," *The Western Horseman* (May–June 1945): unnumbered copy.

68. Gordon Moore, Crawford, Nebraska, letter to Phil Livingston, October 30, 1996.

69. Summary of Training Activities at Fort Robinson, Nebraska 1947, mimeographed Government sheet.

70. General Information Letter (QMGOR 454.L), November 12, 1946, mimeographed Government sheet.

71. General Information Letter (QMGOR 454.1), December 18, 1946, mimeographed Government sheet.

72. "Periodic Ophthalmia Control Achieved," *The Blood-Horse* (January 4, 1946): 1314. Also, Brig. Gen. R. A. Kelser, "This is not Speculation," *The Blood-Horse* (March 16, 1946): 685.

73. Col. F. W. Koester, "New Army Method of Branding," *The Blood-Horse* (June 1, 1948): 1261–1262, 1282.

74. "Lip Tattoo Branding," *The Blood-Horse* (August 17, 1946): 503.

75. "Remount Services to Move," *The Blood-Horse* (December 21, 1946): 1739.

76. "Remount Division Status," *The Blood-Horse* (August 16, 1947): unnumbered copy.

77. Public Law 494, 80th Congress, Bulletin #18, 7 June 1948.

78. "Remount Group's Plans for Future," *The Blood-Horse* (June 12, 1948): 563–66.

79. Ibid.

80. "The Last Chapter: Wherein War Loses Another Glory," *The Blood-Horse* (April 15, 1948): unnumbered copy.

81. "The Agricultural Remount Service," *The Cattleman* (June 1948): 40.

82. Ibid.

83. "An Expensive Way to Cut the Budget," *The Blood-Horse* (March 5, 1949): unnumbered copy.

84. "Remount Plans New Schedule," *The Blood-Horse* (May 14, 1949): unnumbered copy.

85. "An Expensive Way to Cut the Budget," *The Blood-Horse* (March 5, 1949): unnumbered copy.

86. Ibid.

87. Ibid.

88. Ibid.

89. "Remount Plans New Schedule," *The Blood-Horse* (May 14, 1949): 276.

90. Ibid.

91. Ibid.

92. "Plans for Final Remount Sale," *The Blood-Horse* (October 1, 1949): 14.

93. Sale Catalog, mimeographed copy of sheets. Also, *Arabian Horse World* (June 1949): unnumbered copy.

94. Sale Catalog, mimeographed copy of sheets.

95. "Remount Service Holds Two Horse Sales," *The Cattleman* (August, 1949): unnumbered copy.

96. Ibid

97. Ibid

98. Ibid

99. "Plans for Final Remount Sales," *The Blood-Horse* (October 1, 1949): 14.

100. Ibid.

101. "Plans for Final Remount Sales," 27.

102. Ibid.

103. Ibid.

West Point cadets lead their mascot, the Army Mule, onto the field before an Army–Navy football game on November 30, 1912.

CHAPTER 8

WRAPPING UP THE LOOSE ENDS

"Long have I advocated the retention of at least one full-strength mounted cavalry division, equipped with pack artillery (75mm, mountain howitzer). Such a cavalry division can operate in any weather, in any country, in any climate, and in any terrain. Let us Remount the First Cavalry Division and return it to the United States to serve as a nucleus for expansion, if necessary, or for immediate action in an emergency."

General Jonathan M. Wainwright[1]

While horses and mules were no longer utilized by the military, many ranking army officers were strong in their opposition to complete dispersal. During World War II, cavalry action had been limited but pack transportation proved too useful to be ignored. The fact that the animals could not be easily and quickly transported across the world no longer held true. That was solved by the advent of large transport airplanes and that the technique had been proven in the CBI Theater of Operations. On land, trucks and trailers could rapidly move the animals as far as roads were available, then the unit could unload and function effectively in rough country. These men were convinced that not only would a standing unit be available in case of need, and as a training school for increased personnel and animals, but it would have strong public relations value. A trained cavalry unit for public display would be as valuable to the army as the Anheuser-Busch Brewing Company Budweiser Clydesdale teams were to a civilian firm.[2]

The pleas for retention of some form of cavalry and pack artillery/supply from such generals as Dwight D. Eisenhower, Omar N. Bradley, John P. Lucas and Jonathan

Wainwright fell on deaf ears to post-war leadership. To them, trucks, armor, helicopters and the air force represented modern warfare.[3]

Even though the American army had discarded the horse and mule, other nations had not. A number of the small "brush fire" wars in mountainous foreign countries still depended upon animal transport. Since the threat of a Communist takeover in many of those countries was very real, the American Department of State provided military aid (military advisors, supplies, equipment, weapons) to Greece, Turkey, Nationalist China, Korea, etc. In two instances, that aid included American pack mules, saddles and other equipment.

At the time the Remount was disbanded in 1948, as mentioned earlier, the United States had a military foreign aid program in progress. America agreed to supply Greece with 10,000 pack mules for use against the Russian-backed Communist takeover. The country was mountainous, troops were fighting above the vehicle supply line, trucks and jeeps were in short supply and supplies could only be packed in. It was a classic need for pack transportation.

Military buyers were sent out to purchase mules. The army detailed soldiers to handle and process the animals. Arrangements were made with the Department of Agriculture to utilize the animal processing facilities at Fort Reno,

Photograph courtesy U.S. Army

Hambone, a famous U.S. Army mule, is shown at his retirement from the service in 1950, at the time of the de-activation of the 4th Field Artillery Battalion (Pack) and the 35th Quartermaster (Pack) with Sergeant Cnossen, Fort Carson, Colorado.

Oklahoma. By the time the program ended and military personnel left Fort Reno in December of 1949, approximately 10,000 American mules had been purchased, processed and shipped to Greece.[4]

In 1951, another military aid program was inaugurated, this time to help Turkey. Again, the Army utilized the facilities at Fort Reno. The army's eighty-man 9182nd Quartermaster Technical Service Unit, headed by Colonel M. W. Zwicker, was able to process and ship 806 animals every forty-five days to the port of New Orleans, where they were loaded aboard ship. The program ended in May 1954, with approximately 12,500 horses and mules going to Turkey.[5]

An agreement was made between the Department of the Army and the Department of Agriculture during the fiscal year of 1955 to place the animal processing facilities at Fort Reno on a standby basis. It would be available in case of another foreign aid program.[6] However, such a foreign aid program was never again attempted. By 1990, the processing facilities and much of the Fort Reno Depot, had crumbled to the ground.

Major Fred Burke, one of the purchasing officers for the second foreign aid program, suggested that the Remount program be continued with a different approach. Both Fort Robinson, Nebraska, and Fort Reno, Oklahoma, were self-sufficient as far as raising feed. The Remount Service would not only raise horses and mules there for limited American military consumption, but maintain a cadre of trained personnel to care for them. A pool of animals and experienced personnel would be available if the need arose. The excess animals could be marketed to both national and international consumers.[7] There is no record that the idea was ever considered.

America's involvement in Korea against Red China, 1949–1954, again demonstrated the need for pack mules. The country was mountainous with few roads, hot in summer, cold and wet during the winter. In many places it was all but impossible for vehicular supply. No animals were available from the United States but American troops utilized every usable horse or mule captured from Red Chinese or North Korean forces.[8]

In May of 1951, North of Kumyanjung Ni, the well-known Wolfhound Regiment had thirty-three mules in one machine gun unit. There were many others in the same area. Troops were reluctant to reveal where the captured animals were located for fear they would be denied their use. During the drive north from Seoul, the First Cavalry Division moved their pack animals in 6 x 6 two-and-one-half-ton trucks, just as had been done in Italy and France half a decade before.[9]

In 1951 the third Infantry Division captured a former American mule from Red Chinese Forces. The mule, nicknamed "Francis," carried Preston brand 08K0 on his neck and US on the left shoulder. He was one of the animals which had been shipped to Burma during World War II. The well-traveled mule made the journey over the Himalayan Mountains into China and the Nationalist Army. He was later commandeered by the Red Chinese Army for service in Korea. There, he was again acquired by American troops.[10] Francis was later the prototype of a mule starring in American movies and followed by a television series, *Francis the Talking Mule.*

Another instance of American military use of pack animals in Korea was Reckless. The little Korean mare, acquired by the Fifth Marine Recoilless Rifle Platoon, became a national heroine after a *Saturday Evening Post* article was written about her. In one day during the battle of Panmunjon-Vegas, Reckless carried 386 rounds (over 9,000 pounds) of ammunition in fifty-one trips, a total of thirty-five miles, in spite of injuries. She made all of the trips without a handler, going from the munitions dump to the firing line. The

Photograph courtesy A. J. 'Jack' Campbell
A Remount sale is in process at Fort Robinson following World War II. Horses were disposed of at auction. A. J. 'Jack' Campbell is at center holding a staff. He purchased many Remount animals for resale.

marines thought so much of Reckless that she was promoted to sergeant (later staff sergeant) and eventually taken to the United States. Reckless lived out her life at the Camp Pendleton Marine Base in California as the mascot of the First Marine Division.[11]

There were numerous instances of American military use of pack animals during the Korean campaign.[12] Korea was also the proving ground of the "new Army mule"—the helicopter. The versatile craft could supply hard-to-reach areas, perform scouting operations and was used to fly out wounded soldiers. The problem was that inclement weather would ground a helicopter, and a pack mule just kept right on plodding through fog, black nights, mud, snow and sleet. Helicopters also needed level landing space while a mule could negotiate a steep, rocky hill.

Meanwhile, in May 1953, the Jockey Club yielded to the pressures of American horsemen. The governing body of American Thoroughbred racing agreed to finally register several of the prominent German Thoroughbred stallions brought to America following World War II, along with their get which had been issued racing permits. The following statement was issued:

> At a meeting of the stewards of The Jockey Club held on May 14, 1953, it was decided that *Nordlicht, *Manurai, *Athanasius and *Taj Akbar, and their foals for which racing permits have been issued, will be registered in the *American Stud Book* if their owners shall comply with the usual requirements of its Registration Department.
>
> It now appears that, after an extensive investigation had been made in Germany and elsewhere, the French Stud Book Commission decided to accept the *German Stud Book* as properly kept through 1943, and that *Nordlicht (foaled in 1941), having been sent from this country to France, has now been registered in the *French Stud Book*. He is eligible for registration in the *American Stud Book*.

*Samurai (foaled in 1937) and *Athanasius (foaled in 1931) were registered prior to 1944 in the *German Stud Book* and are in the same position as *Nordlicht, except that they have not been sent to France and there registered. However, the Stewards felt that it would cause unnecessary trouble and expense if the owners of *Samurai and *Athanasius should be required to send them to France. *Taj Akbar has been registered in the *English Stud Book* which is recognized by The Jockey Club, and the original reasons for refusing his registration are considered to be no longer controlling.

Liebwachter cannot be registered because he was foaled in 1944, in respect to which year the *German Stud Book,* because of the destruction of the supporting records, is not acceptable. He was recently sent to France for registration in their book but did not qualify. No racing permits have been issued to his foals as he was imported into the United States as a two year old and had no racing record.[13]

With the Remount Service gone and the government stallions eliminated from competing with privately owned animals, the Jockey Club could finally afford to recognize the truly top individuals and their get. Of course, by the time that the move was made, those few stallions were in private hands and could not benefit the general horse population.

The final animal pack units in the United States Army survived until 1956. Headquartered at Camp Carson, Colorado, were the Fourth Field Artillery Battalion (Pack) and the Thirty-fifth Quartermaster Pack Troop. Both units, the mules and a small number of horses were retained for training purposes to insure a nucleus for rapid expansion in case of emergency. On February 15, 1956, the units were deactivated and the animals sold or transferred to other government agencies,

Photograph courtesy U.S. Army

Hambone "troops the line" past a corral of artillery pack mules, during his retirement ceremony from the U.S. Army in 1950. The artillery last used mules in 1955, Fort Carson, Colorado.

including the Forest Service and the National Park Service. Following the deactivation, Camp Carson was designated as a training ground for a helicopter field artillery unit.[14]

At the deactivation ceremonies, a final review attended by more than 3,000 persons was held at Camp Carson. It honored the long service of the army mule. The last of the army mules, 9YII "Hambone," was mustered out with a suitable ceremony. In addition to representing the army mule, Hambone was honored for his abilities as a "jumper" in horse show competition. The citation read, in part:

> Special commendation is due to you for your extraordinary abilities displayed in jumping events, and for the record of having never lost a mule jumping contest, as well as your phenomenal success in bettering all except the first place winner in a competition with horses at Camp Carson in 1950.
>
> In addition, your exhibition jumping at the International Stock Show in Chicago in 1950, at the Pikes Peak Rodeo in 1954, and at other equestrial functions has been a credit to yourself and the United States Army.
>
> In view of these outstanding achievements, your refusals to perform such menial tasks as carrying a pack and your refraining from associating with other mules are hereby recognized as privileges specifically accorded to you.
>
> Presented at Fort Carson, Colorado, the 15th day of December, 1956.
>
> H. P. Storke, Major General, USA, Commanding[15]

The deactivation of the pack units at Camp Carson left the army with only the mule at West Point Military Academy. The animal served as a mascot and was displayed at sporting events or parades as a symbol of the army. Trotter, No. 583R, a four-gated mule, was transferred from Camp Carson, Colorado, on December 15, 1956, to West Point to assume his new duties. Trotter was just one in a long line of mules who have served as the mascot at West Point. In view of the long service the dependable animal has given the army, it is fitting that a representative act as the visual symbol to the public. A certificate of recognition of his long military service was read during the final review at Camp Carson. It read, in part:

> The presentation of this certificate on the occasion of the deactivation of army mules is accompanied with the firm hope that your retirement will not be plagued with those horrors which, in times past, have caused you to unburden yourself rather hurriedly of riders and other equipment—a glimpse of either of those hideous devices, the umbrella or the bicycle.
>
> Presented at Camp Carson, Colorado, this 15th day of December, 1956.
>
> H. P. Storke, Major General, USA, Commanding[16]

Upon completion of the citations, both mules were returned to their positions next to the reviewing stand. A helicopter, representing the future, flew in front of the stand,

and dipped the fuselage to pay homage to the army mule. The massed units passed in review one last time. As part of the final review, an animal-drawn buckboard carried several old-time sergeants. Following the review, enlisted men mounted on horses brought the colors and guidons before the commanding general. With due ceremony, those flags were lowered and cased, symbolizing the deactivation of both units. Thus, the army said farewell to the dependable mule.[17]

Some military posts maintained a small stable of mounts for recreational use by the soldiers and their families. The stable in Nanking, China, during the late 1940s (operated by the Officers Moral Endeavor Association) was a former Japanese Cavalry barn and the mounts were captured Japanese horses.[18] At Camp Wolters and Fort Hood, both in Texas, horses were kept for the off-duty enjoyment of the military. At Fort Hood, the stables remained open until the end of the Vietnam War in 1968.[19] Other army posts kept saddle horses as well.

When the Remount Service was dispersed, interest in registering Half-bred foals declined. Other equine registries and breeds had become popular (Quarter Horse, Appaloosa, Palomino and Paint) and all had

Photograph courtesy U.S. Army

Officers "troop the line" in an 1890s buggy at Fort Riley, Kansas, 1961.

serious promotion to push interest and registrations. Because there was no promotion, many breeders believed that the Half-Bred Registry had died with the Remount. Only a few, primarily those concerned with producing hunters and polo ponies, continued to use Thoroughbred stallions on grade mares and register the foals.

In 1961 Mrs. Frances Hurlbutt—she and her husband owned the well-known Arabian stallion *Witez II—took over the registry and moved the office to Burbank, California. The name was changed to "The Half-Thoroughbred Registry" to more accurately denote what it was. Almost single-handedly she sparked renewed interest in the Half-Thoroughbred horse, the association, and built up registrations. A number of outstanding hunter-jumpers, polo ponies and stock horses were registered, and for a number of years the association maintained a steady, if not impressive, growth.[20] Interest in the Half-Thoroughbred Association gradually declined during the 1960s as the Quarter Horse boomed in popularity. The American Remount (Half-Thoroughbred) Association was eventually moved to Perris, California. An association with similar aims, *The Part Thoroughbred Stud Book,* was formed and headquartered at Middleburg, Vermont.[21]

Among Thoroughbred-cross horses that achieved renown during the 1950s and 1960s were the show jumper Little Mac, winner of the National United States Equestrian Team Trials in 1953; Candy, a paint that Nancy Sheppard of Globe, Arizona, trick-rode at numerous rodeos; and the well-known stock horse, La Mancha, ridden and shown by trainer and author Charles O. Williamson.[22]

While animal pack transportation was not a planned part of America's involvement in Vietnam, U.S. Special Forces did make use of the time-tested mode of supply. In 1959–1960, Colonel Richard F. Krueger, a U.S. Army military adviser, was in charge of supplying troops in the dense, jungle-covered highlands. He experimented with pack animals. With no mules available, he used small Asian horses and old French-made packsaddles. The colonel claimed that the pack trains were used only on training maneuvers, but pack transportation would have been effective "if it had only been given a chance to prove itself."[23]

Photograph courtesy U.S. Army

The "Old Trooper" Cavalry Monument, Fort Riley, Kansas, was dedicated on a cold rainy day in 1959.

Beginning in 1958, Special Forces successfully used pack animals extensively and effectively for patrol operations in the wooded plains and highlands of Central Vietnam. Trained in unconventional warfare, the Special Forces soldiers followed the footsteps of their grandfathers who had scrounged pack animals and equipment in North Africa, Sicily and Italy, Burma, India and Korea in two previous wars. Naturally, advocates of motorized and air supply kept quiet about use of the "antiquated" four-legged transportation system.[24]

The attempted Russian military takeover of Afghanistan (1979–1987) once again demonstrated the need of animal transportation in rugged country. Afghan fighters, based in Pakistan, supplied forces in their homeland by using pack horses and mules. The animals carried arms and ammunition, rockets, missiles and supplies over the rugged mountain passes that reached 18,000 feet above sea level, floundering through snow and mud. Many animals were lost, not only through overwork, lack of feed and exhaustion but to falls from slippery rocks and Russian artillery or helicopter attacks.[25]

One American, Hub Rease of Gallatin, Tennessee, volunteered to help with the decreasing supply of pack animals. In 1987 he assembled and shipped approximately 1,500 pack mules to Pakistan where they were given to Afghan guerrillas. The animals were transported by air, in 747 aircraft.

Among the supplies that the American mules packed in were Stinger missiles and launchers. In the hands of Afghan guerrillas, they helped clear the air of Russian planes and helicopters. This action helped to contribute to the Russian decision to withdraw from Afghanistan in 1987.[26]

In praise of the American pack mules John Helyar wrote the *Wall Street Journal* in April 28, 1988,

> They have carried tons of equipment, food, medical supplies and more over rugged mountains and long distances, from Pakistan into Afghanistan. They have also carried munitions into battle and continued the mule's long tradition of serving as a vital military operative.... U.S. Representative Charles Wilson, a Texas Democrat and leading guerrilla-aid advocate, [said] "the mules have been absolutely vital. The limiting factor in supplying (the guerrillas) the last three years has been transportation. These mules can carry a lot more and can go a lot longer than anything they ever had before."[27]

As early as 1961, the possible need for animal transport surfaced again in some American military minds. U.S. President John F. Kennedy showed a strong interest in unconventional warfare (as it was fought by 1960) and expanded the Special Forces from 1,500 men to 9,000 men in just one year. Those units were trained to improvise and pack transportation as another means of getting supplies to where they were needed. By 1965, position papers and manuals on the subject appeared in military publications. "Research Notes to the Utility of Horse Cavalry and Pack Animals in Counterinsurgency Operations in the Latin American Environment," written by Hartley F. Dane, Curtis Brooks and Curtin Winsor Jr., and published in May, 1965, presented a twentieth-century historical survey of the use of animals in warfare, solicited professional opinions from military officers, and included maps and related items proving the effectiveness. The conclusions were obvious.[28]

In June 1965, the Special Warfare Agency of the Army Combat Command issued the "Final Draft Study: U.S. Army Requirements for Pack Animals." It appendices lesson plans for teaching animal packing and animal management, terrain, weather and the availability of pack animals in limited and general war. Also included was the suggestion for instructions in packing animals other than horses and mules—donkeys, Asian horses, oxen, water buffalo, yaks, camels, elephants, llamas, dogs and reindeer.[29]

On January 4, 1985, Secretary of the Army John O. Marsh sent a memorandum to Chief of Staff John Wickham asking him for his views on the use of pack mules for the reactivated Tenth Infantry Division and the Vermont National Guard. Marsh countered with, "Why don't we put a small group of mules for testing purposes in the Tenth Division?" He also added, "It would be very consistent with the role and image we have in mind for this unit. Please keep a closed hold on this, and I would appreciate your views."[30]

Photograph by Helene C. Stikkel

A U.S. Air Force Military Policewoman holds her mount during Secretary of Defense Cheney's trip to the Far East, 1990.

Three months later, in March, Secretary Marsh told Wickham to quietly establish a group to undertake a serious study of the subject. As with most military projects, a "closed hold" was not kept and the media heard about the proposal. Reporters and television commentators proceeded to cover the subject in a humorous manner which did not reflect favorably on the progressive "army of the 1980s." The final decision in 1984 was not to use them. The excuse was that the project would be too expensive. Probably the real reason was fear of criticism and laughter from the media, Congress and the mule-illiterate public about the army being "old fashioned."[31] The majority of old mule men from World War II would have probably said, "Image be damned. We have yet to win a war without mules."[32]

The Marine Corps evidently felt the same way. In 1993 a course in animal packing was added to the USMC Mountain Warfare Training Center, located near Bridgeport, California. While the mule packers course is an official training activity, students are cautioned that there will be no logistical support when they return to their units. If such transportation is needed in the field, they will have to improvise using local animals and equipment—just as Americans did during World War II and in Korea.

In the words of the Student Handbook:

> The Marine Corps will not be sending animals and tack with you into the theater of operation. Thus, you will have to procure the animals from inhabitants. You are going to have to rely on your own initiative and imagination for tack.[33]

The marines have always been able to rely on their own initiative and imagination when it came to battle. They know that pack mules can operate under conditions which would ground aircraft and can go anywhere that a man can go without the use of his hands.

In 1993 the Jockey Club moved to establish a registry for Thoroughbreds and Half-Thoroughbreds in non-racing events. The reason was to maintain pedigree records on animals which performed in sporting events. In other words, the purpose was to re-activate the old Half-Bred/Remount Association with a new name and under the control of the Jockey Club.

In making the arrangements, the Jockey Club Director of Registration, Roger Shook observed:

> The Thoroughbred is such an exceptional all-around athlete. And today, more and more breeders and trainers of "sport horses" are looking to Thoroughbreds and Half-Thoroughbreds for those natural attributes which make them excellent performers in so many disciplines, from show jumping to dressage, combined training and polo.
>
> The problem is that, without a central registry, there is no way to identify which Thoroughbred bloodlines and crosses are more successful than others in the performance horse arena. It has almost been a hit and miss situation. The PTR will not only take away a lot of guesswork and provide information to assess quality better, but of equal importance it should help to stimulate a market for Thoroughbreds which has been generally little-recognized.
>
> This is a natural. The Jockey Club has the equipment, the personnel, expertise and experience to establish this registry, and do it well. The PTR responds to a need widely expressed throughout performance horse circles. It will benefit Thoroughbred breeders, and will be good for the Thoroughbred breed as a whole.[34]

Working with the American Horse Shows Association, the United States Combined Training Association, the United States Dressage Federation and other equestrian organizations and breed registries, the PTR was designed to incorporate a central data base relating Thoroughbreds and Half-Thoroughbreds to performance in non-racing events.

The idea sounds familiar, doesn't it?

America has not completely forgotten the cavalry and remount heritage. Old Remount Depots, museum displays, monuments to army horses and cavalry re-enactment groups pay tribute to the four-legged soldiers and their handlers of yesterday.

The Branch Remount Depots are still there but all have suffered different fates:

Fort Reno, Oklahoma—transferred to the United States Department of Agriculture and used as a research station for beef cattle. Over the years the facilities have crumbled to the ground and little is left other than the buildings surrounding the old parade ground.[35]

Aleshire, Front Royal, Virginia—used as a beef cattle research station after transfer to the USDA. In 1975 the facilities became the Research Center for the Preservation of Endangered Species of Wildlife administered by the National Zoo. The buildings have been well maintained and give the visitor an accurate picture of what the depot must have been like during the Remount days.[36]

Fort Keogh, Montana—the depot was designated as a U.S. Range Lifestock Experiment Station in 1925. It is still being used as such, although little remains to show the Remount influence.

Fort Robinson, Nebraska—after transfer to the USDA the facilities were used as a beef cattle research center. In 1956 the Nebraska Historical Society opened the Fort Robinson Museum in the 1905 Post Headquarters and portions of the fort complex were set aside for recreational use. By 1972 the USDA was moved out and the entire depot transferred to the state of Nebraska as the Fort Robinson State Park. It is now used for recreation and is open for visits and trail rides.[37]

Pomona Remount Depot, California—the property was returned to the University of California and is now the campus of the California Poly Technic College, Pomona. Arabian horses are still bred there and housed in the stables originally build by Mr. W. R. Kellogg.[38]

The Cavalry Museum, Fort Riley, Kansas, traces the history of the American horse soldier from 1775 to 1950 through displays, artifacts, uniforms and equipment, paintings, sculpture and photographs. Located at the site of the Cavalry Headquarters and School, the Cavalry Museum is housed in the building which served as General George Custer's headquarters.

Adjacent to the Museum is the Cavalry Research Library containing reference material, biographies of cavalrymen and numerous books pertaining to the cavalry and Remount Service.

Standing next to the parade ground at Fort Riley is the bronze statue of The Old Trooper. This represents a cavalry trooper of the 1880s and his horse. The monument pays tribute to the cavalrymen and their horses who have served during the 175 years of American military actions.

Near the Old Trooper monument is the grave of Chief, the last horse to carry an army Preston Brand and be listed on government rolls.

Fort Riley is also the home of the U.S. Horse Cavalry Association. Formed in 1976, the Association is dedicated to preserving the memory and history of the cavalry.[39]

The Patton Museum of Cavalry and Armor, Fort Knox, Kentucky, is dedicated to the memory of General George S. Patton Jr., who utilized cavalry tactics with tanks in his successful campaigns in North Africa and western Europe during World War II. It not only traces the evolution of armor taking over the functions of the horse cavalry, but exhibits equipment, photographs, paintings, tanks and other military artifacts. In addition, there are many mementos of General Patton.[40]

Numerous other museums around the country display cavalry saddles and equipment, uniforms, photos and other reminders of the impact that the cavalry, and horses, have had upon the military.

While the horses are gone from the military there are still reminders of their long service. At various army posts monuments have been erected to individual cavalry mounts commemorating their contributions to an era that is long gone.

On the wall of the old State, War and Navy Building, Washington, D.C., is a bronze tablet commemorating the horses and mules which died during the great European War, 1914–1918, put up by the American Red Star Animal Relief. It was unveiled on October 15, 1921, during a ceremony when General Willard A. Holbrook, former Chief of Cavalry, made the acceptance speech on behalf of the U.S. Government.[41]

At historic Fort Sam Houston in San Antonio, Texas, is a monument to Pat, who entered the Army in 1912. He was purchased at Fort Reno, Oklahoma, by Major General John F. Present as his private mount. Later he was purchased by Major General Charles G. Trent as a gift for his son, First Lieutenant Joseph Trent. When the younger Trent was killed the General sold the horse to the army. Pat served with Headquarters Battery, Twelfth Field Artillery until October 10, 1938, when he was retired from active duty and turned out to pasture. Afterwards he was used only in military funeral processions. He died on Texas Independence Day in 1953. An impressive stone marker marks his grave, inscribed:

Pat

Foaled 1908

U.S. Army 1912

Died Mar. 2, 1953

Age 45 Years[42]

Whiskey, a bay gelding who was one of the famous "characters" of the army and who spent his entire career at Fort Snelling, St. Paul, Minnesota, is described in Chapter 5, page 143.

On the campus of Washington and Lee University, situated at Lexington, Virginia, rest the bones of America's most famous war horse. Traveller, ridden by Confederate

General Robert E. Lee, is buried adjacent to the Lee Chapel and Museum, where lie the remains of his famous rider. A marker has been placed over the grave by the Daughters of the Confederacy.[44]

An on-going reminder of the horse in the military is seen regularly at Arlington National Cemetery, Washington, D.C. In keeping with the old, old military tradition that a soldier should go to his grave behind horses, the 200-plus-year-old Third Infantry, known as the "Old Guard," maintains the Caisson Platoon. Headquartered at Fort Myer, Virginia, the Caisson Platoon provides the caissons, horses and uniformed personnel for military funerals. Active duty soldiers, retired veterans and honored citizens are carried to their graves at Arlington National Cemetery behind the six matched gray horses. The caisson detail also represents the U.S. Army in parades, military pageants and presidential inauguration ceremonies.

Each caisson, which originally served as an ammunition carrier with a cannon hitched behind, is pulled by a six-up (three pairs of two horses abreast). Only the horses on the near (left) side are ridden but each animal carries a saddle. Behind the box is the "limber," which carries the flag-draped casket, where the cannon once rode in the 1918 vehicle. There is also a lead horse, ridden ahead and to the left of the caisson team. In the case of a general or a cavalry officer, a riderless caparison horse brings up the rear. This horse is black, fitted with a flat saddle, saber and shiny black boots arranged in the stirrups as if the officer were riding backwards—looking back over his military career.[45] These forty-three animals are the last of their kind on army rolls and regularly perform a task fitting to the long tradition of the horse with the military.

By the 1960s renewed interest in America's history and the cavalry had brought about the formation of military re-enactment groups. The majority are civilian but an occasional military post fields a platoon. The most popular time frame represented is the period from 1870 through 1895, the Indian Wars with the troops arrayed in army blue with cavalry yellow stripes on the pants legs. The Civil War period is also favored with the weekend soldiers in their correct uniforms.

While there are many reminders of the cavalry and the Remount Service still with us, the most important legacy is the horses. America has more well-bred horses today than ever before, and a large proportion of them trace back to Remount stallions. Without good breeding from those stallions, the quality would not be so high. Daughters of such stallions, when crossed with Quarter Horse, Palomino and Appaloosa mares, have given the breeders of today a cornerstone to build on.

Chapter 8: Sources and Notes

1. Mel Bradley, *The Missouri Mule* (Columbia, Missouri: University of Missouri Press, 1991), 433.

2. Ibid.

3. Ibid.

4. Anna Waller, "Horses and Mules and National Defense," (Department of the Army, Office of the Quartermaster General, XVIII-3-009, 1958), 39.

5. Ibid. Also, John Dexter, "Exit the Mule," Fort Reno Oklahoma newspaper (December 13, 1953): 7.

6. Waller, "Horses and Mules and National Defense," 39.

7. Dick Spencer, "Just Whittlin'," *The Western Horseman* (May, 1952): 7.

8. Waller, "Horses and Mules and National Defense," 31.

9. Ibid.

10. Ibid.

11. Eve Iverson, "The Marines Are Looking for a Few Good Mules," *The Brayer* (undated copy): 93–94. An old marine story, told to author Phil Livingston by Fred Davies about Reckless, probably happened. When the First Marine Division was loading aboard ship to leave Korea and was marching Reckless up the gang plank, the captain of the ship hollered that no horse was coming on his ship. Confronted with a cocked 45 automatic pushed against his nose by a marine colonel, the captain reconsidered and Reckless came aboard. When the ship got to San Diego, the USDA representative said that without ninety days in quarantine, health papers, records of shots, the proper export/import papers, etc., the horse could not come into America. He was told that either Reckless came ashore or the Division Commander would turn the still armed marines loose. The first move they would make would be to drop him into the harbor and there was no doubt that he would not be able to swim to shore. The civil servant decided that any necessary paperwork was in order, the mare was in excellent health and should be transported to Camp Pendleton. There were no repercussions from his superiors. Reckless lived out her life in rather plush retirement quarters at Camp Pendleton. Phil Livingston also relates that at his father's funeral in 1996, he asked the gunnery sergeant in charge of the firing squad detail from Camp Pendleton if he had ever heard the story. He smiled and quietly commented that, "The word was out that Reckless would come ashore." Fred Davies, Weatherford, Texas, former marine stationed at Camp Pendleton, California, remembering Reckless.

12. Waller, "Horses and Mules and National Defense," 31.

13. News release, *The Blood-Horse* (May 23, 1953): unnumbered copy.

14. Waller, "Horses and Mules and National Defense," 71.

15. Ibid.

16. Ibid.

17. Ibid., 73.

18. Phil Livingston, memory of riding at the OMEA stables, 1948.

19. Debbie Garrison, Farmersville, Texas, Fritz Hunsucker, Weatherford, Texas, Jimmy Light, Piester, Texas, conversations with Phil Livingston.

20. Phil Ray, "The Remount Registry," *The Western Horseman* (October 1964): 64–65.

21. *Horse Industry Directory* (American Horse Council, 1984).

22. Ray, "The Remount Registry," 64–65.

23. Emmett M. Essin, *Shavetails & Bell Sharps* (Lincoln: University of Nebraska Press, 1997), 196.

24. Ibid.

25. Hunter Penn, "Afghan War Horses," *The Western Horseman* (January 1988): 32–39.

26. Bradley, *The Missouri Mule*, 434–437.

27. Ibid., 437.

28. Essin, *Shavetails & Bell Sharps*, 196.

29. Ibid., 197–98.

30. Ibid.

31. Ibid.

32. Bradley, *The Missouri Mule*, 434–37.

33. Iverson, "The Marines Are Looking for a Few Good Mules," 93–94.

34. Press Release from the New York Jockey Club, June 18, 1993.

35. Observations from visit by authors.

36. Ibid.

37. Ibid.

38. Ibid.

39. Ibid. Also, Cavalry Museum Information brochure, Fort Riley, Kansas and U. S. Horse Cavalry Association brochure, Fort Riley, Kansas.

40. Information brochure form Patton Museum.

41. Waller, "Horses and Mules and National Defense," 45.

42. "Speaking of Texas," *Texas Highways* (November 1993): 3.

43. Aileen Kilgore Henderson, "A Stout Heart," *Equus* (undated copy): 50, 55.

44. James C. Lee, "Traveller—the War Horse," *The Western Horse Magazine* (undated copy): 37.

45. Waller, "Horses and Mules and National Defense," 67. Also, Cristine Anthony and Allison Rogers, "Horses of the Old Guard, *Equus* (August 1996): 33–34, 38.

AP Photo

A riderless horse is led in President John F. Kennedy's funeral procession on November 25, 1963. The boots reversed in the stirrups symbolize a fallen hero.

The body of President John F. Kennedy is borne from the White House on November 24, 1963.

of registration papers from one of the equine breed associations was an important sales tool. The most popular, and the fastest growing, of the breed associations was the American Quarter Horse Association. Organized in 1940 by a group of horse-raising cattlemen, AQHA breeders utilized many Remount-bred horses as foundation stock during the early years. Those broodmares were already on the ranches and were often

Photograph courtesy of Phil Livingston

Chalk (Royal HiBars AQHA 239236 foaled March of 1985) traces his lineage back through five generations to the Remount stallions, to Southern Gent (TB) on the top side of his pedigree and to Uncle Jimmie Gray (TB) on the bottom side. The gray color comes down from Joe Bailey's King who was used by the Pitchfork Ranch on daughters of Southern Gent in the late 1940s.

crossed with Quarter Horse stallions to produce Appendix-registered (a horse with a registered Quarter Horse sire or dam and by, or out of a Thoroughbred-cross individual) foals. A few Remount-bred mares were in use in some areas as late as the early 1960s. Many of the horses registered in Volumes I, II, III, IV and V of the *AQHA Stud Book* had their dam listed as being sired by a Remount stallion or were by a Remount stallion. The same was true with the early Appaloosas and Palominos (the latter often "double registered" in both the AQHA and the PHBA). When registered

Quarter Horse mares, that traced back to Remount stallions, were bred to Palomino and Appaloosa stallions, the Remount base was broadened to include *all* western horse breeds.

Along with the demand for registration papers came a changing conformation to meet the interest in the showring. No longer was a horse standing 15 to 15-2 hands, with a prominent set of withers, a slim neck and functional feet and legs the ideal. Judges at early Quarter Horse shows were awarding ribbons to animals that stood 14-2, were exceptionally "beefy," thick necked and with low withers. Termed "Bulldogs," these horses became the criteria for several years. It was a case of the showring dictating form, rather than function. Only in areas where horses were ridden for work did the Remount-type stay in favor. By the middle 1950s the "Bulldogs" were losing their popularity and a more refined horse was taking their place. Since then, the halter horse ideal has become larger (15-2 to 16 hands), has a pencil neck and fine-boned legs and small feet.

The argument over equine conformation even divided the fledgling American Quarter Horse Association. By 1945 a group of Quarter Horse breeders had split off from the AQHA and formed the National Quarter Horse Breeders Association. Those individuals favored a more functional type of animal, one with speed, agility and athletic ability over the "Bulldogs." A large percentage of the horses registered in the two studbooks printed by the young association (before it merged back into the AQHA in 1949 and the horses assimilated[1]) list horses sired by, or out of mares sired by "Gov't. Remt. Stallions." Often the stallion was named. This proved that the Remount breeding had a definite influence on the American Quarter Horse, as well as the other breeds that utilized the same foundation stock.

By the middle 1950s, the AQHA was recognizing the impact of Thoroughbred blood (often descended from Remount stallions) and terming that type of animal a "middle of the road" Quarter Horse. A decade later, the old Bulldogs were gone and the desired conformation was once again a larger, more athletic type of animal. That was the "Half Bred" or Remount type. The wheel had turned again. The majority of horsemen had no idea of the Remount breeding behind their animals.

The influence of the Remount stallions on the western horse population is difficult to document. A number of the mares registered in the early days of the AQHA were listed as "Dam-riding type" or "Dam by Thoroughbred stallion." Since many of those mares were owned by former Remount Agents, it is probable that they were sired by a Remount stallion. Only when the name of the sire of the mare—frequently a Remount stallion— is given is it possible to list the breeding correctly. The number of early Quarter Horses which do show close-up Remount breeding in their pedigrees is substantial.

Photograph courtesy of the King Ranch
Romolino (TB), by Ariel and out of Flying Duck, was a Remount Service stallion standing at the King Ranch during World War II.

Perhaps the most influential Remount stallion in the early days was Uncle Jimmie Gray (TB). Although he died nine years before the formation of the AQHA, he contributed strongly to the speed found on South Texas quarter tracks. Fifty-seven of his sons and daughters[2] found their way into the stud books. Numerous grandget were later registered, carrying on his blood in the modern Quarter Horse. Uncle Jimmie Gray's impact was so strong that in 1947 he was listed in the Yearbook of the American Quarter Racing Association as the Leading Maternal Grandsire of Register of Merit race horses. Sired by the great Bonnie Joe (which made him a half-brother to Joe Blair, the sire of Joe Reed P-3), Uncle Jimmie Gray was foaled in 1906. After a successful racing career, he was purchased by the Remount Service in 1921 and sent to the Pfefferling Brothers Horse and Mule Barn in San Antonio, Texas. He lived out his life there, dying in 1932. During his eleven years at stud he sired such horses as: Alamo; Tommy Gray, the sire of the speedy Chain Lay; Major Speck, sire of Lady Speck, Gallant Maid, Lane's Flicka and Major D; Golden Girl, the dam of Flicka; Highball; Jimmie Gray, Jr.; Jiggs; Major Gray and a host of others found in the pedigrees of modern Quarter Horses.[3] A large percentage of mares originally registered by the pioneer breeders Whitehead and Wardlaw, Del Rio, Texas (Nos. 7146–7217) were out of mares foaled from 1936 to 1944, and sired by Bay Jimmie Gray by Uncle Jimmie Gray (TB).[4] Those mares were daughters of various Quarter Horse and Remount Thoroughbred stallions.

Another Remount stallion who left his mark was King Plaudit (TB), a son of the 1898 Kentucky Derby Winner Plaudit. He sired the palomino Plaudit who, in turn, sired 187 AQHA-registered foals. Among those were the famed Question Mark who once defeated Shu Fly; Colorado Queen; Mexicala Rose; Scooter W., World Champion Racing Stallion in 1948; Miss Helen, the dam of Gold Mount; Santa Maria; Smokey Moore; Cimarron; Rey and Golden Plaudit. King Plaudit also sired the AQHA-registered Lucky Plaudit; Lucky Strike; Beulah S; Queen Plaudit and countless polo and army mounts, ranch geldings and broodmares. A number of his granddaughters by Plaudit went into the broodmare bands owned by Hank Wiescamp of Alamosa, Colorado and Warren Shoemaker of Watrous, New Mexico. Through Plaudit, the influence of King Plaudit (TB) on both the Quarter Horse and the Palomino has been huge.[5]

Photograph courtesy The Quarter Horse Journal
Oklahoma Star, P-6, the foundation Quarter Horse was by Dennis Reed (TB), a Remount Service stallion. Oklahoma Star sired 119 AQHA-registered foals and founded a family of show and performance horses.

Dennis Reed (TB) made his strong impact on the Quarter Horse through his half-bred son, Oklahoma Star P-6. Owned for many years by Ronald Mason, Nowata, Oklahoma, the bay stallion sired 119 AQHA-registered foals from fourteen crops, in addition to an uncounted number of grade sons and daughters. He produced such well-known stallions as: Congress Star, Starway, Osage Star, Nowata Star, Star Deck, Oklahoma Star Jr., Double Star and Sizzler. Through them, the blood of Dennis Reed became widely spread. The Oklahoma Stars not only made a reputation in the show ring but were highly regarded as rope horses by rodeo contestants.

Doc Horn (TB), a stakes winning son of Flying Squirrel, passed on his speed to many racing Quarter Horses during his years as a Remount stallion in Louisiana.

Among his get were Della P, who produced both Bardella and Lightning Bar when bred to Three Bars (TB), the great Randle's Lady, Rosita and Rozella. All were Quarter Horses that raced and won during the 1940s and 1950s. Della P's grandson Doc Bar established a dynasty of cutting horses in the 1970s and 1980s.[6]

Captains Courageous (TB), by Stimulus by Ultimus. His best known daughter was the speedy Miss Bank ROM. Another was Miss Choya, who accumulated seventy-nine AQHA Performance points, an ROM and a Superior at Cutting. He also sired the stallion Rey, who in turn sired Frontera Sugar, the dam of Sugar Bars who was responsible for many outstanding race and performance horses. [7]

Fleeting Time (TB), who was a grandson of Ultimus, had only sired a single daughter his contribution to the Quarter Horse would have been substantial. That daughter, Nellene, was bred to Joe Reed P-3 and produced the prepotent Joe Reed II, who in

Photograph courtesy Phil Livingston

T-Bird, the product of a Remount stallion handled by Jewel England of Florence, Arizona, and a Quarter-type mare, was a hard-knocking calf and head horse during the 1960s.

turn sired such greats as: Leo, Joak, Little Sister W, Joe Queen, Mr. Joe Big and Joe's Last. Another daughter, Black Beauty Pollard, produced Cactus Comet AAA. A son, Buddy Nile, was used by the premier breeder Coke Roberds, Hayden, Colorado, and also sired a number of quality individuals.[8]

Chimney Sweep (TB), by Whisk Broom II, sired the well-known Brush Mount, as well as a number of other top horses, both registered and unregistered, during his years at the CS Ranch. The majority of his daughters out of Little Joe Springer mares went back into the broodmare band and continued to carry on the line of speedy individuals who could perform under saddle.[9] Hank Wiescamp used a number of Chimney Sweep (TB) daughters during his early career as a breeder.[10]

Maple Prince (TB) this son of Sweep contributed strongly to the quality of mares used by Colorado horseman Hank Wiescamp during his early days in the horse business. His gelded sons were either sold to the army, went for polo mounts, ranch horses or light carriage horses. His daughters, which included Rose O Lani out of Mexicala Rose, Red Ruth and Cherioca, were outstanding broodmares. Wiescamp also used the Remount stallions Galus (Arabian), Lani Chief (TB) who sired Slipalong Wiescamp, Coventry (TB), Captain Alcock (TB), Advantage (TB), Light Carbine (TB) and Reighlock (TB).[11]

Remount stallions that were popular in West Texas during the late 1930s and

1940s included: Pride of India (TB) by Delhi (his daughters were especially valued as dams of polo ponies); Runflor (TB); King O'Neil II (TB) and Buggins (TB), both used by the Burnett Estate; and Hackberry (TB) who sired the fine Olympic jumper Slippery Sam. Those stallions, and others like them, sired many military and ranch geldings while their daughters were added to broodmare bands on Southwestern ranches.[12] The produce of those daughters were frequently registered in the American Quarter Horse Association.

Most frequently, the close-up Remount influence in early Quarter Horses is found in the dam's pedigree. This substantiates that the horse colts were gelded and ridden or sold. The fillies were put into the breeding bands to continue the improvement of western horses. Many of their sons and daughters were registered in the AQHA after it was formed in 1941. A few examples of their off-spring, from the Consolidated AQHA Stud Books 1, 2, 3, 4 and 5, are: (Remount Stallions in Bold Face type)

402. NOBODY'S FRIEND, blk. h., foaled 1939; breeder-owner King Ranch, Kingsville, Texas.

Sire: Boojum (TB) by John P. Grier (TB) by Whisk Broom II (TB)

Dam: Pal 169 by Alamo by **Uncle Jimmie Gray (TB)**

Photograph courtesy Western Livestock Journal

Shu Fly is shown with her foal, Bold Fly. Shu Fly, a Quarter Horse mare foaled in 1937, was sired by the Quarter Horse Buck Thomas P-12 and out of Lady Luck by Booger Red by Rancocas (TB), a Remount Service stallion, and bred by Loyd Miller, Chamita, New Mexico.

717. SHU FLY, ch. m., foaled 1937; bred by Lloyd Miller, Chamita, New Mexico; owned by Hepler Brothers, Carlsbad, New Mexico.

Sire: Cowboy P-12 by Buck Thomas by Peter McCue

Dam: Lady Luck by Booger Red by **Rancocas (TB)**

2nd Dam: TB Mare.

722. JOE HANCOCK'S STEELDUST, gru. h., foaled 1932; bred by Tom Burnett, Iowa Park, Texas; owned by B Bar Cattle Co., Knox City, Texas.

Sire: Joe Hancock 455.

Dam: Mare by **Slipalong (TB)**

2993. SMOKEY HEATH, s.h., foaled 1940; bred by A. H. Fike, Waelder, Texas; owned by Sproul A. Morris, Mountain Home, Texas.

Sire: Joe Bailey P-4

Dam: Raggedy Ann by **Fleeting Time (TB)**

2nd Dam: Lady Run by June Bug.

5137. JOHNNIE K., s.m. foaled 1944; breeder-owner Ramona Merritt, Federal, Wyoming.

By Old Red Buck 9.

Dam: Blondie (TB) by **Night Club (TB)**.

7178. CLEMIE, b.m., foaled 1944; breeder-owner Whitehead & Wardlaw, Del Rio, Texas.

By Brownie Red 3272 by Booger Red by **Rancocas (TB)**

Dam by Bay Jimmie Gray by **Uncle Jimmie Gray (TB)**

2nd Dam by Johnny Walker

8681. MISSY JO, s.m., foaled 1945; breeder-owner Charles Springer Cattle Co., Cimarron, New Mexico.

By Little Joe III 505

Dam Mare by **Donnay (TB)**

8974. SANDY LADY, pal. m., foaled 1945; breeder-owner H. J. Wiescamp, Alamosa, Colorado. By Nick Shoemaker 1095

Dam: Dark Maid by **Erskin Dale (TB)**

2nd dam Belleflower by Old Joe by Harmon Baker

9183. TETONWAN, gr. m., foaled 1943; bred by Geo. McGinley, Keystone, Nebraska; owned by Wm. J. Gentry, Gering, Nebraska.

By Blue Jacket 2737

Dam: mare by **Reno Kaffir (TB)**

9383. RED VINE, s.m., foaled 1943; bred by Dell Owen, Meeker, Colorado; owned by John A. Hansen, Rawlins, Wyoming.

By Buddy Nile by **Fleeting Time (TB)**

Dam: Flower Girl by **Dazzler (TB)**

10,183. LECK'S GYPSEY GIRL, s.m., foaled 1944; breeder-owner Jay Leck, Carlsbad, New Mexico. By San Dionisio 703

Dam Gypsey by **Gov't. Remount Stud**

2nd dam Flossie by **Gov't. Remount Stud**

The pedigrees of the above horses, and others like them, prove that the use of Remount stallions was widespread among western horse breeders during the years between the two world wars. Many of those horsemen stayed in operation, utilizing a broodmare band built on the Remount-bred daughters, and Quarter Horse stallions until they went out of business in the 1950s or 1960s.

Similar Remount stallion influence was found in the stud books published by the

National Quarter Horse Breeder's Association. Representative pedigrees are: (Remount Stallions in Bold Face type)

5005. MISS TIPTON, s.m. foaled Jan. 1946; Owner: Roy Blankenship, Tipton, California; Breeder: Harvey Foster, Dexter, New Mexico.

Sire: Norfleet Pride NQHBA 47 by Lord Lubbock NQHBA 164 by **Line Up (TB).**

Dam: Cotton Lee (McCue breeding)

5008. COTTON, s.h. foaled Spring 1944; Owner: B.R. Farmer, Wauchula, Florida; Breeder: T.T. East, Kingsville, Texas.

Sire: Sancho by Old Sorrel

Dam: Red Roan East NQHBA 792 by Lobo by **Lovely Manners (TB).**

5016. BUDDY GRAY, b.h. foaled June 12, 1945; Owner: Yale Siminoff, Chandler, Arizona; Breeder: Same

Sire: Jimmie Gray NQHBA 503 by Bull Dog by **Uncle Jimmie Gray (TB)**

Dam: Beauty by Clabber by My Texas Dandy

5021. MIDGET (RAMSEY), s.m. foaled Jan. 1943; Owner: Dr. Minton T. Ramsey, Abilene, Texas; Breeder: M. E. Marburger, Bridgeport, Texas.

 Sire: Billy The Kid NQHBA 1976 by **Elmindorf (TB)**

Dam: Cheta (Marburger mare)

5032. QUICK SAND, pal. h. foaled April 15, 1945; Owner: Sam Brunswig, Benkleman, Nebraska; Breeder: Frank N. Tortorice, Trinidad, Colorado.

Sire: Silver Streak NQHBA 809 by Smokey by Plaudit by **King Plaudit (TB)**

Dam: Joyce by Peter Joyce (TB).

5041. BLACK ROCKET, blk. g. foaled April 1, 1946; Owner: Junior Hazzard, Belle Plains, Kansas; Breeder: Same

Sire: Red Miller NQHBA 541 by **Prince Barton (U.S. Govt. Remount TB)** by **Sir Barton (TB).**

Dam: Queen S. by **Alex Jr. (TB).**

5108. FLYING AMBER, s.m. foaled April 15, 1942; Owner: M.A. Van Cleave, Springfield, Oregon; Breeder: G.B. Matthews, Canadian, Texas.

Sire: Avery by **Sonny Basil (TB)** by Basil (TB).

Dam: Matthews Q.H. mare by **Bat-'em-Out (TB)** by James P. Silo.

5148. TEDDY, b.m. foaled April 12, 1939; Owner: Carl B. Bently, Fulshear, Texas; Breeder: Same

Sire: Baldy Bentley by **Stamper (TB).**

Dame: Mare by Boots by **Pride of India (TB).**

5157. GOLD CHIEF, pal. h. foaled July 1940; Owner: Frank Loomiller, Longmont,
Colorado; Breeder: Frank Eckstine, Steamboat Springs, Colorado.
Sire: Ding Bob NQHBA 220 by Brown Dick by *****Deering Doe (TB).**
Dam: Queen by **Dalston (TB).**

In 1949, when the National Quarter Horse Breeder's Association merged with the
American Quarter Horse Association, the horses registered in the NQHBA were
assimilated in the *AQHA Stud Book.* Their Remount heritage runs in the veins of many
of today's Quarter Horses.

Besides the increasing demand for registered horses there was another factor which
contributed to the demise of Remount-bred horses. A searing drought settled on the
Southwest (Texas, Oklahoma, New Mexico) from 1951 to 1957 and burned the pastures

dry. Ranches which had raised their own
saddle horses—frequently out of Remount-
influenced mares—had no grass to feed
them and sacrificed the horse operation in
order to keep cattle. Other ranches went out
of business completely, selling all livestock.
By the time that the drought broke, many
long-time horse breeders were no longer in
operation. Those that did stay in the
business, concentrated on the growing
registered Quarter Horse market. Only a few
of the larger cattle ranches continued to raise
their own saddle horses and many of them
registered their mares with the AQHA in
order to sell the surplus stock more easily.

An offshoot of the drought was that
ranches began to cross-fence, making the
pastures smaller and easier to work. They
utilized stock trailers to move horses
around and did not need as big a remuda as
before. Rather than raising their own
horses, many operations decided that it was

Photograph courtesy Phil Livingston

*Marion's Girl, AQHA No. 27,822, World Champion Cutting
Horse was sired by Silver Wimpy and out of Joan Scarbauer by
Tallwind (TB), a Remount stallion which stood at the Scarbauer
Cattle Company in West Texas for a number of years. She is shown
with her owner, Marion Flint of Midland, Texas.*

easier, and cheaper, to buy remounts as needed. While ranch horses didn't need registration papers, there wasn't the large-scale demand for the animals that had been

prevalent before 1950. Fewer people raised horses in volume and those that did usually turned to a registered Quarter Horse stallion to head a small broodmare band. Only a limited number of operations, like the Burnett Estate, Waggoner Ranch, R. A. Brown Ranch, Wardlaw Ranch, Moorehouse Ranch, Green Ranch, the Triangle, the Pitchfork, King Ranch and Bell Ranch continued to maintain mares to raise their saddle horses and offered the excess for sale.

Photograph courtesy Western Livestock Journal

Knocky, sired by King Raffles (TB), a Remount Service stallion handled by Tommy Chochran, Gatesville, Texas, was an AQHA Champion in both Reining and Calf Roping during the 1950s. Knocky is shown with Doc Spence up.

With the army out of the buying picture and the number of ranch horses declining, breeders turned to the growing pleasure and show horse market. Buyers in those areas demanded registered Quarter Horses. Appaloosas and Palominos were also popular. Horse operations aimed at the show market became prevalent, rather than being integrated with cattle raising.

Countless well-known Quarter Horse stallions and mares trace their ancestry back to one or more Remount stallions. The legacy of the program designed to produce acceptable cavalry remounts has given American horses a basis of good breeding that could have been obtained in no other way. Some of those horses are:

Doc Bar—this cornerstone of a cutting and halter horse dynasty was sired by Lighting Bar by the great Three Bars (TB). His paternal grandam was the speedy Della P. by Doc Horn (TB), a Remount stallion who also sired Rosita and Rosalita. In 19 foal crops Doc Bar sired 485 AQHA-registered get who amassed a total of 2,492 halter points and 4,569.5 performance points, 27 AQHA Championships, 1 ROM in Racing, 118 ROM's in Performance, 9 Superior Halter Awards, 20 Superior Performance Awards and 2 World Championships.[13] The influence in the cutting world has been impressive with numerous sons, daughters and grandget winning championships and an untold amount of money.

Oklahoma Star P-6—one of the original Twenty Horses registered in the AQHA was by Dennis Reed (TB). He sired 119 AQHA-registered get including Sizzler; Star Deck; Little Star; Osage Star, the maternal grandsire of Palleo Pete AAA; Nowata Star who sired

Star Duster (who also traces back to the Remount Stallion Master Gould TB); and Oklahoma Star Jr. who produced 131 foals which won 5 AQHA Championships, 11 Performance ROM's, 1 Racing ROM and 2 Superior Halter Awards as well as Sandy's V who carried Jane Mayo to World Champion Barrel Racing titles and the famous bulldogging mare Baby Doll.[14]

JOE REED II—sire of a sprinting family was out of Nellene by Fleeting Time (TB), a Remount stallion. He was the 1942–43 World Champion Quarter Racing Stallion. Out of 25 foal crops, Joe Reed II produced 347 foals that earned 1 AQHA Championship, 49 Halter Points, 79 Performance Points, 4 Performance ROM's, 66 Race ROM's, 66 Race ROM's and 6 Superior Race Awards. Among his get were: Leo, the sire of such great horses as Leola, Sweet Leilani W, Robin Reed, Flit (the dam of King's Pistol), Leo Tag, Croton Oil and Garrett's Miss Pawhuska; Little Sister W; Whisper W; Joak; Lady Gray; Poison Ivy; Joe Queen; Tonta Lad and the World Champion Cutting Horse, Joe's Last.[15]

Barbra B—the Quarter racing mare who defeated the Thoroughbred *Fair Truckle at Hollywood Park, California in 1947 in addition to twice outrunning the celebrated Miss Bank in match races. She was sired by B'ar Hunter II by B'ar Hunter (TB) who stood in Oklahoma in 1942 and out of a daughter of Waggoner's Rainy Day. In addition to earning a ROM at racing, she was the dam of: Barbara Tex ROM by My Texas Dandy Jr.; Pelican Gill; Barbara Grace by Glass Truckle (TB); Captain Crusade by Glass Truckle (TB); Adrienne by Bar Tonto; Richie ROM by Glass Truckle (TB) and Joe B Less ROM.[16]

Quick M Silver—He had a double dose of Remount influence. His sire, Brush Mount, was by Chimney Sweep (TB). His dam, Red Bonnet Moore, was by Smokey Moore by Plaudit by King Plaudit (TB). As a race horse, Quick M Silver started 75 times and collected his ROM and Superior Race Horse title. In 19 foal crops his sired 261 offspring that earned 75 Halter points, 165 Performance points, Performance ROM's, 59 Racing ROM's, 1 Superior Halter, 1 Superior Performance and 2 Superior Race Awards. Among those that won their ROM's on the track were Quick Tex, Miss Penley and Quick O Silver.[17]

Skipper W—the result of Hank Wiescamp's long and well planned program to produce outstanding horses. The stallion was by Nick's Shoemaker by Nick and out of Skipalong Wiescamp by Lani Chief (TB). In 18 crops, Skipper W sired 132 registered foals who won 13 AQHA Championships; 1,392 Halter points; 586 Performance points; 19 Performance ROM's; 7 Superiors at Halter and 1 Superior Performance. Included among those foals were: Skipper's King; Skipperette; Skip's Reward; Skipadoo; Skipette; Skipper Jr.; Skipity Skip; Silver Skip; Sailalong; Skippa String; Skipper's King and Skipper's Smoke.[18]

Jesse James—considered to be one of the great cutting horses, this dun stallion was out of Reno May by Reno Bay (TB). He was 1951 NCHA Reserve Champion Cutting Horse and earned his AQHA Superior in Cutting. With only 143 foals from his 24 crops, he produced 1 AQHA Champion, 16 Performance ROM's and 1 Superior at Performance Award winner. His talented get included: Fanny James; Cindy James; RL Banjo Eyes, Martin's Jessie; Jaime Jess; May Wood; Red Miller James; Collins James; Collins Jessie and Daisy James. Most of his get would "look at a cow."[19]

King's Pistol—1957 NCHA World's Champion Cutting Horse, AQHA Champion and AQHA Superior Cutting Horse was out of Flit, by Leo by Joe Reed II out of Nellene by

Painting by Orren Mixer

King's Pistol, an AQHA Champion, AQHA Superior Cutting Horse and 1957 World Champion Cutting Horse, was sired by King and out of Flit, a granddaughter of Joe Reed II, who was out of Nellene by Fleeting Time (TB).

Fleeting Time (TB). In addition to being a World Champion at cutting, the bay stallion was a top ranch horse. As a sire he was responsible for: King's Michelle, 1962 NCHA Reserve World Champion Cutting Horse and World Champion Cutting Mare; Pistol Toter AQHA Champion; Pistol's Mike; King's Pistola; Pistol Lady 2 B and the 1968 and 1971 AQHA High Point Reining Stallion Pistol's Machete. He sired the kind of horses that a person could ride.[20]

Lightning Bar—AQHA Champion and Racing ROM—a prepotent sire out of Della P by Doc Horn (TB). He not only ran well but sired a herd of good horses during his 8 years at stud including 5 AQHA Champions, 8 Performance point earners, 4 Performance ROM's, 4 Superior Halter awards and 1 Supreme Champion. A few of his get included: Lightning Rey; Cactus Comet AAA—AQHA Champion out of Black Beauty Pollard by Fleeting Time (TB); Pana Bar, AAA+, AQHA Champion, Co-Champion Running 2-year-old; Light Bar AAA; Lightnin Bar J and Doc Bar. He also sired Glamour Bars, the dam of the great Impressive.[21]

Sugar Bars—AAA Race Horse out of Frontera Sugar by Rey by Captains Courageous (TB). He sired 867 foals in 19 years with his offspring winning 30 AQHA Championships, 2,574 Halter points, 4,465 Performance points, 93 Performance ROM's; 139 Racing ROM's, 9 Superior Halter awards and 27 Superior Performance awards. He sired: Bar Face AAA; Sugar Leda; Bar Flit; Oto; Bit O Sugar; Mr. Cabin Bar; Counterplay, and Little Bit A Sugar. Others were: Classy, the speedy Connie Reba, Connie Reb, Bars Bailey and Jewel's Leo Bar (Freckles) who became a cutting horse legend.[22]

Mr. Gun Smoke—this sire of cutting and reining horses had a triple infusion of Remount breeding which went back to Fleeting Time (TB) through Joe Reed II, King Plaudit (TB) through Plaudit, and to Dennis Reed (TB) through Oklahoma Star P-6. Mr. Gun Smoke was the sire of: Smokin' Pistol, a top cutting horse, Hollywood Smoke, One Gun, Kits Smoke, Miss Hickory Smoke and Political Smoke.[23]

There is absolutely no doubt that the high quality government stallions made available to breeders from 1920 to 1948 definitely influenced America's light horses for the better. The program originally founded to provide a pool of usable cavalry mounts gave breeders a genetic base to produce an outstanding animal. A horse which would serve as a functional cavalry mount was also more than suitable for ranch, sporting and pleasure use. Such horses could be sold at a premium, even at a time when an average animal had little value. Those breeding programs laid the groundwork for the generations of American horses to come and established the criteria for quality.

America's horsemen owe a debt of gratitude to the forward thinking and dedicated men who staffed the U.S. Remount Service, devoted their lives to the development of quality horses and fought to maintain the program. While their goal was a military acceptable animal, the standards they put in force were accepted by the entire nation. Without their efforts, and the civilian breeders who worked with them, America's light horses would most probably be sadly lacking in overall quality and usability. Those individuals left a legacy to be honored by the horsemen and women who follow.

Chapter 9: Sources and Notes

1. Don Hedgepeth, *They Rode Good Horses* (Amarillo, Texas: American Quarter Horse Association, 1990) 21.

2. AQHA Get-of-Sire computer printout, September 1997.

3. Ralph Dye, "Uncle Jimmie Gray Made His Mark," Lone Star Horse Report (April 1995): unnumbered. Also, AQHA Get-of-Sire computer printout, September 1997 and Yearbooks of the American Quarter Racing Association, Tucson, Arizona, 1943, 1944, 1945, 1946 and 1947.

4. AQHA Combined Stud Books 1, 2, 3, 4, 5. American Quarter Horse Association, Amarillo, Texas.

5. Diane Simmons, *Legends* (Colorado Springs, Colorado: The Western Horseman, 1993), 130. Also, AQHA Get-of-Sire computer printout, September 1997.

6. Jim Goodhue, Frank Holmes, Phil Livingston, Diane C. Simmons, *Legends, Volume 2* (Colorado Springs, Colorado: The Western Horseman, 1993), 64. Also, AQHA Get-of-Sire computer printout, September 1997 and 1947 Yearbook of the American Quarter Racing Association, Tucson, Arizona.

7. Simmons, *Legends* (Colorado Springs, Colorado: The Western Horseman, 1994) 150. Also, AQHA Get-of-Sire computer printout, September 1997.

8. Goodhue, *Legends II*, 150. Also, AQHA Get-of-Sire computer printout, September 1997.

9. Simmons, *Legends*, 149. Also, AQHA Get-of-Sire computer printout, September 1997.

10. AQHA Get-of-Sire listing, September 1997.

11. Frank Holmes, *The Hank Wiescamp Story* (Colorado Springs, CO.: The Western Horseman, 1996. Also, AQHA Get-of-Sire computer printout, September 1997.

12. Ibid. Also, AQHA Get-of-Sire computer printout, September 1997.

13. Col. Joseph H. Dornblaser, "Remount Breeding in the Southwest," *The Cattleman* (September 1946): 161.

14. Simmons, *Legends*, 64. Also, AQHA Get-of-Sire computer printout, September 1997 and 1947 Yearbook of the American Quarter Racing Association, Tucson, Arizona.

15. Goodhue, *Legends II*, 74–87. Also, AQHA Get-of-Sire computer printouts, September 1997.

16. Simmons, *Legends*, 149. Also, 1947 Yearbook of the American Quarter Racing Association, Tucson, Arizona.

17. Ibid., 72.

18. Ibid., 135. Also, AQHA Get-of-Sire computer printout, September 1997.

19. Goodhue, *Legends II*, 64. Also, AQHA Get-of-Sire computer printout, September 1997.

20. Ibid., 100. Also, AQHA Get-of-Sire computer printout, September 1997 and AQHA Get-of-Sire Record for Reno Bay (TB), September 1997.

21. Ibid., 106. Also, AQHA Get-of-Sire computer printout, September 1997.

22. Ibid., 142.

22. Ibid., 150.

23. "Mr. Gunsmoke," *Cowhorse Magazine* (August 1983): unnumbered copy.

Photograph by James Cathey

Jesse James, AQHA NO. 2,257 cuts a cow in 1951 with Matlock Rose in the saddle. Jesse James was sired by Red, a Quarter Horse, and out of Reno May by Reno Bay (TB), a Remount Service Stallion. Jesse James was the 1951 National Cutting Horse Association Reserve World Champion Cutting Horse.

Photograph courtesy America's Horse

Quarter Horse broodmares of the Green Ranch, Albany, Texas in 2002. These well-conformed individuals, tracing back to Fleeting Time (TB) through Leo and to Del Rey (TB) through Hollywood Gold, are typical of the Remount influence on today's light horses. The Green Ranch horses, of Billy Green, Albany, Texas, received the 2002 AQHA/Bayer Best Remuda Award.

⚘ Acknowledgments

There is no way to list all of the wonderful people who contributed to this book. Old friends and perfect strangers dug deep in their memories to share their part of the Remount story with us. Other researchers on the subject opened their files. Magazine personnel carefully read back issues of their publications and sent copies of pertinent material for us to work from or loaned photographs. Fellow writers, including several who were not horsemen, read the manuscript and made comments that improved it. Without the help and encouragement of all of these individuals there is no way in which this material would have seen print.

Mil gracias' amigos …

Dr. Lee T. Railsback, Manhattan, Kansas, who shared his experiences with both the 2nd Cavalry Division in 1941–42 and the China-Burma-India theater in 1943–44 where he was in charge of flying mules over the "Hump" into China.

Lanham Riley, Aledo, Texas, old friend, top horseman, world class roper and former Remount cowboy during 1942–43. He rode many a pitchin' remount horse at Fort Reno, Oklahoma, and Front Royal, Virginia.

A. J. "Jack" Campbell, Douglas, Wyoming, auctioneer, premier horse breeder and a former Remount Agent, cavalryman stationed at Fort Robinson during World War II and purchaser of many Remount horses when they were sold following the War in 1946.

H. J. "Hank" Wiescamp, Alamosa, Colorado, Outstanding Quarter Horse, Paint and Appaloosa breeder. His early program was based upon a group of mares of Remount breeding. His memories helped to provide a firm foundation for this book.

Ray K. Erhard, Glen Allen, Virginia, researcher and writer on the Remount story who kindly made his material available to us.

Lynn Mayes, The Black and White Works, Fort Worth, Texas, she graciously copied a "whole herd of photos" as well as proof reading on the entire manuscript.

Thomas R. Buecker, Curator of the Fort Robinson Museum, Crawford, Nebraska, he and his great staff opened the doors to the entire post and supplied us with reams of information. As an enthusiastic supporter he personally suggested, and sent, vital research material on Fort Robinson and related areas of the Remount.

Terry Van Meter, Director, United States Cavalry Museum, Fort Riley, Kansas, we came for knowledge on the Remount and he gave us the keys to the library. His staff couldn't have been more cooperative.

Patricia S. Bright, Adjutant, U.S. Cavalry Association, Fort Riley, Kansas, if she couldn't answer a question, she knew who to ask.

✓Pat Close, Managing Editor of *The Western Horseman*, Colorado Springs, Colorado, encouragement, copies of articles and the use of countless Cavalry photographs from their extensive magazine files.

Maxie Cameron, Farm Operations Manager, Conservation and Research Center, Front Royal Remount Depot, he grew up on the Depot, showed us the entire operation as no one else could have and shared his memories of the Remount years.

Lee O. Hill, Sr., Rogers, Arkansas, Chief of the U.S. Remount Service who shared his memories of the program.

Henry King, Fort Worth, Texas, old friend and fellow horse journalist who read the manuscript, made suggestions and kept pushing for the completion of the project.

John McCord and Neil Ross (both of Fort Worth) and Tad Mizwa (Houston), writers all, for critically reading and rereading the manuscript, offering suggestions and the constant encouragement.

Dan Taylor, Doole, Texas, horseman and top roper of the 1950s who dug through old photographs to find examples of his Remount-bred calf roping horse, Red Bird.

Bob Rothel, Weatherford, Texas, horseman, cowboy, roper and polo player. He was part of the "tail end" of the Remount experience and was lucky enough to ride many Remount-bred horses during his years in West Texas. He shared those experiences with us.

Major Raymond Smith, Retired, Alexandria, Virginia, old friend, horseman and student of military history. He capably made his way through the National Archives in Washington D.C. and sifted through piles of reference cards to locate many photographs of Army horses and mules in action.

The family of Colonel C. D. Ramsel, U.S. Army, Retired; Duncan, Oklahoma, for making his papers available to us. As the last Chief of the U.S. Remount Service, Colonel Ramsel was acquainted with many of the procedures and practices, as well as the important events that took place between 1921 and 1947 when the Remount Service was abolished.

Ray Graves, Duncan, Oklahoma, a top horseman who took an interest in the project and steered us towards Colonel Ramsel and his valuable contributions. His start in the horse business was with Remount-bred animals during the early 1950s.

Harry Reed, Fayetteville, Texas, top horseman for many years who has been associated with three of the landmark Appaloosa stallions—Bright Eyes Brother, Top Hat H. and Prince Plaudit (who goes back to Remount breeding). He supplied Remount material that his father had received during the 1920s when he was standing Remount stallions.

Bill Culbertson, Ft. Collins, Colorado, First Horse Extension Specialist, Colorado State University, Associate Professor (Horse) Emeritus, long-time friend, horseman, artist and Remount enthusiast. He located priceless research material as well as offered encouragement and suggestions.

General Wayne O. Kester, Retired, Golden, Colorado, he gave of his memories of his days as a Veterinary Officer in the Remount Service as well as commenting on the contributions that the horse has made to the military service.

Ferd Good, Belton, Missouri, decendant of the Owans Brothers Horse and Mule Sales, the firm which sold so many horses and mules to military buyers over the years. Thanks for his interest and assistance.

L. J. "Buster" Burns, Jr., Yoakum, Texas, horsebreeder, polo player, race horse man and former Buyer of Remount Horses in addition to serving in the China-Burma-India theater during World War II. His comments about "Half-breds" and "Remounts" and how they fit into the horse world of the 1930s added an important dimension.

Dave Ramely, Silver City, New Mexico, for allowing us to use his information regarding the Remount stallions used on the Bell Ranch as well as permitting us to review an unpublished manuscript detailing the Thoroughbred as the seedstock for western ranch mounts.

Gordon Moore, Crawford, Nebraska, retired Remount soldier and horse trainer. He shared memories of his service at Fort Robinson during World War II with us as well as providing photographs of stallions and the Depot.

✓ Melvin Bradley, Professor Emeritus, Animal Science, University of Missouri, Columbia, Missouri, and author of the source book, *The Missouri Mule* who took the time to read proof, offer suggestions and allowed us access to his research on the Missouri Mule during War Time.

Aaron Dudley, Chino, California, former Editorial Director of the *Western Livestock Journal,* journalist, horseman, long-time friend and mentor. He went over the manuscript with his eagle eye and added his memories of the Remount horses. His encouragement over the years has had much to do with this project.

N.Y. "Jack" Plume, Yoakum, Texas, old friend, horseman and South Texan who told of the Remount stallions scattered across South Texas during the 1930s.

Clark Imlay, Grantsville, Utah, who took the time to tape record his experiences at Fort Robinson, Nebraska during World War II as well as remembering the Remount-bred horses on his grandfather's Utah ranch during the 1930s. As a high school teacher, he helped start the journey that resulted in this book.

Jane Pattie, Aledo, Texas, well-known author of numerous articles on horses and their use, western equipment and history as well as the definitive volume on *Cowboy Spurs and Their Makers.* She furnished encouragement as well as research material.

Fred Davies, Weatherford, Texas, roper, horseman and traveling partner who was always ready to listen to the "Remount Story" and had constructive suggestions to contribute.

Ralph Dye, Lovington, New Mexico, horseman, historian, one of the founders of the Quarter Horse Association of West Texas, employee of the American Quarter Horse Association, Executive Secretary of the American Paint Horse Associan and fellow writer. His constructive comments and knowledge of the early years of the AQHA were major assistance.

Dick Bannon, Agoura, California, former Advertising Director of Crow Publications. His suggestions gave us another view of the horse industry to consider.

Pat Graves, Vernon, Texas, for compiling the Stallion and Agent from Remount records, magazine articles and handwritten notes, as well as computer-formating the material.

Junior Gray, Graham, Texas, a top cutting horse trainer who remembered riding sons of former Remount stallions back in the 1950s when he first began cinching his saddle on other people's horses. "They were some of the best that I ever rode," he commented.

Curtis Jones, Morgan, Utah, the shared interest in the Remount influence on today's light horses resulted in stories and old photos from Northeastern Utah. Without his help much of the information from his area would have been lost.

Jim Crocker, Fort Worth, Texas, top photographer, horseman and friend, who found Remount information, took photographs and pushed for the completion of the manuscript.

Calvin Allen, Weatherford, Texas, Saddlemaker, horseman and military history buff. He opened his book and equipment collection for both information and photographs.

Chuck DeHaan, Graford, Texas, old friend, top horseman and talented artist contributed colorful interviews [conversations] with former Remount buyers, and his great painting for our cover.

Andrea Laycock Mattson, her excellent book *Reference to the Thoroughbred Roots of the Quarter Horse*, Premier Publishing, Wamego, Kansas, provided the names of many Thoroughbred Remount Sires used during the program and helped to establish their contributions to the Quarter Horse, Paint, Palomino and Appaloosa horses of today.

Barbara Mills, Weatherford, Texas, who grew up in the Virginia "Horse Country" and rode a number of Remount-breds. Her memories of the horses, and the people who used the horses, provided an insight of the way the animals not purchased by the Army were considered in the sporting horse field. Her comments on the manuscript were also greatly appreciated.

W. B. "Woody" Woodruff, Jr., Decatur, Texas, a member of the Mars Task Force and a historian. He provided rememberances of the dependable pack mules during the Burma campaign of 1944 as well as a number of reference books on the same subject.

Munrow Tumlinson, Cresson, Texas, a top horseman and rope horse trainer who remembered the quality of the Remount-bred horses following World War II.

Dr. Richard Galley, DVM, Aledo, Texas, equine veterinarian, roper and good friend who took the time to read the manuscript, suggest improvements and offered encouragement.

George Costa, Weatherford, Texas, for reading with a critical eye and offering both constructive critisism and encouragement.

David Huey, Weatherford, Texas, a military history fan who gathered photos and made his reference material available.

Theresa Brown, Fort Worth, Texas, for her expertise in handling the computer programming involved in producing this book.

Fran Vick, Dallas, Texas, an exceptional editor who put our manuscript in fine order and gave insightful advice.

Theresa Anderson, Fort Worth, Texas, who ran innumerable copies of research materials, filed, re-filed, and retrieved materials when needed.

The Amon Carter Museum, Fort Worth, Texas, whose wonderful Frederick Remington paintings provide a fine art view of cavalrymen and their mounts.

Isabel Lasater Hernandez, Bedford, Texas, our talented graphic designer who put the manuscript in final form.

Bright Sky Press, Albany, Texas, for publishing the result of twenty years' research and work.

Carol Livingston and Joy Roberts, two wives who lived with this long project, read proof, offered suggestions and sat through many an "after dinner discussion" on Remount horses.

GLOSSARY OF TERMS

American Remount Association—an organization founded in 1919 and headquartered in Washington D.C. It was dedicated to enhancing the public awareness of the Remount-bred horse for sporting use and to encourage the breeding of such animals. By the middle 1930s, the Remount Association had approximately 4,000 members, both in the United States and abroad.

animal husbandryman—an individual well-versed in the production of domestic animals. In this case, an individual employed by the Department of Agriculture to advise on the production of horses suitable for Remount purposes.

Appropriation Act of 1911—U.S. Congress appropriates $50,000 to the Department of Agriculture for the formation of the Remount Program. This appropriation was used to purchase suitable stallions as well as pay for their maintenance.

artillery rider—a large horse, 15–16 hands in height and weighing 1,200–1,300 pounds, that was very active. These horses were utilized for both saddle and light draft work, pulling caissons (two-wheeled ammunition cart with a light cannon behind). Each two- or four-horse team had riders on the near (left) horses hence the term "Artillery Rider."

bell mare—a white or gray mare, wearing a bell strapped around her neck, that was used to lead pack strings of mules. The mules would bond with the mare and follow her wherever she went.

blooded stallions—stallions that were purebred, one of the "light horse breeds" such as: Thoroughbred, Arabian, Saddlebred or Morgan.

Board of Arbitration—a Board created early in the Remount Program (1912) to fix the prices paid for Remounts bred in each state. This Board was administered by the Bureau of Animal Industry, Department of Agriculture through the Chief of the Animal Husbandry Division.

bog down—become stuck in the mud.

bone—used to describe the size of the bones of the legs and the fact that a horse with a large, dense leg bone is less prone to "break down" or become unserviceable under hard use. A heavy-boned horse, in relationship to size, is much more likely to stay sound than a light-boned horse.

Branch Remount Depots—the military posts situated in various parts of the United States where Remount horses and mules were sent after purchase, conditioned and maintained and then issued to the using units. Government stallions were also quartered there when not issued to civilian agents.

Breeding Bureau—created in 1906 by the New York Jockey Club to place Thoroughbred stallions in every county of New York State. The stallions were to be bred to local mares for the nominal fee of $10 in an effort to improve the light horse population.

Breeding Center—a small area where an interest was displayed in breeding better horses and where Remount Service stallions were assigned to civilian agents to meet this interest.

caballero—the Spanish term for "Gentleman on Horseback." One of the upper class, reflecting the fact that at one time, only the wealthy could afford to ride horseback.

cadre—the basic staff officer group necessary to staff a military post or form a new unit.

caisson—a light, two-wheeled ammunition cart, with a cannon behind, hitched to four-horse team. There was a seat for two men on the caisson, with one mounted on each of the left-hand horses, for a four-man cannon crew.

cash crop—a product which was raised and sold for cash, such as corn, wheat, cattle or horses and mules.

Chief of Remount Service—the officer, originally a general but later a colonel, who was in charge of the entire Remount Service and reported to the head of the Quartermaster Corps.

chunks—light, active work horses in the 1,200–1,400 pound size range that were used on many farms or in the military to pull wagons.

"cinched big"—a horseman's term describing a horse with a deep heart girth and a set of well-sprung ribs. Such a horse has a large lung capacity and this increases the animal's endurance.

contagious infectious abortion—an infectious disease carried by mares which causes them to abort the fetus or give birth to a weak foal. An outbreak of this disease in a band of broodmares would seriously hamper any breeding program.

contract civilian personnel—civilian individuals working for the military on posts and under contract to the army for a specified term of duty.

crossed sabers of cavalry—the military insignia representing the mounted arm of the army (two crossed sabers) which was worn by all cavalrymen. It is still used, superimposed with a front view of a tank, to designate the Armored Corp.

dealers—individuals buying and selling large numbers of horses, often order buyers or the operators of regional auction barns.

dehorsed—the dismounting of the cavalry immediately preceding and during the early years of World War II. Following the "dehorsing," cavalry was fought as mechanized infantry.

depots—a military term describing army posts used to provide supplies for the troops (i.e., Remount Depots, Quartermaster Depots, Ordinance Depots).

Division of the Missouri (Department of the West)—the military area from Texas to the Canadian Border and from the Mississippi River to Utah where the western military campaigns of the 1860–1890s were carried out. This was primarily a cavalry war and was the proving ground of American horseflesh for the period.

dourine—equine syphilis caused by an animal parasite resulting from contact with other horses. Army remount purchases were routinely tested and treated for the disease.

drag hunt—similar to a fox hunt except the dogs follow a scent trail laid down by a "drag" or sack filled with something to leave a trail instead of the real animal. The "drag" will go across open country, over fences or creeks just as a real fox would. The riders follow the dogs, jumping any obstacles in the way.

dragoons—infantry troops which were mounted on horses and functioned as cavalry. The forerunner of cavalry in the American Western campaigns.

East Prussian (breed)—a breed of horse developed in East Prussia during the late 1800s. It was a large, functional animal well-suited for military purposes. A number of East Prussian stallions were imported to the United States and used in the U.S. Remount Breeding Program.

en masse—an unorganized attack by an entire group charging at the enemy and, most probably, riding over it.

flanking movement—a military tactic where the attacking force comes against the enemy on the side of the defensive line, as opposed to the front. This disrupts the defending force and makes the overrun easier.

flexibility—1) the ability of the horse to effectively maneuver in response to the rider's signals. This is accomplished through the animal's natural athletic ability and through training. 2) the rider's ability, due to his seat on the horse, to not only ride securely but to move his upper body to handle either weapons or a lariat. This was accomplished through the use of stirrups and then adjusting them short enough so that the rider can raise up in the stirrups and move his body around. The Spanish horsemen adopted this type of seat from the invading Moors in the Twelfth Century and called it *la jineta*.

"form follows function"—the form of the animal, tool or building is created to do the most effective job for which it was designed: i.e., cavalry horses with heavy bone; strong, hard feet; plenty of lung capacity and sturdy conformation—all designed to provide an effective mount which could withstand hard use without becoming crippled.

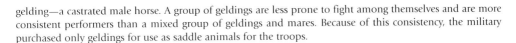

four-up—a team of four horses, hitched in pairs with one pair in front of the other. Field Artillery teams used to pull caissons with cannons behind always had a rider on the near, or left-hand horse.

frontal attack—the attacking force charges directly at the massed forces of the opposing army. The idea is to overrun, scatter and destroy through speed, force and firepower.

garrison life—the social life of military families, as well as single men, living on military posts or "garrisons." For many years, army posts were isolated away from towns and life there was fairly self-contained.

gelding—a castrated male horse. A group of geldings are less prone to fight among themselves and are more consistent performers than a mixed group of geldings and mares. Because of this consistency, the military purchased only geldings for use as saddle animals for the troops.

Genesee Valley Breeder's Association—an organization formed in Glen Avon, New York in 1906 to document the pedigrees of Half-Bred horses, the result of New York Jockey Club Thoroughbred stallions bred to native mares. The reasoning behind placing Thoroughbred stallions at stud in New York state was to improve the quality of light horses. In 1918 the Genesee Valley Breeder's Association pedigrees were given to the Half-Bred Registry founded by Mrs. Herbert Wadsworth.

glanders—a contagious respiratory disease characterized by a nasal discharge and tumors in the nasal passages, lungs and other internal organs. It is communicable to man, dogs, cats, rabbits and guinea pigs. There were severe losses of military horses to the disease during World War I. All horses purchased for military use were routinely tested for glanders (see malliend).

grade—refers to a horse that is not registered in an accredited breed association.

half-bred horse—an animal sired by a Thoroughbred stallion and out of a grade, or unregistered, mare of some other breed.

Half-bred Stud Book—a stud book, or registry of breeding ancestry, of horses sired by Thoroughbred stallions, and out of grade or unregistered mares, that were suitable for military and sporting use. The registry was founded in 1918 by Mrs. Herbert Wadsworth and was authorized by the Jockey Club of New York.

heavy cavalry—cavalry equipped with large horses, body armor, swords and lances. Their primary function was to bring weight and speed to a frontal attack, crushing and scattering the enemy forces.

herdsmen—men who devote their lives to handling herds of cattle and sheep. This was a way of life for the Mongols and other nomadic tribesmen and their portable villages followed the growing grass for pasturage.

IC—a military horse or mule condemned to be either sold or destroyed was branded with the IC, standing for "Inspected and Condemned."

jack—a male donkey or jackass. Bred to mares (female horses), a jack produces mules which were, and are, desirable for draft, pack and military purposes.

la brida—a Spanish term describing a style of riding with very long stirrups (no bend to the rider's knees). Since the rider has no "spring" to his legs, his mobility in the saddle is limited.

leaders—the lead pair in a four or six-up hitch.

Lend Lease Program—a program activated before and during World War II by the United States Government to provide supplies and materiel to the Allied nations which did not have either the farm land or the factories to produce needed products.

levies—a governmental requisition (actually the taking) of products or animals for military use.

light cavalry—a highly mobile, lightly armed and armored force utilized primarily in scouting or hit-and-run tactics.

military specifications—a list of specifications, for men, animals, weapons or equipment, which would meet the needs of the military. Army horses and mules were not purchased unless they filled the specifications outlined for a specific purpose.

malliend—testing for glanders (disease). All military horses and mules were tested for glanders when they arrived at the Remount Depots for conditioning and issuing.

mixed breed mares—a combination of several breeds; grade.

mobile fire power—fire power (cannons) which could rapidly be moved from location to location as needed to augment an attack, rather that being situated at one spot.

"mother up"—a term used to describe horses and mules bonding to a bell mare, just as a foal bonds to its dam. This trait made it relatively easy to control large groups of pack mules.

native horses—horse indigenous to an area.

number branded—horses branded with an identifying number, i.e., paint branded at time of purchase for identification at the Remount Depot or hot-iron branded for permanent identification.

officer's charger—the highest type of military mount, often pure or almost pure-blood Thoroughbred. A horse of very high quality.

pack string—a line of loose pack mules or horses trained to follow a bell mare. The men that packed the animals and handled them rode either horses or mules and were responsible for loading, unloading and caring for several animals in the string. When pack animals were attached to infantry each mule had a handler

who led the animal and did the packing and unpacking.

Periodic Ophthalmia (Moon Blindness)—a recurring inflammatory infection of the eyes that usually results in permanent blindness.

post—an army base. A soldier was "posted" to a new location.

Preston Brand—the permanent identification brand on a horse's or mule's neck. This number was prefixed with a letter denoting which of the Remount Depots initially processed and issued the animal. This number stayed with the horse during the entire military career.

prizes of war—the term applied to the stallions and mares taken from the German military breeding farms and brought to America following the close of World War II. These animals were representatives of some of the finest breeding in Europe.

processing center—a military post, normally a Remount Depot, where horses and mules were collected, conditioned and then issued to the units.

Punitive Expedition—in 1916, Poncho Villa raided Columbus, New Mexico. Units from the 11th and the 13th

Cavalry crossed into Mexico, under the control of General John J. Pershing, to pursue and destroy the Mexican outlaws. It is remembered as one of the most grueling tests of military horses and men in America's history.

purchasing boards—government-appointed boards (groups of men) who were responsible for purchasing horses and mules for the military. Since these were politically controlled, frequently the quality of animals provided to the army was not of the necessary quality.

ranch remuda—the saddle horses (remounts) on a ranch.

Remount Depots—military posts, or a location on a post, where horses and mules were collected, conditioned and then issued to the units. There were four Branch Remount Depots which dispersed animals to the different units and posts: Front Royal, Virginia; Fort Reno, Oklahoma; Fort Robinson, Nebraska; and Pomona Quartermaster Depot, Pomona, California.

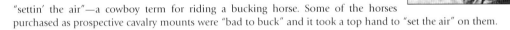

school horses—cavalry mounts (usually the older, settled animals) assigned to military schools or colleges for the use of training recruits in the art of horsemanship.

Second Cavalry Regiment—formed in the 1840s and one of the initial Cavalry Regiments. It was "posted to Texas" in the 1850s to protect settlers against raids from Mexican bandits and Indians.

"settin' the air"—a cowboy term for riding a bucking horse. Some of the horses purchased as prospective cavalry mounts were "bad to buck" and it took a top hand to "set the air" on them.

showings—a scheduled gathering of individuals wishing to show, and sell, their horses to the army. Military purchasing agents would be on hand to evaluate, and then purchase the animals which met army specifications. These showings were held at various locations throughout the purchasing areas of each Remount District.

slashing charge—a cavalry charge with the soldiers armed with sabers and slashing the enemy as they overrode them.

steeplechase—a horse race over jumps. These obstacles could be rail fences, hedges, stone walls or water jumps.

supply pack train—a pack train of mules carrying supplies during a prolonged march.

Texas Rangers—a police force formed in Texas in the 1830s for the purpose of controlling bandits and Indians. They were renowned for traveling with little excess equipment and covering large areas in rapid time.

The Blood-Horse—a magazine published in Kentucky that documents the developments within the Thoroughbred breeding and racing world. The publication also kept the public aware of the U.S. Remount Service and informed it of impending congressional developments which might affect the use of horses within the military.

traveling inspector—an inspector employed by the Breeding Bureau charged with inspecting breeding stallions and keeping the Department of Agriculture advised of their condition and the quality of their foals.

troop horse—a horse assigned to use within a cavalry troop.

tsetse fly—an African fly that carries sleeping sickness (an equine disease) and transmits it through its bite. During the Boer War, many horses and mules died because of sleeping sickness.

U.N.R.A.—the United Nations Relief Act passed by the United Nations and designed to help other countries recover from the ravages of World War II. Part of the program was to help farmers in areas where they needed seed, fertilizer or animals to provide power. The United States was the major participating power and donated many surplus military horses and mules.

windbroken—a horse that has noisy and difficult breathing; one whose breathing is impaired.

wheelers—the pair of horses or mules hooked immediately in front of the wheels in a four or six-up hitch. This pair is separated by the tongue (which is attached to the front wheels of the wagon) and actually guide the vehicle.

CHRONOLOGICAL DATE LINE OF ANIMAL USE BY THE AMERICAN MILITARY AND THE U.S. REMOUNT SERVICE

July 28, 1863—Union Army sets up the Cavalry Bureau within the Office of the Quartermaster General to remedy the remount supply/purchase/distribution problem. Receiving and distribution stations activated at: Griesboro, South Carolina; Washington, D.C.; Nashville, Tennessee; Harrisville, Pennsylvania; Wilmington, Delaware and St. Louis, Missouri. The Bureau operates during the balance of the Civil War but is closed at the war's end for reasons of economy. The direct requisition/purchase/delivery system used prior to 1863 is reinstated with the expected poor results.

1868—The Remount Depot concept proposed in the Quartermaster General's annual report for the 1868 year. It recommended that military horses bred in the eastern states be shipped to Texas to acclimate them (on a government-owned farm) and a year's supply of remounts be kept for issue to the troops serving in the theater. This was during the years of the Indian Campaigns when large numbers of cavalry mounts were needed. It was also suggested that all the mares in the service be collected and sent to such a farm, money appropriated to purchase a few good stallions, and the army raise its own remounts. The cost would be less and the quality better than the animals purchased on the open market and they would be acclimated to the area in which they would be used. There is no record that either recommendation was ever considered.

1884—The Quartermaster General recommends in his annual report that a Remount Depot be established at Fort Leavenworth, Kansas, for the purchase of military horses (riding and draft), training and conditioning them before issue to troops. This would provide a pool of suitable animals to be issued as needed. There is no record that such a depot was established.

1899–1902—British army purchases more than 185,000 American horses and mules for export and use during the Boer War in South Africa. This seriously depletes the supply of military-acceptable horses in the United States.

1904—Realizing that the quality of America's horse population is low, the United States Bureau of Animal Industry begins the development of a strain of utility horses. This is done in cooperation with the Colorado Agricultural Experiment Station utilizing Standardbred, Saddlebred and Morgan stallions crossed on native mares. The program is carried out in Colorado, and later in Wyoming.

1906—Colonel Joseph Battell donates to the U.S. government his farm at Middlebury, Vermont, as well as the Morgan horses bred there. The farm was deeded to the Bureau of Animal Industry and was the first official government horse breeding program.

May 1906—The Jockey Club of the State of New York creates the Breeding Bureau, placing Thoroughbred stallions in every agricultural county of the state. This is for citizen benefit and is an attempt to up-grade the light horse population. The stallions are to be bred to local mares at the nominal service fee of ten dollars. The resulting records of Half-bred horses are a basis for the *Half-Bred Stud Book* which is developed in 1918. The Genesee Valley Breeders Association is formed in Avon, New York, the same year.

1907—Major General James B. Aleshire, Quartermaster General of the U.S. Army, reports to Congress on the problems facing military acquisition of suitable horses and mules. He strongly recommended that this duty be assigned wholly to the Quartermaster Corps. Standards of suitability to function, prices, overall procurement, conditioning, training and distribution to the using services can be maintained in a more orderly, economic and systematic manner.

1908—The U.S. Remount Service is activated, as a part of the Quartermaster Corps, United States Army, through the efforts of Major General James Aleshire. The original purpose is to put the acquisition, processing and distribution of military horses and mules to the using units under the control of a single department of the army. Specifications, ages and quality for the various classes of horses and mules are set. Area Purchasing Boards are staffed and established at: Boise, Idaho; Front Royal, Virginia; Lexington, Kentucky; Sheridan, Wyoming; San Angelo, Texas; Colorado Springs, Colorado and Sacramento, California. These offices are staffed by experienced cavalry officers and military veterinarians.

May 1908—Fort Reno Quartermaster Depot, Fort Reno, Oklahoma, is acquired and designated as the first processing/distribution center for military horses and mules. 8,406 acres of land is set aside from public domain for this purpose.

1910—The Remount concept (providing well-bred stallions to the public for use on privately-owned mares to develop a supply of military-acceptable horses and mules for possible purchase) is presented to the Office of the Quartermaster General of the U.S. Army and to the Bureau of Animal Agriculture, U.S. Department of Agriculture for testing and evaluation. The idea is approved with the provision that the stallions will stand at government farms. Congress appropriates $50,000 to the U.S. Department of Agriculture for the formation of the Remount Breeding Program. Requests are made to leading civilian horsemen soliciting donations of suitable stallions as well as the army purchasing stallions.

August 30, 1911—Land (4,100 acres) in the Shenandoah Valley of Virginia is acquired for Front Royal. The acreage was designated as a Branch Remount Depot and laid out to effectively handle large numbers of horses and mules. Because of the impending military situation with Mexico (revolt against the existing government and potential trouble with Mexican bandits), Fort Sam Houston, San Antonio, Texas and Fort Bliss, El Paso, Texas, are designated temporary Remount Depots.

1912—Fort Keogh, Miles City, Montana, is designated a Branch Remount Depot. During World War I, 1914–1918, more horses and mules were processed at Fort Keogh than any other Depot. Following World War I, Fort Keogh was abandoned by the military and the Remount function transferred to Fort Robinson, Nebraska. Fort Keogh is later designated as a Department of Agriculture Range Experiment Station.

1913—Thirty-five Thoroughbred stallions acquired and based at Front Royal, Virginia, to begin the Remount Program. Five of these stallions were donations from Mr. August Belmont and one from Mr. Johnson Camden. Horsemen desiring to breed their mares to one of the stallions could do so by taking the mare to Front Royal and paying a minimum stud fee.

1913–1918—Representatives of numerous European armies are in the United States to purchase horses and mules for military use in World War I. They purchased approximately 100,000 head and spent approximately $11,000,000, providing a financial windfall for American breeders. This took a large percentage of the better animals out of the country.

1914–1918—U.S. Army purchases more than 500,000 horses and mules during World War I. The demand, and lack of better quality animals emphasized the fact that America did not have a pool of horses and mules which were acceptable for military use. A planned breeding and procurement program was necessary.

1914—The Bureau of Animal Industry, assisting the Department of the Interior, begins a horse breeding program on the Cheyenne River Indian Reservation, South Dakota. The idea is to give the residents a product to sell as well as improve horse stock. Standardbred, Saddlebred and Percheron stallions are put into service on the native mares already on the reservation.

1916—Under the command of General "Black Jack" Pershing units of both the Eleventh and Thirteenth

Cavalry cross the Mexican Border after the bandit Poncho Villa raids Columbus, New Mexico, on March 9, 1916. During the short campaign, termed the "Punitive Expedition," American cavalry units crisscrossed the Mexican state of Chihuahua with orders to disperse and destroy Villa's outlaw bands. This is remembered as one of the most grueling cavalry campaigns in history.

1918—Mrs. Herbert Wadsworth establishes the *Half-bred Registry and Stud Book.* This Registry is open to horses sired by registered Thoroughbred stallions that are suitable for military, polo, hunting and jumping and other sporting events. It is authorized by the Jockey Club of New York and under the control of the Genesee Valley Breeders Association, Avon, New York.

1919—Following the close of World War I, the Remount Program is revised in order to be more practical for mare owners. Instead of all stallions owned by the Remount Service being located at one spot (Front Royal, Virginia), they are distributed to all three Branch Remount Depots (Front Royal, Virginia; Fort Robinson, Nebraska; and Fort Reno, Oklahoma). From the depots they are then assigned to civilian agents. Regional mare owners can take their mares to a stallion located near their home. In some cases, agents with large broodmare bands utilized a stallion exclusively on their ranches. In this way, more mares could be bred, all over the country, and a larger pool of military-acceptable animals developed.

November 1919—The American Remount Association is formed, with an initial membership of eighty-eight. It was dedicated to enhancing the public awareness of the suitability of Remount-bred horses for sporting use. In addition to military personnel, membership included many individuals prominent in Thoroughbred breeding and racing. A bi-monthly magazine, *The Remount*, is published.

November 22, 1919—Fort Robinson, Nebraska, designated a Branch Quartermaster Remount Depot with 23,040 acres and a capacity for approximately 12,000 horses. This phased out Fort Keogh, Montana, as a Remount Depot.

1921—The United States Congress appropriates funds for the revised government horse breeding program for the 1921–22 fiscal year. Five Purchasing and Breeding Headquarters (Kansas City, Missouri; Lexington, Kentucky; Sacramento, California; Ft. Reno, Oklahoma; and Boise, Idaho) are designated to regionally administer the program. Three Intermediate Branch Remount Depots (Front Royal, Virginia; Ft. Robinson, Nebraska; and Ft. Reno, Oklahoma) are in operation to process, condition and issue the horses and mules. The value of the 160 stallions being utilized in the Remount Breeding Program was estimated at $440,000.

April 1924—U.S Range Livestock Experiment Station is established at Fort Keogh, Montana. This becomes the second U.S. Government Morgan Horse Breeding Farm. Horses raised there are to improve stock horses rather than provide military remounts, although it is probable that some of the offspring was purchased by the army.

July 1924—The U.S. Army adopts the Preston System of branding and identifying horses and mules. This is a one letter/four digit series branded on each animal's left neck. This number, along with the individual Descriptive Card, made possible an accurate record for each animal. *See Appendix v.*

1929—The U.S. Army Horse Breeding Program is well-accepted and producing both the necessary quantity, and quality, of horses to keep the military mounted during a time of war. The Remount Service purchases approximately 100 stallions annually to add to the stallion battery or replace older individuals.

1930—The U.S. Remount Service announces that the Army Horse Breeding Program is responsible for the production of approximately 12,000 foals per year with an estimated value of $2,000,000. Some 10,000 of these horses are utilized annually by the civilian market.

1931—A sub-committee of the Committee of Appropriations, U.S. House of Representatives, recommends a reduction of the Horse Breeding Appropriation from $150,000 to $120,000 for the 1931 Fiscal Year. This reduction is approved.

December 2, 1931—Pierre Lorillard Jr., President of the American Remount Association, makes the following announcements: 1. The Government appropriation has been reduced to $120,000. While this will allow the

Breeding Program to continue, it leaves no room to purchase either more stallions or remounts for cavalrymen. 2. There are 641 Remount stallions in service in forty states. 3. Since the Breeding Program began in 1921, there have been a total of 185,000 mares bred to Remount stallions, producing 126,900 foals. 4. Value of donated stallions and breeding stock is estimated at $350,000.

January 2, 1932—The Remount Association announces that approximately forty percent of military mounts have been sired by Remount stallions.

January 1, 1933—Congress appropriates $82,500 for the purchase of military remounts.

1935—Records of the Half-Bred Registry are transferred to the American Remount Association with the approval of the American Jockey Club. This enabled breeders to register the offspring of Thoroughbred Remount stallions, increasing the value of the foals.

1935—Fourth Cavalry transformed into a "horse-mechanized" Reconnaissance Regiment utilizing motorcycles and scout cars in conjunction with horses. Portees are also introduced. These tractor-trailers are capable of carrying 8 horses, men and equipment (a squad) and can rapidly move the unit to an unloading point at the end of roads so that they can unload and perform their mission.

1938—The last of the U.S. Army Infantry regiments are mechanized. Infantry officers are no longer mounted on horses. Only the cavalry, field and pack artillery still utilize horses and mules and they used large truck-trailers (portees) to transport the animals.

1939—A vaccine for eastern and western Equine Encephalomyelitis developed for use in army horses. This proved to be a breakthrough for all future virus vaccine production, including the development of tetanus toxoid for humans.

April 27, 1940—The Remount Association announces that in 1938, Program stallions were bred to a total of 16,492 mares with a resulting 1939 crop of 10,193 foals for a 61.8% production rate.

January 1941—The U.S. Remount Service becomes a separate branch of the Quartermaster Corps, responsible for supervising the Army Horse Breeding Program, assigning Remount stallions to civilian agents, purchasing, processing and issuing horses and mules to the various military units.

1941—Over 700 Remount stallions are standing for public service, either at one of the three Branch Remount Depots or with civilian agents. This is the maximum number of stallions that the Remount Service will have in service at one time.

1941—Tetanus toxoid tried on U.S. and French army horses with success. The American Surgeon General approves it for use on humans and all troops are immunized. The result—minimal losses of humans due to Tetanus during World War II.

September 1941—The German army has over 791,000 horse in military reserve for use in Russia during the planned winter campaign of 1941–42.

September–October 1941—U.S. Cavalry units successfully demonstrate during Louisiana maneuvers that cavalry can effectively function in rough terrain and play an effective part in modern war.

December 7, 1941—The Japanese air force attacks the American Naval Base at Pearl Harbor, Hawaii. The United States declares war on the three Axis powers of Japan, German and Italy. Prior to this, Japanese forces in China are dependent upon horses for cavalry and field artillery use during the campaigns of the 1930s.

January 1, 1942—During the 1941 fiscal year, U.S. Army horse buyers inspect 70,515 potential army Remounts and purchase 23,989 for military use or buildup to meet the coming world-wide conflict.

January 16, 1942, Morong, the Philippines—A platoon of the 264th Cavalry Regiment, Philippine Scouts, under the command of U.S. Army Lt. Edwin Ramsey, charges and routes Japanese forces. This was the last mounted cavalry charge in American military history.

April 1942—The Fourth Cavalry is "dehorsed" and assigned to the rapidly developing Armor branch. The Sixth Cavalry is also "dehorsed" and utilized as mechanized infantry.

1942—The U.S. Coast Guard draws more than 3,000 horses from the Remount Service for beach patrol. This was the major use of horses in the United States military during World War II.

1942–1945—Horses utilized for guard duty at prisoner-of-war camps, military bases, defense plants and sea ports. Some military bases and hospitals maintain horses for recreational use.

1942, Tunis, North Africa—U.S. Army leases and purchases local pack mules for use against the German army in the decisive mountain campaigns.

March 1942, New Caledonia—The Ninety-Seventh Field Artillery Battalion is brought to full strength and then assigned to New Caledonia, less animals. The battalion was later sent to Guadalcanal where 300 pack mules shipped from the Fort Reno Oklahoma Remount Depot are used. The mules carried both pack howitzers (broken down on six mules) and supplies to the front lines.

1943, India—The U.S. Army ships 8,000-plus mules and horses to India to be used as pack and saddle animals against the Japanese in Burma and China.

May 1943—The historic First Cavalry Regiment is "dehorsed" and utilized as mechanized infantry during the balance of World War II.

August 1943, Sicily—U.S. Army utilizes locally purchased and leased pack mules to supply troops during mountain fighting against German and Italian forces.

September 1943—Following the conclusion of the Sicilian Campaign, General L. K. Truscott forms both a Provisional Cavalry Reconnaissance unit and supporting pack animal units for use in Italy utilizing animals captured in Sicily. These units are shipped to the Salerno beachhead and immediately put into service. Following the surrender of Italy, both mules and packers from the Italian army are pressed into service. Eventually 15,000 pack mules were utilized, including 2,900 shipped from the United States and assigned to the Tenth Mountain Division.

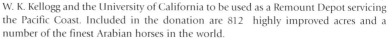

October 1943—Kellogg's Arabian Horse Farm, Pomona, California, donated to the U.S. War Department by W. K. Kellogg and the University of California to be used as a Remount Depot servicing the Pacific Coast. Included in the donation are 812 highly improved acres and a number of the finest Arabian horses in the world.

November 1943, Algeria, North Africa—French Foreign Legion wagons and mule teams are leased by the U.S. Army, through the Lend Lease Program, to unload and load from C-47 airplanes. Supplies are flown to Algiers and then transshipped for the Italian and European campaigns.

February 7, 1944—The 5307th Composite Unit (Provisional), known as Merrill's Marauders, begin their 600-mile trek behind Japanese lines to liberate the airport at Myitkyina, Burma. The purpose was to provide an Allied staging area. They began with 360 American pack mules and 340 pack horses from Australia. The Myitkyina is captured on May 17.

March 1944—The Fifty-sixth Brigade, Texas National Guard, and the Second Cavalry are "dehorsed."

March 8, 1944—The Seventy-seventh Brigade (the Chindits), organized and led by British General Orde Wingate, embarks on a harassing mission behind the Japanese lines in Burma with 9,052 soldiers and 1,360 pack mules. Additional supplies during the mission are to be supplied by air drop. One thousand five hundred men and their mules are flown in by American gliders. In spite of crash landings, in which ninety men and several mules were killed, the mission was a success.

April 1944—Nearly 800 American mules are shipped to Hawaii for use in a landing force on the Chinese mainland.

May 27, 1944—The Army Horse Breeding Program produces a total of 11,066 foals during 1943.

June 10, 1944—The One Hundred Twenty-fourth Cavalry Regiment is "dehorsed" and shipped to India. It is assigned to the Mars Task Force and utilized to clear Japanese forces from the area surrounding the Burma Road. This route will allow supplies to move freely from India into China.

August 12, 1944—The U.S. Remount Service is consolidated into four districts to facilitate administration.

1944—The Coast Guard Beach Patrol is de-activated and 3,000-plus horses sold at public auction.

December 1944—The U.S. Air Force flies 1,582 American Army horses and mules over the Himalayan Mountains ("The Hump") in C-47s to Kunming, China, for use by the Chinese Nationalist Army against the Japanese.

February 1944—The U.S. Air Force flies an additional 1,100 mules from India over the Himalaya Mountains and into China for use by the Chinese Nationalist Army against the Japanese. The two series of flights require 600-plus trips by the airplanes.

January 1945—U.S Remount Service advertises that it is looking for replacement stallions to be used in the Army Horse Breeding Program.

May 1945—After the conclusion of the Italian campaign, the Thirty-sixth Infantry Division is transferred to France to fight against Germany. The unit takes 200 pack mules for use in the French Alps. The 6742d Quartermaster Remount Depot is also transferred to France and sets up facilities to handle 600 mules and 50 horses. A herd of 900 American army mules is given to Chiang Kai-shek's Nationalist Chinese Army. These mules are driven over the mountains 750 miles from Myitkyina, Burma, to Kunming, China, in three series of 300 mules each. These mules developed surra (a contagious, fatal disease) and are destroyed on August 20.

August 2, 1945—Colonel Fred L. Hamilton, Chief of Remount Services, U.S. Army, is ordered to Europe to inspect and select breeding stock for the American Remount Program from captured German military horses.

October 29, 1945—153 German military horses, including 65 European Thoroughbreds, are imported to the United States from Europe as "Prizes of War."

December 1945—The Foreign Liquidation Committee is given full authority to dispose of the 2,000–3,000 horses and mules, plus equipment at the Shillong, Assam, India Remount Depot. A large levy of horses and mules was sent to Calcutta and then shipped to Poland, Yugoslavia, Rumania and other European countries as part of the American Lend-Lease Agreements. A second shipment of mules was sent to China and the Philippines.

April 1946—The 800 mules stationed in Hawaii are shipped to China and donated for use in the UNRRA farming and rehabilitation programs. The majority of these mules are too "snorty" for Chinese farmers to handle and are eventually slaughtered.

September 1946—An additional 300 horses are brought from Europe as "Prizes of War." This includes European Thoroughbreds, Half-Breds, Anglo-Arabs, Arabians and Lippizaners.

1946—The Remount Service demonstrates lip tattooing as a means of permanent identification instead of hot iron branding. The Jockey Club considers it as a means of identifying Thoroughbreds.

1946—Veterinarians working with the U.S. Remount Service at Front Royal, Virginia, show that Periodic Ophthalmia (Moon Blindness) is related to diet and that Riboflavin is necessary to prevent it. Riboflavin is a part of prepared horse feed ever since.

December 18, 1946—Chief of Remount Colonel Fred L. Hamilton announces that the 1947 stud fee for Remount stallions will be raised to twenty dollars to off-set the increased costs of maintaining the animals.

June 16, 1947—Congress passes an emergency appropriation of $350,000 to maintain the Army Horse Breeding Program until it can be transferred to the Department of Agriculture.

April 12, 1948—The U.S. House of Representatives passes House Bill No. 3428 which transfers the Army Horse Breeding Program from the Army Quartermaster Corps to the Department of Agriculture effective July 1, 1948.

July 1, 1948—U.S. Army Horse Breeding Program is transferred from the Department of the Army to the U.S. Department of Agriculture. The Secretary of Agriculture is directed to administer it in such a manner as he deems will best advance the livestock and agricultural interest of the United States. The Department of Agriculture changes the name of the U.S. Remount Service to the "The Agricultural Remount Service." It is to be administered by a separate unit within the Agricultural Research Administration.

November 1, 1948—Aleshire Remount Depot, Front Royal, Virginia, is closed as far as horses are concerned. It is to be operated as a beef cattle research center.

February 1949—Civilian stallion agents receive a letter from H. A. Marston, Department of Agriculture, ordering all government-owned stallions to be readied for shipment back to the depots for public sale. Government horses on the various depots are to be immediately sold and the Remount Service completely liquidated.

April 5, 1949—Senator Wayne Morris arranges a meeting with the Secretary of Agriculture, the Chief of Remount and a number of Congressmen and Senators. He convinces them to delay the liquidation of the Remount Service until October 31, allowing agents to keep their stallions until the end of the 1949 breeding season. Disposition of the existing Remount Depots was also made public at this time.

May 25, 1949—First public sale of Remount stallions, including European horses imported as "Prizes of War," at Fort Reno, Oklahoma. One hundred forty-two horses are offered for sale. This move spells the end of the government horse breeding program. Other sales follow until all stallions and breeding stock are disposed of.

June 3, 1949—One hundred twenty-nine Remount Service horses are offered for public sale at Fort Robinson, Nebraska. This includes recalled stallions, brood stock and young horses.

October 8, 1949—First shipment of Austrian and Hungarian horses (Prizes of War) repatriated to Europe.

October 18, 1949—Public sale of stallions, saddle horses and breeding stock at Front Royal, Virginia.

October 21, 1949—Public sale of stallions, breeding stock and saddle horses at Fort Robinson, Nebraska.

October 25, 1949—Sale of Remount horses, including stallions and mares (primarily Arabians) to the general public at Kellogg's, Pomona, California.

October 28, 1949—Fort Reno, Oklahoma, the first Remount Depot, is the site of the last sale of Remount horses.

October 31, 1949—The Army Horse Breeding Program has been completely liquidated with all animals, property disposed of and personnel transferred or retired.

December 1949—U.S. Government purchases more than 10,000 pack and draft mules from American breeders to send to Greece under a military assistance program. These mules are processed through Fort Reno, Oklahoma, before shipment.

June 25, 1949—Korean War breaks out. United Nations/North Korean/Red Chinese troops all utilize pack mules whenever they can be found. Some of the mules captured from the Red Chinese by American forces can be traced through their Preston Brands to be U.S. Army stock shipped to India and then flown over the Himalayan Mountains into China for service against the Japanese during World War II.

1951–1952—U.S. Army purchases American horses and mules for Turkish military assistance program. Over 12,000 animals are processed through Fort Reno, Oklahoma. Problems are encountered finding sufficient animals that are satisfactory for military use.

June 23, 1953—The Jockey Club agrees to accept offspring of German Thoroughbred stallions for registry in *The Stud Book,* providing that they qualify as far as proof of ownership is concerned.

February 15, 1956—Deactivation of the Fourth Field Artillery Battalion and the Thirty-fifth Quartermaster Pack Company at Camp Carson, Colorado. These are the last military units in the U.S. Army using horses and mules, other than the burial detail at Fort Myers, Virginia.

February 6, 1976—Black Jack, the last horse bred and foaled under the Quartermaster Remount Program, dies at Fort Myers, Virginia. He was a part of the ceremonial burial detail there. Black Jack carried the final Preston Brand assigned, 2V56, which indicated that he entered military service at Front Royal, Virginia.

1958–1960—U.S. Army Special Forces Military advisors in Vietnam use pack animal transportation when necessary.

1961–1984—The army periodically "reconsiders" the use of pack animal transportation training. The idea is finally discarded in 1984 when the media begins criticize the army as "old fashioned."

1993—The U.S. Marine Corps begins to teach a course in animal packing to students at the USMC Mountainwarfare Training Center, Bridgeport, California. The Jockey Club establishes the Performance Horse Registry for Thoroughbreds and Half-Thoroughbreds used in non-racing events. This is simular to what the Half-Bred/Remount Association was doing during the 1920s and 1930s.

PRESENT TIME—The Caisson Platoon, H Company, Third Infantry Regiment "The Old Guard," stationed at Fort Myers, Virginia, is the only official mounted unit in the American military forces. It maintains approximately thirty-five horses for use in military funerals at Arlington National Cemetery. Various military posts maintain small units of cavalry as a public relations program. These units are equipped in the manner of 1870s troopers and pay tribute to the "Indian fighting cavalry."

CHIEFS OF THE U.S. REMOUNT SERVICE 1917–1957

Colonel John S. Fair

Colonel Matt C. Bristol

Colonel Fletcher Hardeman

Colonel Frank S. Armstrong

Brig. General Henry C. Whitehead

Colonel Robert Sterrett

Colonel Charles L. Scott

Colonel Ernest G. Cullum

Colonel Warren W. Whiteside

Major John F. Wall

Lt. Colonel Stephen C. Reynolds

Colonel Henry R. Smalley

Colonel Thomas J. Johnson

Colonel Edwin N. Hardy

Colonel E. M. Daniels

Colonel Frank L. Carr

Colonel John L. Horner, Jr. (Acting)

Colonel Fred L. Hamilton

Colonel T. E. Whitehead (Acting)

Colonel R. E. Ireland

Major Lee O. Hill

Major Curtis D. Ramsel

Courtesy: Horses and Mules and National Defense, Department of the Army, Office of the Quartermaster General, 1950.

U.S. REMOUNT SERVICE AGENTS

This is not a complete list of all the agents who stood Remount stallions over the years. Complete files of civilian agents were not available. A number of these stockmen stood several different stallions over the years while others only had one. It was through the efforts of these men and women that the quality of American horseflesh was improved during the quarter of a century that the remount program was in existence.

ALABAMA
Horn, J. L., Livingston

ARIZONA
Bailey, Lewis, A., Grand Canyon
Bourdon, William R., Taylor
Cecil, Russell, Gooding
Colter, Bert J., Springerville
Davis, W. J., McNeal
Dick, Sam, Yuma
Ellsworth, Rex, Safford
Eubank, W. H., Young
Flake, James, Snowflake
Flake, Marshall H., Snowflake
Fuller, C. Clark, Pinetop
Harelson, C. L., Glendale
Hinton, Dan, Fort Thomas
Kinney, J. C., La Osa Livestock Co., Red Rock
Lorenz, Wm. H., Scottsdale
McCauley, C. D., Winslow
Naegle, A. C., Vernon
Palmer, Irving, Willcox
Sands, Louis, Grand Canyon
Shawn, Tom, Yuma
Spence, Wm. A., Springerville
Tenny, H. C., Higley
Vail Cattle Co., Sonoita
Wilson, Robert T, Flagstaff

ARKANSAS
Anderson, Joel, Tuckerman
Barnes, Edgar, Rogers
Burnett, Oliver, Fort Smith
Cabe, Horace C., Gurdon
LaVezzi, John S., Beaver
Prince, Oscar E., Pochantas
Smith, Jess T., Garland

CALFORNIA
Armsby, J. K., Loqust Farm, Morgan Hill
Balfe, Harry, Clovis
Bare Ranch & Cattle Co., Eagleville

Blakeley, Ambrose C., Lemoore
Botts, J. H., Bradley
Brown, J. W., Williams
Brown, Varion, San Ardo
Cardinet, George H., Jr.; Concord
Chandler, E. R., Dorris
Clark, A. N., Oroville
Clough, A. H., Los Molinos
Collins, R. D., Pebble Beach
Davey, Wm., (Ed. Q. McVitty), San Miguel
Dibblee, T. Wilson, Lompoc
Doughtry, F. A., Salinas
Ellinwood, Vernaus, Sonora
Footman, W. F., Raymond
Fragie, L. R., Merced
Gilmore, E. B., Wasco
Gregoire, Dale E., Napa
Hartwell, Charles A., Pleasanton
Harwood, R. E., Milford
Howell, C. E., University Farm, Davis
Hubbs, C. E., Simon Newman Co., Newman
Huffman, Fred H., Alturas
Jack, R. E., Company, Cholame
Johnson Bros., Alturas
Johnston, Fred, Standish
Lanphear, Guy, Proberta
McClelland, J. H., Standish
McKee, Earl A., Three Rivers
Neilson, A. J., O'Neals
Owens, H., Bieber
Patterson, R. L., Visalia
Pennington, L., Redding
Piercy, O. V., Squaw Valley
Pollard, R. Lee, Sanger
Powers, Harold J., Eagleville
Roberts, E. G., El Centro
Roberts, J. R., Oakdale
Santa Margarita Land & Cattle Co.,
    Santa Margarita
Scott, A. B., Upper Lake
Seeley, Raymond, Blythe
Smith, Paul Stark, Stockton,

Thomas, Dr. W. W., Merced
Thomas, E. Willard, Pleasant Grove
University of California, Davis
Vestal, T. H., Pittville
Vincent, H. G., Glennville
Wardlow, LeRoy, Prado
Wason, Thomas C., Fresno
Wemple, Claude, Milford
White, Osborne, Healdsburg

COLORADO

Alexander, James W., Silt
Anderson, Ben G., Craig
Anderson, Geo. E., Gunnison
Baker, W. O., Lake City
Beirne, Harry L., Model
Big Horn Land & Cattle Co., Cowdry
Blanchard, John, Steamboat Springs
Blaney Ranch, Granby
Braiden, W. A., La Jara
Brooks, Ralph, Castle Rock
Buchanan, W. E., Sterling
Calloway, Joe, Mesa Verde National Park
Campbell, A. J., Greeley
Clark Brothers, Lamar
Cole, Allyn, Lamar
Colorado State Reformatory, Buena Vista
Cummings, James, Trinidad
Curtis Bros., Sedalia
Cusack, C. F., Denver
Dameron, Thomas, Pueblo
Delaney, Ed., Price Creek

Dodge, Bob, Kim
Drake, Fred, Loveland
Dunn, Paul, Meeker
Eccher, Joe; Almont
Eshe, Mrs. Jacob, Rifle
Fender, A. K., Akron
Fowler, Jane, Lamar
Goss, J. W., Pueblo
Grant, E. H. Littleton
Gray, Warren H., Norwood
Grubb, J. Frank, Gunnison
Hahn, A. W., Mesa
Hall, Mac, Saguache
Hanssen, John, Westcliff
Hayden Ranch, Malta
Henry, R. W., Chrome
Higgins, Kenneth, Parker
Highby, Louis R., Greenland
Hill, Victor, Joes
Hixon, E. H., Rocky Ford
Hoover Bros., Elbert
Hopkins, Bernard, Glenwood Springs
Horn, Leonard, Wolcott
Hotchkiss, John Virdie, Ridgeway
Howarth, Herbert, Englewood
Hoyt, John H., Denver

Hull, Virgel, Arapahoe
Hutchins, Gilbert H., Ragged Mountain
Hutton, Roscoe, Burlington
Isaacson, Donald F., Elizabeth
Jack, Cleo, Denver
Jacobson, Chris, Walden
Johnson, R. W., Parker
Johnston, M. C., Nathrop
Keithley, Earl, Silt
Kester, J. E., Willard
Kilbourn, O., West Simsbury
Kirkpatrick, R., Utleyville
Lamb, W. T., Jr., Center Hill
Lamont, R. P., Jr., Larkspur
Lemon, H. R., Durango
Lewis, R. W., Colorado Springs
Light, Leo, Snowmass
Lilley, Chas. W., Virginia Dale
Lindauer Ranch, Grand Valley
Linger, H. K., Hooper
Luce, R. C., Gulf Hammock
Mahaffey, E. H., Grand Valley
Mann, J. C., Rand
Marx, Fred, Lamar
McDaniel, Guy, Thatcher
McDonald, R. W., Glenwood Springs
McIlvaine, Chas., Eads
McPherson, Thos. B., Masters
McPhilliamy, J., Colorado Springs
McLennan, A. J., Simla
Mendenhall, H. B., Rocky Ford
Miller, C. E., Wray
Moore, Kenneth, Gunnison
Moore, Walter A., Dove Creek
Moore, W. A., Cortez
Nelson, H. R., Center
Nicoll, George, Monte Vista
Oldland, Ernest, Meeker
Paddock, E. E., DeBeque
Paepoke, Walter P., Larkspur
Paine, Charles, Antonito
Patterson, A. E., Norwood
Perry, C. E., Gainsville
Peterson, Ivor C., Granby
Phipps, L. C., Jr., Denver
Powell, Vaughn, Steamboat Springs
Pring, Ed, Colorado Springs
Riddle, A. E., Paradox
Riley, Victor, Walden
Roberds, Dr. Kingsley, Crawford
Ross, A. O., Deora
Roth, Chas., Olney Springs
Schaefer, Conrad E., Weldona
Sheffield, Clyde, Ragged Mountain
Sickles, Chas. C., Creede
Sims, Mrs. McDonald,
    Fort Garland
Slane, Ray, Doylville

Slane, Ray, Gunnison
Smith Bros., Conifer
Snider Bros., Piceance
Stephens, O. E., Littleton
Strang, Stephen B., Golden
Stratton, Myron, Farm, Colorado Springs
Taylor, G. L., Lamar
Thatcher, J. H., Pueblo
Thompson, Bert, Durango
Thompson, Gid R., Villas
Trampe, Sheldon, Gunnison
Vader, R. I., Gunnison
Van Tuyl Bros, Gunnison
Venuti, R. E., Bayfield
Walker, William, Lamar
Weiscamp, "Hank", Alamosa
Westbrook, I. K., Pagosa Springs
White, John F., Bighorn Cattle Co., Coalmont
Widmer, Jack, Julesburg
Wilbur, Arthur, Meeker
Willsea, Chas. A., Grand Junction
Wilson, Cecil, Strasburg
Wyman, J. N., Meeker
Whittingham, John, Montrose

CONNECTICUT
Drummond, Miss Lucy H., Lakeville
Kilbourn, O. P., West Simsbury
Russell, Samuel, Jr., Middletown
Welch, Maj. Wm. H., New Haven

FLORIDA
Brown, Wesley W., Tampa
Carleton, T. N., Wauchula
Horne, Jack, Ocala
Kempfer, George H.
Lamb, W. T., Jr., Center Hill
Luce, R. C., Gulf Hammock
Milan, M. A., Miami
Perry, C. E., Gainesville
Rose, Carl G., Ocala

GEORGIA
Elder, J. G., Chickamauga
Jones, N. W., Glenwood

IDAHO
Adair, George, Potlatch
Allen, Buck, Salmon
Anderson, Kenneth, Moscow
Benson, L. H., Leador
Berret, Reed L., Roberts
Billings, Dewey, Homedale
Black, Jos. R., Bruneau
Butler, Arthur, Bliss
Carlile, Ira, Cambridge
Caudle, Helen E., Twin Falls
Cecil, Russell, Gooding

Clawson, Julion, Rupert
Cook, Geo. F., Gooding
Cranney, M. W., Oakley
Crothers, Milton, Oreana
Dennison, Olivere., White Bird
Detton, C. R., Leadore
Dobson, Len, Horseshoe Bend
Fausett, Al, Mayfield
Finney, F. A., Woodland
French, Lowell L., Rupert
Glidden, A. M., Bruneau
Graham, Robert, King Hill
Hagenbarth, D. V., Spencer
Hamilton, Merle, May
Hatch, R. O., Bancroft
Hickman, Dr. C. W., Moscow
Hill, A. F., Grace
Hitt, John C., Malta
Howard, Merrill W., St. Anthony

Hunt, Gilbert, American Falls
Jacobs, M. M., Boise
Kelley, Lyman B., Caldwell
Kerr, G. W., American Falls
Lee, Worth S., Mountain Home
Martin, C. V., Major, Caldwell
McBeth, Victor, Twin Falls
McClain, Frank, Mamer
Miller, H. S., Parker
Mulkey, Doyle L., Baker
Nettleton, Hugh, Murphy
Nordby, Herman, Lewiston
Ostner, Ed., Boise
Rigby, Ivan, Pegram
Roche, Edmund B., Pocatello
Roy, F. S., American Falls
Showell, Rollin, Stone
Sims, Elmer, Lemhi
Smith, Carl M., Holbrook
Smith, Willard, Sr., Holbrook
Spivy, W. A., Boles
Straw, Ellis, Montpelier
Tews, Clarence, Hailey
Thoreson, Freeland, Weiser
Thurston, Harry L. Pocatello
Trude, Sam A., Ashton
Watson, Jesse, Weiser
White, Dr. T. W., Malad
Wilson, I. R., May
Wilson, Lynn, May
Young, Raymond W., Salmon

ILLINOIS
Edmonds, L., Univ. of Illinois, Urbana
Ketcham, Frank W., Skokia
Logsdon, Thomas O., Shawneetown
Pinch, Wm., Lake Villa
Seaman, George G., Taylorville

INDIANA
Berghoff, Polen A., Fort Wayne
Hurwich, M. L., South Bend
Newman, Lowell L., Fort Wayne
Rafferty, W. A., Morocco
Zody, Carl, Franklin

IOWA
Bailey, Glen F., Maquoketa
Chatterton, W. W., Wapello
Green, Max H., Oakland
Hansen Dr. R. T.(DVM), Vinton
House, Guy, West Union
Lynn, Walter A., Grundy Center
Means, H. H., Corning
Spear, Jack A., Tipton
Yates, Austin, Moulton

KANSAS
Allen, J. O., Hardtner
Blair, H. H., Atlanta
Bland, F. O., Gove
Bloom, John, Medicine Lodge
Bradley, E. G.; Wichita
Bronson, Bert, Bunkerhill
Brown, Bert, Byers
Brown, Elmer, Halstead
Brunner, Henry, Onaga
Buckle, Wm. R. H., Stafford
Burnside, John H., Garden City
Burton, C. E., Coffeyville
Butcher, C. E., Cimarron
Christy, R. B., Strong City
Connell, O. J., Jr., El Dorado
Couch, Oren; Garden City
Counter, Thos. A., Oberlin

Dennis, J. A., Ottawa
Dewey, Chauncey, Brewster
Dickson, F. A., Quenemo
Drennan, Ralph, Bloom
Drum, Frank, Westphalia
Durbin, Jack, Moline
Forrest, G. H., Oswego
Freeman, M. A., Dighton
Fuson, Nick F., Wichita
Geyer, Elmer R., Marienthal
Gibbons, J. G., Cunningham
Good, S. E., Hardtner
Harmon, George W., Anthony
Hendricks, Wesley, Cunningham
Hiebert Bros., Hillsboro
Hines, Jay, Scott City
Hosman, L. J., Potwin
Jackson, Ralph, Florence
Johnson, H. C., Ellinwood
Jones, Don, Alta Vista
Lee, O. S., Altamont
Longan, Geo. R., Kenneth

Lowe, H. E., Weskan
Martin, Paul G., Topeka
Maser, Peter, Shields
McBride, Earl, Lewis
Mollet, Mark E., Arkansas City
Moomau, Cleve, Kismet
Mulhern, Sheridan, Summerfield
Murray, Dr. C. W., La Cygne
Myers, Dan, Wakefield
O'Daniel, Fred, Westmorland
Pratt, J. B., Syracuse
Raserm Kebm, Jetmore
Rhodes, Lloyd W., Protection
Robbins, E. C., Belvidere
Roberts, E. C., Strong City
Robinson, J. D., Pleasanton
Rorick, W. D., Johnson
Ryan, L. B., Abilene
Smith, Guy T., St. Francis
Staatz, Wes, Juction City
Tarrant, Alton, Bucklin
Taylor, George, Bloom
Tucker, W. O., Wamego
Ulrich, B. L., Manhattan
Vickers, J. A., Wichita
Waddle, W. H., Blue Mound
Webb, Dr. G. Farrell, De Soto
Weisner, W. J., Manhattan
Wells, R. J., Frankfort
West, Laurence E., Ruleton
Wheatcroft, J. E., Utica
Woodworth, Henry, Dodge City

KENTUCKY
Boyd, C.H., Madisonville
MacDonald, J.W., Campbellsville
Massey, Eddie, Burna
Platt, A. H., Versailles
Remount Purchasing & Breeding
    Headquarters, Lexington

LOUISIANA
Bernstein, Arnold, Monroe
Brewton, J. H., Goldonna
Cormier, Hadley, Breaux Bridge
Daughenbaugh, Gordon, Iowa
Girard, F. E., LaFayette
Glynn, Richard, Arbroth
Goster, Henry L., Newellton
Hoffpauir, N. S., Crowley
Magee, J. A., Sunny Hill
McQuerry, I. H., Columbia
Morein, Claude, Ville Platte
Rendall, Allen, Shreveport
Roberie, Wilson, Washington
Speaker, J., Tallulah
Speyrer, Antony, Arnaudville
Young, A. V., Shreveport

MAINE
Griffin, O. B., Caribou
Startton, H. F., Corinna

MARYLAND
Bedford, Mrs. Dean, Fallston
Bonsal, Frank. A., Jr., Glyndon
Covington, T. F., Cordova
DuPont, Wm., Jr., Fair Hill
Floyd, A. F., Bethesda
Gosnay, Stanley P., Cecilton
Hubbard, W. R., Chestertown
Lamborn, Maj. Louis E., McDonogh
Leonard, Maj. Henry, Brown
Phelps, Wm. P., Upper Marlboro
Riggs, Augustus, Cooksville
Ring, John J., Westover
Tilghman, William H., Salisbury

MASSACHUSETTS
Brainerd, John B., Jr., Belchertown

MICHIGAN
Kinch, Frank, Grindstone City
Lewis, Col. Joseph H., Lansing
Vernor, James, Jr., Lapeer
Wing, W. S., Three Rivers
Wright, Alex M., Birmingham

MINNESOTA
Anderson, B., Pipeston
Albinson, J. C., Worthington
Backus, Charles K., Metamora
Clarkson, Worrel, Withrow
Densmore, Dwight L., Beulah
Fick, H. Q., Upjohn Farms, Richland
Gale, Richard P., Mound
Huebner, Felix M., Jackson
Long, Frank L., Minneapolis
Murphy, F. E., Breckenridge
Rasmussen, Dr. Hilmar, Balaton
Weston, Chester, Concord

MISSISSIPPI
Cooper, R. L., Louisville
Causey, S. C., Brookhaven
Dean, M. L., Columbus
Dunn, Mrs. A. C., Meridian
Legett, A. T., Magnolia
Penny, J. C. Horse Farm, Hamilton
Stockett, R. N., Jackson

MISSOURI
Ball, W. W., Salisbury
Bond, Dr. Van II, Hornersville
Cox, Edwin, Fayette
Davis, True, South St. Joseph
Duncan, M. J., Ruth

Ellis, Jewel E., Cleveland
Flater, John B., Lucerne
Freet, Wilbur, Fairfax
Hamilton, Jim, Mexico
Holloway, Wayne, Milan
Jones, Dr. B. L., Osgood
Kappelman, A. H., Waverly
Kemper, James M., Kansas City
Longan, George B., Kansas City
Low, H. M. C., Belton
McKitterick, Dr. J. W., Greenwood
Mott, J. H. H., Carthage
Rigby, R. A., Chadwick
Sale, Phil, Gentry
Schaeffer, R. W., Hannibal
Stipp, Horace P.,
      Rocky Comfort
Thornburg, J. C., Galt
Walsh, Edw. J., St. Louis
Weakley, Wm. B., Clarksville

MONTANA
Aldridge, Mrs. R. D., Bozeman
Badgett, George, Ashland
Beattie; S. R., Hamilton
Blackfoot Indian Reservation, Browning
Blackford, A. M., Piniele
Boissevain, G., Greenough
Bones Bros. Ranch, Birney
Boothman, Glen, Libby
Brewster, Warren, Birney
Brown, Albert G., Birney,
Brown, Joe, Birney
Butle, Julius W., Bozeman
Campbell, F. C., Browning
Carey, Henry, Sheridan
Carrel, Jack, Birney
Crow Indian Res., Crow Agency
Daily, Eben, Ashland
Ditty, Geo. E., Dillon
Dunning, Forest, Ashland
Dunning, Luther, Ashland
Edminson, Dr. E., Great Falls
Elk Horn Ranch, Ennis
Fish, Herbert, Dodson
Flathead Indian Agency, Dixon
Fraser, R. B., Billings
Galbreath, Galen, Browning
Godfrey, John, Malta
Halvorson, Oliver D., Bainville
Haywood, Edna, Gopher
Hedges, J. P., Ekalaka
Hemphill, Burton C., Libby
Hibbard, A. T., Helena
Hinton, Elmer, Roundup
Hodgens, T. M., Ennis
Hodges, Wetmore, Ennis
Irion, A. J., Coalwood

Irion, A. J., Olive
Irion, L. G., Olive
Kelsey, A. R., Stacey
King, Fred, Otter
Lewis, Fred, Browning
Lewis, Waldo, Broadus
Mackey, F. P., Billings
Marsh, E. F., Nibbets
Mason, L. G., Lavina
McAllister, J. A., McAllister
Metlen, Dale E., Armstead
Mock, Alvin E., Roundup
Moore, A. M., Marion
Morledge, Dr. Roy V., Billings
Murphy, Joseph B., Ovando
Nay, Frank, Dillon
Newton, Harley, Gage
Nicholson, C., Hamilton
Noffsinger, G. W., Glacier Park
Norman, M. H., Hilger
Olson, John, Ashland
Olson, E. O., Lewistown
Orcutt, Bruce, Beebe
Parkins, Frank, Lee
Phillips, Bud, Dodson
Pittman, Roy H., Ashland
Power, C. B., Wolf Creek

Quirk, W. L., Billings
Ramer, J. C., Coalwood
Rehbein, Alfred, Sr., Lambert
Ross, H. B., Jordan
Schall, W. E., Arlee
Scott, Winfield, Ridge
Secrist, Earl G., Hill
Smith, Ralph, Billings
Smith, W. Latham, Hardin
Sun Ranch, Cameron
Tate, R. T., Jr., Ashland
Thexton, A. E., Ennis
Thomas, Bert W., Lodge Grass
Tingley, O. C., Big Sandy
Tingley, Oliver, Big Sandy
Tonn, Wm. & Sons, Miles City
U.S. Range Livestock Exp. Sta., Miles City
Van Cleve, Paul L., Jr., Big Timber
Wallstein, Ernest, Mill Iron
Woodley, J. H., Helena
Wortman, Lloyd, Ennis

NEBRASKA
Abbott, C. J., Hyannis
Anderson, C. L., Cody
Aplan, Frank F., Rushville
Applegate, Harvey, Sutherland
Arnold, Thomas F., Nenzel
Arnot, H. F., Herriman
Bates, A. F., Halsey
Beltner, F. D., Bayard

Bourret, J. S., Harrison
Brennemann, Rolf, Hyannis
Buechle, Otto, Valentine
Butterfield, Ivan, Pawnee City
Chamberlain, J. L., North Platte
Cook, W. Harvey, Broken Bow
Cooksley, Ivan V., Anselmo
Crossfive Cattle Co., Gordon
Crouse, Wm., Arthur
Duffy, Elwood, Long Pine
Fawn Lake Ranch Co., Gordon
Fight, W. A., South Omaha
Foley, Dr. J. H., Hay Springs
Fox, George C., Bayard
Garner, L. C., Arcadia
Graff, Leslie, W., Johnstown
Hamilton, Lloyd L., Thedford
Haney, Jim, Hyannis
Haskell, Ilene, Elsmore
Haumont, Frank, Berwyn
Headgecock, Geo. F., Marsland
Herian, J. F., Antioch
Hossack, J. Q., Omaha
Hull, Lyle F., Gordon
Hunter, R. L., Marsland
Jones, A. C., Rose
Kime, A. G., Ashby
Kime, A. G., Cody
Lakeview Ranch Co., Chambers
Lewis, Albert, Harrison
Mainard, J. S., Mitchell
McClaran Bros., Cody
McGinley, Geo., Jr., Keystone
McMillan, T. W., Milburn
Melton, Alan S., Wallace
Minor, Harry, Hyannis
Monahan, Earl, Hyannis
Myer, C. Louis, Omaha
Payton, G. L., Almeria
Pierson, A. H., Mitchell
Pinney, B. C., Crawford
Porter, Grove, Nebraska City
Reel, Paul H., Spencer
Remount Depot, Fort Robinson
Rogers, D. L., Harrison
Shadbelt & Arnot, Merriman
Shaw, Troy, Burton
Snyder, F. G., Broadwater
Southwick, H. J., Friend
Stanek, Mrs. L. D., Pawnee City
Stanley, Frank, Ringgold
Trego, Mose, Sutherland
Wickman, J. A., Eli
Wilson, Dr. F. L., Stuart
Wisner, Mrs. D., North Platte
Wright, Lew H., Chadron

NEVADA

Adams, Ruth Wiseman, Wells
Agee, R. G., Wells
Anderson, R. T., Metropolis
Bernard, Yerington
Boies, Oran F., Metropolis
Boies, Oran F., Wells
Calloway, Currant,
Claser, Walter, Halleck
Delmue, Albert M., Ursine
Dodge Bros. Construction Co., Fallon
Eager, Ray, Lamoille
Ensign Hill, Metropolis
Gansberg, Chris, Gardnerville
Garat, Henry, Whiterock
Griswold, C. W., Elko
Hylton, Lee, Jiggs
Kane, William, Wells
Laing, C. A., North Fork
Maestrette, Don, Austin
Magee, Richard, Austin
March, W. A., Manhattan
Marvel, E. R., Battle Mountain
McCleary, Frank, Winnemucca
Mink, J. W., North Fork
Ringling, Clark, Winnemucca
Robinson, Melbourne, Cleveland Ranch
Romeo, Albert, McGill
Schoer, G., Wells
Sewell, C. A., Elko
Shiller, Jack, Indian Road Ranch, Mindin
Steele, R. M., Wells
Stewart, F. B., Winnemucca
Thornal, Thomas, Steptoe
Utah Construction Co., Montello
Waltz, Ed. P., (Gerlach & Waltz), Gerlach
Wilson, Clarence, El Rancho Santa Margarita,
    Yerington

NEW HAMPSHIRE

Brown, W. R., Berlin

NEW JERSEY

Haskell, A. L., Red Bank
Macauley, Thos. J., Farmingdale

NEW MEXICO

Arrott, James W., Sapello
Baker, E. J., Roswell
Billings, G. F., Roswell
Blancett, Linn, Aztec
Bloom, J. E., Roswell
Booth, J. S., Lake Valley
Bradshaw, Kenneth L., Belen
Burnham, C. W., Crown Point
Burris, Weldon, Cambray
Cain, Memory H., Deming
Calley, Sim, Wagon Mound

Calvin, J. Frank, Santa Fe
Coats, Walter, Hope
Culberson, Victor, Whitewater
Davenport, J. E., Espanola
DeBaca, F. C., Jr., Mosquero
Dow, Watts & H. M., Roswell
Driggers, W. H., Santa Rosa
Dunn, Jack, Texico
Galway, Ney C., Ocate
Gray, Chas. L., Nara Visa
Grimsley, Sam, Tyrone
Hall, Tom, Hatch
Harrington, V. P., Albuquerque
Hartley, F. N., Mora
Hendricks, Clement, Roswell
Hindi, Brahaim A., Duran
Jenkins, J. R., Carono
Johnson, Dean, McGaffey
Joy, E. E., Hope
Kirk, L. A., Thoreau
Lee, F. W., Albuquerque
Lee, Floyd W., Grants
Lewis, Rudger, Ramah
Loyd, G. B., Barton
MacWherter, John, Dunlap
Major, Malcolm S.,
    New Laguna
McGrath, M. W., Silver City
McLain, Sam, Ricardo
Means, Sam F., Silver City
Messer, G. W., Corona
Minnick, J. H. "Jim," Cimarron
Mitchell, T. E. & Son, Mosquero
Mohler, D. M., Clovis
Moore, Cecil, Grant
Moore, Walter W., Raton
Mossman, B. C. "Cap," Roswell
Munsey, W. E., Portales
New Mexico Military Institute, Roswell
Nutt, Kirby E., Lovington
Paltenghe, Garfield, Santa Fe
Parker, Joe, Hope
Presley, Kelsey, Crownpoint
Reynolds, Dewitt C., Watrous
Reynolds, R. M., Lordsburg
Saunders, Col. H. P., Roswell
Springer, E. T., CS Ranch, Cimarron
Sullivan, Charles, Monticello
Sutherland, Theodore, Roswell
Tallee, Tom, Vermejo Park
Taylor, J. V., Carrizozo
The Bell Ranch, Bell
The Philmont Ranch, Cimarron
Tres Ritos Cattle Co., Three Rivers
Troutman, Guy, Tucumcari
Walter Bros., Aragon
Watts, Edgar, Hope
Westbrook, I. K., Thoreau

Wilson, Brownlow, Cimarron
Wilson, W. A., Correo
Woofer, Paul, Magdalena

NEW YORK
Bailey, Geo. S., Glen Head, Long Island
Bonis, Myron, Southampton, L.I.
Genessee Valley Breeders Association, Avon
Luce, Sanford R., Dansville
McMillan, W. D., Ithaca
Smith, Leon H., Saugerties
Schoonover, Leonard M., Vestal
Sqn. A. Armory, N.Y.N.G., New York

NORTH CAROLINA
Crowell, R. Church, Asheville
Dick, J. Lawson, Burlington

NORTH DAKOTA
Annear, J. Wilbur, Gorham
Bieri, Walter, Blaisdell
Docksteader, Ben, Mikkel
Fitzlaugh, Dr. D. B., Killdeer
Goebel, Alvin, Lehr
Harding, Harry, Pettibone
Heaton, L. E., McKenzie
Ingalls, Elgy, Judson
Jensen, Ralph, Killdeer
Kongalie, Axel, Towner
Metzger, Ivan V., Williston
Montgomery, Dr. R. G., Cogswell
Mosser, Ralph, Trotters
Mostad, C. A., Jamestown
Natwick, Herbert, Bantry
Neuens, J. W., Medora
Patterson Land Co., Bismarck
Schnell, Ray, Dickinson

Seibold, John, Cathay
Shigley, Dr. F. M., Rollette
Smedberg, Carl, Fort Trotten
Sullivan, John F., Mandan
Tetly, Ed., Medora
Tkachenke, Gus C., Grassy Butte
Wachter, Eugene, Bismark
Whittmeyer, C. C., Lehr
Wrightman, Arthur, Williston

OHIO
Evans, Merle D., Massillon
Fleischmann, Julius, Blue Ash
Foster, Richard, Croton
Kerr, Paul, Defiance
Milet, John, Cincinnati
Thacher, Col. E. S., Columbus
Todd, Frank P., Miamiville

OKLAHOMA
Acton, Owen E., Lovell
Alexander, W. G., Laverne
Alton, Frank, Claremore
Armstrong Bros., Mangum
Barber, F. A., Hydro
Bennett, E., Marshall
Bibb, B. A., Cyril
Boggess, R. E., Ochelata
Buster, Tom, Porter
Campbell, H. L., Tuttle
Carlisle, W. A., Cherokee
Cheaney, Leonard, Snyder
Clark, Coris A., Weatherford
Clark, Harry, Boise City
Cole, S. J., Gate City
Conner, Ike, Ringling
Converse, L. E., Mutual
Coonrod, F. M., Mannford
Cooper, F. M., Custer City
Cothran, Hugh, Antlers
Creach, J. F., Hammon
Crotzer, John L., Kingfisher
Crousen, W. S., Marlow
Crow, Joe F., Bartlesville
Culbertson, J. C., Muskogee
Derdeyn, M. H., Pernell
Donelson, R. L., Burbank
Donovan, C. M., Edmond
Drummond, A. A., Hominy
Dubois, E. D., Gracemont
Edgington, Frank, Optima
Eggleston, Ed, Bishop
Evans, W. A., Muskogee
France, Jesse, Watonga
Francis, Wm., Elk City
Gilchrist, Edward, Glencoe
Giles, F. E., Norman
Giles, L. C., Norman
Ging, H. C., Aline
Goodman, M. W., Apache
Greer, A. P., Woodward
Haddan, Elmer, Pryor
Hallock, Geo. H., Regnier
Halloway, Paul, Arnett
Hancock, W. E., Arnett
Harned, P. R., Talihina
Harper & Turner, Scullin
Heavner, E. J., Tulsa
Helm, J. W., & J. J., Antlers
Henderson, D. L., Ponca City
Holloway, Paul, Grant
Hooser, N. H., Tuskahoma
Jarvis, H. T., Fairfax
Jones, Percy, Davis
Ketch, Frank L., Cache
Kuyrkendall, J. O., Atoka
Lasater, Luke L., Pauls Valley

Leahy, Rogers, Pawhuska
Mayer, W. J., Stonewall
Miller, P. N., Waynoka
Monroe, F. L., Claremore
Myers, John W. R., Dover
Oklahoma A. & M. College, Stillwater
Osment, T. F., Chelsea
Palmer, John F., Pawhuska
Paul, Homer, Pauls Valley
Paul, Robert E. L., Pauls Valley
Powell, Howard, Enid
Pratt, Vernon L., Hugo
Pursley, W. M., Rush Springs
Reed, Charles L., Alva
Remount Depot, Fort Reno
Rodgers, Paul B., Sr., Coalgate
Schreiber, Leo, Chandler
Shupe, C. D., Buffalo
Smith, Hugh C., Okmulgee
Smith, Raymond, Guymon
Snell, R. E., Jr., Dustin
Sparks, B. C., Ardmore
Stallings, L. A., Ringling
Stinnett, E. H., Guthrie
Thomas, C. S., Lawton
Thomas, J. D., Gage
Turner, M. E. Eufaula
Tyler, A. Z., Braggs
Wade, Lawrence O., Sardis
Wait, L. L., Spavinaw
Westheimer & Dause, Ardmore
Willoughby, B. H., Texola
Woodman, Roy, Gould
Wren, H. N., Talihina
Wyatt, Frank T., Alva

OREGON
Alcorn, M. D., Olene
Allen, J. H., Long Creek
Bidwell, H. C., North Powder
Blacker, Walter, Halfway
Bosserot, Vern, Burns
Brewer, Roy, Ontario
Brothers, Conley, Cove
Carloa, Homer E., Suntex
Davis, Conley, Watson
Dimmick, Neil G., Nyssa
Edwards, A. J., Salem
Fairbanks, C. C., Eugene
Green, W. H., Enterprise
Hadley, M. G., Eugene
Helyer, W. C., Kent
Houston, Frank, Redmond
Jeppesen, Marvin S., Keating
Jordan, M. W., St. Helena
Lemons, Byron; Mt. Vernon
Mills, I. M., Paulina
Mortimore, Howard, Fossil

Nash, Carrol, Dayville
Ohles, Sam, Terrebonne
Redsull, Whitton A., Ontario
Reed, Charles O., Adams
Rizor, Sam, Robinette
Sherlock, Ned, Lakeview
Stanbro, R. J., Prairie
Thompson, Jos., Hereford
Trowbridge, C. A., John Day
Wagner, G. H., Scappoose
West, Willis, Astoria
Whited, Alfred, Unity
Whiteley, Halfway
Withers, Vancil A., Paisley
Zurcher, W. W. & Sons, Enterprise

PANAMA CANAL ZONE
Walker, M. L., Balboa Heights

PENNSYLVANIA
Chase, E. B., Radnor
Clapp, Roger E., Spruce Creek
Clothier, Wm. J., Phoenixville
Deubler, Dr. E. C., Newtown
Fitting, Samuel E., Harrisburg
Fuller, J. W., Catasauqua
Haubesm, Nagkib B., York
Leitzinger, Wm. A. E., Clearfield
Mack, J. S., Homer City
Mather, C. E., West Chester
Miller, Edward T., Lock Haven
Minor, S. G., Dunns Station
Mitchell, E. B., Harrisburg
Montgomery, R. L., Villa Nova
Sharp, D. B., Berwyn
Sharp, David B., Berwyn
Wetzel, Donald L., Newtown Square

PUERTO RICO
Association Hispica Puerto Rico, San Juan
Central Aguirre Sugar Co., Central Aguirre
Luce & Co., Central Aguirre

SOUTH CAROLINA
Barnette, W. A., Greenwood

SOUTH DAKOTA
Aaberg, John, Hot Springs
Albright, C. H., Blunt
Anderson, Alvin, Avance
Barthold, F. R., Bridger
Bearry, Clarence, Fort Pierre
Berry, Governor Tom, Belvidere
Brickley, Henry, Hermosa
Burki, Albert, Blunt
Butler, F. O., Hot Springs
Chaffee, Francis, Union Center
Cooper, J. J., Sturgis

Cooper, Malcom, Sturgis
Cooper, Norval, Wendt
Dickinson, Col. Henry, Nashville
Dockter Bros., Hosmer
Drame, D. G., Reliance
Erck, Carl L., Mobridge
Fogh, Hans, Strool
Fogh, Nels, Strool
Forbes, J. Lee, Sturgis
Frame, David G., Reliance
Gant, L. V., Geddes
Gatzmeyer, Merle, Buffalo Gap
Hablutzel, U. J.
Hahne, Frank, Trail City
Haley, James L., Hereford
Hall, C. F., Hot Springs
Heppner, Geo. L., Rumford
Hinman, Albert E., Rapid City
Holcomb, Gene, Harding
Humphrey, Bert, White River
Ireland, H. S., Martin
Kaupp, Oswald J., Gegory
Knutson, Jos. M., Presho
Kruger, Wesley O., Aberdeen
Lane, Dennis, Buffalo
Lei, Ernest, Murchison
Looby, H. A., Martin
Mackey Bros., Buffalo
Malcolm, Kirk W., Newell
Meredith, W. H.,
Morell, Fairpoint

Muth, F. C., Morristown
Nylander, Alfred, Lebanon
O'Neil, Henry, Midland
Payton, G. L., Millboro
Pine Ridge Indian Agency,
    Pine Ridge
Pitts, Arvel, Custer
Powers, H. A., Belle Fouche
Ramey, James, Wanblee
Ruby, Frank A., Zeona
Schomer, Joe, Jr., Fort Pierre
Schriner, Edward J., Custer
Scott, Gaylord W., Plankinton
Selland, Oscar, Letcher
Shelving, Robert, Hardin
Shipman, E. G., Fairfax
Shires, Al, Onida
Shoemaker, Arthur, Hermosa
Shoun Bros., Viewfield
Sloan, Stanley, Interior
Sterling, Robert, Hayes
Stoecker, Fred, Fort Pierre
Thompson, Lewis E., Wessington Springs
Towne, Geo. I., Leslie
Trople, Frank, Ft. Pierre
Tubandt, W. A., Tulare
Turner, Robert E., Fort Pierre

Turner, Robert E., Hot Springs
Tyler, A. B., Pierre
Vroman, Col. J., Buffalo
Weyler, Laurence, Belle Fourche
White, Ed. F., Oelrichs
Whitmeyer, C. C., Aberdeen
Wright, Lew H., Manderson

TENNESSEE
Grissom, Roscoe, Columbia
Johnston, S. K., Chattanooga

TERRITORY OF HAWAII
Brewer, C. & Co., Kapapala Ranch, Pahala
Carter, A. W., (Parker Ranch), Kamuela
Dillingham, W. F., Island of Oahu
Kaunakakai, Geor. B., Molokai
Kilauea Sugar Company, Kilauea, Kauai
Rice, Harold, Paia, Maui Island

TEXAS
Aldwell, Lea, San Angelo
Alexander, Minor, Abilene
Alexander, T. H., Eldorado
Andrews, V. E., Lipan
Anson Estate, Christoval
Appelt, Oscar, San Angelo
Arledge, J. W., Santo
Asher, G. C., Menard
Bade Bros, Sterling City
Bales, A. A., Lampasas
Barnes, H. C., Andrews
Barrett, I. F., Trenton
Barron, Pat, Winters
Bassett, C. N., El Paso
Bell, A. J., Meadow
Bell, J. R., Cotulla
Benavides, Alfonso, Laredo
Berny, C. J., Edinburg
Bierschwale Bros., Comfort
Bierschwale, D. H., Dilley
Bierschwale, Walter, Johnson City
Blackstone & Slaughter, Sheffield
Bonner, Brice R., Eureka
Brainard, E. S. F., Canadian
Brewer, Geo. A., Dallas
Broome, Geo., San Angelo
Brown, Jack, Truscott
Brownlee, Houghton, Fairland
Brownson, T. J., Whitsett
Burchell, Tom, El Paso
Burnett, S. B., (Triangle Ranch) Fort Worth
Burns, Denman J., Owens
Burns, L. J., Jr., Yoakum
Burson, J. H., Silverton
Caldwell, T. J., San Angelo
Callaghan Land & Pastoral Co., Laredo
Callan, James, Menard

Callaway, Oscar, Comanche
Carpenter, J. W., Dallas
Carroll, M. W., Jr., Dallas
Cartledge W. R., Comanche
Casey, W. D., Toyah
Cauthorn, Dan, Sonora
Christian, D. W., Big Spring
Coates, Fleet, Ozona
Cochran, M. F., Huntington
Collins, John, Fort Stockton
Conley, W. M., Quanah
Cooper, Earl, Beaumont
Cooper, W. A., Langtry
Corder, J. M., Sanderson
Couch, S. E., Ozona
Currie, W. J., Garden City
Custer, J. L., Spofford
Daggett, Walter M. "Port," Pecos
Danz, Louis, Johnson City
Davidson, W. J., Wharton
Decker, C. M., Kyle
Douthitt, J. W., & Sons, Henrietta
Dromgoole, H. A., Eagle Lake
Dublin, Francis, Midland
Dublin, Jho., Midland
Duncan, H. B., Burnet
Dunman, Theo., Novice
Easley, Hartley, Crowell
Eastland & Newby, Brackettville
Eaton, A. J., Avery
Edison, J. A., Hamilton
Edwards, Paul, Laguna
Eidson, Miller, Judkins
Fairman, M. E., Christoval
Fields, J. W., San Angelo
Fields, John, Sonora
Fischer, Willie, Fischer Store
Fisher, W. L., Marfa
Flowers, M. D., San Angelo
Floyd, B. W., Midland
Foster, W. L., Sterling City
Franklin Bros., Tilden
Friend, Warren, Girvin
Garcia, M. E., Raymondville
Garner, J. W., Rankin
Gibbons, J. W., Richland Springs
Gillis, Roger, Del Rio
Greer & Geesey, Wellington
Greer, Robert, Blum
Griffin, Mrs. Dorthea C., Lawn
Griffin, Mrs. Phil, Goldsboro
Hall, G. M., San Angelo
Hallcomb, Paul M., Ozona
Harkey, Jim, Girvin
Hausser, A., Eagle Pass
Hemphill & Walters, Mertzon
Henderson, A. R., Vancourt
Henderson, J. W., Ozona

Hoover, A. C., Ozona
Howell, Joe, Wimberly
Huggins, J. F., Pierce
Hunt, Bryan, Sonora
Hutchins, J. F., Pierce
Ingham, B. B., Ozona
Jenkins, F. J., Rocksprings
Johnson, Howard, Dryden
Johnson, W. B., Crowell
Jones, D. T., Brackettville
Jones, O. P., Midland
Jowell, Myrl, Porterville
Keete, J. F., "Skeete," Sterling City
Kincaid, E. B., Sabinal
Kincaid, J. Bert, Ozona
Kirby, J. C., Lometa
Kleberg, Robt, J., Jr. (The King Ranch),
    Kingsville
Knickerbocker, Gen. A. B., Austin
Koonsman, J. J., Snyder
Landa, Henry, San Antonio
Lasater, Ed. C., Falfurrias
Lee, John P., Tankersly
Lee, Pat, Ozona
Linthicum, Eugene H., Barnhart
Martin, Pat, Eldorado
Matador Land & Cattle Co., Channing
Maxwell, R. H., Haskell
Mayes, Hudson, Fort Stockton
Mayfield & Caldwell, Sonora
Mayfield, Eugene, Aspermont
McCutcheon, W. W., Fort Davis
McDaniel, Ronnell, Garden City
McDowell, L. S., Big Spring
McElroy, Earl, Alpine
McFadden, W. P. H., Beaumont
McHenry, J. F., Christine
McMurtry, J. H., Clarendon
McRoey, R., Carrizo Springs
Meador, W. E., St. Jo
Means, Cole A., Valentine
Mertz, Len M., San Angelo
Miller, J. P., Coleman
Miller, R. C., Fluvanna
Miller, Rob, Ozona
Millspaugh, S. S., Ozona
Minnick, J. M., Foard City
Moore, W. M., San Saba
Morriss, A. G., Mt. Home
Munger, L. S., Buffalo Gap
Nail, J. H., Jr., Albany
Nance, Tom, Midland
Nasworthy, R., San Angelo
Nichols, T., Truscott
Nixon, Zeb V., Luling
North, W. G., Cuero
O'Keefe, Joe T., Sierra Blanca
Oliver, John H., Menard

Owen, Thos. H., Baird
Patterson & Rieck, Roosevelt
Pattie, R. C., Seminole
Pfefferling, Ed, San Antonio
Pitchfork Land & Cattle Co., Guthrie
Pool, J. W., Marfa
Poole, Hogue, Cotulla
Postell, O. H., Brackettville
Proctor, Foy, Midland
Pursley, Mrs. Gertrude, Jayton
Pyle, T. M., Longfellow
Rahl & Woody, Goldthwaite
Reagan, Rocky, Beeville
Reese, John W., Floresville
Reid Bros., Fort Davis
Remount Headquarters, San Angelo
Renfroe, J. E., Menard
Renfroe, M. P., Sonora
Reynolds, N. B., Snyder
Reynolds, W. W., Ft. Worth
Richards, F. M., Brady
Rishworth, W. I., Center Point
Roach, H. N., Shamrock
Robertson, Ben, Ozona
Roe, Fred, Jr., Robert Lee
Rogers, B. G., Foard City
Roper, Aaron, Vineyard
Rose, Pat, Brackettville
Sampson, Dick, Clairemont
Sansom, Marian, Est., Fort Worth
Sartin, Henry D., Sulphur Springs
Scaling, G. W., Fort Worth
Scharbauer Cattle Co., Midland
Scott & Hooper, Falfurrias
Scott, J. W., Vega

Seale, Frank B., Benchley
Sellers, R. E., Del Rio
Sheen, Winston W.,
    Ft. McKavett
Shelton, Malcolm, Amarillo
Shirley & Offield, Crowell
Short, Jos. W., Jr., Bandera
Sikes, L. E., Pandora
Skeete, J. F., Sterling City
Smith, Geo W. Jr., Celina
Smith, Howard C., Mason
Snyder, D. W., George West

Sorell, J. E., Voca
Sorrell, W. D., Menard
Speer, Leo, Dickens
Springer, W. A., Aspermont
Stadler, Jno. H., Brackettville
Steward, D. N., Texarkana
Stiles, Martin, Annona,
Storey, H. D., Cotulla
Swenson Land & Cattle Co., Stamford
Taylor, G. F., Juno
Taylor, Marvin, Tokio

Taylor, W. H. San Saba
Taylor, W. H., Pontotoc
Texas A & M College, College Station
Thompson, Philip, Sterling City
Thompson, R. E., Stinnett
Tredwell, J. M., Menard
Turner, Ainslie, Water Valley
Turner, Percy W., Water Valley
Tyson, V. D., Goldthwaite
Waddell, J. M., Odessa
Waida, E. V., Victoria
Walker, Geo. P., Jr., Center Point
Walsh, F. T., San Antonio
Waring, R. S., San Angelo
Watson, Felix H., Junction
Weathersbee, R. A., Del Rio
Weston, O. D., San Angelo
Wheat, Ira L., Rocksprings
White, C. T., Brady
White, G. R., Brady
Whitehead, Forrest C., Del Rio
Wilkinson, Chas. M., Menard
Willis, B. H., Beaumont
Wynke, Guy E., Junction
Yoakum, Dan W., Vernon
Young, Jack, Midland
Young, R. A., Crane
Zirkle, Dr. R. M., San Angelo

UTAH
Aiken, S. L., Castle Dale
Andrus, Roscoe, Marion
Bailey, C. W., Escalante
Beebe, Gilbert, Altonah
Beebe, Reed, Junction
Brown Bros., Grantsville
Burke, Jesse, Vernal
Carling, Elmer, Fillmore
Colton, Hugh W., Vernal
Cuff, Robert L., Marysvale
Esplin, Fern, Orderville
Fenton, R. L., Parowan
Findlay, Alex, Kanab
Flanders, Joe, Payson
Gardner, Lester, Neola
Grant, R. B., Honeyville
Guymon, F. Marion, Huntington
Guymon, W. A., Huntington
Hanchett, Voyle, Richfield
Henderson, Geo., Joseph
Hinckley, Lawrence, Lynndyl
Holyoak, Alvie, Moab
Huff, Archer, Spanish Fork
Jenkins, Cecil, Roosevelt
Johnson, Byron, Castle Dale
Kelly, Francis, Fillmore
Kenner, R. E. L., Manti
Larsen, V. Blain, Spring City

Lowry, J. L., Manti
Moody, L. R., Deseret
Murdock, D. N., Heber
Nelson, S. T., Cedar City
Paxton, Taft, Kanosh
Quartermaster Stables, Salt Lake City
Rasband, G. T., Heber City
Redd, Chas., La Sal
Rogerson, John, Panguitch
Rosenvall, Alan, Salt Lake City
Seely, J. Leo, Mt. Pleasanton
Shakespear, Harmon, Tropic
Singleton, J. H., Gandy
Smith, P. M., Manti
Smith, T. Howard, Veyo
    (Blake Mayberry, Mgr)
Snow, Earl, Orangeville
Spilsbury, A. P., Cedar City
Stewart, B. J., Kamas
Stookey, L. A., Clover
Story, Chas. E., Eden
Thurgood, Joseph S., Layton
Thurston, Bert, Morgan
Titensor, Lowell C., Richmond
Utah State Agricultural College, Logan
Warburton, Ernest, Etna
Wardle, Jed, Ouray
Warnick, Reed W., Pleasant Grove
Watts, C. W., Kanosh
Weston, Norman, Laketown
Whitelock, L. F., Farmington
Wilson, Gordon N., Payson
Wood, Brown, Tremonton
Young, Grant, Salt Lake City

VENEZUELA
Military Attache of Venezuela,
    Washington D.C.

VERMONT
Cortland, A. Van, Brandon

VIRGINIA
Allen, David, Berryville
Allen, Dr. L. M., Berryville
Butler, Arthur, Bliss
Byers, C. W., Ft. Defiance
Cecil, Russell, Gooding
Chapman, T. H., Boyce
Clatterbuck, Joe, Dayton
Crouch, C. M., Aldie
Crouch, T. Walter, Middleburg
Dobson, Len, Horseshoe Bend
Dowden, O. B., Orleans
Field, Catesby T., Glouchester
Furr, H. E., Aldie
Hazen, M. C., Nokesville
Hepner, Oliver, Sterling

Herring, H. W., Nokesville
Hinckley, A. P., Orleans
Holtzclaw, T. C., Hampton
Humphrey, Dr. F. M., Philamont
Iselin, C. O., Jr., Middleburg
Iseman, I. I., Harrisonburg
Jett, J. M., Nineveh
Keister, Wm. E., Fairfax
Keyser, J. E., Flint Hill
Larrabee, S. L., Warrenton
Lewis, John D., Upperville
Lyne, H. O., Orange
Marine Barracks, Quantico
Miller, C. J., Jr., Washington
Moore, Lindsley L., Ringgold
Mulkey, Doyle L., Baker
Palmer, A. J., Brookneal
Payne, Chas. B., Culpepper
Randolph, Geo. A., Keene
Ray, Benton G., Happy Creek
Scott, J. Holland, Bridgetown
Sharp, F. W., The Plains
Shaw, Albert, Jr., Sterling
Taylor, Forest T., Staunton
Taylor, John E., Staunton
Utterback, T. W., Markham
Vickers, Reginald J., The Plains
Washington, M. M., Nokesville
Weir, James, Boyce
Willis, H. C., Rapidan
Wisecarver, C. E., Berryville

WASHINGTON
Armstrong, Herb, The Valley Farm
    Harrington
Baker, Dr. W. M., Sprague
Bartlett, O. O., Deer Park
Bergevin, Clem, Walla Walla
Biggs, Ivan, Eureka
Blende, Dr. O. O., Winthrop
Coffin, Stanley, Yakima
Farron, W. M., Harrah
Flower, C. F., Sunnyside
Fries, J. Jacob, Brewster
Grote, Joe Jr., Dayton
Hensel, A. J., Waterville
Hjaltalin, Sig, Bellingham
Jurgensen, Rolf, Wilbur
Matthews, Grove, Curlew
McLellan, Robert, Nine Mile Falls
Miller, Ward E., Omak
Morris, Lawrence, Monse
Stafford, Clyde, Wenatchee
State College of Washington, Pullman
Turner, Leslie, Addy
Woodard, Ross, Loomis
Yeackel, Joseph, Centerville

WEST VIRGINIA
Bentz, Ralph, Martinsburg
Traynham, Dr. B. L., Sweet Springs

WISCONSIN
Engbretson, W. E., Wild Rose
Litza, Daniel F., Milwaukee
Pabst, Fred, Oconomowoc
Rothermel, W. G., Menomonee Falls
Terry, Charles R., Sussex

WYOMING
Allison, C. A., Weston
Atherton, N. B., Lawver
Behunin, Orson, Burnt Fork
Bennett, Tom, Marshall
Berger, John, Oshoto
Berry, C. P., Recluse
Boner, Harry, Hat Creek
Brock, William B., Buffalo
Byrne, C. Leslie, Piedmont
Cammon, Clarence, Buffalo
Campbell, A. L., Lysite
Carey, C. D., Cheyenne
Carey, Robert D., Careyhurst
Carmin, Lem, Douglas
Claytor, I. M., Split Rock
Cox, Mark T., Cheyenne
deRham, Mrs. Chas., Jackson
Dew, Jack, Cora
Dodge, George, Rock River
Driskill, J. L., Hulett
Elliott, Jack, Cheyenne
Foss, F. W., Diamondville
Foster, M. C., Pine Bluffs
Foxton, J. H., Glendo
Gibbs, Fred O., Wheatland
Gratiot, J. T., Lander
Hagemeister, Lee D., Dwyer
Hickey, Joe, Lonetree
Horton, Frank, Buffalo
Huyler, C. D., Wilson
Hylton, Dr. J., Douglas
Hylton, Roy H., Douglas
Jasperson, C. W., Thayne
Jensen, Chris, Midwest,
Johnson, Chester, Alcova
Jones, T. J., Wheatland
Kendrick, Sen. John B., Sheridan
Lamb, Robert L., Sheridan
Larom; I. H., Valley
Mahoney, P. S., Buffalo Creek
⠀⠀⠀Live Stock Co., Arminto
Matheson, H. R., Teckla
McCarty, Ed, Chugwater
McDonald, Kenneth, Arminto
McGill, Owen D., Wheatland
Meigh, Robert J., Highland

Miller, Russ E., Buffalo
Morrison, E. H., Diamondville
Morton, Jack, Douglas
Neponset Stud Farm, Sheridan
Nicholas, Ridgely, Sheridan
Nicholas, Ridgley, Big Horn
Nylen, Gus, Douglas
Nylen, Gus, Orin Junction
O'Reilley, Mrs. Hazel, Horse Creek
O'Reilly, Mrs. Hazel, Cheyenne
Reavis, Thos. H., Sheridan
Schmidt, Karl F., Dull Center
Scott, J. G., Jackson
Shultz, Fred, Lander
Shumaker, Carl F., Casper
Smyth, S. Watt, Big Horn
Snyder, Simon, Painter
Spear, Wm., Sheridan
Spurlock, A. L., Alcova
Starr, J. W., Medicine Bow
Sun, Tom, Rawlins
Todd, Roger, Ucross
Valdez, Mark E., Lusk
Van Auken, W. G., Buffalo
Warren Livestock Co., Cheyenne
Welch, Art, Cowley
Yonder, Frank L., Torrington
Yonder-Marsh Co., Chugwater

REMOUNT STALLIONS—1921–1947

This is a partial listing of the stallions utilized by the United States Remount Service Horse Breeding Program from when it was organized in 1908 until it was phased out in 1948. Unless otherwise noted, the stallion listed is Thoroughbred. The prefix "Reno" denotes horses bred at the Fort Reno Remount Depot, Oklahoma; "Virginia" denotes horses bred at the Front Royal Remount Depot, Virginia and "Pomona" denotes horses bred at the Kellogg's Arabian Horse Farm during World War II. Each line contains the stallion's name, and when known, color, year foaled, sire and dam.

Listings have been compiled from the various "stud books" published by the Remount Service, the Fort Reno Daily Log, 1938–1941, material from Fort Robinson, Nebraska, lists and articles published in The Blood Horse, articles in various livestock publications of the period, 1921–1948, the National Quarter Horse Breeders and the American Quarter Horse Association stud books and catalogs listing the horses being sold at the Remount Dispersal Sales. The authors feel that this is not a complete list. All of the annual "stud books" or sale catalogs are not available and there is no way to obtain a complete stallion inventory. Over the years, records have become lost or destroyed due to fire or other circumstances.

Some of the later stallions were, interestingly, sired by individuals which had been donated to the Remount Service previously. Since many of the younger stallions were listed as donated by civilian horsemen, it is probable that they were foaled *before* their sires were donated to or purchased by the Remount.

A number of Remount stallions appear in Volume 1 (Nos. 1–27,000) of the AQHA stud book. A few figure prominently while others are only listed a few times. Some of those individuals are: Dennis Reed through his son Oklahoma Star P-6; King Plaudit through his son Plaudit; Uncle Jimmie Gray; Brettenham through his grandson Bear Hug; Fleeting Time through Clover Leaf and Joe Reed II's dam Nelline; Deering Doe through Brown Dick; Red Bug; Chimney Sweep; Master Gould; Pride of India; Lantandos through Red Landandos; Line Up; Buggins, King O'Neil II and Rancocus. Most probably their input can be attributed to the volume of operations conducted by the individuals who stood them.

Because of the number of appearances in the stud book by individual stallions, the United States Army Horse Breeding Program did make a major contribution to the

:an Quarter Horse and through that breed, to the Appaloosa, Palomino and Paint
:s we have today.

An asterisk (*) Indicates that the individual was imported to the United States. A
number (number) indicates Army serial number Preston Brand.

*Under the plan for the encouragement of the breeding of light horses, authorized by
Congress, and operated by the Remount Service, Quartermaster Corps, U.S. Army*

Reprinted from Stallion Distribution List—1948 Breeding Season

Aanad (Arabian)—Ch. 1938—Aabab—Nadirat
Abbadon (0P6)—Ch. 1944—Rifuas—Ferafa
Abbott (Morgan)—Ch. 1930—Monterey—Klyona
Above Par—Ch. 1934—Wise Counsellor—My Best
　　Girl
Accountant—Filligrane
Achill—B. 1920—Achtol—Belle Isle
Acropolis—1927—Short Grass—Grecian Bend
Adalid—Ch. 1910—Amigo—Lady Diamond
Adamad—B. 1926—Adalid—La Madre
Adanor—Ch. 1922—Adalid—Norette
Adams Express—Ch. 1908—Adam—Frederica
*Adept (A0012)—(European) Br. 1944—
　　Arjaman—Annemone
Admiral Bayley—Br. 1919—Disguise—Sea Air
Adevo—1920—Adalid—El Cheva
Advantage (7K97)—Ch. 1932—*Carlaria—Betty
　　Ames
Aga Khan—1921—*Omar Khayyam—Gravitation
After Me—1936—Stimulus—Katrina
Ah Ben (Arabian) Gray—1924—Azra—Dahura
Air Chief—1926—Pluvious—Risponde
Air Force—1933—Diavolo—Flying Squadron
Air Man—1926—Waterbay—*Calomal
Akbar (Arabian) Ch. 1942—Rabiyas—Ferafa
Alarm Clock—1929—Spur—*Jessant
Albert H.
*Alcazar—1931—Achtoi—Priscilla Carter
Aldeano—B. 1924—Al Bloch—Edith Inez
Alex, Jr.—Ch. 1917—Alex the Great—Bronzewing
Alexander Hamilton—1918—Sweep—Sweet Clover
*Alfred The Great—Br. 1931—*Teddy—Iberia
Algernon (55B2)—Ch. 1925—Fair Play—Lady Algy
Alhaamed—1936—Alcazar—Maaroufa
Allan Luck
All American—Ch. 1920—Pluvius—Margaret
　　Lowry
Allair Gold—1930—*Star of Gold—Pentecost's Last
Allen's Choice—Ch. 1922—Malamont—Great
　　Dolly
All Over—1919—Zeus—Lassie
Allumeur—B. 1911—Meddler—Strike a Light II
Almadel Jr. (223F)—Ch. 1931—Almadel—Blanche
　　Epine
Al Noble
Al Strauss—1918—Uncle—Serpentaria

Altawood
Altimeter—Br. 1926—Sporting Blood—Evil
Ambassador 4th—1911—Dark Ronald—Excllenza
American Eagle—Ch. 1915—The Manager—Star Cat
American Smile—1930—American Flag—
　　Laughons Eyes 2nd
Ammon (Arabian)—B. 1944—Farana—Hazzadina
Ampelos—1928—Craigangouer—Casuarina
Angel Jim—Ch. 1908—Tarquin—Gulliana
Ann Dolly—1927—Chatterton—September Moon
Anotherone—1933—Whichone—Circus Rider
Anticipate—B. 1917—Plaudit—Antipathy
Antigo II
Anton Cermak—Ch. 1926—*Polymelian—Lady
　　Winsome
Appreciate—Ch. 1926—McGee—Foyer
Appretry—B. 1939—Apprehension—Coventry Girl
Apron String—Eck Davis
Ardwan (Arabian)—B. 1921—Rodan—Fahreddin
Arena—*Sun Briar
Argonne—1915—Sunflower—Sunglass
Arjac—1936—Jacapo—Lady Argos
Areomail—Br. 1925—*Jack Stuart—Jennie Wood
Arnold—B. 1914—Peep O'Day—Victoria M.
Ashton—Ch. 1919—Electioneer—Francolin
Ashby—B. 1921—Mediator—Golden Meteor
Ashland Boy—Br. 1937—Aga Khan—Ashland Babe
Ask Me Another—1939—Vulcain—Schoolgirl
Astraled—1919
*Athanasius (A0039)—Br. 1931—Ferro—Athanasil
*Auftakt (A0016)—B. 1944—Janitor—Adrienne
Aurun—1925—Mushroom—Roual Anne
Autumn Bloom (39A3)
Autum Mark—1932—Mark Master—Autumn Leaf
*Aventin—Ch. 1929—*Teddy—Abbazia
Avery—Sonny Basil
Avalon
Avondale—Ch. 1923—Beiloc—Arrogance
Axmetic—Br. 1929—*Axenstein—Cosmetic

Baababi (Arabian)—Ch. 1942—Rabiyas—Raab
B'ar Hunter—B. 1928—Black Servant—*Bit of
　　White
Babolina—1935—Durbar—Bona
Bachelor Bird—1923—Bachelor's Double—Bird i'
　　the hand

Bachelor's Bliss—Blk. 1914—Tredennis—Lady Black

Bachelors Honor—1925—Bachelor's Double—Bayora

Back Fence—1933—Sullivan Trail—Mis Kittens

Bad Guess—Ch. 1929—*Craigangower—Quince Bush

Bad Lands—1922—*Athling 2nd—St. Aelwena

Baggage King—Ch. 1922— Blind Baggage—King Belle

Bah's Boy—Ch. 1920—Ecouen—Fille de Guerre

Baffling—1921—*North Star 3rd—Bandoura 2nd

Bahka (Arabian)—Ch. 1921—Mahon—Badine

Balamour 2nd—

Balance Wheel—B. 1919—Ben Brush—Whisk Broom

Baldy Chatty—Chatterton

Ball Boy

Balls T

Balroma—1926—Ballot—Edroma

Balustrade—B. 1916—Hanbridge—Oriental Queen

Baltus—1926—Polygnotes—*Bouton de Nacie

Ball Sport—B. 1930—Polante—Kaffir Maid

Banco—1926—Black Servant—Betty Beall

Band Time—1929—High Time—Brandymo

Bank Roll—1927—Coventry—Banksia

Barbaritan—Ch. 1935—Berrilsand—Barbara Whittier

*Barberry 2nd—B. 1932—Beresford—Toybridge

Bari (3P1) (Arabian)—Grey 1945—Alyf—Treyf

Barney Lucas—1910—Dr. Curtis—Massacre

*Barred Umber (580F)—Grey 1931—Sansovino—Barrulet

Barracuda—Ch. 1919—Trap Rock—Balancoire

Barrier—Ch. 1920—Madman—Elasticity

Barrington—B. 1923—Light Brigade—Five Aces

Barrons (42M2)—1933—Lantados—Dental

Barron Barton—1935—Sir Barton—Hay Market

Bartender—B'ar Hunter

Bartosol—Sir Barton

Barushan (Arabian)—B. 1921—Sinbad—Baraza

*Basalt (A0040)—Bl. 1943—Athanasius—Bastini

Bataan (Arabian)—Blk.—*Czubuthan—*Ba—Ida

Bat 'Em Out—Ch. 1923—James P. Silo—Bartender II

Bathorse—Ch. 1928—*Durbar II—Believe Me Boys

Battering Ram—B. 1928—Bubbling Over—Knockaney Bridge

Battersea—Ch. 1920—Mont d'Or—Sunflower

Battle Cry—B. 1921—War Call—Beetle Bug

Battle Royal—1927—High Time—Scramble

Battlewick (0Y9)—Ch. 1942—Battleship—Hotwick

Bay Barton—1934—Sir Barton—Sea Romance

Bay Beauty—B. 1926—Black Toney—Blushing Beauty

Bay Flight—1935—Carmelus—Flight Car

Bay Meteor—B. 1930—Meteorite—Irmalee T

Bazigha—(Arabian)—Ch. 1919—Abu Zeyd—Butheyna

Beachcomber—Br. 1911—Rock Sand—Fairy Slipper

Beach Orphan—Semprolus

Beal—B. 1935—Swope—Lady Bunting

Beau Gallant—1898—*Light Brigade—Bonita Belle

Beau Geste—1924—*Omar Khayyam—Sand Dune

Beau's Ship—Ch. 1943—Battle Ship—Beau's Gal

Beauregard—B. 1925—Black Toney—*Doreid

Beck Forth—1932—Dan 4th—Maybeck

Behave Yourself—1918—Maratho—Miss Ringlets

Belamore—1909—Rock Sand—Beldame

Belcross—Blk. 1921—Rock View—Sainville

Belfry II—1908—*Rock Sand—Beldame

Bellini—Br. 1920—Chouberski—Basse Terre

Belphre—1922—Ballot—Latonia

Benares—1931—Durbar 2nd—Mary Maud

Ben Gow—B. 1915—Neil Gow—Fruition

Bennington (Morgan)

Ben Royal—Ch. 1915—Flis—Rosebud III

*Bergkristall (A0018)—Ch. 1944—Aventin—Bachstelze

Bernie Harding—Ch. 1925—The Wanderer—Virginia Flannery

Bereavement—1928—Aga Khan—Widow's Weeds

Besom—Ch. 1925—*Golden Broom—Perfection

Bet A Million—*North Star III—Bit o' Love

Bet Mosie—B. 1919—*North Star III—Santa Anna II

Betelguese—1923—*North Star III—Thanid

Betelouese—Ch. 1922—*North Star III—Tranid

Better Still—Ch. 1919—*North Star III—Sweet Alice

Bewithus—1924—Black Toney—Doreid

Biff—B. 1931—Broadside—Wildwood

Biff Bang—1917—Textile—Byf

Big Blaze—B. 1921—Campfire—Queen of the Hills

Big Blow—Br. 1929—Wildair—*LaGrisette

Big Flag—1936—Big Blaze—Yellow Flag

Big Horn—1932—Gordon Russell—Eagle Arbie

Big Jim—1925—J. Garfield Buell—Eugenia Graves

Big Luke—1927—Secret Greetings—Arma L.C.

Big Light—B. 1934—Lee O'Cotner—Largo Light

Big Mack—1935—Macaw—Brassiere

Big Sink—*Paicines—Star Bertha

Big Spring—1927—Snob 2nd—Resist

Billbo—Ch. 1933—Bagenbaggage—Little Indian

Billy Boy—Br. 1936—Caddy Boy—Dorothy Jester

Billy McLaughlin—1918—Wrack—Lady Elite

Biloxi—1925—Sporting Blood—Alfadir

Bimbo—1928—Flying Ebony—Clover

Birdsell—Ch. 1934—Spearpoint—Beatrice G.

Birley M.C.—Ch. 1924—North Star III—Daisy Signal

Bit Bolder—Ch. 1919—Cunard—Winning Widow

Bit O'Peace (62M)—B. 1947—Peach Chance—Smatterings

Bivouac—Br. 1939—Fitzgibbon—Straw Bonnet

Black and Blue—B. 1928—Black Servant—Mary Grace
Black Bottom—1925—Friar Rock—Continent
Black Bug—Br. 1923—Norito—Brown Bee
Black Dick—1898—Sir Dixon—Merdin
Black Dove Br. 1928—Black Servant—Paloma
Blackfoot 2d—Br. 1934—*Rosolio—Cherokee Lil
Black Jacket—Br. 1920—Black Toney—Friar's Carse
Black Sole—B. 1928—Diligence—Meteuse
Black Tar (Arabian)—Ch. 1943—Katar—Niht
Black Warwick—Blk. 1931—Eternal—*Book Lore
Blithe Wood—B. 1924—War Call—Turn Turtle
Blue Bull—Br. 1923—Louie—Osage Lass
Blue Ash—Ch. 1927—Lord Martin—Ashtoreth
Blue Blitzen—1929—Eternal—*Reggilf—Aver
*Blue Don—B. 1926—Blue Ensign—Donna Inez
Blue Gauntlet—Ch. 1928—*Epinard—Columbia
Blue Larkspur—1926—Black Servant—Blossom Time
Blue Trace—B. 1936—Trace Call—Blue Dora
*Bluecoat—Grey 1920—Clydebridge—School
Bo Gordon
Bo McMillan—Ch. 1920—Ballot—Nettie Hastings
Bob—Ch. 1919—Orb—Panlita
Bob Humphrey—Ch. 1925—*Crimper—Queen Blonde
Bob Kay—1922—Robert Kay—Star Snip
Bob Romanesque (Morgan)—
Bob Shannon—B. 1927—Sporting Blood—*First Attempt II
Bob Tail—Helmet—Miss Ringletts
Boola Boola—1907—Ben Brush—the Mecca
Bolliver Bond—B. 1922—Light Brigade—Medaena
Bomar—Jean ValJean—Forest Nymph
Bone Dry—B. 1917—Beachcomber—Melton Mowbray
Boneby—Boneface—Niobe
Bonnie Jack—B. 1921—Wrack—Mary's Aunt
Bonnie Wrack—B. 1926—Bonnie Jack—Francis P.
Bonneville—Ch. 1936—*Lord of Law—Clementina
Boom—1924—*Huon—*Flying Jib
Boone's Knoll—Br. 1922—Brown Prince II—Macaroon
Borderland—Blk. 1922—St. Rock—Continent
Bordeaux
Boro Poker—Br. 1934—Desperate Desmond—Dinah's Dimple
Boston Fair—1936—Bostonian—Fairest
Boston Hill—Br. 1929—Bostonian—Lady Churchill
Bostwar—1936—Bostonian—Tulwar
*Botanic—B. 1923—Braxted—Auctioneering
Botanical—1926—*North Star 3rd—Bed of Roses
Boulder—Blue Larkspur—*Ephye
Bradley Boy—B. 1924—Major Bradley—Uscita
Bramstar—1925—Starhawk—Bramble Rose
Brave Bob—Br. 1922—Grand Parade—Lady Eager

Breast Plate—1923—Olambala—Simburst
Breezy Bill—1936—War Instigator—Little Fay
Breezy Player—1945—High Breeze—Little Player
Brettenham—1907—The Solicitor—Miss Used
Brian Boy—Grey 1923—Royal Canopy—Corveno
Bright Bud—Ch. 1940—Lord Autumn—
Bright Haven—*Bright Knight—Rock Haven
Brilliant Cast—Ch. 1921—North Star III—Macroon
Brilliant Jester—Br. 1917—Black Jester—Lady Brilliant
Bristol—1924—Brown Prince 2nd—Alverda
Bro. Compton—1913—Dr. Mack—Luna Beall
Broad Silk—1925—Bondage—Biddy McGee
Broadway Jones—Black Toney
Broccoli—B. 1928—*Epinard—Red Cross Girl
Brookland—Ch. 1915—Star Shoot—Dike
Broom—1924—*Huon—Flying Jib
Broomburg—Navigator
Brother Batch—B. 1918—Vulcain—Barbie
Brother Thomas—1934—Broadway Jones
Brown Derby—Br. 1922—Helmet—Mrs. F.C. Hogan
Brown Sugar—*Brown Prince II—Sweet Alice
Bruberry—1927—Brumado—Alderberry
Bubbling Over—1923—*North Star 3rd—Beaming Beauty
Buck Garrett—1923—Richety—Lucky Miss
Bucky Harris—1923—*Hourless—*Clef de Fer
Buckeye Poet—Br. 1927—Black Toney—*May Bird
Buckskin—B. 1939—Swashbuckler—*Beeuma
Buckthorne—1928—Top Hat—Steady Lady
Budlure—1937—Buddy Beaver—Golden Lure
Bud McDougal—Ch. 1918—Trap Rock—Run of Luck
Buggins—Br. 1930—Brown Bud—Brenda
Bug of Trinka (93M)—B. 1948—Red Bug—Reno Katrinka
Bull Boy—1932—Basil—Prudy
Bull Dog Tenacity—Br. 1921—North Star III—Biscuit Tertoni
Bulse—Ch. 1913—Disguise—Nethersole
Bunty—1942—Bunting—Dark Flower
Bulletin—1923—Atwell—Marsand
Burke's Boy—Br. 1923—George Smith—Deleusinia
Burning Blaze—1929—Big Blaze—Mexican Tea
Burning Glass—1925—Assagai—Dancin Son
Bushnell Lad—B. 1915—St. Amant—Allumetta
Bus Boy—1929—The Porter—Keltoi
Buster (04Y4)—B. 1939—Bull Dog—*Felina 2nd
Buzz Saw—Br. 1921—Meridian—See Saw II
By Hisself—1922—Man O'War—Colette
By The Stars—Br. 1916—Divination—Horoscope

Caath—B. 1935—Apprehension—Coventry Girl
Cabalero—Br. 1923—Cruzados—Letty Ree
Cabildo—Br. 1927—*Johren—Marguerite H.
Calabasas—B. 1939—Omaha—Percussion
Camas King—Ch. 1936—Snow King—Kango Dunn

*Campito—Ch. 1936—Alma Tadema—Kamara

Candy Mark—1928—Hall Mark—Candy Girl

Canmore—B. 1920—Marathon—Canice

Canmore Jr.—B. 1925—Canmore—Drucy B.

Cannae—B. 1923—Hannibal—*Orange Lilly

Cannon Shot—Br. 1921—War Shot—Purer

Cant Kost—B. 1916—Cantilever—Koster Girl

Canyon—Ch. 1919—Harmonicon—Welsh Maid

Captain Alcock—Ch. 1917—Ogden—Mallard

Captain Bridge—Ch. 1924—Setback—Flo Hargrave

Captain Costigan—Ch. 1920—Vandergrift—Bastante

Captain Hershler—B. 1917—The Manager—Fleeting Fashion

Captain Jinks—Gr. 1933—Mr. Jinks—*Chanelle

Captain Kinnarney—B. 1921—Dick Finnell—Idle Day

Captain Mosie—1926—Bet Mosie—Ben Daugharty

Captain Whitehead—B. 1913—Tad H—Deerfoot

Captain's Courageous—Ch. 1928—Stimulus—*Sea Dream

Carbineer

Care—1924—Comrade—Coralle

*Carmelus—B. 1928—Ellangowan—Carmel

Carpan—Ch. 1934—*Light Carbine—Mizanna

*Carneval—B. 1942—Antonym—Countessa La Motte

Carlton G—1907—Carlton Grange—Resignation

Carthage—Ch. 1922—Archaic—Rockwater

Caslium—B. 1934—Chicaro—Cop's Maid

Castleton—B. 1919—Sweep—Bell of Arcadia

Catalyte—Ch. 1936—Stimulus—*Catalpa

Cattail—1930—Sweep—Kitty Puss

Celtic Lad

Celtney—B. 1919—Jim Gaffney—Irish Queen

Centimeter—1918—Meelick—Regea

Cermaics—1916—Ballet—Wajolica

Cervlean—Ch. 1923—Broomstick—Sky Bird

Chance Flag (38M)—B. 1946—Perehance—Princess Flag

Chance Meeting—B. 1930—Chance Play—Continental

Champ de Mars—1924—*War Star—Yellow Blossom

Chappaqua, Jr.—Ch. 1914—Chappaqua—Yrsula

Chappie—1924—Golden Maxim—Bimeby

Chariot1927—Thunderer—Walf

Charlbury—Ch. 1922—Tad H.—Albia

Charlemagne—1925—Gay Crusader—*Princess Sterling

Charles B. Hall—Br. 1925—Donnaconna—Fritter

Charles Edward—Ch. 1904—Golden Garter—Flora Mac

Charmer—1928—Lucullite—Siren

Chatmoss—Br. 1929—Chatterton—Blue Moss

Chatty—1928—Chatterton—Countess

Chattillion (8M3)—Ch. 1944—Pillory—Lady Chatterton

Check Signal—B. 1935—Chicaro—Out Step

Checko—B. 1921—Ormondale—Checkers

*Cherry King II—Ch. 1925—Sun Star—Maid of Kent

Chevachie—B. 1921—Adalid—El Cheva

Chicho A Gar

*Chico—B. 1937—Umidwar—Athasia

Chucko A Gar

Chief Flag—Ch. 1939—Flag Pole—*Indian Maid

Chief John—B. 1928—Sir John Johnson—The Reaper

Chief Lally—B. 1915—King James—Rossiare

Chief Mourner—B. 1932—*Sir Gallahad III—Widow's Weeds

Chileula—Br. 1938—Chilhowee—Eulawa

Chilhowee—1921—Bollet—Bourbon Lass

Chilly Beau (78V)—B. 1939—Chilhowee—Beau's Gal

Chimney Sweep—Br. 1927—*Whisk Broom II—Polly Flinders

Chipping Norton—B. 1922—Tad H.—Clover Night

Choral Sand—1939—Sands of Time—Ave Maria

Choice Land—1938—R. Choice—Ashland Lady

*Cicerone (A0081)—B. 1935—Oleander—Countess Maddalena

Cirland

Clansman—B. 1919—Uncle—Katrine

Clarion Call—Ch. 1934—Ed Crump—Rowesgold

Classy Lad—Sir Charles

Claude M.—Ch. 1921—Enfield—Sassy

Clean Gone—B. 1916—Olambala—Lizzie Gilman

Clermont Jr.

Clever Seth—B. 1921—Seth—Pickaninny

Clock Tower—Br. or Blk. 1938—*Snob II—Daylight Savings

Clonsilla—1923—Sundian—Jelly

Cockalorum—1926—Snob II—Genevieve B

Cock O' The Walk—Ch. 1910—Peep O'Day

Coco J.—Ch. 1939—*Brig O' Doon—Contusion

Cockney—1921—Great Britian—L'Avenir

Cold Check—Ch. 1929—High Time—*La Planche de Briante

Colonel Orrie—1938—Scamp—Slient Moments

Colonel Rivers—B. 1922—Alvescot—Himera

Combustor—B. 1921—Hand Gernade—Rural Delivery

Comic—Ch. 1928—John P. Grier—Valentine

Comet—1923—Gnome—*Starflight

Commissioner Cahill —B. 1921—Everest—Beauty Bright

Compadre—Colin

Consort—Br. 1919—Celt—Silent Queen

Convoy—1917—Uncle—Orsina

Copper Chief (Morgan)—Ch. 1939—Tehachapi Allen—Ella Linsley

Cook's Memorial—B. 1935—In Memoriam—Deirdre

Coot II—1928—Phalaris—Concertina

Copy Cat—B. 1935—Apprehension—*Garden of Allah II
Coq d' Esprit—*Coq Gaulois—Duley
Coq Ola—1941—Coq d' Esprit—Olacream
Coral Reef Jr.—Ch. 1933—Coral Reef—Ragamier
Corindy—1945—Port au Prince—Cindy 35
Corsair—Recommend
Cotton Club—B. 1931—Brown Bud—Hold Me
Coventry—1922—Negofol—Sun Queen
Coverwood—1926—Trap Rock—Little Sweeper
Crack Favor—Br. 1937—Crack Brigade—*In Favor
Crack O'Day—1937—Hunky Dorey—Black Bessie
Cragsman—B. 1920 Lomond—Bieasdale
Cranford (Morgan)—1932—Mansfield—Evdora Crawford
Credit Balance—1930—Chaffinch—Princess Bush
Creeper—1927—*North Star III—Crimson Rambler
Crystal Chimes—Crystal Pennant
Crystal Pennant—1924—Pennant—Crystal Isles
Crystal Shiek—Ch. 1934—Crystal Pennant—Yucca
Cresent Pole (6Y4)—Ch. 1943—Flag Pole—Olacream
Crow Butte—B. 1939—B. 1939—Fitzgibbon—Dorothy Marie
Cruzard—B. 1923—Cruzados—Famosa
Crystal Chimes—Ch. 1939—Crystal Pennant—Belltop
Curfew—B. 1918—Ten Point—Lights Out
Curland—Ch. 1920—Golden Maxim—Eva K
Custas—1922—Huston—Minnie Lucas
Czardon—B. 1916—Royal Realm—Zoara

Daareyn (Arabian)—Grey 1940—*Raesyn—Raab
Daedalus—Ch. 1915—Aeronaut—Princess Chic
*Dahoman I (A0007) (Grade Arabian)—K. Dahoman I—558 Luna VIII
*Daimyo—B. 1921—Gay Crusader—Osaka
Dainger Lewis—Ch. 1935—*Carlaria—*Peline II
Dakota Note—1929—War Note—Keo May
Daljo—B. 1925—Daedalus—Lady Johnson
Dalston—1911—Sir Huron—Binda
Damascus (P83) (Arabbian)—Ch.1943—Rabiyas—Rayza
*Dan IV—Ch. 1918—Ex Voto—Delhadarra
Danburn (V60)—Ch. 1934—*Dan IV—Runfire
Danby—B. 1922—Star Master—Lady Algy
Dan Bunty—1932—*Dan IV—Bunty
Dan Henry—1929—*Dan IV—Freda II
Dandy Rock—1910—*Rock Sand—Donna Mia
Danger Rock—Ch. 1912—*Rock Sand—Delusion
Danour—B. 1928—Dozer—Wilton Flanna
Dapper Don—B. 1937—Don Leon—Miss Elegance
Dark Angel—*Star Hawk—*Breathing Spell
Dark Demon—B. 1924—Son—in—Law—Milva
Dark Friar—B. 1918—Sweep—Minnie Adams
Dark Hero (24A8)—Blk. 1928—*Herodot—Sunwina

Dark Jest—B. 1923—Black Jester—Ninette
Dark Mystery—1928—Dark Legend—Fairy Moon
Dark Winter—1930—Traumer—Sunwine
Dark Vision—Br. 1929—*Traumer—Sunbranji
Darwin—B. 1929—Jack Hare Jr.—Precious One
Dashalong—1934—Whiskalong—Rash Promise
David B—1933—Just David—Miss Ora
Dear Brutus—Ch. 1923—Achievement—Lady Borgia
Deb's Miller—Yellow Stone
*Deering Doe—1914—Desmond—Action
Deering Step—Ch. 1921—*Deering Doe—True Step
Defense—1914—Star Shoot—Dike
Defense Act—B. 1939—Irish—Maryland Lou
Delarious—1925—Hilarious—Marie T
Delaware—B. 1916—Ormondale—Livonia
Delhi—1901—Ben Brush—Veva
Delman—B. 1915—Fugleman—Delicia
Delmont (Morgan)—B. 1932—Ulysses—Ladella
Delmor—Br. 1921—Delhi—Morion
*Delphinium—1933—Blue Larkspur—Mulliflora
Del Ray—Swedish King
Delwyn—1932—Royal Canopy—Gypsum
Demonstrate—Ch. 1934—Display—Dick's Daughter
Denmark Morgan (Morgan)—1934—Mansfield—Glen Arrow
Dennis Reed—Blk 19ll—Lobos—Bess Chitman
Denny Cooney—1925—Sweep—Hindu Dress
Denver Lad—*Light Carbine
Dennydance—Ch. 1919—Judge Denny, Jr.—Flying Dance
Departed—Ch. 1933—*Teddy—All Gone
Desmond's Day—Br. 1913—Desmond—Palmy Days
Desperate—Br. 1911—St. Frusquin—Donnetta
Despot—Ch. 1922—Flittergold—Destine
Devil Dog—B. 1917—Darley Dale—Mountain Fringe
Devil's Due—Br. 1927—Meridian—Devil To
Dewey (Morgan)—B. 1910—General Gates—Mrs. Culvers
Dick's Smile—B. 1922—Gold Enamel—Smiling Buck
Diego—1926—Setback—Novice Girl
Dinter (East Prussian)—1924—Diebitche—Morena
Dispeller—1930—Brig O' Doon—Alleviation
Divine Kan—Br. 1943—Kanter—Divinity
Dix Fois—1937—Pillory—Soubrette
Do Behave—1931—Behave Yourself—*Yellow Sea
Do Or Die—Br. 1922—Light Brigade—Lady Vulcan
Doc Horn—Ch. 1921—Flying Squirrel—Debutante
Doc Jock—B. 1936—Jock—Edna Cook
Docod—Ch. 1916—Voorhees—Love of Gold
Doctor Howard—Ch. 1918—Handsell—Grace Navarre
Doctor J. P. O'Connell—1927—Omar Khayyam—Barbara Frietchie

Doctor Swartz—1923—Sweep—Toucanet

Doctor Willis—1925—Irak—Nadin M.

Dollar Joe—

Don—1926—Mustard Seed—Kaffir Queen

Donacare—1931—*Donnacona—Spartina

Don Diego—Blk. 1924—Luke McLuke—*Donna Roma

Don Dude (Morgan)—B. 1919—Donald—Kitty Dean

Don McKinley (Standardbred)—Ch. 1912—Mack Henry—Effie Hasty

Don Ricardo—B. 1926—*Donnacona—Confusion

Donday (Morgan)—B. 1919—Donald—Bessie Baker

Donnay (4K32)—B. 1926—*Donnacona—Kiwanah

Door Boy (67M)—B.1947—*Open Door—Reno Katrinka

Door Cap (46M)—B. 1947—*Open Door—Ski Cap

Dorothy Dan—1929—Dan IV—Pajamas

Douai (Morgan)—B. 1921—Dot—Daisy K

Double Cross—Ch. 1919—Superman—Olevia

Double Pay

Double Rambler—*Easton Rambler

Double Reno (47M)—Ch. 1947—Reno Inhale—Reno Panic

Double Swath (06Y3)—Ch. 1945—Paisleypair—Saythess

Douglas S.—B. 1914—Sir Huon—Victoria B.

Dozeless—Ch. 1931—Dozer—Helpless

Dr. Henry—Ch. 1922—Marse Henry—My Nurse

Dr. Mack—1903—Samovas—Clincher

Dr. Maxon—1924—Golden Maxim—Hasty Chick

Dr. Root—Dr. Sam

Dr. Streett—1924—Flying Squirel—Debutant

Dr. West—1924—Dr. Mecum—Toucanet

Dragon II—B. 1915—Friz Herbert—Mistress Penn

Drapasor—

Drawstraws—B. 1936—Clock Tower—Corn Silk

Dreamer—Br. 1921—Manager Waite—Dream Girl

Dress Ship (9F90)—1927—Bunting—Pageant

Drowsy Waters—Br. 1922—Cataract—Bronzewing

Dry Moon—1918—Ulmbola—Honeymoon

Drypool—1937—Fair Bail—Lida G.

Dude Hudson (Morgan)—Br. 1903—Fred Hudson—Velma

Due North (V586)—Ch. 1938—Discovery—Snowshoe

Duke of Lancaster—Ch. 1915—John O'Gaunt—Tamanamass

Duke of Ormond—1907—Orsini—Santutalla

Dundee—1926—Dalston—Dainty Dancer

Dunna—1933—K of K—Senorita Anita

Duplicate—B. 1923—C. Brown—Nora Daly

Durham—B. 1923—Durbar—La Cagoule

Dutch Beau—B. 1935—Bay Beauty—Dutch Girl

Dutiful Don—1927—Drastic—Eugenia Graves

Duval—1909—Lisish—Mary Greenwood

Dwarf—Br. 1921—Setback—Dolly Hayman

Eagle Chief—Br. 1926—Krippen—Verdum Belle

Eagle Pass—Ch. 1934—Night Flyer—Miss Simplicity

Easter Bay—Mad River

Easter Bells—1920—Black Toney—Mission Bells

Easter Martin—1931—Young Martin—Dixie Lou

Easter Time—1929—High Time—Complexion

Eaton Rambler—Ch. 1914—Steadfast—Cyclamen

Ecstasy—1939—Scamp—Stimulation

Ed Stone—1916—Assagai—Bettie Sue

Ed's Star (3J27)—Ch. 1948—Old Master—Jest Mare

Edna May's Choice (Saddlebred)—

Eight O Four—1927—*Negofol—Betty Hanes

El Bardo—B. 1922—Adalid—Bardolita

El Chedal—ch. 1923—Adalid—El Cheva

El Dinero II—Ch. 1922—Uncle—Herodia

Elmer—*Chicle

El Pennant—Br. 1927—War Pennant—El Amiga

El Sakab (Arabian)—Ch. 1915—El Jafil—Narkeesa

Election—B. 1914—Ballot—Sadie S.

Elite—Br. 1919—Dandy Rock—Golden Meteor

Elkwood—Blk. 1916—Elkhorn—Contestor

*Ellanglock—B. 1929—*Ellangowan—Turmglocks

Elmendorf—B. 1915—Ballot —Discipline

El Sabok (Arabian)—

Endeavor—1936—Gordon Russell—Traleta

Endurance—

Enduring—1927—Eternal—Lady Chariot

Enechie Joe—1936—Perchance—Miss Enechie

Energy—B. 1921—*Colonel Vennie—Commensia

Enthroned—1928—Upset—Miss Minks

Ephecian—Hour Glass

Epinique—Ch. 1933—*Epinard—Martinique

Epiphznes—1917—Honeywood—Purse Rose

Erskine Dale—1919—Sweep—Frances Gaines

*Escapade—1929—All Alone—Laughing Eyes

Escott—1930—Escoba—Kittie Mae

Escovar—Br. 1916—Sweep—Valeurcuse

Espatant—B. 1937—Stimulus—Enticing

Espejo—*Swiftfoot 2nd

Esperalid—B. 1924—Adalid—Esperito

Esquire—B. 1918—Meridian—Daruma

Estbartonson—Sir Barton

Et Cetera—B. 1929—Prince of Wales—Melting Star

Eton Rambler—1916—Stedfast—Cyclamen

Evan—1934—Bennington—Lady Sealeet

Ever—Blk. 1929—Eternal—*Bachelor's Choice

Everett—1907—*Goldcrest—Francolin

Excite—1933—Stimulus—Arena

Exhilaration—B. 1935—Sir Andrew—Exhilarate

Eyebrow—1909—Star Shoot—Eyelet

Fahid (Arabian)—Ch. 1923—Sargon—Balkis II

Fair Rochester—B. 1930—For Fair—Lady Rochester

Fair Wind—Fair Play—*Blaircora

Farana (Arabian)—B. 1929—*Nasik—*Farasin
Faris (Arabian)—Ch. 1924—Rizvan—Balkis II
Farmer Jim—1914—Abe Frank—Miss Breeze
Farnley Leader (Cleveland Bay)—B. 1940—
    *Cleveland Farnley—Mulgrave
Fashion Plate —Ch. 1906—Woolsthorpe—
    Fashionable
Father Rock—Ch. 1924—Friar Dixon—Grecian Maid
*Fasching—1925—Dark Ronald—Falada
Fast Company— *Kemano
Fayette C.—Ch. 1915—Fayette—Rose Queen
Fazil (Arabian)—Ch. 1924—Nafia—Badine
Federal—Ch. 1923—Trap Rock—Federal Girl
Fenek V (Arabian)—1932—Fenek—Slieve
Fenek IV (Arabian)—1944—Fenek—Maxim II
Ferados—B. 1923—Cruzados—Feranda
Ferole—B. 1909—Orme—Ferment
Fervor—Br. 1928—Broomstick—Rapture
Feuerbach (East Prussian)—1924—Rembrant—
    Fabula
Feudal Times—B. 1929—*Sir Gallahad III—Fancy
    Light
Fiddle Fit—1928—Sumpter—Unknown F462
Field Marshall—1925—Man O War—Little Flower
Field Officer—1938—Tote—Perfect
Fighting Joe—Br. 1927—Dunlin—*Pearl II
Figuration—Br. 1918—Bogon—Figent
Filemaker—1924—Ambassador 4th—*Filante
Final Appeal—B. 1934—Supremus—*Royal
    Dispatch
*Fine Manners—1924—Souviens—Photime
Fire Chief—1924—Under Fire—Bronzewing
Fire Dog—1924 —Under Fire—Avis
Fire Lane—1926—Runnymeade—Pyrope
Firing Squad—Ch. 1933—Chance Shot—Grief
Firing Point—Br. 1934—Stormy Port—Lady
    Ancestor
First Chip—1900—First Mate—Chippie
First There—
Firthcliffe—1912—Bingara—
Fir Tidy
Fitzgespera—Br. 1929—Fitzgibbon—Espera
Fitzgibbon—Br. 1919—Huron—Rossiare
Fitz Robinson—Ch. 1932—Fitzgibbon—Half—Staff
Fitz Sylvia—1938—Fitzgibbon—Sylvia Mede
Fitzmerry—1939—Fitzgibbon—Merry
Fitzrue—Ch. 1920—Fitzwilliam—Mary Street
Flabene (82M)—Ch. 1948—Flag Pole—Va Bene
Flag's Beau (94M)—B.1948—Flag Pole—Beau's Gal
Flag Bonnent (80M)—Ch. 1948—Flag Pole—Pretty
    Bonnet
Flagelder Red (74M)—Ch. 1948—Red Bug—
    Flagelda
Flagwick (58M)—Ch. 1947—Flag Pole—Hatwick
Flag of Truce—1920—Jim Gaffney—Maltha
Flag Pole—American Flag—Bromotta
Flanders—B. 1934—Herodot—Dutch Girl
Flannel Shirt—B. 1919—King James—Turkey Red II

Flashalong—1939—Chance Shot—Lady Gibson
Flash Rock—1921—*Vulcain—Duck's Pet
*Flechazo—Ch. 1937—Magnax—Titanica
Fleet Bank
Fleeting Time—Ch. 1923—Last Coin—British Fleet
Fletcher M—1915—Hilarious—Mollie Cromwell
Flitlow—Ch. 1921—Flittergold—Loriotee
Flowerful—Br. 1920—Ypsilanti II—Bouquet
Flying Heels—1927—Flying Ebony—Heeltaps
Flying Puritan—1931—Pillory—Benita
Flying Sailor—1930—Navigator—Lucie May
Fogabala—1938—Blenheim 2nd—Marching Along
Footprint—1908—*Rock Sand—Fetish
Forced March—B. 1934—Swift and Sure—Flying
    Squadron
Foregone—1920—Foreground—Anita
Foreign Exchange—Ch. 1927—*Epinard—Money
    Mart
Forever Young—Ch. 1932—Peter Pan—Oreya
Forest Play—1933—Chance Play—Forest Nymph
*Formas—(Half—bred)—Ch. 1936—Lancelot—
    Formamint
Fort Keogh—Ch. 1923—Achievement—Appolita
Fortunate Youth—1927—Lucky Hour—Mollie King
Fourteen
Fourty One—1934—*Spearpoint—Arma L. C.
Forty Winks (OD73)—1934—Twink—Alicia W.
Four Bits—Ch. 1932—*Dan IV—Tidgee
Fourplus (Anglo—Arab)—1937—Walkout—
    Glenwayne
Four Spades—B. 1933—*Dan IV—Queen of Spain
Fox Squirrel—1929—Flying Squirrel—Debutante
Freda 2nd—1918—Torloisk—Menthol
Fredericktown—B. 1921—Pennant—Gentlewoman
Free Hand—Ch. 1921—High Time—Amanuensis
French Canadian—Ch. 1920—Pataud—Phantom
    Light
French Door (26M)—B 1948—*Open Door—Eh
    Bien
Frair's Chance (31M)—B.1946—Perchance—Reno
    Linette
Friar Dixon—B. 1919—Friar Rock—Queen Dixon
*Friar Dolan—Br. 1929—Knight of the Garter—
    LaNeuvaine
Friar's Cowl—B. 1924—*Friar Dixon—Initiatee
Frisco Kid—1934—Jean Valjean—Tesuque
Frizzle—Ch. 1911—Biniou—Frizette
Front Boy—Ch. 1932—Skivesdale—Cimarron
Full Dress—Man O' War
Fullon—Ch. 1920—Friar Rock—Miss Borgia
Funny Face—Ch. 1924—Short Cut—Glen Brier
Fun Maker—1922—Spur—Jest
*Furioso II (3J22) (European)—Br. 1933—Furioso
    VII

G. M. Miller—B. 1907—Lissak—Subdue
Gadar (Arabian)—Ch. 1920—Abu Zeyd—
    Guemura

Galetian—B. 1923—*Trompe la Mort—*Lady
  Galette
Gallant Knight—1927—*Bright Knight—Ethel Gray
Gallantman—B. 1919—Superman—Galanta
Gallant Prince—B. 1932—Gallant Fox—Merry
  Princess
Gallon—B. 1939—*Thorndown—May B.
Gallopin' Son—1930—Busy American—Red Leaf
Galus—B. 1929—Stimulus—Golden Autmn
Gamhuri (Arabian)—B. 1939—Raseyn—Feraga
Gamli—Br. 1917—Myram—Bustler
Ganadore—Br. 1909—The Commoner—Mountain
  Mist
Ganawood—Ch. 1924—Ganadore—Fernwood
Garlouisk—B. 1926—Gargoyle—Freda II
Garrison Flag—B. 1943—Flag Pole—Isabel B.
Gay Comet—B. 1921—Sunstar—Wayward
Gay Gent—1948—Red Bug—Virginia Lassy
Gay Laddie—1930—Sir Luke—Anemone
Gayly—Ch. 1921—Transvaal—Airey
*Gazal III (Arab—Kind)—Ch. 1934—Gazal II—
  Shagya XVII
Gebhat Al Nour (Arabian)—B. 1923—Sidi—Hazen
Gems to Let—Ch. 1924—Parisian Diamond—Letty
  Lind
Gene Autry—Ch. 1939—Major Bowes—Callie
General Grant—B. 1925—American Ace—Prim Lady
General Hadley—1908—Don Orsino—Hortense
  Rhea
General Haig—B. 1916—Dick Welles—My Fair
  Kentucky
General Haldeman— 1924—Thunderstorm—La
  Dolores
General Lee—Ch. 1924—*War Cloud—Nancy Lee
General Parth—B. 1931—General Lee—Parthia
General Pillow—Ch. 1934—*Hourless—Colfin
George Maypole—B. 1928—*Polymelian—Blue
  Jean
Ges Auwil (Arabian)—Ch. 1943—Rifnas—
  Rokhalda
Getalong—Br. 1931—Sleepy Head—Goldie S.
Ghayr (Arabian)—Gr. 1924—Astraled—Guemur
Gibbling
Gibon—Ch. 1921—The Manager—Oreen
Giraldo—1898—Amigo—Indianaola
Give Away—1940—Fitzgibbon—Sweet Charity
Glasstol—B. 1915—Santol—Reveillee
Glaze Over
Glen De Jarnette (Morgan)—Ch. 1916—De
  Jarnette—Frances
Glenerrol Gold—Br. 1941—Time Supply—Alma J.
Glen Oak—B. 1926—Whisk—Hasty Maid
Glen Rock—1930—Kickapoo—Toto
Glentilt—B. 1920—Ecouen—Glorita
G.M. Miller—1907—Lissak—Subdue
Gnome Boy—Ch. 1927—Gnome—Lazy Lady
Gloreous Gordon—B 1933—Gordon Russell—
  Glorita

Gold Bug—B. 1921—Broomstick—Golden Rod
Gold Enamel—1902—*Maddison—Enamel
Goldpen (Morgan)
Gold Trail—Ch. 1934—Sullivan Trail—Golden Dust
Golden Bear—1924—Adalid—Cruzada
Golden Bee—Ch. 1933—Bees—Alys Thayer√
Golden Boss—Ch. 1920—The Boss—Golden Hen
Golden Boy—Ch. 1932—Morvich—Golden Mary
Golden Dust—1924—Golden Brown—Shadow
Golden Fagot—Ch. 1923—Fair Fagot—Golden
  Ramble
Golden Leaf—Elmendorf
Golden Link—1896—Dundee—Ruth
Golden Opportunity—1924—*Golden Broom—
  Substitute
Golden Racket—Ch. 1925—Golden Maxim—
  Brightstone
Golden Seal—Ch. 1933—*Golden Broom—Josie A
Golden Trail—1934—Sullivan—Golden Dust
Goldic—1903—*Goldfinch—Cluc
Gonzalo—Br. 1917—Bard of Hopee— Fanchette
Good Justice—Ch. 1939—*Justice F—Marura
Good Star—1936 Ch.—Epithet—Thistle Star
Goodly—1933—*Waygood—Chesney Lass
Go Play—1933—Mere Play—Laura Frechtling
Goracta—1944—Gordon Russell—Stamp Act
Gordon Russell—Br. 1910—*Marchmont II—
  Tokalon
Gordon Trail—Br. 1938—Gordon Russell—Traleta
Gordon Wells—B. 1925—Gordon Russell—Zadie
  Wells
Gordon's Stamp—Br. 1936—Gordon Russell—
  Stamp Act
Governor of Orleans (Morgan)—B. 1914—Ben
  Lomond—Maid of Orleans
Gowan—B. 1927—Ellangowan—Cissy Brown
*Grain de Cafe—Br. 1922—Bhar El Gazel—Claude
  de France
*Grand Vizier—1928—Teddy—Pointe du Serail
Granary—1926—The Finn—Garner
Granite Prince—1930—Baby Grand—Slim Princess
*Gratteur—Drk. Br. 1923—Macdonald II—Gala
Gray Hat—1933—Kiev—Chapeaulette
Green Melon—1933—Whichone—*Rambling 2nd
Greencomber—Blk 1922—Beachcomber—Elsie
  Green
Greenock—1925—The Porter—Starella
Green Palms—1932—Louverne—Palm Sunday
Greenway's Best—Aloha
Grenadier II—Ch. 1919—Bonspiel II—Golden Queen
Grey Eagle—Gr. 1915—Grey Leg—Memoria II
Grey Friar—1933—Baytown—Marriage Lines
Grey Hill—1924—Tetratema—Betty Hill
Grins—Ch. 1934—Victorian—Laughing Laura
Gudea (Arabian)—1940—Khyber—Gubba
Guest of Honor—1920—Patoud—Bright Star
Guilsborough—B. 1922—Diadumenos—Clare
  House

Gun Rock—Ch. 1914—Rock Sand—Gun Fire

Gus Kruse—Ch. 1917—Regon—Nellie Fitz

Guy Maxey (Standardbred)—B. 1936—Guy Leaf—
Vitha Maxey

Hackberry—Ch. 1926—Wampum—De Prisa

Hadrian—B. 1916—Free Lance—Semprite

Halanda (1V53) (Arabian)—Ch. 1937—Rehal—
Lady Anne

Haldeman—B. 1908—McGee—Long Glen

Hale's Error (3J30)—Ch. 1948—St. Mirth—Lab.
Mare

Half Mast—Ch. 1915—Shorty Skillful—Misty's
Pride

Half Pint—B. 1922—*Spanish Prince II—Kirwanah

Half Rock—Ch. 1917—Rock Sand—Half Sovereign

Hall Mark—Ch. 1920—Sand Marsh—Clarice

Hamilkar (East Prussian)—Ch. 1920—Hazelhost—
Hirtensage

Hampson—Ch. 1925—Peter Quince—Margaret
Hampson

H.M. War—Ch. 1939—Man O' War—Bridgeen
Hansen

Handy Shot—1916—Call Shot—Handy Cup

Haphazard—B. 1923—Escoba—Kaskaskia

Happy Man—Br. 1938—Tote—Merry

Happy Scot—B. 1928—Scotch Broom—Felicitation

Happy Time—Br. 1925—High Time—Little
Blossom

Happy Valley—B. 1915—Plaudit—Top All

Harbinger—1924—Eternal—Grace Harban

Hard Ship—Harmony

Hardwood—Br. 1923—Broomstick—Duckshot

Hardy Jim—Ch. 1936—Sir James—Hardy Fern

Harpost—1929—*Harpenden—Postillion

Harry M.—1923—Elmendorf—Texas Lassie

*Havana Boy—B. 1921—Spearmint—Scared Ibis

Haven (Morgan)—Ch. 1937—Delmont—Topaz

Hawk Jim—(Morgan) Ch. 1929—Linsley—Lady
Spar

Hawthorn Medley—Ch 1924—*Polymelian—
Sweet Music

Hawthorne Hiram—Ch. 1925—Peter Quince—
Lady Rotha

Haymaker—1926—Dominant—Quell

Hazy—Ch. 1922—Ultimus—Perplexing

Hazznas (Arabian) B. 1939—Rifnas—Hazzadina

Headliner—Kilkerry—that's That

Hearalot

Heather Bee—B. 1921—Honey Bee—Sedge

Heathermoon—1911—White Eagle—Virginia Earl

Heel Print— B.—Dark Vision—Minnie Sloan

Helmet—1906—Disguise—*St. Mildred

Hendrick—Br. 1922—George Smith—Auriesville

Henry Grant—Ch. 1937—Sidney Grant—Utah
Nurse

Henry of Navarre—1891—Knight of Ellerslie—
Moss Rose

Hep Kat (Arabian)—Grey 1943—Katar—Pehalf

Hercynian—1929—Naughty Boy 2nd—Turn Turtle

Here's Hoping—B. 1922—Bard of Hope—Tantalize

Hereowee—B. 1939—Chilhowee—Dot's Sugar

Hermis Kemble—Ch. 1919—Prince Hermis—
Fanny Kimble

Herron—B. 1917—Horron—Mizzie

Heuvelton—B. 1934—Hi—Jack—Maid of Honor

Hi Henry—B. 1917—Hilarious—Rosetinge

Hickory—B. 1919—Prince Hermis—Lou Hazel

Hidalgo—1922—Spanish Prince—Minuet

Hidden Rock—Ch. 1924—Trap Rock—Divination

High Ball—1923—Midway—Eye Ball

High Fruit—1928—High Noon—Fruit Cake

High Clover—1931—High Time—Castanet

High Hand—Br. 1920—Fair Play—Houte Roche

High Line—High Time

High Point—Ch. 1933—Transmute—Rondelle

High Prince—1920—*Monte d'Or 2nd—Yermila

High Santa—Ch. 1933—High Cloud—Donna Santa

High Star—1923—*North Star 3rd—Haute Roche

High Step—Ch. 1927—High Time—*High—Born
Lady

Highland Chief—1908—Mortlake—Lucrezir Borgia

Highland Lad (Morgan)—Ch. 1912—Scotland—
Marguerite

Highwayman—1923—*Prince Pal—Holdup

Hill Billy Boy—

Hillside—B. 1923—Trompe la Mort—Gipsey Hill

Hindoo Star—1908—Star Shoot—Sister to Hindoo
Craft

Hiram—Ch. 1925—Peter Quince—Lady Rotha

His Majesty—B. 1910—Ogden—Her Majesty

Historicus—B. 1922—Belloc—Arrogance

Hold Easy—1928—Olambala—Holdup

Home Crest—1906—Water Crest—Sister Jeanie

Homme Rouge (N996)—B. 1936—Richfield—
Shasta Red

Home Sweet Home—Ch. 1914—Ballot—
Homespun Hangover

Homestretch—Ch. 1920—Bard of Hope—Star of
Runnymeade

*Honi Sort—Ch. 1925—Star and Gartar—
Koningin

Hong Kongs—1916—Hovac—Royal China

Honolulu Boy—Ch. 1915—Salvation—Zorita

Hoosier Prince—1929—High Time—*Rosanne

Hootch—Ch. 1922—Polymelian—Home Bird

Horma—1927—Nuri Pasha—Dawn

Hornblende—B. 1938—Hi—Jack—Maliza

*House—1919—Lomond—Wenchal

Howee—B. 1929—Chilhowee—Zeka

H.T. Waters—1921—Polymelian—Lady Winsome

Huffaker—B. 1913—Dick Welles—Outwai

Humanist—1926—Politian—Quite Dark

Humboldt—B. 1920—Atheling II—Celesta

Hunkey Dorey (2M15)—Br. 1933—Scat—April's
Lass

Husband—Ch. 1922—Wormleighton—Daisy Platt
Hush Money—Br. 1926—Danger Rock—Bell Hour
Huxter—1908—Sorcerer—Irony

Iam Good—B. 1937—Goodestone—Sister Relay
I'll Get By—Ch. 1929—Ed Crump—What'll I Do
II. M. War—Ch. 1939—Man o' War—Bridgeen
Ibn Zaid (Arabian) Ch. 1928—Rehai—Rawada
Impropriety—1925—Somekiss—Crimson Square
Indel (05Y9)—Br. 1945—Ariel—Indigestion
Indian Lament—1934—Danour—Bereavement
Indian Name—Blk. 1938—Neddie—Sunaiki
Indian Sky—1932—Sky Raker—Indora
Indian Star—1928—Indian Trail—Starletta
Indian Trail—1920—Delhi—Galaxy
Infidox—1933—Infinite—Paradox
Ingleton—Br. 1927—Helmet—Double Three
Inherit—1932—*Sickle—Maharonee
Inheritor—1928—Sidereal—Chesney Lass
Interrogator—1940—Scamp—Ask Me Another
Intrude—Ch. 1928—Indian Trail—Gertrude
Invergarry—1907—Juvenile—Duchess Lucia
Irish—1926—The Finn—Ohone
Irish Bank
Irish Buzzer—Ch. 1921—Irish Exile—Buzzy Bee
Irish Dancer—Ch. 1917—Celt—Ballet Girl
Irish Holliday—1926—Bunting—Mrs. MC
Irish King—Ch. 1923—Irish Exile—Alessia
Irish Luck—Ch. 1942—Irish—Opportunitist
Irish Mick—1933—Fitzgibbon—Heimick
Irish Shower (M39)—B. 1941—Irish—Shower of
    Roses
Irish Wake—1930—Stimulus—Widow's Weeds
Iron Sides—1925—Man O' War—Bee's Wax
Iron Wood—1924—Assagai—Mint Hill
Izzy's Open (50M)—B. 1947—*Open Door—
    Isabel B.

J. G. Bickel—B. 1922—Alvescot—Marna
J. Garfield Buell—Ch. 1915—Martinet—Mrs. Annie
J. J. Murdock—B. 1913—Contestor—Grotesque
Jack—Ch. 1928—Star Spangled—*Griselle
Jack Beyond—B. 1934—Hi-Jack—Far Beyond
Jack Spratt—B. 1927—*Deering—Doe—Nancy
    Lane
Jack Stuart—Br. 1915—Valens—Sweet Sauce
Jaguar—B. 1927—*St. Germans—Leoperdess
Janissary (Arabian)—Ch. 1916—Jahil—Nessa
Jasper—B. 1925—Craigangower—Sard
Jean LaFitte—B. 1927—Sand Mole—Jeanne Bowdre
Jedran (90F3) (Arabian)—Ch. 1932—Ghazi—
    Baribeh
Jendolan—1943—Friar Dolan—Jenny Camp
Jennie War—1929—War Note—Jennie J. Douglas
Jesse—1917—Clysmis—Miss James
Jim Colito—1932—Angel Jim—Lady Colito
Jim Robin—1929—Jim Gaffney—Sea Robin
Jineill—1928—Jingo—Miss Neill

Jinam—Ch. 1928—Jingo—Amigarit
Jingo—Ch. 1909—St. Simonian II—Edna Gerry
Job—1922—Sans Le Sou—Jenny III
Joe Flores—B. 1929—*Axenstein—Hester Ann
Joe Marrone II—Ch. 1921—Glencairn—Ringling
John Hager—Ch. 1921—Beaverkill—Rose Ring
John F.—Ch. 1928—Ladkin—Pousette
John One—Ch. 1935—Man o' War—On Her Toes
John S. Mosby—1922—Sea King—Puff
John S. Reardon—B. 1918—Ormondale—Antella
John W. Weber—1924—Gnome—Iareena
John White—Br. 1922—The Finn—Adelaide Royer
Johnnycake—Ch. 1933—John P. Grier—
    *Marvella II
Johren—B. 1915—Spearmint—Minenla
Joker—1924—Convoy—Eve
Jokester—B. 1932—*Dark Jest—Vint Daphine
Jouett—B. 1917—McGee—Muff
Joyzelle—1923—Lord of the Hills
Juan Eva—1925—Campfire—Battle
Jubilate—
Judge B. Watkins—Ch. 1905—Nimrod—Little Easter
Judicial—Ch. 1923—McGee—Bonny Doon
Jumna—Br. 1923—Delhi—Florence Webber
Jungle Chase
*Jungherr (A0015)—Br. 1944—Brantome—Jennie
Jupiter—Ch. 1920—Ormondale—One Star
*Jussuf (Arab—Kind)—Grey 1939—Jussuf IV—
    Shagya XXI
Justaheim
Just David—1921—*Atwell—Viola Mabel
*Jusqu'an Boot—1915—Ajax—Roquette

K of K—Ch. 1915—Glasgerion—Mrs. K
Kai Feng—Ch. 1927—Kai—Sang—Dauntless
*Kaiserstuhl (A00190) (Arabian)—Br. 1944—
    Pharis—Croissay
Kalaf (Arabian)—
Kaleidoscope—1928—Golden Broom—Pink and
    Yellow
Kalirice—Br. 1925—Kalitan—Louie Grice
*Kantar—B. 1925—Alcantara II—Karabe
Karachi—B. 1922—Light Brigade—Madras
Katar (Arabian)—1929—Gulastra—Simawa
Katorma (Arabian)—Grey 1943—Katar—Horma
Keen Eye—Ch. 1925—Eyebrow—*Kena
Kearsarge—B. 1933—*Kantar—Ksarine
Kehafe (Arabian)—1930—Nuri Pasha—Ophir
Keltic—1926—K of K—Starlette
Kempland—B. 1913—Monte d'Or II—Reveries
Kenmore's Silver Mackson (Saddlebred) —
Kentucky Cardinal—Ch. 1922—*North Star III—
    *Lucrative
Kenward—1914—*Alvescot—Bashford Belle
Khalaf (Arabian)—1928—Nuri Pasha—Ophir
Khalmer (Arabian)—1938—Khalil—Wetonah
*Khedive 2nd—Roi Hendah—Wetomah
Khordad—1933—Kantar—Ksarine

Khyber (Arabian)—Kaibab—Fath
Kibyr (Arabian)—B. 1943—Sikin—Ferdirah
Kickapoo—1923—Olambala—Cream
Kickapoo Lad—Joe Carey
Kid Hargrove—1923—Colinet—Aureola
Kildare Boy—Br. 1915—Lovette—Lillie Hoy
Kilduggan—Dr. Cardenas
Kilter—Ch. 1923—Johren—Guess Again
Kimball—Br.1933—Lee O'Cotner—Anna Liffy
Kinda (Arabian)—Ch. 1934—*Nuri Pasha—
    Bazvan
Kind Man—1924—Paragon II—Mabel Strauss
*King Aurther—B. 1928—*Sir Gallahad II—Ten—
    Lec
King Basil—1924—Basil—Lamp Post
King Bisquit—B. 1943—Seabiscuit—*Liberte 3d
King Carl—B. 1933— *King Bruce—Lureen
King Charming—1920—Atheling II—Island Queen
King Gorin II—B. 1921—Golden Maxim—
    Yankee Tree
King Heather—Friar Rock
King O'Neill II—1921—*Huon—Duchess of
    Savory
King Plaudit—Br. 1916—Plaudit—Wild Thistle
King Raffles—1938—Raffles—Miss Savage
King Sandan—B. 1943—Virginia King—Lady
    Sandan
King Time—1925—King Charming—Night Time
Kingling II—1913—Ethelbert—Kings Favorite
Kipskin—1919—*Kemano—Sophrony Brown
Kitcat II—B. 1922—Skyrocket—Cat Cleugh√
Knight Club—1929—Sir Luke—L'Easence
*Knight of the Vale—Ch. 1927—Prince Galahad—
    Maida Vale
Kodama (Arabian)—Grey 1934—*Nuri Pasha—
    Dawn
Kolastra (Arabian)—1928—Gulastra—Kola
Koluna—
Koodoo—
Krimkin (Arabian)—Grey 1941—Sikin—Mirza

*La Chevesne—Br. 1914—Arch de Triomphe—La
    Cagouie
La Orb—Ch. 1920—Orb—La Luz
Lad O'Mine—B. 1922—Torchbearer—Sly Wink
Ladkin—Ch. 1921—Fair Play—*Lading
Lamination—
Lamp—Ch. 1925—Adalid—Mary Josephine
Lance Corporal—Br. 1935—*Lancegaye—Lost Agnes
Langley—(Morgan)—Ch. 1918—Hugo—Eudora
Lanson—Ch. 1929—Bubbling Over—Scarab
Lanwades—Br. 1925—He Goes—Aloquin
Laplander—Blk. 1922—The Finn—Black Swan
Lardi—1923—*Light Brigade—Lardella
*Larking—Br. 1926—Hainault—Laragh
*Lartur—4 (Arabian)—Grey 1932—Lartur 10—
    Koheilan IV
Laska—1924—Meridian—Dancing Maid

Last Call—B. 1925—War Call—Oh Fi
Latyf (Arabian)—B. 1939—Sikin—Raab
Laurentian II—Ch. 1916—St. Amarnt—Caroline
    Roche
Law of Law—B. 1929—Son—in—Law—*Lady Grey
Lawrence M—Grey 1933—*Strathleven—Agnes Call
Lawson—1925—Son—in—Law—Frusquin's Pride
Lawyer—1927—Tyster—Entanglement
Lay Low—1910—Laidlaw—Docile
Leather Goods—1935—Quibbler—Red Leather
Leaving Sands—Drifting Sands
*Lebay—1922—Ali Bey—Lady
Leedential—1925—Prudental—Bettie Lee
Lemonade—1926—Lemonora—Hippocreme
Le Pierre De Tanville—Br. 1921—Verwood—
    Philosophy
Lecturer—Ch. 1923—Belloc—Lassair
Legal—B. 1916—Hilaious—Responsful
Leonard B.—1925—Runantell—*Gloire de Vardun
Le Titan—Ch. 1937—*Cherry King 2d—La Tetra
LeVante—B. 1928—*Spanish Prince 2nd—East
    Wind
Leven—*Strathleven
Liberal Lad—1925—Falkirk—Zora H
Liberty Bond
Libyan Sands—Br. 1913—Rock Sand—Linda Stone
*Liebwachter (A0020)—B. 1944—Brantome—Lilac
    Time
Lidalo—B. 1922—Adalid—Nellita
Lieut. Forrester—Accountant
Lieut. Hixon—Ch. 1916—Borghesi—Polandia
Light Arms—1909—Labrador—Light Shot
Light Beau—Ch. 1935—*Light Carbine—Cordon
    Rouge
Light Dew—1928—Light Brigade—Honey Dew
Lindbergh Peavine (Saddlebred)—B. 1927—Radio
    Peavine—Betty Ann
Line Up—1927—Upset—Perling
Lingard—B. 1923—Black Toney—Wayward Lass
Linger—Ch. 1925—Sir Martin—Berryessa
Linsley (Morgan)—Ch. 1918—General Gates—
    Sunflower Maid
Lion Cub—Ch. 1929—Lion D'Or—The Scholar
Lion D'Or—Ch. 1916—Heno—Alle D'Or
Liota—1923—Adalid—Cheviota
Listening Ears—Ch. 1928—Tryster—*Lady Lyon
Little Red—Ch. 1917—Dr. Root—Princess Cunard
Logos—Ch. 1929—Infinite—Grecian
Loch Loyal—Br. 1935—Sir Andrew—Honey Lake
London Pride—B. 1926—Captain Cuttle—Flower
    of Yarrow
Long Bug—1925—Long Tongue—Beetle Bug
Long Run—Ch. 1927—Runnymede—Grace of
    Ogden
Long Time—1932—Paavo—Andgarita
Long Wood—1926—Pandion—Mayonnaise
Lon Martin—Rex Beach
Lonnie Gray—The Sharper

Lookout Ring—Hillarrous

Loradale (5K88)—Ch. 1930—Basil—Eris

Lord Autumn—Ch. 1932—Pennant—Bright Leaf

Lord Brighton—Ch. 1916—Ballot—Miss
    Crittenden

Lord Martin—1921—Sir Martin—Mallard

Lord Meise—B. 1923—Ormondale—Margaret
    Meise

Lord Swift—1928—Hurry On—*Lady in Grey

Lord Quinton—1927—Radames—Britania

Lord Vargrave—Ch. 1922—Polymelian—Berrill's
    Image

Loradale (5K88)—Ch. 1930—Basil—Eris

Los Molinos—1932—*Hand Granade—Tolba

*Lotnik (1V16) (Arabian)—Grey 1938—Opal—
    Mokka

Lough Foyle—B. 1911—Lochryan—Cannera

Lough Swilly—Blk. 1918—Lough Foyle—Bleachers

Louie—Grey 1915—Senseless—Annie Boleyn

Louisita—1933—Gordon Russell—Eagle Arbie

Louverne—B. 1921—Rabclais—Glorita

Love Bug—Ch. 1923—Long Tongue—Beatle Bug

Lovely Manners—Br. 1924—Sweep—*Sournoise

Lousrne—

Luchsinger—B. 1915—Dan Gold—Miss Sayre

Lucknow—Br. 1919—Luke McLuke—Care Ne

Lucky—1918—Hugo—Eunice

Lucky Arcadia—1928—Lucky Hour—Belle of
    Arcadia

Lucky Cargo—Ch. 1935—Almandel—Blanche Epine

Lucky D—Bl. 1927—*All Gold—Montrose Belle

Lucius—Ch. 1914—Isidor—Roxane

Luggage—1927—The Porter—Weary

Luke Dillon—Ch. 1917—Luke McLuke—Francis
    Dillon

Luke Jr.—Till Johnson

Lupie—B. 1939—Debenture—Infiniter

Lutaf (P82) (Arabian)—Ch. 1943—Alyf—Bakmal

Lynchburg—Br. 1909—The Scribe—Rose
    Washington

Macanscat—1937—Scat—Lady Ancestor

Macita—Macaw

MacLean—B. 1921—Meelick—Dona Hamilton

Macanscat—Scat

Marconi—1922—*Omar Khayyam—*La
    Delwrance

Madalid—B. 1923—Adalid—La Madre

Madder Music—Br. 1924—Leonardo II—Helen
    Marie

Madero—Ch. 1935—Gallant Fox—Bonnie Maginn

Madrenor B.—1922—Norito—La Madre

Mad River — 1909—Ethelbert—Goldie Cad

Mad Way—1926—Bull Dog Tennacity—May
    Newman

Maestoso XXII—

Magic Hour—B. 1935—Sortie—One Hour

Magic Orb—Ch. 1926—Flying Orb—Magic Bird

Magic Silence—B. 1918—Magic II—Mum

Magistrate (Morgan)—Ch. 1919—Sealskin—Folly

Mahruz (Arabian)—Ch. 1916—Mahruss—
    Nejdme III

Major Cullum—B. 1924—Setback—Kitty Frank

Makanda—B. 1929—Cherokee—Sweet Lady

Majority—1920—Ballot—Cintrella

Mangler—Ch. 1939—*Brig O'Doon—Contusion

Maori Chief —

Manager Bill—1931—Fair Gain—Forefoin

Manager Waite—Watercress

Mancha—1915—Galloping Simon—Frusquin Belle

Mancho Boy—*Shillelagh 2nd

Mancho Grande—1938—Mancho Boy—Snookie

Man Of Honor—B. 1915—Derring—Miss Cornet x
    Peter McCue

Manulani—B. 1924—Frolic—Walpun

Mark Master—1922—Luke McLuke—Yermila

Master Boss—1935—*Golden Boss—Baby Eve

Mayor House—Br. 1919—Hanbridge—Helma S.

Major B.—Field Marshall

Major Wood—Ch. 1921—Marwood—Jerusha

Majority—Br. 1928—Ballot—Cintrella

Maple Prince—B. 1932—Sweep—Lassair

Marcabala (23K0)—B. 1933—Ariel—Marquette

Marfleet—1935—Fair Ball—Nobilia

Mark Jayhawk—Dk. B. 1941—Mark Master—Toi Kay

Mask Evil—*Masked Marvel 2nd

Master Gould—B. 1916—First Chip—Gracie Gould

Master Hand—B. 1919—Ballot—Shuck H

Marmaduke— Ch. 1921—Boots and Saddles—
    Mae C.

Marse Henry—Br. 1913—Ben Brush—Nun's Cloth

Marse Mouse—Ch. 1915—Marse Abe—Miss White
    Mouse

Marse Hughes—Ch. 1911—Marse Abe—Miss White
    Mouse

Martello—Ch. 1921—Martinet—Hostility

Martis—B. 1927—Sir Martin—Flying Jib

Maynard L.—1921—Hilarrous—Paris Queen

Mazeppa (M63) (Arabian)—Ch. 1941—Gulastra—
    *Balbona

Meadowbrook—Br. 1940—Torchilla—Peggy
    Lehman

Meateor—

Mediator—1908—Meddler—Martha Gorman

Medicine Man

Meditation—B. 1913—Peep O'Day—Coy Maid

Medley—Ch. 1924—*Polymelian—Sweet Music

Melachino

Mellifont—B. 1911—St. Brendan—Meldhre

Melvin—(Morgan)—Ch. 1919—Scotland—
    Sunflower Maid

Menes—Br. 1923—Langraf—Moire

Menifee— 1922—*North Star III—Bourbon Lass

Menneta—1931—Mentor—Senorita Anita

Mentada—Ch. 1927—Mentor—Hamada

Mentor—Ch. 1906—Blackstock—Meta

Mentor Mick

Merchant—Ch. 1914—Star Shoot—Danceress

Merchant Marine—Br. 1918—Friar Rock—Dorothy Gray

Meredith (Morgan)—Ch. 1919—Sealskin—Helen Gates

Merrick's Pal—Ch. 1928—Sun Pal—Castle Jewel

Merry—1923—Polroma—May Day

Merry Task—1907—Octagon—*Merry Token

Meteorite—Ch. 1914—Star Shoot—Hamburg Belle

McDonno—Ch. 1921—McGee—Donno Mamona

Miami Triad—Ch. 1924—Bulse—Triad

Michael Kenna—Ch. 1924—Pataud—Bella Ring

Micro Master (3J32)—Br. 1948—St. Mirth—Lab. Mare

Midnight Chief—Ch. 1923—Swing Loose—Dora Knight

Midnight Watch—1925—On Watch—Roll On

Mikanda—B. 1929—Cherokee—Sweet Lady

Military System—Br. 1916—Poor Boy—Maud Annie

Mill Pond—Ch. 1934—*Royal Minstrel—Lady Daisy

Mill Run—1936—Microphone—Pen

Milton—Peter Quince

Minesweeper (18F7)—Br. 1928—*Sweep—*Sous Marine

Mint Cat—B. 1916—Catmint—Arlette

Mizar—B. 1919—Dick Wells—Milky Way

*Mirbel

Mirzaia—1933—Mirzam—Indaia

Misen Flute—1925—Oreste II—Mistake II

Mi Vida—Leonardo 2nd

Moby—Ch. 1931—Wildair—Sky Blue

Mock Orange—B. 1917—Lonawand—Orange Lilly

Modear—Morvich

Modesta—B. 1922—Ralph—Bonnie Kate

Moiras Boy—Ch. 1931—American Flag—Eastertide

Monday—1929—Hydromel—Rosa Mundi

Monte Carlo—1925—Polymelian—Irish Sweep

Mont Kau—Br. 1937—*Jacopo—Escutcheon

*Monteferrat—1923—Maboul—Conatance d'Antioche

Montserrat II—Br. 1919—Corlander—Monossa

Monument—Dk. Br. 1934—Flag Pole—Chosa Moon

Moon Magic—Br. 1922—Torchbearer—Mirka

Moorcraft—1932—Kickapoo—Sands Cole

Moosehead—B. 1938—*Sir Gallahad III—*Cross of Gold

Mordear—1925—Morvich—Dear Maria

Moreyes—Br. 1927—Morvich—Laughing Eyes II

Morepay—1939—Morley—Pad's Darling

Morley—1927—Whiskaway—Lady Waldeck

Morganatic—B. 1922—His Majesty—Marie Odile

*Morning Star (710A) (Cleveland Bay)—B. 1935—Lord Boughton—Star of Hope

*Mormond Hill—Br. 1934—Brumeux—Polmaise

*Moscado—1926—Beppo—Maud Musk

Morse Code—B. 1928—Sporting Blood—Nellie Morse

Morseth—Ch. 1933—Mortgage—Our Seth

*Mount Beacon

Mountain Elk—B. 1926—Apprehension—Bantry Pass

Move Over—Ch. 1934—Behave Yourself—Malover

Mr. Kirkwood—1924—Squander—Sequrola

Mr. Max—Pennant—*La Marseillaise

Mr. Pepp—Br. 1922—Luke McLuke—Divident

Mr. Whitehall—B. 1934—Chilhowee—Stefally

Mount Beacon—1921—Mount William—Soldier's Breeze

Mount Majella

Muallim (Arabian)—Ch. 1943—Alyf—*Ferdisia

Mufti—1930—Our General—Janie

Multnomah—Br. 1913—Bearcatcher—Marcia A

Murdock's Pride—1924—J.J. Murdock—

Murry River—1930—Mad River—Clara Murry

Mustard Flower—B. 1926—Mustard Seed—Kaffir Flower

Mustard Seed—B. 1919—Peter Quince—Alsike

Mutiny—B. 1920—Wrack—Desirous

My Boy Friend—Ch. 1925—Out and Gone—Fan Tan

My Broom—Br. 1928—My Own—Bromelia

My Standard (57M)—B. 1947—Flag Pole—Menera

Nansen—1929—Stimulus—*Nancy Ann 2nd

Namtro—B. 1921—De Grey—Candy Yankee

Naomha—Ch. 1922—Friar Marcus—My Honey

Natchez—Ch. 1911—Ormicant—Chartreuse

Naseby—Ch. 1934—Wildair—Syrell

Nassak—1925—John P. Grier—Ethel D.

Naughty Boy II—Ch. 1923—Lemonora—Madamoiselle Mai

Navigator—1923—Broomstick—Alster Cross

Nawfal (Arabian)—B. 1922—Nafia—Numera

Neffaj (Arabian)—Ch. 1919—Mahmet—Marian

Nellie's Boy—1929—Sir Charles—Nellie Fitz

Nelombo—Ch. 1923—Nimbus—Naturalisation

New Castle—B. 1925—Stefan the Great—Mintless

Nicodemus—1926—Zria's Charm—

Nigahdar(Arabian)—B. 1920—Rodan—Nanda

Niht—1926—Rodan—Larkspur

Nitro—B. 1936—Stimulus—Malvina B.

Niwad (Arabian)—Grey 1921—Janissary—Najine

Nohant—1918—Rockton—Consuelo II

No Name—R. Choice

Non Conformist—1927—Headstrong—Gaiety Girl

Noon Fire—B. 1921—High Noon—Firefly

Nor Borne—1915—Hastings—Flavia

Nor'easter—1934—*North Star III—*Bunchy

*Nordlicht (German)—Ch. 1941—Orleander—Nereide

Norera—1922—Norito—Espera

Norian—B. 1928—Indian Trail—Norero

Norman Count—B. or Br. 1928—*Phusla—Queen's Maid

Norse—Ch. 1927—*North Star III—*La Grisette

No Security—B. 1938—Plucky Play—Sobieha

North Pole—Ch. 1922—*North Star III—Mixed
    Color
North Star 4th—*North Star III
Northcliff—Ch. 1919—Sea King—Doria
Now Then—Br. 1935—*Dis Done—Meetme
*Numide—
Nuisance—Ch. 1937—Jock—Cassie
Nusik (Arabian)—B. 1939—Sikin—Nusara
Nuyaka—Ch. 1920—Dick Finnell—Annie
    Williamson

*Obajan VIII—(Arab—Kind)—Gr. 1933—Obajan
    VII—Shagya XXII
Oakridge (Morgan)—B. 1917—Red Oak—Roxanna
Oakwood (Morgan)—B. 1921—Troubadour of
    Willowmoor—Folly
Octagon—1894—*Rayon d'Or—Ortegal
Oczeret—
Official—Ch. 1932—Display—Snowy
O'Grady—
Oiai—o—Ch. 1935—Rodgers—Lilaha
Oklahoma Tom—Br. 1920—Dr. Root—Oklahoma
Olaburg—Ch. 1938—Gold Bug—Olacream
Old Baldy—Ch. 1930—*Polymelian—Eagle's Nest
Old Comrad—B. 1933—Lee O' Cotner—Betty B.
Old Dutch—1925—Polymelian—Dust Pan II
Old Forester—B. 1934—Bostonian—Patsie McKim
Old Joe—*Jusqu 'de Bout
*Old Master—B. 1929— Gainsborough—Sergos
Old Smuggler—B. 1922—Golden Maxim—Yankee
    Tree
Old Squirrel—1918—Flying Squirrel—Emily
    Buckler
Old Reb—Dk. B. 1929—Lee O. Cotner—Gloom
Oley—1924—Polymelian—Oleaster
Olin K.—Ch. 1924—Glencairn—Vera Fair
Olnatar (Arabian)—Ch. 1943—Katar—*Babolna
On Fire—Ch. 1936—Stimulus—Nadjy
Oman (Arabian)—Br. 1926—El Sabok—Ana
*Open Door (02Y1)—B. 1935—The Porter—
    Mablonde
Open Heir (55M)—B. 1947—*Open Door—Good
    Heiress
Open Spring (24M)—*Open Door—Laurel Time
Optimist—1921—Tracy le Val—Optima
Orange Juice—Br. 1937—Dark Vision—Yellow
    Sauce
Orator—1923—Whisk Broom II—Prankhurst
Ormesby—B. 1928—*Sir Gallahad III—Chewink
Orient (Morgan)—B. 1921—Troubadour—
    Gertrude
*Oritiz II—Br. 1936—*Asthelstan II—Frivolity
Orphan Boy—1928—Swing Loose—Memorial
    Maid
O'Sullivan—*Oddfellow
Oscar Otis—B. 1936—Ben Homme—Cameo
Otiro—B. 1922—Norito—Reina de Hampton
Otto Friz—B. 1929—Frizzle—Ottaveda

Our Birthday—B. 1917—Golden Maxim—Autolee
Our Irish—B. 1940—Irish—Miss Danour
Our Shadow—Ch. 1935—Danour—Easter Shadow
Our Spot—
Our Watch—B. 1924—On Watch—Zaza
Out Bound—1928—Luke McLuke—In Bounds
OutGuess—Ch. 1929—Lucullite—Budara
Out The Way—Br. 1915—Peter Pan—Sweep Away
Out Play—Ch. 1926—Fair Play—Careful
Output—Ch. 1927—Fair Play—Careful
Over There—B. 1916—Spearmint—Summer Girl
Oxalic Jess—Ch. 1915—Collector Jessup—My
    Nurse

Paavo—1923—The Finn—Planutess
Pablo—Ch. 1921—Glencairn—Bryn Mawr
Padriac—Ch. 1917—Belloc—Anna Patricia
Pagan Pan—Blk 1924—Luke McLuke—*Black
    Brocade
Paget Creek—1930—Secret Greetings—Elk Creek
    Maid
*Palmist—B. 1923—Golden Sun—Palmella
Palmist II—*Palmist
Panover—Ch. 1926—Panhandler—Fringe
Pardner—1909—Cunard—Lady Bache
Parmelee—1924—Polymelian—Fluzey
Parmelee T.—B. 1934—Victorian—Waukalla
Particular—B. 1927—Leonardo II—Facetious
Patches—1917—Ivan the Terrible—Beatrice
Pas De Calais II—Ch. 1919—Bachelors Double—
    Hot Water Bag
Patou Bow—Br. 1932—*Cross Bow—Cicely Kay
Patriotic—Br. 1932—American Flag—Moonlight
Paul Hirtstein—1926—Ballot—Elaine
Paul Leake—Ch. 1924—Enfield—Norma G
Paul Whiteman—B. 1937—*Kantar—Rose Twig
Pauper—1925—Last Coin—Dear Marie
Paycheck—1934—Chance Play—Pencraft
Pea Jacket—Br. 1924—Bluecoat—Daisy
Peace Boy—Ch. 1927—Peace Pennant—First Ballot
Peace Buddy—B. 1928—Peace Pennant—Eris
Peace Penn—1924—Peace Pennant—Mirka
Peace Pipe—1930— Underfire x Loving Cup
Pecan—1929—Peanuts—Miramint
Pennywise—Br. or Blk. 1929—*Bucellas—Fallacy
Perchance—B. 1928—Broomstick—*Perhaps So
Perchene (8M9)—B. 1944—Perchance—VaBene
Perfect—1926—Westward H—Perfect Peach
Perfect Devil—B. 1934—Diavolo—Adequate
Perkins—1926—Westy Hogan—Dress Up
Persimmon's Pride—Ch. 1908—Persimmon—
    Bridal
Peter Hastings—B. 1925—Peter Pan—Nettie
    Hastings
Peter Joyce—B. 1926—Peter Pan—Joyce
Peter Saxon—1932—Saxon—Swiss
Peticence—Infinite
Peto—B. 1927—Peter Pan—Eulogy

Phalady (8Y6)—Br. 1946—*Sultan Mohamed—
　*Lady Phalasis
Phantom Cloud—B. 1928—High Cloud—Phantom
Phantom General—1929—Our General—Phantom
　Blue
Phantom Prince—1923—Prince Pal—Phantom
　Maid
Pharned—B. 1937—*Pharamond II—Nedna
Pharaoh—Br. 1908—Meddler—Hatasoo
Philanthropist—B. 1938—Gordon Russell—Bank
Picorito—B. 1941—Aloha Mood—*Petite 2d.
Pictin—Roan 1922—Wigstone—Altha
Picture Play—B. 1937—Head Play—*Miss
　Gainsborough
Piegan—B. 1920—Polymelian—Jacoba
*Pilot (Arabian)—Grey 1943—Trypolis—Zalotna
Pillar Man—B. 1943—Pillory—Dorothy Marie
Pillory—Ch. 1919—Olambala—Hester Prynne
Pillotta—1924—Spanish Prince II—Game Chick
Pimiento—1917—Sweep—Lemco
Pine Bur—Louis A.
Pines Emblem—1920—Black Pine—May Peep
Pirate Chief—Br. 1925—Brigand—Hadfield
Pirate Gold—Golden Fagot
Pizarro—B. 1916—Bona Rosa—Becky
Plane Jimmie—
Planet—Blk. 1918—Zeus—Black Silk
Planter—Ch. 1922—Sir Martin—Mallard
Plato II—Br. 1918—Polymeius—Mesauge
Play Hooky—B. 1931—My Play—Maggie Hook
Playtime—B. 1927—My Play—Nell Wilder
Plenipotentiary—1927—Planet—Appolita
Plodder—Br. 1916—Borgia—La Calma
Plowshare—Br. 1937—*Sickle—Stagecraft
*Plumb Square—1920—Simon Square—Auburn
　Hill
Poet Meddle—Buckeye Poet
Pogo—Ch. 1920—Glencairn—Caraquet
Pogonip—B. 1922—*Atheling II—Orange Blossom
Point Blank—Ch. 1922—Ten Point—Praline
Polante—1924—*Atheling II—*Polistena
Poly—Ch. 1924—*Polymelian—*Seemly
Polydorus—Frair Rock—Polyanthus
Pomona Abbas (Arabian)—B. 1944—Katar—
　Sonata
Pomona Abd El Kadir (1—1) (Arabian)—Grey
　1944—Alyf—Treyf
Pomona Ahmen (Arabian)—Gr. 1944—*Raseyn—
　*Nakkla
Pop K.—Polante
Poppycock—Br. 1917—Dunbar—Teetotum II
Portden—B. 1929—The Porter—Margaret Ogden
Porterdi (8F86)—Ch. 1928—The Porter—Di
Projectile—*Swift and Sure—Friar Priscilla
Portsul—
Post Haste—B. 1920—Delhi—Mileage
Pot O'Gold—Br. 1926—Pagan Pan—Rainbow
　Division

Powerful—1927—Man O'War—Queen of Jest
Poultney—Br. 1916—Bryn Mawr—Galgris
*Preisrichter (A0020)—Br. 1944—Brantome—
　Patoche
Prepare Away—Br. 1924—Trial by Jury—Annie Webb
Presage—1930—Campfire—Forebode
Pretty Sweeper—1945—Chimney Sweep—Pretty
　Bonnet
Pride of India—B. 1916—Delhi—Dominoes
Prime Minister—1920—Celt—Primula
Prince Barton—1929—Sir Barton—Madras
　Ginghani
Prince Brideau (8Y4)—Ch. 1944—St. Brideaux—
　Princess Flag
Prince Hermis—Ch. 1910—Hermis—Crimea
Prince James—1918—King James—Lacona
Prince Leven—1932—*Strathleven—Spanish
　Name
Prince Pan—1923—Peter Pan—Annagh
Prince Saxon—Ch. 1936—Peter Saxon—Freda
　Wisp
Prisoner—1924—*War Cry—Beartrap
Projectile—1930—Swift and Sure—Fair Priscilla
Propus—1925—*North Star III—Ployantha
Provinzler—Br. 1917—Lycaon—Pro Patria
Protection—1926—Ellangowan—Audit
Prudential—1920—Bard of Hope—Gibraltar
Psychic—Ch. 1939—Psychic Bid—Ready
Psychic Bid—Chance Play
Puchero—Ch. 1930—*Pot Au Feu—Scally
Puddin Cake—B. 1941—Mark Master—Sugar Cake
Pugnacious—1926—Audacious—Domestic
Punjab—1923—Brown Prince II—American
　Beauty
Purchance
Purple Knight—Bright Knight
Pyriform—Br. 1936—Whichone—Oval
Pyx—Br. 1917—Pataud—Okitao

Quick Devil—B. 1935—Diavalo—Double Time
Quick One—Ch. 1929—Campfire—Straw Bonnet

Rabbaz (Arabian)—B. 1921—Sinbad—Remim
Race Riot—Br. 1936—Flying Ebony—Miss
　Simplicity
Raffles—1920—Luke McLuke—Phebe G.
Ragamuffin—Friar Rock
Ragia (Arabian)—1937—Mirage—Indaia
Ragged Sailor—Ch. 1936—Kickapoo—March Time
Rag Man—B. 1924—*McGee—Sweepings
Rainstorm—1925—Thunderstorm—Florsain
Raja Al Mustakbal (Arabian)—B. 1923—Rizvan—
　Rokhsa
Ralco—1917—Rockview—Black Mantilla
Ralet (Arabian)—1930—Raseyn—Sherlet
Ranch Lad—Br. 1939—Heuvelton
Ranococas—1918—Lovelace or Lovetie—
　Phantasma

Rambling Brook—Ch. 1921—Clysmic—Annie Olin

Raphia—1924—Rabelais—La Grelee

Rapid Carrier—1938—Rapidity—Tote

Rapidity—1926—Rapid Water—Mettel Bereaud

Rasakkla (P61) (Arabian)—Grey 1942—*Raseyn—
    *Nakkla

Rashid (Arabian)—B. 1922—Sidi—Ramini

Rasselas—1927—Peter Pan—Poke Bonnet

Ratifier—1923—*War Cry—Mistlebloom

Ray Jay—B. 1919—Assagai—Romange

Rayyis—(Arabian)—Ch. 1932—*Nasik—*Rifla

Ready Standard (56M)—B. 1947—Flag Pole—
    Ready Smile

Recall—Ch. 1922—Argonne—Expectancy

Recluse—B. 1913—Von Tromp—Isolation

R Choice—1932—Zeus—Freda II

Recollection—B. 1923—Jim Gaffney—*Memories II

Red Ant—1929—Nuyaka—Fannie A.

Red Barton—Ch. 1937—Prince Barton—Agnes Ore

Red Bug—1934—Gold Bug—Papoose

Red Easter—1922—Black Pine—Hot Tamales

Red Hans—Ch. 1931—Dozer—Three Stars

Red Mulligan—Ch. 1920—Little Dutch—Cloisteress

Red Racer

Red Rose (28Y) (European)—Ch. 1947—
    *Nordlicht—*Pietrosz

Red Saber (96M)—Ch. 1948—Red Bug—Saber
    Knot

Red Seal

Red Stuart—Ch. 1925—Jack Stuart—Anthem

Red Tomahawk—B. 1925—Assagai—Forbid

Reefer (2M4)—Ch. 1943—Perchance—Stimulation

Rabiyas (P34) (Arabian)—Ch. 1936—Rahas—
    Rabiyat

*Recke (A0079)—Br. 1942—Janitor—Reine
    D'Ouilly

Recommend—

Red Hat—*Under Fire

Red Hand

Red Hot B.—1925—Fletcher M.—Susan D.

Red James—Moronge

Red Wing—Ledalo

Reel

Reflector—Br. 1926—Hall Mark—Orbie Glyn

Refrigerator—1941—Above Par—Ice Cube

Reincocos—Old Mose

Reidalid—Ch. 1923—Adalid—Reina de Santa Anita

Relay—B. 1919—Assagai—Doll

Remolino—B. 1934—Ariel—Flying Dust

Reno Aleck—Ch. 1925—Trial by Jury—Chantlette

Reno Alive—Ch. 1925—Honolulu Boy—Ogoechee

Reno Bay—B. 1926—Captain Ray—Flora McGinn

Reno Bee—Br. 1926—Mock Orange—Brown Bee

Reno Candy—

Reno Commander—1927—Reidalid—Repat

Reno Daze—1928—Trial By Jury—Hat T.

Reno Elmer—Ch. 1939—*Over There—Bartie

Reno Epic—1929—Curulean—Otiron Girl

Reno Eric—B. 1929—Lingard—Bartender II

Reno Filibuster—1930—Lord Meise—Reno Alice

Reno Ford

Reno Gratis—1931—Over Lord—Tax Exempt

Reno Greeting—Ch. 1931—*Optimist—Easter
    Surprise

Reno Hester—1932—Blue Bull—Sherill

Reno Headlight—B. 1932—London Pride—Sarah
    Alethe

Reno Hero—Ch. 1932—Over Lord—Oriental Park

Reno Hurry—

Reno Iban—Ch. 1933—Pablo—Balloting

Reno Idol—Ch. 1933—Stimulus—Forebode

Reno Inhale—Ch. 1933—London Pride—Oriental
    Park

Reno Irritant—B. 1933—London Pride—Mustard
    Flower

Reno Jamboree—B. 1934—Ormesby—Palisade

Reno Jester—

Reno Job—B. 1934—London Pride—Mustard
    Flower

Reno Judge—Blk. 1934—Pagan Pan—Doris Bond

Reno Jupiter—1934—*Friar Dolan—Helen d'Or

Reno Kaffir (D963)—B. 1935—London Pride—
    Mustard Flower

Reno Kandy (D964)—B. 1935—Tush—Dark Quest

Reno Kapok—Br. 1935—Cerulean—Dot Wood

Reno Kerchief—Ch. 1935—*Friar Dolan—
    Sunholme

Reno Kingfish—Ch. 1935—Cerulean—Maid
    Elizabeth

Reno Knockout

Reno Latona—1936—London Pride—U.C. Her

Reno Laughter—

Reno Lee (D01)—B. 1936—*Friar Dolan—Boots
    Last

Reno Legend—B. 1936—High Line—Numa

Reno Link—B. 1936—High Line—Flora G.

Reno Lofty—1936—Cerulean—Lady Edna

Reno Lion—Ch. 1936—Cerulean—Blue Bonnet

Reno Laird

Reno Lord—Ch. 1936—*Friar Dolan—Oriental
    Park

Reno Lusty—1936—*Friar Dolan—Reno Florence

Reno Mallet—Ch. 1937—Cerulean—Blue Bonnet

Reno Magic—Ch. 1937—High Line—Sunholme

Reno Major—B. 1937—High Line—Clara Lou

Reno Mandite—B. 1937—*Friar Dolan—Reno
    Indicted

Reno Marine—B. 1937—*Friar Dolan—Reno Gale

Reno Mecca (D00)—Ch. 1937—*Cherry King—
    Reno Impish

Reno Nero—B. or Br. 1938—*Friar Dolan—Reno
    Hebe

Reno Nitrate—Ch. 1938—High Line—Reno
    Florence

Reno Nor—Ch. 1938—High Line—Reno Alice

Reno Norman—B. 1938—High Line—Flora G

Reno Nome—Ch. 1938—Reno Irritant—Reno Julet

Reno Obey—B. 1939—High Line —Reno Abbey

Reno Omega—Ch. 1939—High Line—Reno Ferment

Reno Omen—Br. 1939—Big Blaze—Flora G.

Reno Oscar—Ch. 1939—Big Blaze—Broadway Mary

Reno Paladen—Reno Riggs

Reno Phillibuster—Reno Legand

Reno Pom Pom—1940—Big Blaze—Reno Indicted

Reno Portent—Ch. 1940—Majority—Reno Kentucky

Reno Riggs—Midnight Chief

Reno Umaydit—Ch. 1944—*O'Grady—Reno May

Reno Upabout— Br. 1944—*O'Grady—Reno Gadabout

Rep—Br. 1918—Picton—Enchantress II

Repulse—Ch. 1922—Spanish Prince—Soria

*Rescate (0N08)—Ch. 1932—Sanstache Sorcerer—Buena Fica

Reticense—1930—Society Scandal

Retrospect—1936—Gordon Russell—Silent Moments

Retusen

Revere—B. 1931—*Sir Galahad III—My Reverie

Revenue

Reviewer—1927—Trompe La Mort—Saffron

Rey De Los Angeles—B. 1924—Adalid—Feranda

Rey El Pleasanton—Ch. 1915—Rey Hindoo—Margie D

Rhntez (Arabian)—B. 1942—El Kumait—Ahvaz

Ribal (Arabian)—Ch. 1920—Berk—Rijma

Rich Phil (7K60)—Ch. 1931—Carom—Empress Wyeth

Richmond's Choice (Saddlebred) Br. 1919—Rex Peavine—Diana Mason

Rieghloch—Ch. 1925—Mighty Power—Princess Thelio

Rifle Shooter—B. 1913—Star Shoot—Babble

Rifnas (Arabian)—Ch. 1932—*Nasile—*Rifla

Rigel—1920—Ballot—Picton's Pride

Rigolo—B. 1924—Rire aux Larmes—Sibola

*Rival 2nd (915A)—B. 1937—*Aethelstan 2nd—Riva Bella

Rivere

Rob—1919—Orb—Panlita

Roband (Morgan)—B. 1921—Red Oak—Birdie K.

Robber Barron—Br. 1934—Desperate Desmond—Ingrid

Robbia Della—Blk. 1921—Red Oak—Bonnie B

Robert Kay—1921—Pepp O'Day—Silk Maid

Robert Mandel—Ch. 1924—Belloc—Gilt Edge

Robespierre (Morgan)—Ch. 1920—Red Oak—Bessie C.

Robinson Boy—B. 1931—Fitzgibbon—Norera

Rock Heather—

Rockledge—Ch. 1922—Half Rock—Mazda

Rockstone

Rockwood (Morgan)—B. 1924—Bennington—Carolyn

Rococo—B. 1918—Marathon—Miss Lida

Rodan (Arabian)—Ch. 1906—Harb—Rose of Sharon

Rodgers—B. 1916—Sweep—Lardella

Rogon Jr.—Ch. 1920—Rogon—Zool

Roguish Pal—Ch. 1941—Roguish Eye—Mayes Lutz

Roi Donovan—Br. 1911—Roi Herode—Miss Donovan

Rolling Rock—B. 1921—Sandbar—Edith B

Roly—B. 1912—Golden Maxim—Lotowana

Romance (Morgan)—Br. 1921—Red Oak—Minnie K.

Romanesque (Morgan)—Ch. 1921—Red Oak—Mariah K.

Roman Punch—B. 1931—Pompey—Polygiot

Rome Haul—Ch. 1934—Greenock—*Barley Water

Ronaq (Arabian)—B. 1940—*Raseyn—Babiyat

Rosario II—B. 1922—Faucheur—Rosanne

Roscommon—B. 1919—Belloc—Rossiare

Rosin (Morgan)—Blk. 1920—Red Oak—Sunset Morgan

Royal Dunbar—Br. 1930—*Dunbar II—Bell Rock

Royal Ease—Gr. 1926—*Royal Canopy—Lazy Lady

Royal Flag—The Manager

Royal Ford—1926—Swinford—*Royal Yoke

Royal Jester—Blk 1917—Black Jester—Primula II

Royal Lad—Ladkin—*Royalty

Royal Light—1927—*North Star III—Breathing Spell

Royal Rascal—1939—Royal Ease—Dura

Ruckus—Ch. 1930—Upset—Virago

Rugby—1921—Broomstick—Rosie O'Grady

*Rumpelmayer—Br. 1926—Dark Ronald

Run Dor—1924—Runflor—Lady Dorinet

Runflor—Ch. 1918—Runnymede—Handsome Florry

Runningwild—Ch. 1921—Olambia—Sunburst

Rushing—In Memoriam

Russmor—Blk. 1934—Bostonian—Grey Watch

Rustam (Arabian)—Ch. 1922—El Bulad—Rhua

Rusty R—Ch. 1934—Red Bug—Mare by Master Gould

S. Bryce Wing—B. 1922—Till Johnson, Jr.—Kickapoo Lass

Saga Flow—1926—Sweep—Miss Jazbo

Sageboy—1925—Chicle—Bonnie Broom

Sahara Wynn—Ch. 1938—Jedran—Agnes Wynn

Sailing B.—B. 1918—Trap Rock—Pecadillo

Saint Rock—

Salutation—1924—Somme Kiss—*Permia

*Samurai—B. 1937—Oleander—Sonnenwende

Sam's Boy—1917—Voter—Light Opera

Sam Frank—Br. 1919—Honeywood—Lady Trinity

Sam French—

Sam Tangle—Br. 1917—Flotsam III—Tangle II

San Marcus—Ch. 1917—Sweeper—Lady Neil

Sand Bed—Ch. 1917—Ogden—Sandpocket

Sandford's Dare (Saddlebred)—B. 1935—Varon Dare—Comming Down

Sands of Time—Ch. 1916—Beach Sand—Alma K.

Sandhills—B. 1923—Meridian—Little Horn

Sangan—Ch. 1923—Long Tongue—Repentant

San Marcus—1917—Sweeper—Lady Sandan

Santa Claus

Santouri—Br. 1935—*Bistouri—Suffrage

Saranan—Ch. 1924—Kalitan—Gold Maid

Saratoga—B. 1912—Ogden—Unsightly

Saret—1935—Pompey—Hilana

Sargon (Arabian)—Ch. 1915—Segario—Najine

Sarko—Br. 1921—Voorhees—Egeria

Sasper—1921—Master Robert—Miss Cynthia

Saucy Sage—B. 1931—Gladiator—Saucy Susie

Saxet—1936—Pompey—Hilaria

Sax Ire—B. 1941—B. 1941—Irish—Sue Saxon

Saxopal—Ch. 1932—Saxon—Fire Opal

Sax Player (6M2)—Ch. 1943—Sir Gordon—Sue Saxon

Saxton—1935—Saxon—Merry

Sazerac—1929—Westy Hogan—Resistance

Scamp—Br. 1919—Son—in—Law—Campanula

Scamper Home—1937—Scamp—Cherry Moment

Scamp's Pride—1938—Scamp—Murdock's Pride

*Scarlet Prince—1927—Triumph or Rose Prince— Pink Daisy

Scat—1924—Chicle—Sketchy

Scorcher—1922—*Frizzle—Sena Lamplighter

Scoreboard—B. 1941—Mark Master—Reno Cassie

Scott Free—Br. 1927—*Wrack—*Latest Fashion

Scotsman—1924—Fireman—Helen Scott

Scoutmaster—1929—Campfire—Susie

Scuppernong—B. 1942—Grog—Sister Hae

Sea Bright—1926—Friar Rock—Seaside

Sea Cliff—Ch. 1931—Brig O'Doon—Shadow Light

Sea Prince—

Sea Romance—1927—Sea Pirate—Romana

Seaton Florio (Hackney)—B. 1918—Malboro— Flora May

*Seidelbast—Blk. 1943—Pharis—Seraphita

Sea Trance—Ch. 1931—Stimulus—*Sea Dream

Sebastian—1926—*Wrack—Brumellian

Secret Agent—1924—Stimulus—Stolen Secrets

Secret Greetings—B. 1918—Luke McLuke—Zahra

Selim—Br. 1920—*Sain—Rezia

Semper—B. 1922—Alvescot—Semprite

Senalado—1922—*Spanish Prince II—Day's Over

Senator Knox(Morgan)—Ch. 1921—Knox Morgan—Senata

Sengaris—*Sir Gallahad IV

*Serajevo—1925—Hapsburg—Hedda

Serf Savin—Br. 1912—St. Savin—Sainvoke

Sergeant Donaldson—Ch. 1928—Whisk Broom II—Assembly

Sergeant Hogan—Platoon

Setback—B. 1907—Ogden—Set Fast

Shag—*St. Germans

Sharkey—Ben Strong

Sharnbrook—B. 1918—Firestone—Daisy C.

Shawnee (Morgan)—B. 1925—Mansfield— Dewdrop

Sheridan—1921—Sweep—Iridescence

Shillelagh II—B. 1917—Irish Lad—Artless

Shilling—Ch. 1917—Seth—Alice Commoner

Shoestring—1927—Omar Khyam—Loriotte

Sickles Man—Dozer Boy

Sidecar—Br. 1930—*Vulcain—Mollie Darling

Sidereal—Ch. 1919—Star Shoot—Old Squaw

Sidney Carton—B. 1936—Blue Larkspur—Mea Culpa

Sidney Grant—*Omond

Sierra King—Ch. 1941—Snow King—Boomette

Sigma Chi—Br. 1923—Runflor—Texas Girl

Siglavy Virtuosa—(Lippizanner)—Gr. 1935— Siglavy Ivanka—Virtuosa

Sign of Time—Ch. 1926—Champlain—Sister Emblem

Silver Fleece—Grey 1933—*Royal Canopy— Marion May

Silver Lip—Ch. 1931—Secret Greetings—Widrig Squaw

Silver Rock—Ch. 1922—Friar Rock—Lady Bedford

Silhouette—Ch. 1923—James P. Silo—Bartie

Silver Gloss—Tiger Gloss

Simon Gallop—B. 1918—Galloping Simon— Gravosa

Sims—1928—Lucullite—The Colonel's Lady

Sing

Singleam—B. 1919—Hesperus—Lady Aritta

Sir Ally—B. 1935—*Sir Gallahad III—Scally

Sir Andrew—Br. 1928—*Sir Gallahad III— Gravitate

Sir Bart

Sir Ben—1929—Sweep On—*Passamaria

Sir Bud—1936—Gallant Sir—Rare Bud

Sir Barton—Ch. 1916—Star Shoot—Lady Sterling

Sir Charles—Br. 1922—Peter Pan—Chulita

Sir Door (25M)—B. 1946—*Open Door—Virginia Lassy

Sirdar—1925—Sweep—Dark Lantern

Sir Flower—Ch. 1939—Fortune's Favorite—Garnet B.

Sir Gordon—Br. 1934—Gordon Russell—Lady Chatterton

Sir Grey Spot—Ch. 1937—Dark Vision—Cathrine Stevenson

Sir Hampton—1897—*Watercress—*Lizzie Hampton

Sir Herbert Barker—B. 1931—*Sir Gallahad III— Minima

Sir Herade—B. 1936—*Sir Gallahad III—Herade

Sir Lanny—1924—*Hand Grenade—Georgia Girl

Sir Norman—Drk. Br. 1933—Insco—Normana

Sir Stuart—B. 1923—War Cloud—Sweetheart II

Sir Tristram—1931—*Sir Gallahad III—Belle of Blue Ridge

Sirwal (Arabian)—B. 1940—Rabiyas—Farasa
Sitar (Arabian)—Ch. 1920—Sinbad—Simawa
*Skald—1924—Alford—Musk of Myram
Skipalong—Ch. 1918—Ballot—Hazzaza
Skipton—1933—Brig O'Doon—Charusan
Skyraker—Ch. 1916—Willonyx—Mountain Jewell
Slambang—1929—General Lee—Peraission
Sledge—B. 1921—Harmonicon—Sledmere
Ski Pole (69M)—Ch.1948—Flag Pole—Ski Cap
Smokescreen—His Majesty
Snap Dragon II—1915—Hampton—Mistress Penn
Snow Flag (71M)—Ch. 1948—Flag Pole—Virginia
    Snow
Snow King—B. 1929—*Sir Gallahad III—*Martha
    Snow
Snug Harbor—1932—Oceanic—Comfy
Social Star—Br. 1918—Brummel—Glad Smile
Socialist—Br. 1923—Kwang Su—La Marsellaise
Socrates—B. 1922—Sarmatian—Daphine
Soggarth Aroon—Br. 1920—Bard of Hope—
    Running Vine
Solar Hawk—1934—Sun Beau—Hawkshead
Soldier Blues (9L7)—B. 1940—Irish—Bereavement
Soldier True—Ch. 1922—Trap Rock—Federal Girl
Solid Chance—1943—Perchance—Glenrock
Some Good—Br. 1931—*Waygood—Oroya
Some One—B. 1937—Whichone—Bequine
*Son—1925—Son—in—Law—Isauria
Son John—B. 1924—DeGrey—Baby Lee
Son of Charley
Son of Fortune—Ch. 1922—Dry Fortune—
    Category
Son of Law—B. 1929—Son—in—Law—*Lady Grey
Son O'Wind—1909—Sea Horse II—Come Along
Song Hit—B. 1928—Dress Parade—Golden
    Melody
Sonny Basil—1928—Basil—Mable Curtis
Soother—Br. 1925—War Fame—Naro
Soothsayer—B. 1914—Dark Ronald—Ariette II
Southern Cross—1919—Luke McLuke—Pamphyle
Southern Gent (53M)—1947—Open Door—
    Virginia Lassy
Southern Saint (20M)—B. 1945—St. Brideaux—
    Virginia Verse
Spanish Ghost (1Y0)—Grey 1942—*Belfonds—
    Queen of Spain
Spanish Gold—B. 1924—Spanish Prince II—Bright
    Gold
Spanish Isle—
Spanish Jean (84KA)—Ch. 1936—*Jean II—
    Malba H.
Spanish Play—1928—*Spanish Prince 2nd—Anna
    Horton
Spanish Title—B. 1933—*Donnacona—Baby
    Buzzard
Sparhawk (Morgan)—Ch. 1913—Dart—Lady L
Sparkling Wit—Br. 1921—Black Jester—Starflight
Spearhead—1927—*Fitzwilliam—Muttkins

Spearpoint—1921—Spearmint—Forget—Me—Not
Special Racket—Ch. 1936—Sun Beau—Alexandria
Speechmaker—Br. 1939—*Justice F—Chat
    Chatterton
Speedy Do Da
Spirit River—1928—Mac Kenzie II—Windigo
Splendor II—1924—Sunstar—Ornow
Spreewalder—B. 1938—Flamboyant—Springflut
Square Set—1914—Duke of Ormande—Dora I
St. Brideaux (04Y5)—B. 1928—*St. Germans—
    Panache
*St. Allen—B. 1917—Bridge of Allen—St. Aelwena
St. Sinecus, Jr.—
St. Mirth (7Y6)—Ch. 1944—St. Brideaux—Reno
    Mirth
Stability—Br. 1935—Blondin—*Pamfleta
Stalstar—Blk. 1925—Gollinet—Starter
Stambul (Arabian)—Grey 1926—El Sabok—Mortfda
Stamp Act—Axenstein—Postage
Stamper—
Star A
Star Hampton—Ch. 1916—Star Shoot—Dorothy
    Hampton
Starab—B. 1934—*Sherab—Bright Shawl
Stars and Bars—1926—Pennant—Remembrance
Star of Villon (92M)—Ch. 1948—Villon—Star Belle
Starset—Ch. 1924—Star Hawk—Set Square
Star Voter—1918—Ballot—Starry Night
Start—B. 1927—Chicle—Initiate
Stepson—Ch. 1915—Uncle—Katrine
Step This Way—B. 1929—All Over—Lizette
*Stevenson 2nd—Bl. 1925—Badajoz—Proponent
Stimjul (515N)—Grey 1937—Stimulus—Gentle Julia
Stimulation—1929—Stimulus—Glyndon
Stone Bell—B. 1921—Wigstone—Bella H
Stone Spout—B. 1927—Gargoyle—Betty Stone
Stony Point—Ch. 1920—Half Rock—Summerhill
Storma Scud—B. 1935—Hard Tack—Blustery
Stormy Dawn—1926—Vulcain—Dawn Star
Stormy Heart—1935—Mancho Boy—Prairie
    Chicken
Stormy Night—1926—Bull Dog Tenacity—Nairn
Stormy Port—1925—The Porter—Storm Nymph
Straight Home—Br. 1922—Jim Gaffney—La
    Chauvier
Straight Shot—Line Up
Straw Bonnet—1924—Roselyon—Straw Lady
Strawman—Dk. Br. 1937—Pillory
Strathcote—Grey 1933—*Strathleven—*Cote
    Rotie II
Stream Bed—1937—*Rolls Royce—Adorada
Stridaway—1884—Glenmore—Spinaway
Street Sweeper (39M)—B. 1946—Chimney
    Sweep—Reno Katrinka
Suburban—B. 1921—Vindex—Rural
Sudha Chance (02M)—Perchance—Sudha Snow
Suleiman (Arabian)—Ch. 1915—Abu Zeyd—Rosa
Sullivan Trail—Wigstone—Speariana

Sully—Ch. 1922—Jim Gafney—Bramble Bush
Sultry—B. 1929—Sun Flag—*Babieca
Sumpter—B. 1922—Sand Mole—Isirose
Sun Broom—Sun Briar—Bromelia
Sun Edwin—1925—Sun Briar—Edwina
Sunfast—1926—*Sun Briar—Hussy
Sunfire—1925—Olambala—Sunburst
Sun Hawk—*Star Hawk
Sun Plume—*Sun Briar
Sun Spice—Br. 1934—Sun Flag—Spices
Sunwood
Suns Way—1928—Sun Briar—Windy Way
Sunny Basil—Ch. 1928—Basil—Mabel Curtis
Sunny Jim—B. 1918—Friar Rock—Lucy M.
Super Cargo—1919—Friar Rock—Sweet Marjoram
Suppliant—B. 1921—Everest—Piliant
Surabia (Arabian)—Ch. 1943—Rabiyas—Suwari
Sure Off—B. 1936—*Swift and Sure—Time Off
Sureyn (Arabian)—Grey 1940—*Raseyn—
    *Cabbett Sura
Survivor—Ch. 1924—Trompe la Mort—Ros Aleen
Surna (Arabian)—1937—Farana—Crabbet Sura
Sustainer—1937—Stimulus—Nettie Stone
Swanton (Morgan)—B. 1925—Bennington—
    Carolyn
Sweeping Star—B. 1930—Sweep On—Order of the
    Star
Sweet Hand—1928—Panhandler—My Sweetie
Swiftfoot II—B. 1912—Thrush—Abbots Ann
Swiftlet—Br. 1933—*Swift and Sure—
    Entanglement
*Swineburne—Ch. 1923—Swynford—Zefu
Swinfield—*Swinburne
Swingby—1931—Swing Loose—Gypsy Poe
Swing Knight—Ch. 1924—Swing Loose—Dora
    Knight
Swing Loose—Ch. 1916—Broomstick—Courage
Swordsman—Br. 1924—Chicle—Wendy

Tagpole—Ch. 1942—Flag Pole—Taglioni
Tad H—1914—Fayette—Millie Young
Tchad—Br. 1916—Negofol—Toia
*Tagfalter (A0034)—Br. 1942—Brantome—Take It
    Easy
*Taj Akbar (A0032)—Br 1933—Fairway—Taj Shirin
Tangara—Br. 1922—Light Brigade—Tanagra
Tantris (East Prussian) 1924—Trinidad—Thalia
Tarpaulin—1928—Supremus—Washoe Belle
Tarry Long (06YO)—B. 1945—Ariel—Tarn
Tarter King—B. 1920—Cantilever—Lovewisely
Temper Wine—
Tenderfoot—1920—Polymelian—Hassock
Teocal—
Thaine—Ch. 1922—Big Boy—Blance Ring
The Bohemian—Br. 1918—Jim Gaffney—Kittenish
The Condor—Ch. 1919—Hesperus—Narcotic
The Creole—1922—Bexant—Louisanne
The Dictator—B. 1919—Dodge—Lipstick

The Greek—B. 1923—Achievement—Grecian Maid
The Inheritor
The Macnah—1916—Sunbright—Sabrinetta
The Moon—1927—Hildur—The Widow Moon
The Persian—B. 1932—Toro—Firewater
The Rollcall—1919—*Lough Foyle—Beth Stanley
The Southerner—*Ormond
The Tallwood—B. 1923—Campfire—Pixy
The Tramp—Br. 1921—The Finn—Kate Adams
Tehachapi Allen (Morgan)—Dk. Ch. 1934—
    Querido—Tab
Theatrical—1929—Lemonora—Eastern Pagean
Theo. Dunman—B. 1915—Meelick—Kitty Smith
Theo Fay—Theo. Cook—Fay—a—Way
Thaine—Big Boy
Thistle D'Or—Ch. 1924— Mont d'Or—Clarice
Thistledown—1916—Olambala—Madchen
Thorndown—B. 1919—Rivoli—Erzsike
Tickwood—B. 1938—Tick—On—Miss Susie
Tiff—Ch. 1923—Hessian—Spanish Dispute
Tiger Cream—1942—Tom Tiger—Olacream
Tiger Cross
Tiger Gloss—1923—Runnymede—Dourquol
Tiger Royal—
Tijanice T—1937—Titus—Janice G
Till Johnson—Br. 1917—Orbicular—Rose of
    Jeddah
Tilka—*Light Brigade
Time Supply—1931—Time Maker—Suplice
Tim O'Brien—Ch. 1924—Sir John Johnson—Bettie
    Louise
Tim McGee—Ch. 1915—McGee—Cheek
Tim Toulin
Time (Arabian)—Ch. 1920—Razzia—Abbess
Time Prince—1935—Time Maker—*Queen of the
    Blues
Tiswild—B. 1931—Wildair—Abbatissa
Titian—1922—Jim Gaffney—Fair Rouise
Titanic
Titus—1927—Infinite—Precipitate
Tomahawk IV—1923—Star Hawk—Mutiny II
Tomerry—1937—Tote—Merry
Tom Green—Br. 1921—Atkins—Nairn
Tom Knight—
Tom McTaggart—B. 1914—Chuctanunda—Teplash
Tom Pendergast—1916—The Friar—La Reve
Tom Tiger—1923—*Stephen the Great—Isabeau
Toney Boots—1934—Bot to Boot—Batwing
Tonto Rock—Br. 1927—Trap Rock—*See Saw II
Top O' the Moon
Tornado Wheel—B. 1924—Balance Wheel—Babe
    Bemish
Tote—B. 1928—*Dark Jest—Portage
Toteaster—Br. 1941—Tote—Easter Shadow
Toteve—B. 1937—Tote—Juan Eve
Totum—1928—Broomstick—Indian Rose
Townsend Boy—1938—Little King—Brown Charm
Toyland—Ch. 1923—Peter Pan—Lucrative

Toyland—Br. 1916—Negofol—Toia
Toyokiah—Ch. 1937—The Okah—Pandion Queen
Trailham (J8)—B. 1928—Indian Trail—Hamada
Traileta—1928—Indian Trail—Cherita
Trailolka—1928—Indian Trail—Amohalko
Tramp (Quarter Horse)—Tubal Cain—
Train Master—1921—Silvery Light—Lottie Lee
Trehal (Arabian)—Ch. 1935—*Rahal—Tref
Trevisco—Ch. 1914—Tredennis—The Test
Trial By Jury—Ch. 1912—Fair Play—Princess Chic
Trimmer—1930— Mad Hatter—Margin
Triple Threat—1929—Supremus—*Triple Sec
*Tristan (A0035)—Ch. 1937—Firdaussi—Valentine
Trolly Car
Trophy—Ch. 1915—Ballot—Miss Crittenden
Troublesome—1905—Planudes—Soubrette II
Truly Rural—Br. 1936—Milkman—Too High
Tubac—1930—My Play—*Reggilf—Aver
Turf God—Ch. 1929—Sting—Turf Star
Turf Writer—Br. 1926—*Polymelian—Irish Sweep
Tuscumbia (Anglo—Arab) Ch. 1936—Walkout—
    Lady Edjelo
Two Trails—Br. 1935—Sullivan Trail—Traleta

Ulysses—1927—Bennington—Artemisia
Umbrella—Ch. 1923—Trap Rock—Shade
Uncas—B. 1916—Wyeth—Codex
Uncertain—1921—Transvaal—Broken Promises
Uncle Sand—B. 1915—Uncle—Golden Sand
Uncle Jimmie Grey—Br. 1906—Bonnie Joe—Mary
    Hill
Uncle Wiggly—1924—Peter Pan—Fan Tan
*Under Fire—1916—Swynford—Startling
Underwriter—Br. 1919—Disguise—Agnes
    Valesquez
Universe—1929—Infinit—Plaid
Unuttered—1937—Gordon Russell—Silent
    Moments
*Upsaiquitch—B. 1918—Faucheur—Aqua Viva
Uptime—1926—Upset—Susan Lenox
Usher (34M)—Br. 1946—*Open Door—*Bay
    Flight
Utopian—B. 1930—*St. Germans—Nixie

Valdina Dandy (Y468)—B. 1937—Blue Larkspur—
    Chicsu
Valentino—B. 1922—Whisk Broom II—Beauteous
Vamoose—Blue Larkspur—
Van Dorn—1910—G.W. Johnson—Costa Rica
Vanquish—Ch. 1926—Victor S.—*Cimea
*Varro—Brn. 1944—Magnat—Vivere
Very Wise—1932—Wise Councellor—Omona
Vetro
Vez—1933—Zev—Sabine
Vicompte—B. 1915—Commoigne—Vitesse
Viernes Santo—B. 1936—Peace Junior—Betty S
Village Sport—Br. 1930—Spur—My Irene
Villon (32F5)—Ch. 1929—Stimulus—Heloise

Vindicated—B. 1931—Flittergold—Pitch Dark
Vino—1930—Sir Luke—Myrtle Hardee
Virginia King—B. 1936—Gold Stick—Queen of
    Spain
Virginia Lamb—
Virginia Shad—B. 1937—Goldbug or Chilhowee—
    Sansonet
Virginia Sweep—B. 1936—Cattail—Jenelda
Virginia Valet—Ch. 1936—Gold Stick—Lucca
Virginia Valor
Virmont—1926—Ormont—Thunderbird
Vioto—B. 1922—Norito—Cheviota
Vito—B. 1925—*Negofo—Forever
Vol—Prince Pal
Vonair—1929—Wildair—Pageant
Voormel—Blk. 1918—Voorhees—Formella

Wabuska—1917—*Honeywood—Princess Zeika
Wag Tale—1927—Chicle—Whisk By
Waif (Arabian)—B. 1926—Nejdran Jr.—Saaida
Walhalla—B. 1924—Verwood—Walkyria
Walkaway
Wampum—1919—Harmonican—Black Eagle
War Burden—1936—Tote—Jennie
War Hero—Man O'War
*Ward—in—Chancery—Warden of the Marches—
    Alimony
War Instigator—1926—War Fame—Instigation
War Note—Ch. 1916—Spanish Prince II—Sun
    Maiden
War Peril—Blk. 1935—Man O'War—*Helsingfors II
War Pennant—Br. 1916—Jim Gaffney—Martha
War Plume—Blk. 1916—Star Shoot—Courtplaster
War Note—1916—Spanish Prince II—Sun Maiden
Wars End—1939—General Lee—Sweetheart Sue
Warfare—Ch. 1922—Lorenzo—Ypres II
Warrior Son—Ch. 1939—Man O' War—Bridgeen
Washakie—1923—Over There—Garner
Watch Charm—Ch. 1921—Spur—Tamira
*Wave of Erire—B. 1919—Greenback—Cliodna
Wave of the Air
*Waygood—1920—Tracery—Ascenseur
Waysco—
Welsh Broom—1928—Whisk Broom II—*Welsh
    Maid
Wealthy Saint (9M9)—Ch. 1945—St. Brideaux—
    Good Heiress
Wee Bunting—1933—Bunting—Pewee Valley
Westerman—Br. 1918—Ildrim—Supposition
Weston—B. 1932—Sun Flag—Madcap Princess
Westy Jim—Westy Hogan
*Witez II (1V17)(Arabian)—B. 1938—Ofir—
    Federacja
Whee—*Wrack
Wheel Right
White Seal —B. 1925—*Assagai—Miss Orilene
White Shield—Ch. 1912—St. Maxim—Louise Wood
White Star—Ch. 1918—McGee—Sweet Charlotte

White Tie—Br. 1934—High Time—*Highland Dell
Wichita Red Wing
*Wigstone—B. 1915—Bayardo—Blue Tint
Wild Tint—1920—Cherry Tint—Bowery
Windy City—Br. 1926—Upset—*Allivan
Winning Grouch—1932—Groucher—Agnes Wynn
Winning His Way—1925—Rameau—Salvatoron
Winter Play—Br. 1929—Leonardo II—Miami Belle
Wise Boy—1937—Good Advice—Light Charge
Wood Prince—Ch. 1928—Blithewood—Reina de
     Hampton
Wood Thrush—1915—Olambala—L'Alouette
*Woszpitt—(Karbardine)—Br. 1939—Prognos—K.
     146 Titanika
Wrattler—1927—*Wrack—Clare Boothe
Wyoming—Ch. 1915—Bryn Mawr—Star of the West

Xerseise—1931—The Porter—Bar le Duc
Xylon—Gr. 1912—Grey Plume—Lady Marie

Yankee Star—Br. 1919—Star Shoot—Yankee Lady
Yellow Horse—Ch. 1932—Paavo—High Heels
*Yen 2d—B. 1929—Legatee—Nan San
Yield Not—1921—Ballot—Temptation
Yo Puedo—1909—W.R. Condon—Lone Princess
Yurucari

Zadeyn (Arabian)—Grey 1940—*Raseyn—
     Sheherzade
Zados—1923—Cruzados—Ardita
Zeb—Buster
Zembrod—1929—Hephaistos—Lady de Jarnette
Zenith
Zeus Laddie—B. 1922—Zeus—Edna Collins
Zeus II—1923—Zeus—Sweet Pea
Zev—1922—Troubadour—Alta
Zewa (Arabian)—1939—Kaszmir—Kostrzewa
Zonite—1924—Donnacona—*Zonia
Zunch—1926—Wormleighton—Anna Lea

Photograph by Scott Trees

*YL Ebony Bey, a registered Arabian descended from *Witez II, is used as a ranch stallion by the YL Ranch, John and Sharon Matthews, Albany, Texas. Through this stallion, and others like him, the legacy of the Remount Service continues into the 21st century.*

Gregg Welch, astride the Green Ranch Haidas Jan, AQHA #3402074, competes in the 2000 NCHA Super Stakes, Fort Worth, Texas.

Pedigrees of Remount-bred stallions and mares

Remount stallions are listed in bold type on each pedigree.

Quarter Horses

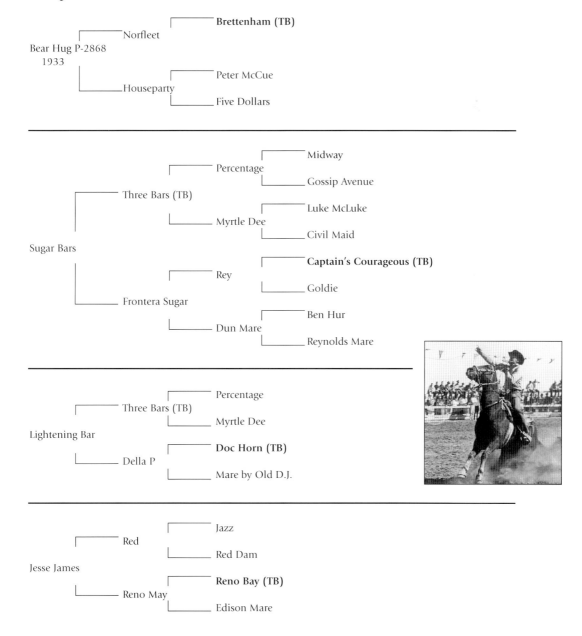

Bear Hug P-2868
1933
— Norfleet
— **Brettenham (TB)**
— Houseparty
— Peter McCue
— Five Dollars

Sugar Bars
— Three Bars (TB)
— Percentage
— Midway
— Gossip Avenue
— Myrtle Dee
— Luke McLuke
— Civil Maid
— Frontera Sugar
— Rey
— **Captain's Courageous (TB)**
— Goldie
— Dun Mare
— Ben Hur
— Reynolds Mare

Lightening Bar
— Three Bars (TB)
— Percentage
— Myrtle Dee
— Della P
— **Doc Horn (TB)**
— Mare by Old D.J.

Jesse James
— Red
— Jazz
— Red Dam
— Reno May
— **Reno Bay (TB)**
— Edison Mare

313

Oklahoma Star P-6
- **Dennis Reed (TB)**
- Cutthroat

Skipper W
- Nick Shoemaker
  - Nick
    - Shiek P-11
    - Sylvia
  - Skipalong Wiescamp
    - **Lani Chief (TB)**
    - Slippers
- Hired Girl
  - Cowboy P-12
    - Yellow Jacket
    - Roan Lady
  - Leche
    - Nick
    - Gold Digger

Joe Reed II
- Joe Reed P-3
  - Joe Blair (TB)
  - Della Moore
- Nellene
  - **Fleeting Time (TB)**
  - Little Red Nell

Barbra B
- B'ar Hunter II
  - **B'ar Hunter (TB)**
  - Rainy Day Mare
- Old Bay Mare
  - Waggoner's Rainy Day
  - Waggoner Mare

Joe Bailey's King P-7260
- Gonzales Joe Bailey P-4
  - Little King
  - Nixon Mare
- Miss Tommy 58-P-470
  - Tom by Midnight
  - mare by **King O'Neil (TB)**

King Glo
- Hyglo
  - **Hygro (TB)**

Music Mount No. 5229
- Gold Mount P-2078
  - Brush Mount
    - **Chimney Sweep (TB)**
  - Miss Helen
    - Plaudit
      - **King Plaudit (TB)**
- Panzy
  - **Madder Music (TB)**

Rebel Cause
- Bankette
  - Miss Bank
    - **Captain's Courageous (TB)**

Croton Oil
- Leo
  - Joe Reed II
    - Joe Reed P-3
    - Nellene
      - **Fleeting Time (TB)**
- Randle's Lady
  - **Doc Horn (TB)**

Blondy's Dude
- Blondy Queen
  - Blondy Plaudit
    - Plaudit
      - **King Plaudit (TB)**

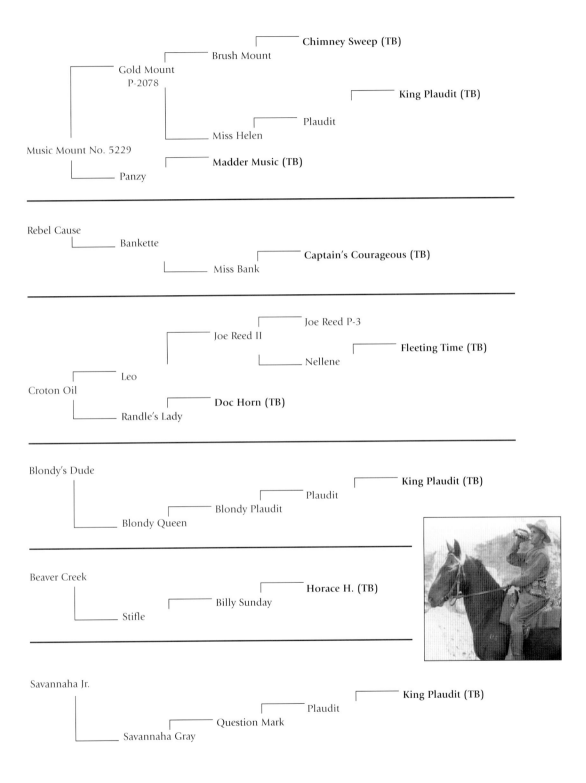

Beaver Creek
- Stifle
  - Billy Sunday
    - **Horace H. (TB)**

Savannaha Jr.
- Savannaha Gray
  - Question Mark
    - Plaudit
      - **King Plaudit (TB)**

Skipa Star
- Skipper's Lad
- Miss Helen
  - Plaudit
    - **King Plaudit (TB)**

Lighting Rey
- Lighting Bar
  - Della P.
    - **Doc Horn (TB)**
- Reina Rey
  - Rey
    - **Captain's Courageous (TB)**

Madden's Bright Eyes
- Gold Mount
  - Brush Mount
    - **Chimney Sweep (TB)**
- Plaudette
  - Plaudit
    - **King Plaudit (TB)**

Sonny Dee Bar
- Win or Loose
  - Mr. Bar None
    - Three Bars
- Chigger Baby
  - Chigger #3042
    - **Sidecar (TB)**
    - Skeeterette x **Fighting Joe (TB)**

Star Duster
- Oklahoma Star x **Dennis Reed TB**
- Lowery's Mabel
  - **Master Gould (TB)**

Miss Bank
- **Captain's Courageous (TB)**

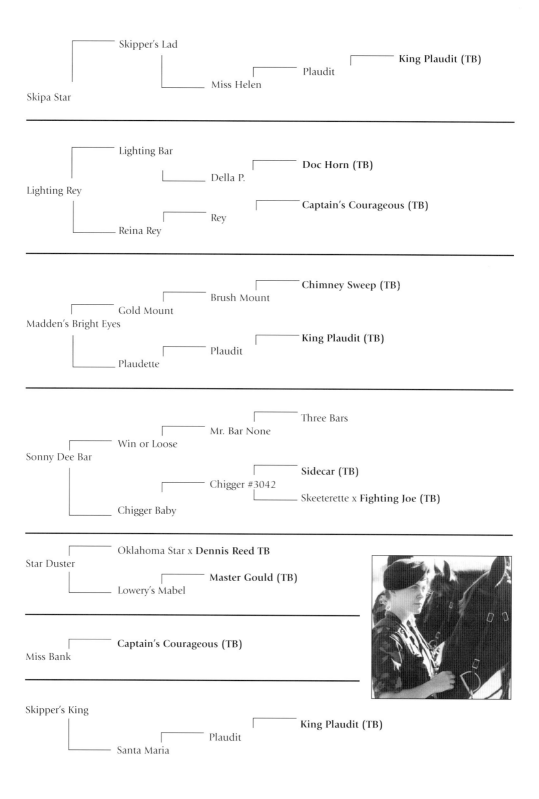

Skipper's King
- Santa Maria
  - Plaudit
    - **King Plaudit (TB)**

Skipper's Lad
└─ Miss Helen
   └─ Plaudit
      └─ **King Plaudit (TB)**

Scooter W.
1948 Champion Running Stallion
└─ Plaudit
   └─ **King Plaudit (TB)**

Quick M. Silver
└─ Brush Mount
   └─ **Chimney Sweep (TB)**

Connie Leo
├─ Leo
│ └─ Joe Reed II
│   ├─ Joe Reed P-3
│   └─ Nellene x **Fleeting Time (TB)**
└─ Connie (TB)
   ├─ **Reno Lion (TB)**
   └─ Fair Lawn

Tiger Leo
├─ Leo
│ └─ Joe Reed II
│   ├─ Joe Reed P-3
│   └─ Nellene x **Fleeting Time (TB)**
└─ Connie (TB)
   ├─ **Reno Lion (TB)**
   └─ Fair Lawn (TB)

Skeeter
World Champion Cutting Horse
├─ **Sidecar (TB)**
└─ Skeeterette
   └─ **Fighting Joe (TB)**

Marion's Girl
World Champion Cutting Horse 1954–56
└─ Joan Scharbuer
   └─ **Tallwind (TB)**

Question Mark
    Plaudit
        King Plaudit (TB)

Plaudit
    King Plaudit (TB)

Buddy Nile
    Fleeting Time (TB)
    Little Nile
        Uncle Jimmy Gray (TB)

Rose O Lani
    Maple Prince (TB)
    Mexicala Rose
        Plaudit x **King Plaudit (TB)**

Night Nurse
    Galus (TB)

My Duster Too
    Star Duster
        Lowery's Mabel
            Master Gould (TB)
    Smokey Duster Too

Leo
    Joe Reed II
        Joe Reed
        Nellene
            Fleeting Time (TB)

Brush Mount
    Chimney Sweep (TB)
    Hula Dancer

Goldseeker Bars *Supreme Champion*

- Nick Shoemaker
- Spanish Nick
  - **King Plaudit (TB)**
  - Plaudit
  - Mexicala Rose
- Spanish Joy
  - Joy Ann

Zan Parr Bars

- Parr Three
  - Three Bars
- Terry's Pal
  - Poco Astro
    - Gold Mount x
    - Brush Mount x
    - **Chimney Sweep (TB)**
    - Music Mount
  - Solo Mount
  - Gold Rondes

Appaloosas

Wapiti

- **Song Hit (TB)**
- Cuadroon

Bright Eyes Brother

- **King Plaudit (TB)**
- Plaudit
- Plaudette

- **Dr. Howard (TB)**

Mansfield Commanche

- **Vinita London (TB)**

Hands Up

- Lucy Polousy

Paints

Sky Hi
└─── Skip Hi
    └─── **Advantage (TB)**

    ┌─── Sky Hi
└─── Skip Hi
Skippa Streak
    └─── **Advantage (TB)**

                                          ┌─ **Chimney Sweep (TB)**
                               └─── Gold Mount └─ Brush Mount
                └─── Cripple Mount
      └─── Tetrak Schooter
Yellow Mount
                ┌─── Moorehouse Yellow Jacket
      └─── Lady Yellow Jacket
                └─── Moorehouse Paint Mare x Yellow Wolf

Palomino

      ┌─── Junior Reed
Mach I *Supreme Champion*
                                         ┌─ **King Plaudit (TB)**
                              ┌─── Nick Shoemaker └─ Plaudit
                ┌─── Spanish Nick
└─── Spanish Joy

AQHA SUPREME CHAMPIONS THAT TRACE TO REMOUNT STALLIONS

Remount stallions are listed in bold type on each pedigree.

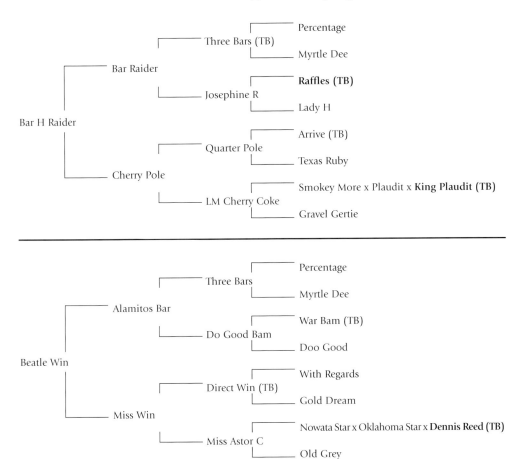

Coldstream Guard
- Afton Creek (TB)
  - Coldstream
    - *Bull Dog
    - Nimble Hoof
  - Sweet Afton
    - Balladier
    - Georgia Marble
- Miss Adeleta
  - Leo
    - Joe Reed II out of Nelline x **Fleeting Time (TB)**
    - Little Fanny
  - Murl L.
    - Moco Burnett
    - Day Break J.

Destiny Jagetta
- Destiny Leo Jag
  - Jaguar
    - Custus Rastus (TB)
    - Mamie Taylor
  - Lady Sophia
    - Leo x Joe Reed II out of Nellene x **Fleeting Time (TB)**
    - Sophia
- Herfano
  - Victory Chief
    - Eagle Chief
    - Flying Victory
  - Brown's Maggie

Desto Bar
- Nug Bar
  - Three Bars (TB)
    - Percentage
    - Myrtle Dee
  - Nugget Hug
    - Bear Hug x Norfleet x **Brettenholm (TB)**
    - Goldienug
- Billie Texas
  - Captain Bill
    - Silvertone
    - Starlight
  - Texas Warrior (TB)

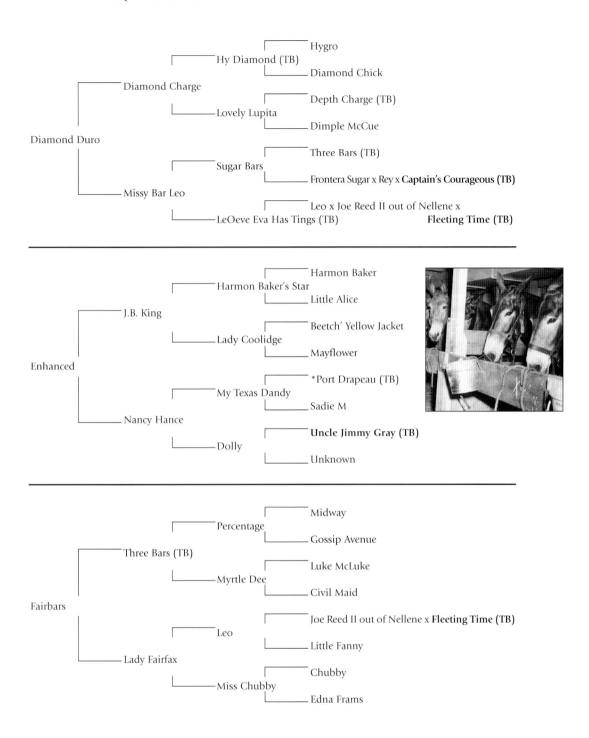

Diamond Duro

- Diamond Charge
  - Hy Diamond (TB)
    - Hygro
    - Diamond Chick
  - Lovely Lupita
    - Depth Charge (TB)
    - Dimple McCue
- Missy Bar Leo
  - Sugar Bars
    - Three Bars (TB)
    - Frontera Sugar x Rey x **Captain's Courageous (TB)**
  - LeOeve Eva Has Tings (TB)
    - Leo x Joe Reed II out of Nellene x **Fleeting Time (TB)**

Enhanced

- J.B. King
  - Harmon Baker's Star
    - Harmon Baker
    - Little Alice
  - Lady Coolidge
    - Beetch' Yellow Jacket
    - Mayflower
- Nancy Hance
  - My Texas Dandy
    - *Port Drapeau (TB)
    - Sadie M
  - Dolly
    - **Uncle Jimmy Gray (TB)**
    - Unknown

Fairbars

- Three Bars (TB)
  - Percentage
    - Midway
    - Gossip Avenue
  - Myrtle Dee
    - Luke McLuke
    - Civil Maid
- Lady Fairfax
  - Leo
    - Joe Reed II out of Nellene x **Fleeting Time (TB)**
    - Little Fanny
  - Miss Chubby
    - Chubby
    - Edna Frams

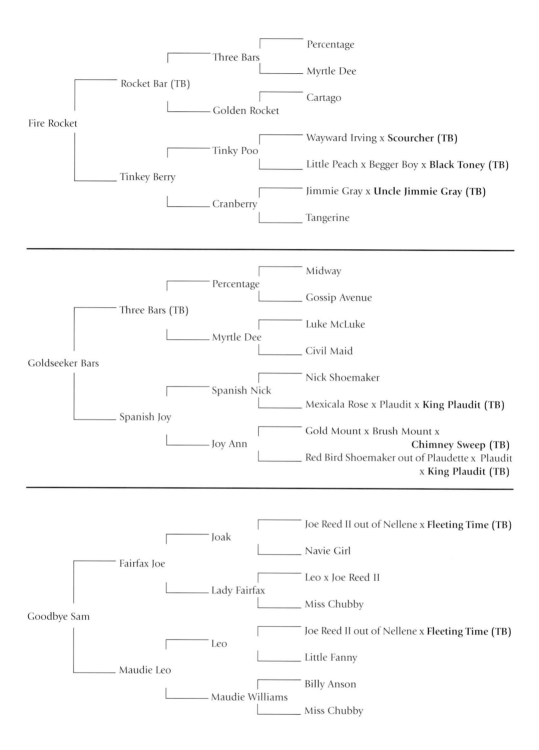

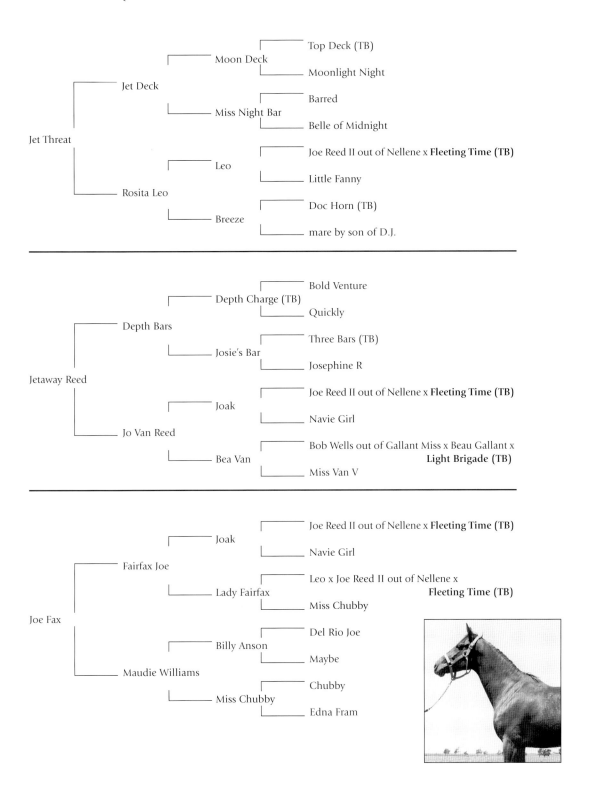

Jet Threat
- Jet Deck
  - Moon Deck
    - Top Deck (TB)
    - Moonlight Night
  - Miss Night Bar
    - Barred
    - Belle of Midnight
- Rosita Leo
  - Leo
    - Joe Reed II out of Nellene x **Fleeting Time (TB)**
    - Little Fanny
  - Breeze
    - Doc Horn (TB)
    - mare by son of D.J.

Jetaway Reed
- Depth Bars
  - Depth Charge (TB)
    - Bold Venture
    - Quickly
  - Josie's Bar
    - Three Bars (TB)
    - Josephine R
- Jo Van Reed
  - Joak
    - Joe Reed II out of Nellene x **Fleeting Time (TB)**
    - Navie Girl
  - Bea Van
    - Bob Wells out of Gallant Miss x Beau Gallant x **Light Brigade (TB)**
    - Miss Van V

Joe Fax
- Fairfax Joe
  - Joak
    - Joe Reed II out of Nellene x **Fleeting Time (TB)**
    - Navie Girl
  - Lady Fairfax
    - Leo x Joe Reed II out of Nellene x **Fleeting Time (TB)**
    - Miss Chubby
- Maudie Williams
  - Billy Anson
    - Del Rio Joe
    - Maybe
  - Miss Chubby
    - Chubby
    - Edna Fram

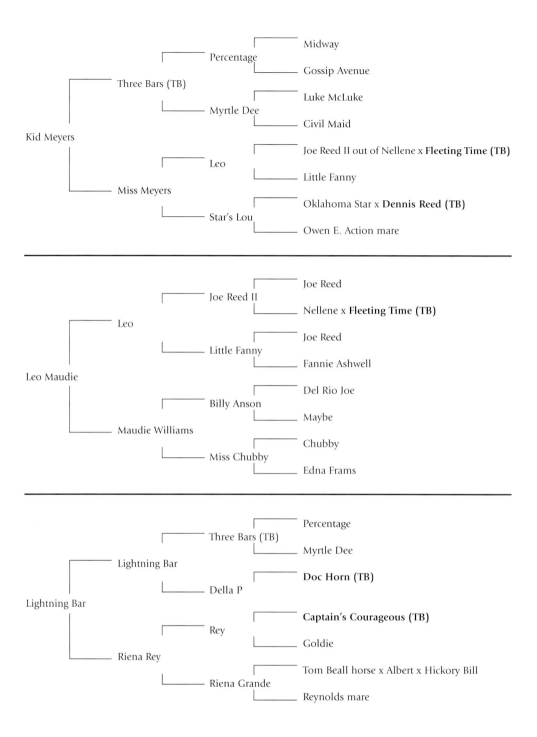

Linda Scotland
- Silver Thistle (TB)
  - Green Flash
    - Green Wave
    - Hot Flash
  - Thistle Cleo
    - Wildair
- Bonnie Scotland
  - **Golden Seal (TB)**

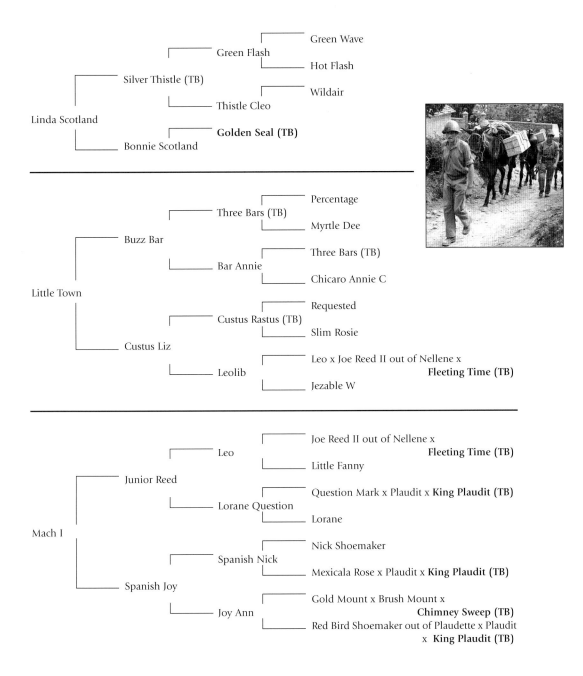

Little Town
- Buzz Bar
  - Three Bars (TB)
    - Percentage
    - Myrtle Dee
  - Bar Annie
    - Three Bars (TB)
    - Chicaro Annie C
- Custus Liz
  - Custus Rastus (TB)
    - Requested
    - Slim Rosie
  - Leolib
    - Leo x Joe Reed II out of Nellene x **Fleeting Time (TB)**
    - Jezable W

Mach I
- Junior Reed
  - Leo
    - Joe Reed II out of Nellene x **Fleeting Time (TB)**
    - Little Fanny
  - Lorane Question
    - Question Mark x Plaudit x **King Plaudit (TB)**
    - Lorane
- Spanish Joy
  - Spanish Nick
    - Nick Shoemaker
    - Mexicala Rose x Plaudit x **King Plaudit (TB)**
  - Joy Ann
    - Gold Mount x Brush Mount x **Chimney Sweep (TB)**
    - Red Bird Shoemaker out of Plaudette x Plaudit x **King Plaudit (TB)**

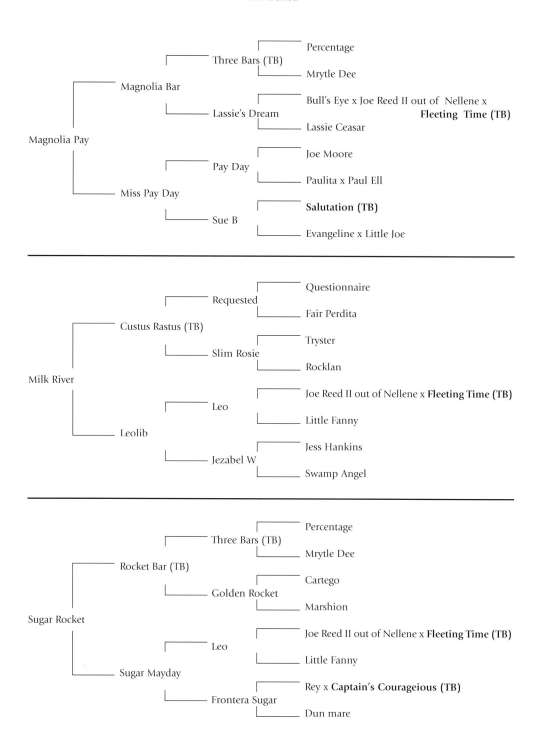

Magnolia Pay
- Magnolia Bar
  - Three Bars (TB)
    - Percentage
    - Mrytle Dee
  - Lassie's Dream
    - Bull's Eye x Joe Reed II out of Nellene x **Fleeting Time (TB)**
    - Lassie Ceasar
- Miss Pay Day
  - Pay Day
    - Joe Moore
    - Paulita x Paul Ell
  - Sue B
    - **Salutation (TB)**
    - Evangeline x Little Joe

Milk River
- Custus Rastus (TB)
  - Requested
    - Questionnaire
    - Fair Perdita
  - Slim Rosie
    - Tryster
    - Rocklan
- Leolib
  - Leo
    - Joe Reed II out of Nellene x **Fleeting Time (TB)**
    - Little Fanny
  - Jezabel W
    - Jess Hankins
    - Swamp Angel

Sugar Rocket
- Rocket Bar (TB)
  - Three Bars (TB)
    - Percentage
    - Mrytle Dee
  - Golden Rocket
    - Cartego
    - Marshion
- Sugar Mayday
  - Leo
    - Joe Reed II out of Nellene x **Fleeting Time (TB)**
    - Little Fanny
  - Frontera Sugar
    - Rey x **Captain's Courageious (TB)**
    - Dun mare

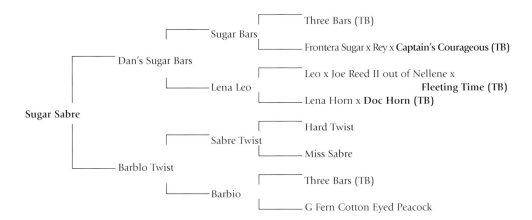

Sugar Sabre

Dan's Sugar Bars
- Sugar Bars
  - Three Bars (TB)
  - Frontera Sugar x Rey x **Captain's Courageous (TB)**
- Lena Leo
  - Leo x Joe Reed II out of Nellene x **Fleeting Time (TB)**
  - Lena Horn x **Doc Horn (TB)**

Barblo Twist
- Sabre Twist
  - Hard Twist
  - Miss Sabre
- Barbio
  - Three Bars (TB)
  - G Fern Cotton Eyed Peacock

ANIMAL IDENTIFICATION SYSTEMS AND PROCEDURES

A. Following the Civil War a descriptive card was made out when a horse or mule was issued to a troop. A description and age at time of issue as well as the identifying hoof brands assigned at the time the animal was issued (ex: No. 26 on left forefoot and 1-D-62 on right forefoot). The hoof brands had to be re-burned each time the animal was shod and there was always room for error. On the I.D. card the animal's breeding, place of purchase and all other information would be unknown except the age at time of purchase. Frequently that age was never changed on the card so there was really no way of knowing how old the horse or mule actually was. By the time that the animal had been through several unit transfers, there was no actual way to accurately identify it.

B. Hot iron branding was the only logical way to identify all military animals. At the time of purchase each horse or mule was number branded (either white paint or silver nitrate solution) which was keyed to the purchase card. This card identified the animal and showed the point of purchase as well as the price paid. The card went with the animal to the Branch Remount Depot.

1. Upon arriving at the Branch Remount each horse or mule was hot iron branded on the left shoulder with a "US" in 3-inch high letters. This identified the animal as belonging to the military. A brand denoting the use (R for Riding, D for Draft and P for Pack) on the croup along with the number of the purchasing officer.[1]

2. Each animal was branded on the front hooves with an identifying number when it was issued to a unit. An example would be Horse No. 52 of Headquarters Troop 3rd Cavalry. He would be branded "52" on the left fore hoof and "C. H. Q. 3" on the right fore hoof. The numbers were only ½ to 1 inch in size, making them hard to see. These numbers, along with a further description, would be listed on what was known as a "Descriptive Card for Public Animals." This information included age, sex, color and identifying marks, along with three drawings on which the special markings were noted. There was NO positive army-wide record of issue beyond the card that was filled out by

the unit company clerk when the animal was issued. These hoof numbers had to be re-burned each time that the animal was shod and frequently a mistake could be made. By the time that a horse or mule had been transferred through several units, any chance of positive identification was lost.[2]

3. In 1924 the army realized the error factor inherent in the hoof branding system and adopted an individual identification brand for service-wide use. Termed the "Preston Brand," after Colonel Guy H. Preston who developed the program, it was a 4-digit combination of 3" letters and numerals branded on the left side of the animal's neck at the receiving Branch Remount Depot. This gave each horse or mule an individual serial number. An identification card was filled out, with the horse or mule's description, age at time of purchase, place of purchase, breeding and the Preston Brand. This card was transferred with the animal from unit to unit.

The combination of three to four numbers and a single letter was sufficient to brand 1,000 horses and 1,000 mules. Example of a single letter/number combination:

A000, A001, A002 through A0999

0A00 through 9A99

00A0 through 99A9

000A through 999A

Using twenty letters of the alphabet, with the necessary numerals, it was possible to brand 80,000 animals. (The letters O, Q, I and G were omitted since they were too simular to O, 1 and C.)

The prefix letter indicated the Branch Remount Depot where the horse or mule began it's military career. The identifying letters were:

Fort Reno, Oklahoma—D, E, F

Fort Robinson, Nebraska—L, M, N

Front Royal, Virginia—V, Y, Z

On Depot—raised animals, the brand was applied at two years age.[3]

The accompanying Identification Card (sample No. v-A) carried all the information regarding the animal, including the service record. A copy of this went with the horse or mule from unit to unit and was used to record the final disposition.

Upon receipt of the original card after final disposition of the animal, the Remount Service noted the same on the triplicate copy, moved the permanent record from the live to the dead animal file in the Quartermaster General's Office and took up the symbol (brand) for reissue. The original record of the animal was forwarded to the Veterinary Corps for use in obtaining data, keeping records or making studies.[4]

4. The hot iron brand "IC" was placed on a horse or mule that was either to be destroyed or separated from the service by public sale. The initials stood for "Inspected and Condemned".[5]

C. Lip Tattoo—In late 1946 the Remount Service announced that each incoming horse or mule in the military would be identified individually by a tattoo on the inside of the upper lip rather than a hot iron brand on the neck. The same series of letters and numbers of the "Preston System" would be used. The lip tattoo system of identification originated at the Pomona Quartermaster Depot (Kellogg's), Pomona, California as a means of identifying the purebred Arabian Horses there. It was tested on several hundred horses and was found to be a positive means of identification.[6]

Sources and Notes

1. Major C. L. Scott, "Preston System of Identifying Horses and Mules in the Army," *The Remount* (July 1924).
2. Ibid.
3. Ibid.
4. Ibid.
5. Colonel C. E. Livingston, Retired, Tujunga, California.
6. Colonel F. W. Koester, "New Army Method of Branding," *The Blood-Horse* (June 1, 1948).

U.S. ARMY OLYMPIC PARTICIPATION—1912–1948

From 1912, the first time that an American Equestrian Team competed in the Olympic Games, until 1948 when the last cavalry team was disbanded, the USET was composed of military riders. As with other countries, the army had the best horses and the best riders to choose from. No individual or company outside of the army lent, subsidized or gave horses to the Olympic Team as is done today. Team candidates were selected from promising graduates of the Cavalry School located at Fort Riley, Kansas. Selection of both horses and riders was made by the appointed Team Captain under the supervision of the Commandant of the Cavalry School, Fort Riley.

Beginning in 1920, the U.S. Olympic Equestrian Teams were selected, organized and trained at Fort Riley, Kansas. In 1935 summer training was moved to Fort Robinson, Nebraska. The higher altitude and cooler climate, along with the rugged topography, made Fort Robinson an ideal training ground for both men and horses. This procedure was followed until the army team was disbanded in 1940. During those years, the Olympic Team candidates and their mounts gave well-attended exhibitions each summer.

Events consisted of the Three-Day Event (horses competed in Dressage; over a 22-mile cross-country course which had to be negotiated in two hours or less; open jumping); the Prix des Nations (jumping over banks, ditches, triple-bar and double obstacles) and Dressage. These three events were divided into individual and team competitions with Gold, Silver and Bronze medals awarded.

1912—Stockholm, Sweden

The U.S. Team won a Bronze medal (third-place) in the Three-Day Event Team competition. The team was composed of Lt. Benjamin Lear on Poppy, Lt. John Montgomery riding Deceive and Capt. Guy Henry on Chriswell.

World War I intervened and there were no 1916 Games.

1920—Antwerp, Holland

Capt. H.N. Chamberlin on Nigra was sixth and Major W. A. West riding Black Boy was seventh in the Individual Three-Day Event.

The United States Event team took a fourth place with Capt. H. N. Chamberlin on Nigra, Major W.A. West riding Black Boy and Major John Barry on Raven. Major Henry Allen riding Don took seventh place in the Individual category. Taking fifth place in the Team Jumping were Chamberlin on Nigra, Karl Greenwald on Moses and Vincent Erwin on Joffre.

1924—Paris, France

Major Sloan Doak on Pathfinder took a third place, the only American entry with any success.

1928—Hilversum, Holland

With victory in the Three-Day Event in sight, the U.S. Army team was disqualified because Major C.P. George, riding Orsella, failed to jump a small obstacle. Under Olympic rules, that disqualified the whole team.

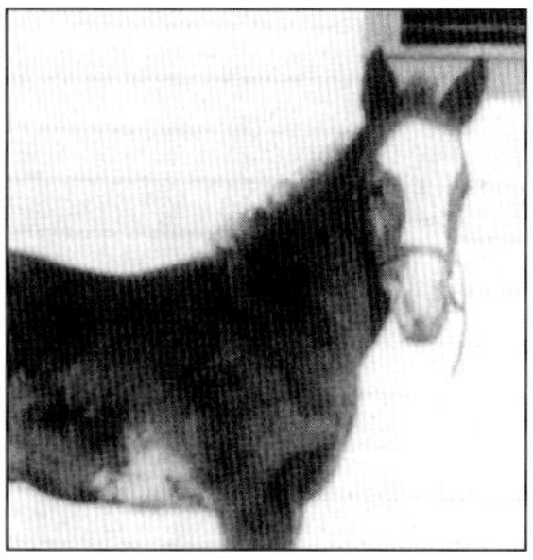

1932—Los Angeles, California, U.S.A.

The Stadium Jumping Course was so hazardous that only five of the 11 mounts entered were able take all 30 jumps over the 18 obstacles. For this reason, no country's Jumping Team (3 riders) completed the course and no team championship was awarded. The U.S. Army Team won the Three-Day Event with Lt. Earl F. Thomson*, Capt. H. N. Chamberlin and Capt. Edwin Argo. Thomson, riding the great Jenny Camp, took the Silver medal in the individual competition.

* Note: At the 47th Annual National Horse Show, Madison Square Garden, New York, Lt. Thomson won the International Individual Military Championship trophy on Tan Bark.

1936—Berlin, Germany

Capt. Earl F. Thomson, riding Jenny Camp, won a Silver medal in the Individual competition (setting a record which still stands) and Capt. Carl Raguse on Dakota earned a fifth place in the individual show jumping. The United States placed fourth in show jumping among the 18 teams, only 7 of which survived the competition.

The Army Equestrian Team was disbanded in 1940, prior to the advent of World War II but was reactivated in 1946 at Fort Riley, Kansas.

1948—Aldershot and Wembley Stadium, England

The U.S. Army Team received the Gold Medal in the Three-Day Event with Lt. Col. Frank S. Henry on Swing Low (who also took second place in the individual ratings), Col. Earl F. Thomson (winner of 3 Olympic Equestrian medals, more than any other USET competitor) and Col. Charles Anderson. Col. Franklin Wing, Jr., riding Democrat*, completed the jumping course with only 8 faults.

*Note: At the age of 19, Democrat was acquired by William Steinkraus after the U.S. Army team was disbanded. Under his handling he went on to win each individual class in the three major horse shows of the 1952 fall circuit: Harrisburg, Pennsylvania; New York, New York; and Toronto, Canada.

PUBLIC LAW 494—80TH CONGRESS, APRIL 21, 1948

An act to transfer the Remount Service from the Department of the Army to the Department of Agriculture.

Be it enacted by the Senate and the House of Representatives of the United States of America in Congress assembled, That, in the interests of economy and efficiency, the records, property, both real and personal, and civilian personnel of the Remount Service of the Quartermaster Corps, Department of the Army, are hereby transferred to the Department of Agriculture, effective July 1, 1948. Prior to that date, the Secretary of the Army and the Secretary of Agriculture shall enter into a written agreement on the property and the personnel covered by this transfer.

Sec. 2.

The Secretary of Agriculture is authorized to receive the property transferred by this Act is directed to administer it in such manner as he deems will best advance the livestock and agricultural interests of the United States, including the improvement in the breeding of horses suited to the needs of the United States; the acquisition by purchase in the open market, exchange, hire or donation of breeding stock and

necessary land, buildings, and facilities; the use of horses in the improvement of the supply of horses available in agriculture; the demonstration of the quality and usefulness of horses through partic-ipation in and lending for use in fairs, shows and other events, otherwise; the loan, sale or hire of animals or animal products through such arrangements and subject to such fees as are deemed necessary by the Secretary to accomplish the purposes of this Act, and

in carrying out such program, the Secretary is authorized to cooperate with public and private organizations and individuals under such rules and regulations are deemed by him to be necessary.

Sec. 3.

Until June 30, 1949, the Secretary of the Army may detail to the Department of Agriculture such military personnel, including officers of the Veterinary Corps of the Medical Department, as he may determine with the Secretary of Agriculture to be desirable to effectuate the purposes of this Act or to safeguard the interest of the United

States. Notwithstanding the limitations continued in existing law, retired officer personnel of the Department of the Army, if employed by the Department of Agriculture for the purposes of this Act only, may receive in addition to their retired pay civilian salary to the extent that the total from both sources does not exceed the pay and allowances received by such persons in the permanent grade last held by them prior to retirement.

Sec. 4.

There is hereby authorized to be appropriated by the Department of Agriculture such funds as may be necessary to carry out this Act. The authority of the Army to conduct a remount breeding program is hereby abolished. Funds appropriated pursuant to this Act shall be available for necessary administrative expenses, including personal services in the District of Columbia, printing and binding, and purchase or hire of passenger motor vehicles.

Approved April 21, 1948.

PROCUREMENT ACTIVITY FEBRUARY 1944, FORT ROBINSON, NEBRASKA

By 1944, approximately 17,000 animals had been disposed of by the Quartermaster Remount Depots through the procurement division of the Treasury Department.[1]

The Monthly Information Letter of Fort Robinson, Nebraska for February 1–February 29, 1944, illustrates the activity.

1. Animals	*Horses*			*Mules*	
a. Received:	Light Riding	Riding	Draft	Draft	Pack & Riding
Sheridan, Wyn. (NWRA)					12
AAB, Alliance, Neb.	1				
Kansas City, Mo. (NCRA)					72
E. St. Louis, Ill. (ECRA)					24
E. St. Louis, Ill. (ECRA)					45
Memphis, Tenn. (ECRA)					60
Twin Falls, Idaho (NWRA)					16
Alamosa, Colo. (SWRA)					18
Total:	1				247
b. Shipped:					
DCGO, Coquille, Ore	22				
Prisoner of War Camp Concordia, Kansas	16		16		
AAB, Alliance, Neb.	1				
Los Angeles PE, Puente, California					283
DCGO, Tillamook, Ore.	22				
Jersey City Stock Yards, Jersey City, N.J.					415
Total:	61		16		698

1. Animals, cont.	Horses			Mules	
	Light				Pack &
c. On Hand:	Riding	Riding	Draft	Draft	Riding
Total:	4,434	3	456	50	2,750

d. Unfilled Shipping Orders:

No. 2 Amended–13th Naval District, Seattle, Wash.	220				
No. 3–AAB, Madras, Ore.	6				
No. 83–12th Naval District San Francisco, Calif.	22				
No. 84–Camp Carson, Colo.	197	5 (Bell)			640
No. 91–Prisoner of War Camp Carlinda, Iowa	4		14		
No. 97–Prisoner of War Camp Atlanta, Neb.	4		16		
Total:	453	5	30		640

e. Sold:

A total of 500 surplus mules and 1,067 surplus horses were sold by public auction at this Depot under the auspices of the Treasury Department on 24th and 25th of February 1944. The auction was conducted by Mr. Ferd Owen of Kansas City, Missouri. Bidding was spirited. The animals were sold at an approximate rate of 3 per minute. The top price for mules was $240 and the low price was $17.50, the average price on riding horses was $61.11 and on horses suitable for light farm work was $52.17. Approximately 200 bidders attended.

1. Stallions.

     a. Destroyed:

     Stallion 55E7 (AEROMAIL) destroyed 14 February 1944, cause—Senility. Number of days on Depot—2 mo., 22 days.

     Stallion 9F90 (DRESS SHIP) destroyed 14 February 1944, cause—Senility. Number of days on Depot—2 mo., 26 days.

2. Breeding

     a. Registration of Half-bred foals:

     Number of registrations obtained—none.

Number of blank applications sent out—none.

Number of persons interviewed—none.

3. Training

Selected 1,095 horses and 500 mules for sale held 24 and 25 February. Processed, trained and shipped 415 British mules. Processed, trained and shipped 283 mules. Processed, trained and shipped 77 horses. Initial driving of 400 draft horses.[2]

Other sales of surplus horses at Fort Robinson Nebraska in 1944 included:

March 23—1,274 horses at an average price of $41.80

September 3—400 horses to Eli Lilly Company for the making of serum at $57.48 per head.

October 26—1,017 horses at an average price of $34.35 and 76 mules at an average price of $91.80.[3]

Sources and Notes

1. "Arms and the Horse," *The Blood-Horse* (May 27, 1944), 747.
2. Fort Robinson Quartermaster Remount Depot Monthly Information Letter, February 1–February 29, 1944, inclusive.
3. Fort Robinson Quartermaster Remount Depot Monthly Information Letters for March, September and October, 1944.

C

D

E

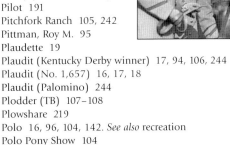

S

Photograph courtesy U.S. Army

Men and horses of the 2nd Cavalry move out for combat maneuvers in South Carolina during 1941. The cavalry ensured military forces maintained mobility in rough terrain that was not suitable for vehicles.